The Politics of International Intervention

This book critically explores the practices of peacebuilding, and the politics of the communities experiencing intervention.

The contributions to this volume have a dual focus. First, they analyse the practices of Western intervention and peacebuilding, and the prejudices and politics that drive them. Second, they explore how communities experience and deal with this intervention, as well as an understanding of how their political and economic priorities can often diverge markedly from those of the intervener. This is achieved through theoretical and thematic chapters, and an extensive number of in-depth empirical case studies.

Utilising a variety of conceptual frameworks and disciplines, the book seeks to understand why something so normatively desirable – the pursuit of, and building of, peace – has turned out so badly. From Cambodia to Afghanistan, Iraq to Mali, interventions in the pursuit of peace have not achieved the results desired by the interveners. Rather, they have created further instability and violence. The contributors to this book explore why.

This book will be of much interest to students, academics and practitioners of peacebuilding, peacekeeping, international intervention, statebuilding, security studies and international relations in general.

Mandy Turner is Director of the Kenyon Institute, at the Council for British Research in the Levant, East Jerusalem, and Visiting Research Fellow at the Middle East Centre, London School of Economics, UK.

Florian P. Kühn is Interim Professor for Comparative Politics at Magdeburg's Otto von Guericke University, Germany.

Routledge Studies in Intervention and Statebuilding
Series Editor: David Chandler

Statebuilding and Intervention
Policies, practices and paradigms
Edited by David Chandler

Reintegration of Armed Groups after Conflict
Politics, violence and transition
Edited by Mats Berdal and David H. Ucko

Security, Development, and the Fragile State
Bridging the gap between theory and policy
David Carment, Stewart Prest and Yiagadeesen Samy

Kosovo, Intervention and Statebuilding
The international community and the transition to independence
Edited by Aidan Hehir

Critical Perspectives on the Responsibility to Protect
Interrogating theory and practice
Edited by Philip Cunliffe

Statebuilding and Police Reform
The freedom of security
Barry J. Ryan

Violence in Post-Conflict Societies
Remarginalisation, remobilisers and relationships
Anders Themnér

Statebuilding in Afghanistan
Multinational contributions to reconstruction
Edited by Nik Hynek and Péter Marton

The International Community and Statebuilding
Getting its act together?
Edited by Patrice C. McMahon and Jon Western

Statebuilding and State-Formation
The political sociology of intervention
Edited by Berit Bliesemann de Guevara

Political Economy of Statebuilding
Power after peace
Edited by Mats Berdal and Dominik Zaum

New Agendas in Statebuilding
Hybridity, contingency and history
Edited by Robert Egnell and Peter Haldén

Mediation and Liberal Peacebuilding
Peace from the ashes of war?
Edited by Mikael Eriksson and Roland Kosti

Semantics of Statebuilding
Language, meanings and sovereignty
Edited by Nicolas Lemay-Hébert, Nicholas Onuf, Vojin Rakić and Petar Bojanić

Humanitarian Crises, Intervention and Security
A framework for evidence-based programming
Edited by Liesbet Heyse, Andrej Zwitter, Rafael Wittek and Joost Herman

Internal Security and Statebuilding
Aligning agencies and functions
B. K. Greener and W. J. Fish

The EU and Member State Building
European foreign policy in the Western Balkans
Edited by Soeren Keil and Zeynep Arkan

Security and Hybridity after Armed Conflict
The dynamics of security provision in post-civil war states
Rens C. Willems

International Intervention and Statemaking
How exception became the norm
Selver B. Sahin

Rethinking Democracy Promotion in International Relations
The rise of the social
Jessica Schmidt

The Politics of International Intervention
The tyranny of peace
Edited by Mandy Turner and Florian P. Kühn

The Practice of Humanitarian Intervention
Aid workers, agencies and institutions in the Democratic Republic of the Congo
Kai Koddenbrock

The Politics of International Intervention
The tyranny of peace

Edited by Mandy Turner and
Florian P. Kühn

LONDON AND NEW YORK

First published 2016
by Routledge
2 Park Square, Milton Park, Abingdon, Oxon OX14 4RN

and by Routledge
711 Third Avenue, New York, NY 10017

First issued in paperback 2017

Routledge is an imprint of the Taylor & Francis Group, an informa business

© 2016 selection and editorial material, Mandy Turner and
Florian P. Kühn; individual chapters, the contributors

The right of the editors to be identified as the authors of the editorial
material, and of the authors for their individual chapters, has been
asserted in accordance with sections 77 and 78 of the Copyright,
Designs and Patents Act 1988.

All rights reserved. No part of this book may be reprinted or
reproduced or utilised in any form or by any electronic, mechanical,
or other means, now known or hereafter invented, including
photocopying and recording, or in any information storage or
retrieval system, without permission in writing from the publishers.

Trademark notice: Product or corporate names may be trademarks or
registered trademarks, and are used only for identification and
explanation without intent to infringe.

British Library Cataloguing-in-Publication Data
A catalogue record for this book is available from the British Library

Library of Congress Cataloging-in-Publication Data
The politics of international intervention : the tyranny of peace /
edited by Mandy Turner and Florian P. Kühn.
pages cm. – (Routledge studies in intervention and statebuilding)
Includes bibliographical references and index.
1. Peace-building. 2. Peacekeeping forces. 3. Intervention
(International law) 4. Humanitarian intervention.
I. Turner, Mandy, editor.
JZ5538.P653 2015
327.1'17--dc23
2015010063

ISBN 13: 978-1-138-31052-0 (pbk)
ISBN 13: 978-1-138-89127-2 (hbk)

Typeset in Baskerville
by Cenveo Publisher Services

Contents

Acknowledgements	ix
Contributors	xi

Introduction: The tyranny of peace and the politics of international intervention — 1
MANDY TURNER AND FLORIAN P. KÜHN

PART I
Exploring peace — 19

1 **International peace practice: Ambiguity, contradictions and perpetual violence** — 21
   FLORIAN P. KÜHN

2 **Geographies of reconstruction: Re-thinking post-war spaces** — 39
   SCOTT KIRSCH AND COLIN FLINT

3 **Still the spectre at the feast: Comparisons between peacekeeping and imperialism in peacekeeping studies today** — 59
   PHILIP CUNLIFFE

4 **Lineages of aggressive peace** — 77
   MICHAEL PUGH

5 **A double-edged sword of peace? Reflections on the tension between representation and protection in gendering liberal peacebuilding** — 94
   HEIDI HUDSON

PART II
Imposing peace 115

6 **UNTAC, peace and violence in Cambodia** 117
CAROLINE HUGHES

7 **Securing and stabilising: Peacebuilding as counterinsurgency in the occupied Palestinian territory** 139
MANDY TURNER

8 **Waging war and building peace in Afghanistan** 163
ASTRI SUHRKE

9 **War and peace in Côte d'Ivoire: Violence, agency and the local/international line** 179
BRUNO CHARBONNEAU

10 **Enemy images, coercive socio-engineering and civil war in Iraq** 197
TOBY DODGE

11 **Libya in the shadow of Iraq: The 'Old Guard' versus the *thuwwar* in the battle for stability** 218
NICOLAS PELHAM

12 **Defending neoliberal Mali: French military intervention and the management of contested political narratives** 229
BRUNO CHARBONNEAU AND JONATHAN SEARS

13 **Intervention and non-intervention in the Syria crisis** 251
CHRISTOPHER PHILLIPS

Index 272

Acknowledgements

This book was three years in the making. It started life as a special issue of the journal *International Peacekeeping* in August 2012, entitled 'Where Has All the Peace Gone? Peacebuilding, Peace Operations and Regime Change Wars' (vol. 19, no. 4). We would like to thank Taylor & Francis for permission to re-use many of the articles, albeit updated and extended. The starting point of this special issue was to critically interrogate the practices of international 'peacebuilding' and 'peace missions' to highlight the violence that inheres in their attempts to enforce socio-economic and political changes on societies. We felt that the 'peace prefix' was applied to all sorts of activities that were, in fact, incredibly violent. This underlined for us the ambiguities of the word 'peace' itself, and prompted us to seek to explore both the concept, the development of the practices used to institute 'peace', and experiences of its implementation through international intervention. We held two panels on this topic – one at the International Studies Association annual convention in San Diego, 1–4 April 2012, the second at the British International Studies Association conference in Edinburgh, 20–22 June 2012. Both panels, which included contributors to the special issue and this book, received important critical feedback, which further enriched our discussion of this topic. This edited volume includes updated versions of all but two of the articles in the special issue, as well as five new chapters.

There are many people we would like to thank for helping to make this book possible. We would first of all like to thank Michael Pugh, who was crucial in helping us nurse the special issue of *International Peacekeeping* into existence and persuading us to develop it into this book. We are extremely grateful for the immense support, warmth, professionalism and camaraderie that Michael has given us both over the years. We would also like to thank the contributors to this edited book for their patience and support for this project: Bruno Charbonneau, Philip Cunliffe, Toby Dodge, Colin Flint, Heidi Hudson, Caroline Hughes, Scott Kirsch, Nicolas Pelham, Christopher Phillips, Astri Suhrke and Jonathan M. Sears. It has been a privilege and a pleasure to work with you.

We would also like to thank the following people for other assistance along the way: Berit Bliesemann de Guevara, David Chandler, Vanessa Farr, Nicola Pratt, Eric Herring, Roger Mac Ginty, Oliver Richmond, Tony Chafer, Gilbert Achcar, Nicolas Lemay-Hébert, Jesper Nielsen and Jana Hönke.

We offer our sincerest gratitude to everyone mentioned here as they all played a huge part in creating, what we hope, will be an important contribution to the study of intervention and the imposition of peace.

Mandy Turner and Florian P. Kühn
Jerusalem and Berlin

Contributors

Bruno Charbonneau is Associate Professor of Political Science at Laurentian University, and Director of the Center for Peace and Humanitarian Missions Studies at the Université du Québec à Montréal, Canada. His research examines the international politics of West African conflicts and peace interventionism. He wrote *France and the New Imperialism: Security Policy in Sub-Saharan Africa* (2008), and co-edited *Peace Operations in the Francophone World* (2014), *Peacebuilding, Memory and Reconciliation* (2012) and *Locating Global Order* (2010). His work is available in several edited books and academic journals, including recent publications in the *Review of International Studies, International Peacekeeping, Journal of Intervention and Statebuilding* and the *Canadian Journal of Political Science.*

Philip Cunliffe is Senior Lecturer in International Conflict at the School of Politics and International Relations, University of Kent. His most recent book, *Legions of Peace: UN Peacekeepers from the Global South*, was published in 2013. He is the editor of *International Peacekeeping.*

Toby Dodge is the Kuwait Professor and Director of the Middle East Centre as well as being a Professor in International Relations at the London School of Economics and Political Science. He is the author of *Iraq: From War to a New Authoritarianism* (2013) and *Inventing Iraq: the Failure of Nation Building and a History Denied*, (2003).

Colin Flint is a Professor of Political Science at Utah State University, US. His research interests include geopolitics, militarisation, just war theory and the spatial analysis of conflict. He is editor of *Spaces of Hate: Geographies of Hate and Intolerance in the United States* (2003) and *The Geography of War and Peace* (2004), and co-editor (with Scott Kirsch) of *Reconstructing Conflict: Integrating War and Post-War Geographies* (2011). He is the author of *Introduction to Geopolitics* (2012) and co-author, with Peter J. Taylor, of *Political Geography: World-Economy, Nation-State and Locality* (2011).

Heidi Hudson is Professor of International Relations and Director of the Centre for Africa Studies at the University of the Free State, Bloemfontein, South Africa. She is a Global Fellow of the Oslo Peace Research Institute

(PRIO), in Norway and serves on the executive committee of the Feminist Theory and Gender Studies section of the International Studies Association (ISA). Heidi is co-editor of *Post-Conflict Reconstruction and Development in Africa: Concepts, Role-Players, Policy and Practice* (2013), with Theo Neethling. Over the years she has contributed several chapters in books and has published numerous articles in, among others, *International Peacekeeping, Security Dialogue, Security Studies, Politikon, Agenda, Strategic Review for Southern Africa* and *African Security Review*. She is co-editor of *International Feminist Journal of Politics* and serves, among others, on the editorial board of *International Peacekeeping, Politikon, The Australasian Review of African Studies* and *Africa Insight*.

Caroline Hughes is Professor of Conflict Resolution and Peace, and the academic director of the Bradford Rotary Centre for International Studies, University of Bradford. Her research interests combine a critical analysis of the politics of international post-conflict intervention, aid and development with expertise in Asian politics. In particular, she focuses on the ways in which aid and peacekeeping interventions are mediated by national and local-level social structures and ideologies in post-conflict contexts. Recent books include *The Politics of Accountability in South East Asia: The Dominance of Moral Ideologies* (with Garry Rodan; 2014) and *Dependent Communities: Aid and Politics in Cambodia and Timor-Leste* (2009).

Scott Kirsch is Associate Professor of Geography at the University of North Carolina at Chapel Hill, US. He is author of *Proving Grounds: Project Plowshare and the Unrealized Dream of Nuclear Earthmoving* (2005) and co-editor (with Colin Flint) of *Reconstructing Conflict: Integrating War and Post-War Geographies* (2011).

Florian P. Kühn is Interim Professor for Comparative Politics at Magdeburg's Otto von Guericke University. He has published research on risk, security and development in South and Central Asia as well as the narrative foundations of interventionism in several journals, including *International Peacekeeping, International Relations, Canadian Foreign Policy Journal, Peacebuilding*, and *Zeitschrift für Außen- und Sicherheitspolitik*. He published *Security and Development in World Society* (2010), which was awarded the German Middle East Studies Foundation's dissertation award 2010 and, together with Berit Bliesemann de Guevara, *Illusion Statebuilding* (2010). He is co-editor of *Journal of Intervention and Statebuilding*.

Nicolas Pelham is *The Economist*'s correspondent in Jerusalem, and a writer on Arab affairs for the *New York Review of Books*. From 2005 to 2010 he was the Israel/Palestine senior analyst for International Crisis Group, where he covered the rise of the region's national–religious movements. He began working as a journalist in Cairo in 1992, and then joined the BBC Arabic Service. He joined *The Economist* in 1998, and has worked as the paper's

Contributors xiii

correspondent in Morocco, Amman and Baghdad. He is the author of *A New Muslim Order* (2008), which traces Shia resurgence in the Arab world, and co-author (with Peter Mansfield) of *A History of the Middle East* (2010).

Christopher Phillips is Senior Lecturer in the International Relations of the Middle East at Queen Mary, University of London, and an Associate Fellow at the Chatham House Middle East and North Africa programme. He has a PhD in International Relations at the London School of Economics, specialising in contemporary Syria and Jordan. He has lived for several years in Syria and conducts regular research trips to Jordan, Turkey, Lebanon and Egypt. He has written for various publications including the Guardian, CNN, the Huffington Post and Open Democracy and has appeared on the BBC, Channel 4 and al-Jazeera discussing the Syria crisis. His first book, *Everyday Arab Identity: The Daily Reproduction of the Arab World* was published in 2013.

Michael Pugh is Emeritus Professor, University of Bradford, and Visiting Professor at the Institute for Management Research, Centre for Conflict Analysis and Management, Radboud University Nijmegen. He was Leverhulme Emeritus Fellow (2011–2012) and founding editor of *International Peacekeeping*. He has written extensively on peace and conflict and is the co-editor, with Neil Cooper and Mandy Turner, of *Whose Peace? Critical Perspectives on the Political Economy of Peacebuilding* (2008). He is the author of *Liberal Internationalism: The Interwar Movement for Peace in Britain* (2012) and 'Local Agency and Political Economies of Peacebuilding' (*Studies in Ethnicity and Nationalism*, 2011).

Jonathan M. Sears is Assistant Professor of International Development Studies at Menno Simons College (affiliated with the University of Winnipeg), Manitoba, Canada. From a multi-disciplinary background in political studies, philosophy, and anthropology, Jonathan teaches development ethics and theory, aid policies, African politics, and political theory. His recent publications include 'Seeking Sustainable Legitimacy: Existential Challenges for Mali' in *International Journal: Canada's Journal of Global Policy Analysis* (September 2013).

Astri Suhrke is a Senior Researcher and political scientist at the Chr. Michelsen Institute, Bergen, and Associate Fellow at the Asia-Pacific College of Diplomacy, The Australian National University, Canberra. She has worked on the social, political and humanitarian consequences of violent conflict, and strategies of response, including concepts of human security and peacebuilding. Her current special topic is strategies of post-war reconstruction and statebuilding, with particular reference to Afghanistan. She has led research projects funded by the Research Council of Norway: The Multilateral Aid System (2001–2003); Aid in Post-Conflict Situations (2003–2005) and Violence in the Post-Conflict State (2005–2008). Astri has participated in projects commissioned by the

Norwegian Ministry of Foreign Affairs, various UN agencies and state international development agencies, and the World Bank. Her publications include *When More is Less: The International Project in Afghanistan* (2011), *The Peace In Between: Post-War Violence and Peacebuilding* (co-edited with Mats Berdal, 2011) and *Roads to Reconciliation* (co-edited with Elin Skaar and Siri Gloppen, 2005).

Mandy Turner is the Director of the Kenyon Institute (Council for British Research in the Levant) in East Jerusalem and a Visiting Research Fellow at the Middle East Centre, London School of Economics and Political Science. Her research focuses on the political economy of war-torn societies, with a country focus on the occupied Palestinian territory on which she has published widely. She is co-editor, with Omar Shweiki, of *Decolonizing Palestinian Political Economy: De-development and Beyond* (2014), and co-editor, with Michael Pugh and Neil Cooper, of *Whose Peace? Critical Perspectives on the Political Economy of Peacebuilding* (2008/2011).

Introduction
The tyranny of peace and the politics of international intervention

Mandy Turner and Florian P. Kühn

> So we look at the issue of intervention or not and seem baffled. We change the regimes in Afghanistan and Iraq, put soldiers on the ground ... We change the regime in Libya through air power ... In Syria, we call for the regime to change, we encourage the opposition to rise up ... Then there has been the so-called Arab Spring. At first we jumped in to offer our support to those on the street. We are now bemused and bewildered that it hasn't turned out quite how we expected.
>
> Tony Blair, speech on the Middle East, Bloomberg, London, 23 April 2014

On 23 April 2014, the Middle East Quartet representative and former UK prime minister, Tony Blair, delivered a keynote speech at Bloomberg, the financial media organisation, in London. His main focus was to explain the failure of Western intervention in the Middle East to bring peace, democracy, religious freedom, and open market economies. The huge conundrum, argued Blair, was that despite all the boots on the ground, the airstrikes, the implementation of forceful regime-change, international involvement in societal reconstruction, and political encouragement – these countries continue to be wracked by instability, violence and extremism. Blair's conclusion is that the reason for these failures is that they are common victims of a wider 'Titanic struggle' going on between modernity and radical Islam.[1] For Blair, even the rise of Da'esh (ISIS) in Iraq and Syria is regarded as having been caused by domestic problems, not by the Western invasion of Iraq and the destabilising reconstruction strategy implemented thereafter.[2] While we reject his Orientalist framework and conclusions, we find Blair's speech interesting for two simple reasons. First, Blair identifies and voices the confusion that resides within the discourse of Western policymakers over why something so normatively desirable – the pursuit of, and building of, peace – has turned out so badly. From Cambodia to Afghanistan, Palestine to Mali, interventions in the pursuit of peace have not achieved the desired results. Second, Blair's speech shows that international elites will continue to misunderstand why these interventions fail – and why they will continue to lead to such tragic situations as represented by Iraq and Libya in 2014.

This is because these Western elites will continue to blame the 'other', the 'local', the 'savage' – for preventing peace, for creating instability, for wreaking chaos on the order they are trying to impose – and they will continue to disregard and ignore the central role of the actual type and experience of intervention upon these societies. Indeed, George Joffe, one of the Iraq specialists who advised Blair in the run-up to the invasion in 2003, revealed that the prime minister was uninterested in the complexities of Iraq and the potential for destabilisation preferring instead to see it as a crusade against evil,[3] much like his US counterpart at the time, President George W. Bush, as analysed by Toby Dodge in Chapter 10 of this book. From the comfort of their metropolitan worldview and narrative, the interveners thus absolve themselves of responsibility and see their missions as legitimate.

This type of thinking has its foundations in Western liberal political thought, in particular, the writings of John S. Mill, Alexis de Tocqueville and John Locke.[4] De Tocqueville, for example, in his analysis of French colonialism in Algeria, advised colonisers and interveners thus:

> What can be hoped for, not to suppress the hostile sentiments that our government inspires, but to weaken them; not to make our yoke liked, but to make it seem more and more tolerable; not to annihilate the repugnance that Muslims have always displayed for a foreign and Christian power, but to make them discover that this power, despite an origin they condemn, can be useful to them.[5]

Such a perspective, based on the heuristic ordering principle that urges the 'superior' to engage in 'helping' the 'inferior' in order to foster 'modernity', stability and 'bring' peace, has created a disconnect between understanding the politics of intervention and the violent results it produces. This book thus seeks to understand how peace – and interventions to impose, protect and advance it – became such a hegemonic, tyrannical project. Revealing the hierarchies and power relations enshrined in intervention requires an analysis of its practices in contrast to its purported ideals, in order to highlight the forceful and violent ways through which such politics is conducted. Towards this end, the chapters critically explore the politics and practices of intervention and peacebuilding, and the politics of the communities experiencing intervention.

We take as our starting point a rejection of the traditional 'well-trodden dichotomies and dilemmas between, for example, interests vs. rules (or norms), selectivity vs. consistency, intentions vs. capacity, legitimacy vs. legality, and surgical action vs. quagmire'.[6] These debates reside within the largely policy-based focus of conventional studies, which privileges the needs and priorities of Western policies and practices, and which also focuses its gaze on military intervention, including the recent debates that have taken place under the rubric of 'responsibility to protect' – the doctrine advanced by the International Commission on Intervention and State Sovereignty

(ICISS) in 2001.[7] We seek to move beyond this restrictive definition of intervention, instead starting from the principle that intervention takes many forms, and includes the full spectrum of tools and policies to structurally influence and change others' policies and/or polities, as well as how the politics of intervention themselves are designed and implemented. Interventions, as we understand them, mean the involvement in the internal politics of a nation-state or community by an external body (particularly by another state or by an international institution) which thus widens the boundaries to cover a multitude of actions in addition to military operations – such as blockades and sanctions, diplomatic or financial support for certain political elites, as well as aid and economic policies. It can also include requests for colonisation or acceptance of it by local elites, as was the case in Bosnia Herzegovina.[8]

Therefore, while some of the empirical chapters in this book focus on a direct international peacebuilding intervention and/or peace mission, others utilise a wider conception of what constitutes intervention. The latter explore the ways in which regional and international actors influence particular conflict contexts and interact with local actors in ways that are perhaps not always directly visible but are nevertheless designed to steer things in particular directions. This may involve covert military support or political influence as was witnessed in the first few years of Syria's revolution and descent into civil war analysed by Christopher Phillips in Chapter 13 of this book. Widening out the definition of intervention – and identifying which groups cooperate and find an interventionist policy 'useful' in accordance with Tocqueville's dictum – thus allows us to capture a variety of actions that would otherwise remain hidden, but are no less important. And yet with this widening out, comes risks – as it makes it more difficult to draw a clear distinction between regular everyday relations between states and intervention *per se*. And perhaps therein resides the real conundrum of intervention. It happens so regularly that to regard it as an exception to the discourse of sovereignty that governs the modern international system and how we understand it is an ideological position, to follow Slavoj Žižek's definition of ideology as 'a lie which pretends to be taken seriously' and hinges on the enabler's complicity.[9] This means that certain ideas and beliefs are enshrined in 'normalcy' in ways that obscure responsibility for economic and political policies and practices. These ideas therefore, in turn, become an intricate part of this 'reality' by being written into socio-political practices and institutions.[10] Stephen D. Krasner was therefore right to refer to sovereignty as 'organised hypocrisy' – it being continually invoked as the governing principle of international order while being continually contravened.[11] And yet a focus on sovereignty, which underpins the academic discipline of International Relations and thus most studies of intervention, largely shrouds the unequal power relations and racialised forms of imperial power that the international system rests upon. It also shrouds the privileging of private property and capitalist relations, which requires establishing laws that protect and guide these relations.[12]

States display a remarkable ability to cover up their violent origins as well as the power relations enshrined in their institutions and laws.[13] Furthermore, institutionalised power sanctions particular social ideas and projects the state 'into the minds' of citizens through education and support for certain forms of economic reproduction and political organisation, while suppressing others.[14] Opening a set of opportunities while closing down others means expanding a particular, capitalist, way of governing the peace to a global scale. Indeed, the most powerful actors in the international system argue that international stability occasionally requires violent intervention in the pursuit of peace – or rather the pursuit of a form of peace that favours their privileged positions. The use of military violence as well as more subtle and invisible technologies of control and co-option of elites is one way of ensuring that the framework survives and is further enshrined in the epistemology of international relations. The practices and impacts of military occupation are widely reported on – largely because of its highly visible repercussions on Western societies in terms of traumatised soldiers or the kidnapping of humanitarian workers.[15] But disruptions and changes in social practices in societies experiencing intervention are less well-observed or understood. And even less well understood is how these societies perceive and deal with intervention, as well as an understanding of their political and economic priorities, which often diverge markedly from those of the intervener. So, while some forms of intervention remain largely hidden from public view, it is our contention that grey suits in government offices can have as big an impact as soldiers' boots on the ground. Indeed, the research of Mark Duffield and Graham Harrison on aid and development reveals how Western donors discipline and direct by inserting their own advisors into key ministries in aid-recipient governments.[16] Restricting the definition of intervention to military action would therefore miss 'the way in which overtly coercive practices may be superseded by more subtle rational-bureaucratic means of reordering and control'.[17]

The contributions in this book, particularly the empirical case studies, largely focus on the post-Cold War period, because intervention in the pursuit of peace in this epoch has been 'undertaken by a sufficiently unified core which has frequently demonstrated its will to use force to reorder the periphery'.[18] Nevertheless, despite this focus, several thematic chapters in Part I explore a longer historical experience of intervention and the wider conceptual understanding of it that this necessitates. Intervention has a long biography – as Lawson and Tardelli point out, it lies at the heart of the modern international system.[19] And so it is our contention that by adopting a wider conceptual and longer historical lens, themes come into focus that would remain hidden or ignored in the current debate. This wider historical and conceptual understanding of intervention is intricately interconnected with another key critique in this book: that the current overwhelming research focus on the concept and practice of liberal intervention and the 'liberal peace' ignores the fact that intervention in the pursuit of peace and order existed long before the end of the Cold War and the perceived defeat of alternatives to liberal capitalism.[20] Writers within this framework have, of course, identified the origins of the liberal peace and liberal interventionism within philosophical debates that reach back far beyond this current historical period.[21] And yet the research undertaken and arguments put forward continue to remain firmly placed within a research agenda in which the parameters are limited to a debate between two camps: those who seek to defend and advance the liberal peace (and make it 'better'); and those who seek an alternative in either the 'post-liberal', the 'local-local' or the 'hybrid peace'.[22] Many of the chapters in this book engage with this important contemporary debate; however, we are at pains to stress that we place our analyses of liberal peace interventions within a broader historical and conceptual understanding of intervention and peace.

This book therefore analyses intervention as an embedded international social practice and focuses on its deep sociological grammar. This is developed through conceptual and thematic exploration, and an extensive number of in-depth empirical case studies. There is a focus on empirical analysis, provided by people who have researched the countries in question for many years, to avoid the tendency in much writings on intervention to 'exclude or marginalise consideration of the people targeted'.[23] This is powered by the adoption of an explicit decolonising approach. Many of the chapters, therefore, do not merely focus on the *interveners* but also the *intervened*. A focus on the former is not only inadequate for an analysis of the politics of intervention, but reproduces a perspective that analytically privileges the West and silences the subaltern. Recent writings on opposition to international peacebuilding interventions have unfortunately replicated this problem by identifying neoliberalism as an 'international imposition', and the 'local' as being more authentic and likely to resist.[24] Neoliberalism, for sure, dominates the political economy of the international system, but treating 'the international' as a static, homogeneous category loses sight of how different actors, both international and local, shape neoliberalism through the interaction of various forms of power and resistance. Some chapters, such as Bruno Charbonneau's on Côte d'Ivoire (Chapter 9), even problematise the analytical distinction between 'interveners' (and their automatic designation as 'international') and 'intervened' (and their automatic designation as 'local'). By tapping into the epistemological resources of state orders, newly empowered elites often try to re-shape national narratives and legitimising myths.[25] Local elites also seek to adopt, adapt, utilise and/or reject neoliberal strategies – the analysis of which constitutes a strong theme in many chapters in this book. We do not, however, lose sight of the fact that often when local elites step out of line, international and regional actors attempt to make them conform.

Two important points emerge from our approach, and from the studies in this book. The first point is that intervention should be understood *sociologically* as constituting the pursuit of the expansion and protection of capitalist social relations and institutions. The extension of capitalist social forms has been, and remains, inseparable from conquest and war, and the imposition of a particular kind of 'peace'.[26] The debate on the 'liberal peace' is therefore, for us, merely the most recent conceptualisation of this deep grammar of intervention. It is a momentary concept that allows us to understand the current priorities of Western states and their foreign policy interventions. The second point that emerges from our approach is that intervention is inscribed and inherent within the Western-dominated international system, and constitutes a core method by which the capitalist West tries to both integrate the periphery into the capitalist system *while* protecting itself from the conflicts emanating from transformations in this periphery. Such an analysis does not ignore the role of colonial and imperial violence in the emergence of capitalist social forms but rather takes this violence as its starting point. 'Colonial difference' is therefore the product of 'power' and 'positionality', and not the result of 'culture or historical exceptionalism'.[27] The 'standard of civilisation',[28] the 'clash of civilisations',[29] the 'liberal peace'[30] and the 'war on terror'[31] are, for us, ideological moments in the justification of Western violence.

States are driven by the necessity to collect funds to finance their own institutions that, in turn, favours capitalist 'economies of scale' and economic and political expansion. The extension of capitalism to new spheres – both territorially and socially (and its continual defence) – requires the establishment of institutions and social relations to facilitate capitalist investment and infrastructure to extract resources and the flow of profits back to the metropole. While trade capitalism, one of the characteristics of early colonialism, rested on violent expropriation, the transition to equivalent structures of capitalist exchange requires the dominance of production capital (rather than trade capital). For all societies, this transformation from subsistence and small scale to specialised and industrialised production (which empowers some, while disempowering others), demands a violent process of dispossession. This process, which Marx calls 'primitive accumulation', required to institute capitalist social relations, is not, however, the final experience of dispossession. Indeed, dispossession is not constituted in one single isolated event or act but can happen in any society at any time – and is part of a continual historical process of political struggle as capital reacts to ensure its dominance and profitability. The concept of accumulation by dispossession, developed by David Harvey,[32] is therefore utilised explicitly by a number of chapters in this book, while others allude to the process through empirical reconstruction and analysis. For example, in chapter six on Cambodia, Caroline Hughes argues that while the key transitions for Western peacebuilders were war to peace and communism to capitalism – for locals, another transition was of equal or greater concern, that being instituted by a rapacious process of capitalist primitive accumulation which was transforming resource governance and landholding through violent dispossession experienced by workers and the poor. Market reforms and the institution of liberal forms of ownership and citizenship underpinned and powered this process. Recognising and analysing such social processes, we contend, are crucial to understanding what type of peace is being implemented – and who is benefiting from it.

From a historical-structural point of view, the process of transformation – which should ideally equalise relations – is interminably prolonged (perhaps even impossible) as industrialised countries remain dominant, with the gap in terms of capital density even widening.[33] While the international system is made up of sovereign states equal in law, in reality some are more powerful than others because of uneven development. The uneven and combined process that characterises the expansion of capitalist social forms creates instability by playing out huge disparities of power. This drives a structural imperative for intervention as a managing exercise in which the capitalist core seeks to manage the conflicts, to protect itself, and to violently contain the transformation as it is unfolding.[34] The European powers initially performed this role and the main goal of their actions around the globe was to create favourable frameworks for capitalist expansion and to prevent local regimes emerging that opposed the dominance of European capital. After World War II, the USA emerged as global hegemon, with the European powers in minor roles. In this period, the Communist Soviet Union provided a visible opposition to the structures and values of the Western-dominated international system and was a barrier to the establishment of a global Pax Americana.[35] The ability of developing countries to play the two superpowers off against each other helped to obscure the strong colonial and imperial roots of the UN, which was marginalised during this time.[36]

While the state is enshrined as the principal actor of world politics, its practices transcend national borders through the establishment of formal and informal networks of power that guide and influence the politics of the nation-state, both domestically and internationally. Such clusters – which include security communities, fora such as the G8, and international institutions – limit, enable and prescribe the options available to collective actors, from states to firms, to social movements. Multilateral institutions have, in the process, become vehicles for Western interests portrayed as universal values. For over 30 years, neoliberalism has been promoted by western states which have made use of their power to influence and epistemologically code the politics of international bodies. Since the 1980s, the World Bank and the IMF have been pushing a particular neoliberal form of development and political organisation, which circumscribes the type of policies that states can follow.[37] After the collapse of the alternative Soviet model of political economy in the early 1990s, Western organisational forms and conceptions of peace could again become internationally hegemonic. These beliefs and structures were strengthened through their adoption and implementation by a newly energised UN, and thereafter they became deeply embedded in the architecture of global governance and imperial multilateralism. The UN is a particularly important actor as the main forum in the post-Cold War era for the discussion and implementation of peace strategies; it also provides the bulk of agencies and funding as well as interventionist expertise supporting social engineering and transformations. The UN has therefore played a strong legitimising role – through its purported neutrality – in helping these Western ideas become hegemonic and embedded in the ideology of international NGOs and human rights practice, as noted by some of the chapters in this book.

Our analysis therefore contests that there is more than a fleeting connection between the colonial *mission civilisatrice* and modern intervention practices. And not just because it is largely former colonial powers who have assumed the leadership in establishing an order which decolonisation de jure but not de facto managed to establish. Intervention is therefore, for us, a method of 'policing (colonial) differences globally'.[38] Such a conclusion punctures the purity of liberal ideology that capitalist social forms promote a pacific domestic and international polity. A peace that seeks the extension, imposition and defence of capitalist social relations by necessity excludes and oppresses, delegitimises and criminalises alternative ideas of order. It is a violent, tyrannical peace.

Structure of the book

The book is divided into two parts: 'Exploring Peace' and 'Imposing Peace'. Part I has five chapters which focus on critical enquiries into the origins and historical development of the concept of peace and how it has been pursued. Part II has eight chapters, each of which interrogates a particular international intervention or peacebuilding mission. While all of the contributions vary in their analytical underpinnings, they all critically unpack the politics of international intervention and highlight the violence that inheres in attempts to enforce socio-economic and political changes from the 'outside' in the quest to build a particular type of peace.

Part I – 'Exploring Peace' – offers analyses of: the origins and development of the liberal concept and practice of peace; the origins and development of the concept and practice of post-war/post-conflict reconstruction; comparisons made between contemporary peacebuilding and the imperial practices of European empires; how the UN became a promoter of Western values and liberal social forms; and the application of liberal feminist ideas to the politics of intervention and peacebuilding.

In Chapter 1, Florian P. Kühn explores the origins and development of the dominant conceptualisation of peace that has its historical roots deep in Enlightenment thought and in the emerging practices of nation states during the period since. This liberal version of peace, he argues, reifies and legitimises the Western social forms of the sovereign state and the capitalist market – and securitises the 'not-yet-liberalised Other' thereafter deemed non-equal. In this worldview, Kühn posits, intervention and the use of violence thus become justified – and so peace (and war) work to expand the 'liberal world' through the imposition of Western social forms globally. While the liberal way of peace is a policy and practice driven by a narrative of non-violence, this chapter argues that it does, in fact, serve to disguise violent techniques of global governance employed to manage the security of this structure while extending its reach. It is therefore an aggressive politics pursuing the preservation of the existing peace of the powerful – a 'managing exercise that aims to protect the capitalist core from the non-liberal periphery'.[39] Kühn argues that the politics and practices of peace in the current period – often labelled the 'liberal peace' – are the result of a combination of long-standing liberal internationalism *and* late twentieth century neoliberalism. The politics of peace, which relies on technologies of control and co-option of elites, reflects the power of liberalism; it is a victor's peace which renders alternative forms of peace unthinkable. The chapter concludes by arguing that only by scrutinising the current liberal myths as well as the structures of domination that they preserve might we be able to resurrect a concept of peace that has emancipatory potential.

Chapter 2, by Scott Kirsch and Colin Flint, continues to scrutinise these liberal myths by deconstructing the history of the concept and practice of post-war/post-conflict reconstruction (PCR). They make a strong case for the application of a geographical approach 'to identify and explore the false dichotomies of war and peace', and posit that periods of war are also periods of construction, while PCR is a process of conflict in which relations of power shaped through war become embedded in the peace. To develop these arguments, Kirsch and Flint trace the history and practice of PCR from the US during and after its civil war through the inter-war and post-World War II periods, up to the post-Cold War world. Their analysis of PCR in the US shows how the Federal government's attempts to impose a particular form of state, economy, culture and society on the southern US states in the nineteenth century, provoked violence from sectors of that society set to lose from the changes – in today's parlance they would be referred to as 'spoilers'. Kirsch and Flint then go on to chart how the concept and practice of PCR became an essential political tool for the US as it moved to exert its power globally, and then became pervasive as a form of ensuring Western dominance embedded in the language and practice of international institutions such as the World Bank, the IMF and the UN. The waging of war and peace is, they argue, a constant feature of a society driven by the intertwined 'social processes of capital accumulation, imperialism, state formation, and militarisation'.[40] The chapter concludes by emphasising that PCR is a hegemonic strategy which confirms the politics of the 'winning side' and generates conditions for accumulation by dispossession.

Philip Cunliffe, in Chapter 3, explores the comparisons made between UN peacebuilding operations today and historical practices of imperialism and colonialism. He starts with the basic observation that the legitimacy of contemporary peacebuilding is often seen to hinge on the extent to which it transcends historic practices of imperialism. He then offers a critique of how these comparisons are made in the extant scholarship, and argues that supporters of peacebuilding deploy an under-theorised and historically one-sided view of imperialism. Claims that the aims and modalities of peacebuilding (disinterested/consensual and multilateral) are different from colonialism (driven by profit/strategic motives and unilateral) reveal a fundamental misunderstanding of the latter, argues Cunliffe, largely because this has been reliant on a scholarship that has long been critiqued and surpassed. He concludes that while there are many differences, there are also many similarities that 'spontaneously conjures up the spectre of imperialism: peacekeepers are set to pacify unruly but marginal territories, using deterrence and force, and propagating ideals and institutions that are consonant with the values espoused by the most powerful members of the international system'.[41] Cunliffe makes a strong case for a research focus which analyses the rise of imperial multilateralism and the institutions it deploys, given that the UN, rather than facilitating mediation between competing national or political projects, now facilitates conformity with one political order: liberal government and market-capitalist society. By doing so, Western peacebuilding practice thus 'restricts the range of options available to post-conflict societies'.

The importance of the UN as an instrument for the promotion of a particular model of development is the subject of Chapter 4 by Michael Pugh. In his survey of international operations fostered via or by the UN since the end of the Cold War, Pugh focuses on two developments that he argues signifies an aggressive peace: the militarisation and codification of violence as peace, and the institution of a hegemonic coercive political economy of peacebuilding. Peace operations, Pugh observes, have increasingly merged with counterinsurgency campaigns where regime change wars, endorsed by UN resolutions, echo nineteenth century imperial wars in which violence is deemed necessary to induce peace. Indeed, he makes the basic observation that the vast majority of peace missions have occurred in the territories of former European empires – but are implemented under the rubric of the more innocuous labels of the 'international community' and 'humanitarianism'. Often pathologised as 'failed states', these sites of intervention are thereafter subjected to a political economy formula of de-regulation, privatisation, marketisation, and international competition – codified in peace agreements, implemented by transitional administrations, or promoted by aid donors. Both aspects of this aggressive peace, pursued by drivers of liberalisation, 'protects the political economy preferred by institutions with power'.[42] The first stages in developing a non-violent and non-coercive political economy of peacebuilding would therefore involve reforming the institutions of advanced capitalism and global governance, although Pugh is sceptical of this possibility. The chapter concludes by arguing that these dual aggressive aspects of contemporary peace operations reveal a contradiction in liberalism – that its purported and self-proclaimed values of 'tolerance' actually mask principles and practices that are exclusionary.

Unpacking another example of the way in which liberalism functions as a form of exclusion is the focus of Chapter 5 by Heidi Hudson, who critically analyses international discourses on the politics of inclusion/exclusion, protection, as well as sexual and gender-based violence (SGBV). Hudson shows how the adoption of liberal feminist discourse and its mainstreaming by peacebuilding agencies function to produce exclusionary outcomes in peace processes, particularly as regards the politics of representation, in terms of how 'truths' about the 'strange' (them) in relation to the 'familiar' (we) underpin the gendered logic of Western protectionism. Utilising a postcolonial-feminist approach, she argues that women of the global south are regarded as passive and victimised – and in need of protection by their Western 'sisters' – thus illustrating the disempowering effect, and Orientalist underpinning, of such instrumentalist interpretations of women's agency. Hudson concedes that intervention has never been justified purely in gender terms; nevertheless, she shows how the appropriation of liberal feminism under the banner of 'saving' oppressed women has fed into the overall discourse. Indeed, Hudson posits that the way in which gender is framed in peace interventions is symptomatic of the way in which discourses about the representation and protection of women within the liberal intervention model are constructed and institutionalised. Furthermore, the discourse around SGBV in liberal peacebuilding has led to a focus on awareness-raising, rather than on the economic, political, social and cultural structures of patriarchy that ensure women's disempowerment.

Part II – Imposing Peace' – offers analyses of eight experiences of intervention and their aftermath up until 2014, structured in terms of historical implementation: the United Nations mission in Cambodia 1991–1993; Western peacebuilding practices in the occupied Palestinian territory after 1993; the international intervention in Afghanistan after 2001; international and regional interventions in Côte d'Ivoire after 2002; the US intervention in Iraq after 2003; regime-change intervention in Libya in 2012; French intervention in Mali in 2013; and international and regional intervention in Syria from 2011 to 2014.

In Chapter 6, the first of the case studies, Caroline Hughes analyses the first UN peacekeeping mission with a dedicated human rights component and a complex peacebuilding mandate – the United Nations mission in Cambodia (UNTAC), 1991–1993. She skilfully shows how the usual critique of this mission – that it did not have enough power to deal with spoilers in the incumbent regime – is misguided. Instead, Hughes offers a political economy analysis that charts the institution of a form of predatory rapacious capitalism which integrated Cambodia into the regional economy through policies and practices of large-scale dispossession that accelerated social and economic inequality, and created vast environmental destruction.

Liberal peacebuilders, she argues, not only failed to prevent this, but acted in ways that facilitated it, particularly in their focus on promoting individualistic liberal forms of citizenship and property ownership which legitimised, powered and underpinned the transformation of regimes of resource governance and landholding by a corrupt elite. Indeed, Hughes reveals that most complaints to the UNTAC Human Rights Component were related to land conflicts, but they disregarded them. The struggles of workers and the poor against this process and other practices designed to dispossess and repress were undermined by the promotion of a liberal conception of 'civil society' as constituting professional organisations that scrutinise state policy, not as class-based movements that defend collective interests. Hughes concludes that the primary outcome of the UN mission was the securing of a relationship between Cambodia's authoritarian elite and Western donors that created a violent political economy of power and reintegrated Cambodia into the regional capitalist economy.

Mandy Turner's analysis of peacebuilding in the occupied Palestinian territory (oPt) in Chapter 7 reaches similar conclusions. Since 1993, the oPt has been the site of extensive Western donor involvement in a non-sovereign context (but did not involve full UN control) which was neither post-conflict nor post-colonial. Peacebuilding practices are analysed by Turner in the realms of governance, security coordination and neoliberal economics – and she concludes that they have operated as another layer of pacification techniques that have complimented Israel's methods of control and helped to institute a new political economy serving the interests of a colonial peace. She argues that donor policies in the past 20 years have had one underlying goal: to secure and stabilise. This has meant that democracy, human rights and even economic development have been downgraded or ignored, if and when they have become an obstacle to ensuring this main underlying principle of peacebuilding in the oPt. Turner therefore makes the case for reconceptualising peacebuilding as counterinsurgency by charting their commonalities, particularly their shared goal of creating a particular form of political economy that stabilises *from the inside* in collaboration with a section of local elites who benefit from its implementation. Turner concludes by arguing that Western aid and donor practices are now intricately intertwined and embedded within the processes of colonisation and fragmentation taking place in the oPt, while at the same time purporting to reduce (or manage) its impacts. All of this has helped to secure a 'victor's peace'.

In Chapter 8, Astri Suhrke argues that there were two huge contradictions in the politics of international intervention in Afghanistan; the first involved simultaneously waging war and building peace; and the second involved building a rentier state dependent on donors while promoting a system of democracy where the government is accountable to the people. Widely regarded within the UN system as a just and necessary war for peacebuilding and stabilisation, Suhrke charts how the US-led intervention rapidly lost support, and led to a scaling back in 2014. She makes the important observation that, in the initial phases of the intervention, the aid and human rights communities were vocal advocates for a strong international military presence, although they were vehemently opposed to attempts by the military to jeopardise their neutral humanitarian space. But while visions of peace generated political support for intervention, violence undercut efforts to create the structures necessary for this peace. In order to reach demand for rapid results, interveners adapted measures that undermined basic precepts of statebuilding and peacebuilding thus illustrating the underlying tensions in the security-peacebuilding nexus, which increased as the mission went on. For example, to develop Afghan military capacities, NATO forces started re-arming the militias which disrupted the statebuilding process outlined as part of the transformative project codified in the Bonn Agreement. Nevertheless, however, the intervention fulfilled some important US foreign policy objectives by eventually ensuring the institution of a regime supportive of Western strategies in the region, as indicated by Afghanistan being conferred the status of Major Non-NATO Ally of the United States, which would help to protect US military power in the region.

In Chapter 9, Bruno Charbonneau analyses the peace interventions in Côte d'Ivoire from 2002 that led to regime change in 2011. He makes the important but oft ignored point that violence in the context of international peace interventions is rarely problematised: it is associated with the conflict belligerents, while that deployed by peacekeepers is conceived as 'peace operations' that mitigate, subdue or deter the belligerents' violence. This, he argues, is the result of a discrimination between 'local' and 'international' considered theoretically necessary to understand interventions – and which underpins the question of legitimate political agency. Charbonneau, however, critically scrutinises this division by showing how France, the ex-colonial power, was already an intricate part of 'local' and 'regional' dynamics and structures; while the involvement of ECOWAS and the African Union indicate the importance of regional actors in the intervention. The French–UN use of force in 2011 was premised on the assumption that it was employing legitimate violence in the pursuit of peace, whereas France's decision not to intervene in 2002 was regarded by Laurent Gbagbo as a betrayal, who thereafter portrayed France and other international actors as colonialists. Charbonneau observes how the framing of and subsequent policymaking vis-à-vis violent crises is often a joint endeavour of political elites who, alongside calculations of their political and social interests, play the game of violence for their own purposes. 'Local transnationalised actors' can therefore 'benefit or aggravate the relationship between an international militarised peace agenda and capitalism'[43] as exemplified by Gbagbo's use of anti-colonialist and nationalist rhetoric. And so local elites defy characterisation of being passive recipients of Western concepts and practices, as they can, in fact, also shape these visions. The ways in which violence was deployed in Côte d'Ivoire, argues Charbonneau, responded to these competing claims to legitimacy, agency and authority.

Chapter 10 focuses on Iraq. Toby Dodge argues that the origins of Iraq's post-war political settlement can be traced back to the ideational understanding of Iraq under Saddam Hussein shared by the dominant decision-makers in the US Bush administration. The Ba'ath regime was seen through a 'diabolical enemy image' which drove a moral sense of urgency and encouraged the US to pick certain groups to form Iraq's new ruling elite and to exclude others. This was the cause of the ensuing civil war, not 'ancient hatreds' as is commonly argued. Dodge reconstructs the US's foreign policy decision-making process through a constructivist lens, in which the creation of the 'other' drove the enemy image, whose power was enhanced by long-standing Orientalist and racist Western assumptions. As the situation was regarded to be a struggle between 'good' and 'evil', the outright subjugation of the enemy was pursued through a 'victor's peace'. Once the military struggle was over, state power was used to 'cleanse' society of the vanquished foe by purging the old order. The head of the US-led Coalition Provisional Authority, L. Paul Bremer, had paramount authority across the land, and the reform programme was targeted at Ba'ath Party members, which was then extended to the Sunni community as a whole. This policy of exclusion drove the country into civil war and explains the upsurge in violence in Mosul in June 2014. One side, Iraq's new ruling elite, with US support, fought to impose a victor's peace through the violent suppression of former members of the old regime. The other side (i.e. those excluded) therefore launched an insurgency to overturn the post-war political order. Dodge concludes that 'the rise of Da'esh [ISIS] and Iraq's renewed civil war [in 2014] spring directly from the profound mistakes made by the US occupation'.[44]

International thinking and experiences of Iraqi 'de-Ba'athification' heavily guided the practices of the National Transitional Council in post-revolutionary Libya, as Nicolas Pelham argues in Chapter 11. In attempting to avoid 'reliving the Iraq war', the NTC made a conscious decision to integrate the 'old guard' into the new order, but in the process alienated those who had led the rebellion. The fledgling central authority thus drove the post-Qaddafi instability by failing to secure the buy-in of the rebel militias (*thuwwar*) into their post-conflict vision of a civilian order. Pelham shows that little attempt was made to structurally integrate the militias, who were increasingly viewed less as liberators and more as looters and hooligans – and more emphasis was placed on 'reining them in'. Politically, they were excluded as government was dominated by the old elite and returnee exiles. Economically, they were increasingly deprived of their assets – the ports, border terminals and airports. And in the security sector, the potential outsourcing of Libya's national defence to foreign private security companies was perceived as a threat to the *thuwwar*'s hope of recruitment into state security services. Locked out of employment opportunities in government, security, and the private sector, the *thuwwar* thus turned to smuggling, which enhanced their autonomous coping mechanisms and hastened the erosion of state control.

Promises to decentralise and bridge the inequality between Tripoli and the provinces also went unfulfilled, and corruption was rife – both of which further fuelled instability. Pelham concludes that the failure to demobilise the *thuwwar* and offer them a stake in the new order was the proximate cause of the descent into violence that Libya subsequently faced.

Bruno Charbonneau and Jonathan Sears's analysis of Mali in Chapter 12 challenges the dominant formulations of Mali's 2012–2013 crisis and questions the rationales for the French and international responses. The authors show how the discourse of global Islamist terrorism overlay the complex dynamics of Malian politics and erased the context-specific dynamics that led to the crisis. They situate Mali's weak state capacity in its ongoing failure to consolidate a hegemonic national political identity, and its development problems in neoliberal economic restructuring (imposed by the World Bank and IMF) that further centralised power, concentrated wealth, and intensified divisions between rural and urban and within urban settings. Mali's persistent governance problems, condoned for decades by donor partners keen to further Mali's tutelage in neoliberal economic development, combined with increasing socio-economic cleavages to threaten state integrity from within. French intervention in this context, argue Charbonneau and Sears, is a clear example of the relationship between global militarised practices and transnational neoliberal governance. Furthermore, donor insistence on Mali being a secular state has foreclosed Islam-based discourses of moral authority and legitimacy which have greater local traction. The chapter concludes by arguing that the neoliberal mode of good governance favoured by donors and secured by international military intervention risks inhibiting rather than enabling the building of a durable and democratic peace in Mali.

In Chapter 13, Christopher Phillips analyses international and regional responses to the Syrian crisis. He makes two key points: firstly, that an expanded understanding of intervention is required in this context; and secondly, that the concurrent crisis in Libya played an influential role in shaping the response of both rebels and members of the UN Security Council. Up until mid-2014, Syria was regarded as an example of non-intervention but, argues Phillips, while the crisis has domestic origins, from the very beginning regional and international powers utilised an arsenal of intervention tools (that included diplomatic protection, finance, weapons and manpower) either in support of Assad or his enemies to shape the nature and scale of the crisis. He also shows how the situation in Libya was a crucial comparator for key actors in the Syrian context. Indeed, Phillips begins by asking the important question: why was there direct Western military intervention in Libya but not in Syria? While many analyses invoke the importance of the 'responsibility to protect' doctrine (R2P), Phillips instead concludes that it was perceived 'national interests' that drove intervention in Libya, not R2P. Indeed, as Phillips argues, the difference between Libya and Syria remind us that military intervention is dependent on the will of the five permanent members of the UN Security Council to act. The situation in Libya, however, raised expectations among the Free Syrian Army about the possibility of direct military intervention. Russia's stance on Syria was also influenced by the Libyan experience – in which it regarded NATO to have overstepped the UN mandate by pursuing regime change rather than humanitarian protection. Nevertheless, other P5 members, particularly the US, were also reluctant to intervene militarily in Syria. Eventually, the rise of Da'esh (ISIS) prompted a military response, but this has taken the form of targeted strikes, such as in Pakistan and Yemen, rather than boots on the ground.

Conclusion

Intervention is a central and constant strategy in the international system in the pursuit of a particular type of peace and stability. Intervention, we argue, should be understood *sociologically* as being driven by the pursuit, expansion and protection of capitalist social relations and institutions. This deep social grammar underpins the West's motivation to shape the world in its own image – based on the ideological belief that Western capitalist social forms are the most advanced, efficient and pacific forms of organising society. Underpinned by a racist worldview described by Rudyard Kipling as the 'white man's burden', such political action in pursuit of what is deemed to be higher goals absolves interveners of responsibility for the violence that is inherent in the process. Indeed, by explicitly re-framing international intervention in the language of responsibility, as is the current fashion, contemporary policymakers are practicing an intellectual 'outsourcing' of violence, apparently oblivious to their own aggressive politics. 'The savage wars of peace', as Kipling referred to them, are not therefore regarded to be of the white man's making. And yet such ideological justifications cannot mask the self-interest, especially the ordering principle ascribed to liberal capitalism, which is the basis for the saviour role that Western states have adopted, and has led them to pursue goals of peace that demand the subjugation (and self-subjugation) of others. This conclusion is clear from the chapters in this book. The domestic pacification of societies and their refashioning into capitalist social forms within a hierarchy of international inequality is a repressive endeavour. The peace that is being advanced, imposed and policed is, we have argued, a tyrannical, aggressive and unequal peace. Visions and strategies for a new inclusive and pacific type of society and international system have thus never been more urgent.

Acknowledgements

We would like to thank Michael Pugh for helpful comments made on an earlier draft. However, all errors and views expressed are our own.

Notes

1 Tony Blair, 'Why the Middle East Matters: A Keynote Speech by Tony Blair', 23 April 2014 (at: www.tonyblairoffice.org/news/entry/why-the-middle-east-matters-keynote-speech-by-tony-blair/).
2 Tony Blair, 'Iraq, Syria and the Middle East: An Essay by Tony Blair', 14 June 2014 (at: www.tonyblairoffice.org/news/entry/iraq-syria-and-the-middle-east-an-essay-by-tony-blair/).
3 Mehdi Hasan, 'Tony Blair Bears "Total Responsibility" for ISIS, Says Academic Who Advised Him on Iraq', *Huffington Post*, 17 June 2014 (at: www.huffingtonpost.co.uk/2014/06/17/iraq-tony-blair_n_5503110.html).
4 John Stuart Mill, 'A Few Words on Non-intervention', in John Stuart Mill, *Essays on Equality, Law and Education*, ed. by John Robson, Toronto: University of Toronto Press, 1984.
5 Alexis de Tocqueville, 'First Report on Algeria (1847)', in Alexis de Tocqueville, *Writings on Empire and Slavery*, ed. and transl. by Jennifer Pitts, Baltimore, MD: Johns Hopkins University Press, 2001, pp. 129–173, in this book, p. 145.
6 John Macmillan, 'Intervention and the Ordering of the Modern World', *Review of International Studies*, vol. 39, 2013, pp. 1039–1056, in this book, p. 1040.
7 This is despite the fact that the ICISS conceptualisation was originally conceived as being more than military intervention to include the 'responsibility to prevent, react and rebuild'. International Commission on Intervention and Statebuilding, *The Responsibility to Protect*, Ottawa: International Development Research Centre, December 2001.
8 We are grateful to Michael Pugh for this point.
9 Slavoj Žižek, *The Sublime Object of Ideology*, Verso: London, 1989.
10 Ilan Kapoor, *The Postcolonial Politics of Development*, London: Routledge, 2008, p. 61.
11 Stephen D. Krasner, *Sovereignty: Organized Hypocrisy*, Princeton, NJ: Princeton University Press, 1999.
12 China Miéville, *Between Equal Rights: A Marxist Theory of International Law*, Chicago, IL: Haymarket Books, 2006; Jens Siegelberg, *Kapitalismus und Krieg: Eine Theorie des Krieges in der Weltgesellschaft [Capitalism and War: A Theory of War in World Society]*, Hamburg/Münster: Lit Verlag, 1994, pp. 54–55, 105.
13 Ernst Cassirer, *The Myth of the State*, New Haven, CT: Yale University Press, 1946, p. 286.
14 Pierre Bourdieu, *Practical Reason: On the Theory of Action*, Cambridge: Polity Press, 1998.
15 Interventions also have a decisive impact on the states from which interventions emanate, are conducted, financed, mandated and politically controlled; however, this is not the focus of this book. See Berit Bliesemann de Guevara and Florian P. Kühn, *Illusion Statebuilding*, Hamburg: Edition Körber-Stiftung, 2010.
16 Mark Duffield, *Development, Security and Unending War: Governing the World of Peoples*, Cambridge: Polity Press, 2011; Graham Harrison, *The World Bank and Africa: The Construction of Governance States*, London: Routledge, 2004.
17 Macmillan (note 6 above), p. 1044.
18 *Ibid.*, p.1054.
19 George Lawson and Luca Tardelli, 'The Past, Present and Future of Intervention', *Review of International Studies*, vol. 39, 2013, pp. 1233–1253.
20 Mark Mazower, *No Enchanted Palace: the End of Empire and the Ideological Origins of the United Nations*, Princeton, NJ: Princeton University Press, 2009; Francis Fukuyama, *The End of History and the Last Man*, New York: The Free Press, 1992.
21 Oliver P. Richmond and Jason Franks, *Liberal Peace Transitions: Between Statebuilding and Peacebuilding*, Edinburgh: Edinburgh University Press, 2009;

Roger Mac Ginty and Oliver P. Richmond (eds), *The Liberal Peace and Postwar Reconstruction: Myth or Reality*, London: Routledge, 2009.
22 Oliver P. Richmond, *A Post-Liberal Peace*, London: Routledge, 2011; Roger Mac Ginty, 'The Local Turn in Peacebuilding: A Critical Agenda for Peace', *Third World Quarterly*, vol. 34, no. 5, 2013, pp. 763–783; Roger Mac Ginty, *International Peacebuilding and Local Resistance: Hybrid Forms of Peace*, Basingstoke: Palgrave Macmillan, 2011.
23 Meera Sabaratnam, 'Avatars of Eurocentrism in the Critique of the Liberal Peace', *Security Dialogue*, vol. 44, no. 3, 2013, pp. 259–278, in this book, pp. 264–265.
24 Mac Ginty (note 22 above); Richmond (note 22 above).
25 Berit Bliesemann de Guevara (ed.), *Myths in International Politics*, Basingstoke: Palgrave Macmillan, 2015, forthcoming.
26 Christopher Cramer, *Civil War is Not a Stupid Thing: Accounting for Violence in Developing Societies*, London: C. Hurst & Co., 2006; Eckehart Krippendorff, *Staat und Krieg: Die historische Logik politischer Unvernunft* [*State and War: The Historical Logic of Political Unreason*], Frankfurt am Main: Suhrkamp, 1985; Siegelberg (note 12 above).
27 Sabaratnam (note 23 above), p.263.
28 Gerrit Gong, *The Standard of Civilisation in International Society*, Oxford: Oxford University Press, 1984.
29 Samuel P. Huntington, *The Clash of Civilizations and the Remaking of World Order*, New York: Simon & Schuster, 1996.
30 Beate Jahn, 'The Tragedy of Liberal Diplomacy: Democratization, Intervention, Statebuilding (Part I)', *Journal of Intervention and Statebuilding*, vol. 1, no. 1 (March), 2007, pp. 87–106; Beate Jahn, 'The Tragedy of Liberal Diplomacy: Democratization, Intervention, Statebuilding (Part II)', *Journal of Intervention and Statebuilding*, vol. 1, no. 2 (June), 2007, pp. 211–229.
31 Alastair Finlan, *Contemporary Military Strategy and the Global War on Terror: US and UK Armed Forces in Afghanistan and Iraq 2001–2012*, New York: Bloomsbury, 2014, pp. 181–198.
32 David Harvey, 'The New Imperialism: Accumulation by Dispossession', *Socialist Register*, vol. 40, 2007, pp. 63–87.
33 Krippendorff (note 26 above), pp. 139–156; Ha-Joon Chang, *Bad Samaritans: The Myth of Free Trade and the Secret History of Capitalism*, London: Bloomsbury, 2008.
34 Mandy Turner, 'The Expansion of International Society? Egypt and Vietnam in the History of Uneven and Combined Development', unpublished PhD thesis, London School of Economics, 1999.
35 Richard Saull, *Rethinking Theory and History in the Cold War: The State, Military Power and Social Revolution*, London: Frank Cass, 2001.
36 Mazower (note 20 above).
37 Ha-Joon Chang (note 33 above), pp. 26–28.
38 Robbie Shilliam, 'Intervention and Colonial-Modernity: Decolonizing the Italy/Ethiopia Conflict through Psalms 68:31', *Review of International Studies*, vol. 39, pp. 1131–1147, in this book, p. 1135.
39 Florian Kühn, 'International peace practice: ambiguity, contradictions, and perpetual violence', in this book, p. 29.
40 Scott Kirsch and Colin Flint, 'Geographies of reconstruction – re-thinking post-war spaces', in this book, pp. 53–54.
41 Philip Cunliffe, 'Still the spectre at the feast: comparisons between peacekeeping and imperialism in peacekeeping studies today', in this book, p. 73.
42 Michael Pugh, 'Lineages of aggressive peace', in this book, p. 87.
43 Bruno Charbonneau, 'War and peace in Cote d'Ivoire: violence, agency and the local/international line', in this book, p. 181.
44 Toby Dodge, 'Enemy images, coercive socio-engineering and civil war in Iraq', in this book, p. 197.

PART I
Exploring peace

1 International peace practice

Ambiguity, contradictions and perpetual violence

Florian P. Kühn

Why is it called 'peace'?

In international relations 'peace' is an ambiguous term and can have enigmatic meanings. While bearing mostly positive connotations, peace has become a key legitimising tool in international relations, especially in the politics of the UN regarding state stabilisation and regime change. Programmes of post-conflict reconciliation, peace conferences and policy to establish mechanisms for managing and transforming conflicts abound. This is striking because the notion of 'peace' was discredited during the Cold War era – when 'peace' was routinely evoked by Soviet leaders, and peace activists in the West were held to be subversive.[1] How then did peace become instrumental for legitimising international interventions, violent politics including bullying of allies, and increasing disregard of sovereignty?[2]

In this chapter, the notion of peace is traced through its changes and related to the common and most dominant form of social relations, the state. This is a limited approach given ample and mutually related theories and concepts of peace.[3] However, international relations (IR) traditionally includes significant components of thinking about war and its absence, portrayed as peace. This self-conception relies on the solid assumption of a state as a container of social relations. While IR's notion of national politics may have changed, the state remains centred in derived concepts of peace: state domination is viewed as juxtaposed to other, potentially un-peaceful, sub-state and transnational social relations. This reflects a historical change of meaning, from spiritual to worldly: formerly, *eternal peace* was a transcendental condition, which became possible immediately, mundanely enshrined in states. Peace and war became binaries and mutually exclusive.[4]

At the same time, ontological and epistemological problems arise when trying to clarify what peace actually means politically. To approach the puzzle of why aggressive politics have come to be viewed as supporting peace in Western, but also wider UN, policy circles, I argue that the state of non-violent politics between the members of a Western security community[5] has amounted to understanding politics as 'world domestic policy'.[6] The states of the Western security community have increasingly come to view problems outside as challenges to the community. In turn, the security community, led by the United States and supported by liberal intellectual research institutes, assumed governance tasks in countries beyond. Representing a 'can-do' attitude,[7] based on an Enlightenment understanding of the world as open for transformation by a subject,[8] these states set out to create their social environs.[9] Expanding the 'domestic' peace enjoyed within the community by identifying and transforming spoilers of peace or replacing illiberal regimes has required the development of a mode of governance assuming authority beyond institutionalised international law.

Although by no means global, Western integration and cooperation has developed a super-state structure, which shapes global governance bolstered by the combined power of nation states. Practising 'peace' through this structure combines both the characteristics of states as well as of the international system: formally segregated states share interdependencies to an extent that none of them could meaningfully act on their own in the 'international' sphere, while legitimisation and political control remain bounded nationally. While the governance super-structure has limited political scope (resembling the 'night-watchman state'[10]) and works in selected places only, it guides political norms and repertoires of political action, and governs some segments of world society while neglecting others.

Reminding ourselves of the basic principles of liberal thought is necessary for unpacking the core function of contemporary practices of peace. We need to go back to Locke's basic claims of freedom as being identical with property, organised guarantees of property rights and consensual execution of such rights. In Beate Jahn's words, '[p]rivate property constitutes individual freedom and individual freedom requires government by consent whose main task in turn is the protection of private property and thus that of individual freedom'.[11] That a person owns himself (and less so herself), as Locke argues, is granted as a natural right by (the Christian) god, which implies a god-given legitimisation of things appropriated. Property, for liberals, is what freedom hinges upon.[12] A Lockean state of nature poses dangers to wellbeing, as property is not guaranteed and so property protection is the main reason to consent to common government. The free individual 'seeks out, and is willing to joyn in Society with others who are already united, or have a mind to unite for the mutual *Preservation* of their Lives, Liberties, and Estates, which I call by the general Name, *Property*'.[13] The liberal portrayal of the interests of this small group (i.e. property owners) as common interests is replicated by Western states who propagate their own ordering role and policy aims as universally desirable.[14] If property is essential for individual rights, then the humanitarian debate and cosmopolitarian ideals are an effigy stalking horse for global capitalist expansion. According to Andrew Sartori, 'self-contradictory' liberal thought makes possible this expansion through the application of violent social orders of exploitation and expropriation while simultaneously promoting epistemological individualism and broad representation in decision making.[15]

Peace and, by extension, war thus work to legitimise the expansion of the liberal world. Peace, understood in this way, is a teleological concept which may well remain void of clear definition. The end-state need not be pinned down, as the process of making peace will determine its form. It is supposed to be designed in the open and participatory way that liberal societies ascribe to themselves. But in practice, the liberal way of peace is a result of power structures and epistemic influence. Indeed, the process of making, keeping, or enforcement of peace is a violent endeavour, resembling war in many aspects. The distinction between declaring war and making peace is thus blurred, rendering peace another version of war.[16] Regime change is the most violent end of this continuum (as experienced in Afghanistan, Libya and Iraq), but there are more nuanced ways in which it has been pursued. In the name of security, violence is employed – essentially to preserve the existing peace of the powerful.

The chapter is split into four sections. The first analyses the genesis of peace as a concept and relates it conceptually to the state and politics. I then explore how Western peace practice has been informed and dominated by these anti-emancipatory and reductionist notions of peace. The third section elucidates the need to constantly adapt and re-invent peace in a changing world. The chapter concludes by arguing that peace should be understood as a historical and constantly evolving concept, open for ideational competition and requiring further critical interrogation. This implies questioning dominant definitions as influenced by and serving the purposes of powerful interests and structurally conservative actors.

A short genealogy of peace

How peace is understood is intrinsically linked to the development of modern statehood. Michael Howard explains how distinguishing between domestic and foreign politics preceded understanding peace as a mode of international interaction. The creation of order by warrior elites, which then required legitimacy, 'produces domestic peace, and also legitimizes the conduct of war'.[17] When society was riddled by power rivals such as church, feudal landlords, and kings who competed over funds, control and legitimacy, feuds were frequent and characterised politics.[18] Only the state with its – often forceful – claim to a monopoly of violence was able to pacify society by virtue of its organisational capacity to accumulate the means of mass violence. Creating a pacified container for social relations, states had to begin to convey war or non-violence between these 'like units'[19] – creating a system of states.[20] To possess the means of violence against internal and external rivals was essential for the development of European states' specific form.[21] While this violent legacy and its historicity tends to be forgotten in all states' narratives, Jahn argues that the intellectual constitution of the 'international' as outside legal arrangements and rights guarantees allowed the appropriation of foreign land to be legitimised. The people in possession of that land had forfeited their rights by not protecting it. The sovereign state, in this reading, is a liberal invention derived from the property rights it ought to protect; it bundles power to compete with the war-like outside world.[22]

What is important is the self-legitimisation of the state and its elites once political interaction was institutionalised. For the modern state, which was to become the seminal template for social structures, a myth of rationality took hold with the Enlightenment. Law supports the relevance of the rulers rather than emanating from social necessity: 'by claiming that political action follows rational decision-making, political parlance masks the banality and ritualistic character of most political interaction'.[23] On the global scale, these states' mode of economic reproduction – based on money and surplus production – outcasts other forms, as Pierre Clastres described for subsistence based societies.[24] The production of surplus allows the allocation of resources for organised mass violence and, 'for the most part, they [the states] relied heavily on capital and capitalists as they reorganized coercion'.[25] Such professionalisation of violence, subsequently, led to developing strategic and tactical concepts within hegemonic structures of knowledge production.

The Westphalian norm of sovereignty prescribed a system to be 'at peace' when war did not occur, though war was possible at any time under anarchy. The international level thus appropriated the characteristics of what Hobbes had described as the state of nature: 'For WAR, consisteth not in battle only, or the act of fighting; but in a tract of time, wherein the will to contend by battle is sufficiently known: ... during all the time there is no assurance to the contrary. All other time is PEACE.'[26] Hence, war is what may occur on the international level, whereas a state's attempts to domesticate violence meant that power struggles were not war.[27] Historically, some philosophical strands have viewed peace as the default mode of social relations, while others have counted it as a temporal, and desirable, deviation.[28] It seems plausible, however, to argue that the fatefulness of war as one of the four horsemen of the Apocalypse disappeared with the gradual formation of the modern state: from something that comes over a society to something that politics can avert. An Enlightenment assumption that the world is open to be fashioned according to men's ideas makes it possible to think of politics and thus peace as something to be designed.[29] Peace becomes a process of constant political interaction, shaped by human will and decisions which are expressions of individual freedom.[30]

Ontologically tied to statehood, peace thus becomes a concept based on reason and something that can be precipitated. For Immanuel Kant, a League of Peace could be established as a federation of republics whose citizens controlled the means of war. The political system was the prerequisite for inter-state peace; its creation the state's most noble task.[31] However, Kant believed the league would need defending against the 'outside' world that was characterised by either lack of adequate (that is peace-inducing) government or lack of reason. Reason was the basis of enlightened forms of statehood in the first place and necessary for societies, and states, to be viewed as equal.

Against non-equals, argued John Stewart Mill, intervention could be justified: '[t]o suppose that the same international customs, and the same rules of international morality, can obtain between one civilized nation and another, and between civilized nations and barbarians, is a grave error'.[32] According to Mill, there is always a difference between the civilised and the barbarian; akin to democracies and non-democracies in current parlance. Risks that resemble the unpredictable nature of the uncivilised stem from the latter, and their 'failed' and 'failing' states. This, then, constitutes an order, determined by a 'standard of civilisation' or membership of a 'security community',[33] what Edward Said describes as 'Othering' with regard to orientalist framings that distinguishes between 'us' and 'them'.[34] It allowed the culturally different to be regarded as non-rational, child-like, and unable to self-govern.[35] Such binary ordering is not limited to a region or culture,[36] but enshrined in liberal Western thinking.[37] Such reductionism – creating binaries, dichotomising categories and universalising members of each category – characterises academic disciplines that embody Western modes of knowledge production. Conceptualising global politics in this way is therefore a necessary result of existing epistemic structures.

In the normative discourse about international law for example, inherent power relations are hidden by the generalisation of norms that are abstracted from existing conditions. Law acquires a weight and momentum that disguises its origins. Not only are Western states the major funders of the UN system and international bodies, but their mode of knowledge production dominates the epistemic 'software' of global institutions concerned with peace (see Chapter 4 of this book). Beyond a lip service acknowledgement that governance can take multiple forms, the benchmark for full statehood is essentially about whether state domination is durably established internationally. Domination in this sense means institutionalised power that allows governing on a recurrent basis instead of relying on ad hoc opportunities to impose on others. Weber was aware that his sociology of domination (as opposed to ubiquitous power[38]) is an abstraction, carving out ideal types for solely analytical purposes.[39] In practice, the ad hoc is more popular than official discourse has it. In global politics, however, the institutional capacity to exert domination has become the measuring rod for statehood – and, by extension and in ever prevalent quantifying spirit, for 'rating' states. Hierarchy, thus, derives from the functional qualities of states.

Paradoxically, that qualities are commonly quantified in social science leads to a ranking of states according to indices of weakness.[40] Beyond the circular reasoning that a state is unable to fulfil its supposed tasks because it is not a full member of the 'international community', such indices underpin risk assessments that pave the way for interventionist policies. With apparent scientific accuracy, judgements about risks – for states, the international system and individuals – are objectified and Western superiority reified.

Social conditions become open to comparison, thus elevating the Western ideal type. In the realm of international policy, this means mapping a lack of a legitimate monopoly of violence, social and political unrest or population movement, and assuming that these factors indicate non-peaceful environments. The more complex social figurations seem to be, the easier it is to declare such polities 'states at risk'.[41] States are classified 'weak' if they are unable to adapt to changing economic, social and environmental circumstances.[42] These factors cement hierarchical conditions of power and illustrate an implicit bias towards the *status quo* and against perceived threats to arrangements formed only about 50 years ago when territorial-style colonialism ended.

Western peace practice

The politics of peace associated with interventions and statebuilding that focuses on capitalist re-production and re-design of administrations, along with ideas of security sector reform, rule of law and policing of citizens, is largely a Western endeavour.[43] Its historicity is largely ignored in peace research. Based on democratic peace theory and an understanding of civil society resembling the thoughts of the Scottish Enlightenment thinker, Adam Ferguson,[44] peace in the twentieth century became conceived as rooted in civilian participation in politics. By voicing interests and taking part in decision-making based on reason and guided by self-interest, citizens were trusted to conduct politics internationally.[45] What Kant described as a 'league of peace' is indeed very similar to a security community. There is no legally-binding obligation to conduct relations peacefully, but practice excludes war as a means of politics. However, law-based politics is the consequence of a republican constitution; thus, Kant's idea of a law-based integration of the states comprising the 'league' is a teleological vision of a future world federal 'state of nations' (*civitas gentium*) once all states are democratic.

This thinking entails three critical aspects. First, it locates the individual tightly within state boundaries, extending its assumed rationality (expressed in abstract economic models and equally abstract law) to social relations.[46] Beyond personal forms of interaction, such as clientelism or other affinities, political abstractions open up state activity for structured repetition. Second, Kant saw that states, were they to be completely absorbed in a suprastructure, would run into problems in representing the sovereign people. However, he expected that states governed by interest-driven citizens would increasingly cooperate, form contractual relations and shape an environment of security of expectations conducive to business. Third, the institutions, regimes and common practices between states become a functional equivalent of states. This development of formal and informal integration has been concentrated in Western states, but required cessation of the alternative model and antagonistic ideology of Soviet Communism to fully expand after 1990.

Under the label 'globalisation', many former state functions have been moved to supra-national regulation levels or deregulated and thus effectively privatised. Hence, dominant states are not passive recipients of globalisation, but rather enforcers of an ideology of actively weakening the state.[47] That they have had more say in the process than the relatively powerless ones of the non-Western periphery is axiomatic.[48] As usual, political arrangements made between equals exclude those 'below' Western standards and reproduce Western superiority.[49] This illustrates that instead of having the biggest military, economy, or territory, the formulation and institutionalisation of rules is what constitutes power (or 'empire').[50]

Existing power relations have shaped conceptions of peace. As Mikkel Rasmussen argues, the salience of democratic peace theory is a result of the undisputed position of the West in the global order after 1989.[51] Not only did Western organisations continue to exist – they expanded. NATO's accession process incorporated the majority of former Warsaw Pact states, but enlargement also meant including fields other than state security. Likewise, the UN spearheaded a process of redefining peace in tight conjunction with respect for the continuing influence of militaries and Cold War security institutions. The Westernisation and securitisation of peace formed the narrative constituents of democratic peace. Within that paradigm, the formation of civil societies in the non-Western world was required. Led by the United States, but essentially as one group of powerful allies, Western agencies began programmes of democratisation, entailing the belief that this would eventually lead to a more peaceful world.[52] Essentially, the West had only one vision of peace, and this meant that only it was able (and challenged), to make peace. As Rasmussen remarks, '[b]ecause the West defined peace in terms of the "domestic peace and regular policy" which it believed were a mark of its civil societies, the West could not accept that peace was possible with non-civil societies. One could of course end wars with non-liberal states, but such a peace could never last'.[53]

To keep a lid on conflicts, military-led approaches to peace-making and peacekeeping became dominant by virtue of military-led knowledge production in think-tanks and research institutes, flanked increasingly by cohorts of UN and NGO aid agencies. Their policies are guided by ideas of development through growth and progress by individualisation, secularisation and modernisation (albeit implicit), and the rationalisation and marketisation of social relations.[54] Figuratively speaking, the state sits in the midst of these ostensibly teleological goals and corresponding programme planning, positioned centrally between the components of peace, and between the local and the international spheres.[55] In the endeavour to establish and maintain peace, 'peace' is understood as a policy rather than a defined concept.[56] Peace becomes an institutional exercise, to be implemented by bureaucrats and technocrats. An impressive professionalisation can be observed in the way that executive organisations portray their work in public. Application for and management of funds has been mainstreamed with economic logics (including aid consultancies and organisational capacity building). Many organisations have become involved in awareness-raising and advocacy, most have incorporated pragmatic appearance and target definition while practically sticking to a 'can do' attitude.[57] Note, however, that this is mainly aimed at the domestic publics of donor countries, while local projects suffer from this 'split constituencies'[58] problem: Logics of projects often contradict the expectations of different publics, as local recipients often see themselves as the ones who ought to determine projects' aims, while donor agencies have to make sure their funders/tax payers have the impression it is them who are making the decisions.

Political accountability for the process is limited by merging aspects of peace (for example, by conflating development and security[59]), by diffusing decision-making channels, moving executive responsibilities to inter- or supra-national institutions, and by restrictive information policies including embedding of the press. Furthermore, military services are often outsourced and thus removed from public and parliamentary oversight. Reconstruction programmes are hardly evaluated. The assumption that progress in one area automatically helps in another joins a paradoxical belief that progress can be achieved wholesale. Failure can be blamed on the local context, which is depoliticised by external target-setting and deprived of policy co-determination.[60] Consequently, the 'success' of aid campaigns often seems to be a question of how a project is presented, and it is hard to tell if change in a host country occurred through aid agency involvement or in spite of it.[61] Governance reforms, intended to strengthen a capacity to channel social conflicts, mostly seem unsustainable and dependent on external funding and oversight. This condemns internationals to remain indefinitely or risk local recidivism. Such institutional redesigning tends to create 'Potemkin states', façades behind which social life follows logics other than those of the Western ideal-type state.[62]

On a societal level, peace politics aims to manage and control the individual. On the one hand, individuals are assumed to be interest-driven and rational, and ought to carry the weight of societal organisation; on the other, individuals in non-Western societies are held to be irresponsible. Citizens who do not use Western-style political paths are viewed as political risks.[63] Typically, there is a deep distrust of local agency in conflict-ridden societies. Politically, 'the poor cannot always be trusted to make the right decisions. ... In their rejection of a system in which they have no stake, the poor are prone to pick up leaders they do not deserve and global liberal governance does not want'.[64] Legally, customary law is viewed as an obstacle to legal rationalisation – notwithstanding increasing programmes to incorporate traditional law, which aims to streamline it in rational ways. Culturally, religious norms hinder the state's secular abstractions. Customs which appear highly regressive and economic patterns assumed to work along the lines of 'greed and grievance',[65] rule the lives of the non-Western 'other' who needs to be disciplined, educated and policed until Westernised progress is achieved.[66] In Western countries, similarly, the individual seems to be a lot less trusted in everyday political practice than one would expect given the West's liberal roots.[67]

These phenomena can be read as integral to a class struggle from above which transcends national borders and non-spatial social demarcations. The driving interest of a global capitalist class acting within structures established by Western states, is to influence international policy in order to avert change or, if that seems impossible, to manage it.[68]

Peace and war as functions of capitalist consociation

On a global level, the politics of peace carries significant ambiguities – of both long-standing liberal internationalism and twentieth century neoliberalism. Over several hundred years, capitalist expansion has gone hand in hand with capitalism's consolidation – that is, increasing cooperation between states characterised by capitalist consociation.[69] As sketched above, the politics of peace reflects the power of liberalism. Capitalist consociation with associated ruptures and transformative influences on traditional forms of society, remains the driving force of modernisation and 'has had a global dimension affecting all previously existing societies, although uneven in degree, time and space'.[70] While competitive and monetised material reproduction replaces other economic forms, abstract politics, enshrined in law-based social relations, compete with symbolic (and religious) orders, as do state and non-state political arrangements. Because different, modern and pre-modern forms exist together, one may speak of 'the "contemporaneity of the non-contemporaneous" in these ambiguously accelerating or retarding dynamics'.[71] As part of this transformative process, the politics of peace is a manifestation of the unfolding historicity of international relations. The ongoing integration of the capitalist West fosters a culturally rooted construction of 'us' and 'them', based on what Barry Buzan and Richard Little have termed the 'zone of peace' and the 'zone of conflict',[72] and Kees van der Pijl in a political-economic perspective calls the 'Lockean heartland' of Western cooperative networks.[73] The density of information and economic and social transactions has vastly increased since Deutsch and his colleagues famously counted letters crossing the Atlantic to identify a 'security community'.[74] This includes the cooperation of military forces; it is barely conceivable for a country of the 'Lockean heartland' to go to war without relying on NATO or other integrated institutions as sources of legitimacy, organisational support, and political coordination.

Unsurprisingly, the increasing internationalisation and Westernisation of policymaking, equipped with a cosmopolitan outlook, has produced expansive governance. The politics of peace is a managing exercise which aims to protect the capitalist core from the non-liberal periphery. Relying on technologies of control and co-option of elites, it clearly has an anti-emancipatory impact. In spite of claims to have individualised security through a 'human security' paradigm, 'weak' states or individuals in poor communities have little emancipatory power. Subject to adjustment policies, there is little room for peripheral communities to exact decisive influence on global power structures, institutions, and epistemology. As Tara McCormack puts it:

> In the foreseeable future Moldova or Botswana will not be measuring human security in, say, deprived areas of the US, Britain, Japan or Canada and deciding upon action. Rather, this shift [to human security] can be seen to actually reinforce international power inequalities whereby the weakest and poorest states lose even the formal protection of the pluralist norms of sovereign equality and non-intervention.[75]

Denying states sovereignty when they fail in their 'responsibility to protect' their own populations only seemingly contradicts the treatment of individuals as 'surplus population ... whose skills, status and even existence are in excess of prevailing conditions and requirements'.[76] The internationalisation of peace emanates from assumptions about peace in Western societies (where highly internalised structural forms of violence exist). By locating violence in deviant statehood, the liberal peace paradigm territorialises what is essentially deterritorialised. In order to produce cohesion in, and support for, a prevailing state structure, such fictitious territoriality is required to demarcate people's everyday lives from an imaginary outside world. Virtual relations between elites all over the world, however, fostered by dense connections between academic, economic, cultural, trade, transport, information, and not least ideational transactions, transcend older modes of societal reproduction. The period of broad distribution of gains in welfare may turn out to have been a brief period when the West faced a competing ideological model. The unfolding of the politics of peace since 1990 may signify a normalisation of capitalism, rendering the post-second world war period an anomaly in that Keynesianism enjoyed a limited time-span until the forces of free capitalism imposed less balancing social norms.

The Western model of society – 'its norms, institutions and perspectives on social, economic and political systems' – that is expected to bring peace amounts to a 'victor's peace' forced upon a loser.[77] Such a version of peace might be confused for a realist formulation, since it values system stability over normative aspects of politics. A victor's peace as understood here focuses on agents able to enforce the implementation of an order – at least to the extent of installing an institutional structure through social re-education or forced regime change: 'its absolute end goal is a victor's peace in which all other actors are either subservient or are removed'.[78] Common peace practice seems to be akin to that of a Cold War 'victor' because its enforcement is based on an idea of Western superiority, rendering alternative forms of peace unthinkable. Not only are they unthinkable, they cannot be tolerated in the non-Western world where they would be disruptive for the Western notion of peace. The work of truth commissions, community councils, or reconciliation policy in this regard appears to be a fig leaf to secure consent – supporting management of risks, deterritorialised political authority and the politics of expert technocracy.[79]

In this view, the politics of peace for Western states is not a matter of choice but obligation. As long as such a sense of Western inevitability prevails, ambiguities enclosed in the politics of peace are easily tolerated. The politics of peace thus work alongside what Barbara Tuchman described as the consolidation of false assumptions in the face of the contrary. The more that basic assumptions are rigidified and the higher the stakes have become in the process, the less likely is a 're-examination and rethinking and a change of course'.[80] Non-substantial, cosmetic and legitimising changes in the basic narratives and essentially symbolic politics (such as the human security discourse and its effect of undermining 'self-government and democratic accountability'[81]) mark the politics of peace. Policy declarations are directed at donor audiences whose consent is politically required but whose cooperation and input is a source of risk, and thus, undesirable. Changes in the practise of peace so far have not originated in reconsideration and changes of policy but, if at all, resulted from the politics, and limits, of the purse.

Conclusion: living with ambiguities of peace

The conceptualisation of peace is not ahistoric and has its place and time in concrete policy. Indeed the implementation of a particular form of peace practice lie in it being a function of the consolidation of Western community. It selectively manages violence seen as regressive and risky to the structure of international relations. The puzzle of why the strong felt threatened by the weak after 1990 has its roots in a cosmopolitan notion later epitomised in the human security discourse which left Westerners feeling vulnerable when terrorists struck in New York, London and Madrid.[82] This sentiment helps to legitimise international policy and provides the epistemological basis for the expansion of risk management politics beyond the Western security community (for example, on humanitarian grounds[83]). The superstructure this community represents is the main source of the politics of peace and, correspondingly, of war.

It would be erroneous to understand the Western governance superstructure as a homogenous political space. However, it relies on the depiction of external risks to produce internal cohesion. External risks carry a useful indeterminacy which helps belie the division between capitalist elites and non-elites – regardless of their spatial residence.[84] Such 'debounded' risks may stem from any territory, but can be attributed to risky populations, the poor, the non-capitalist and socially peripheral strata of society. To govern from the 'zone of peace' over a 'zone of conflict' helps to solidify modes of social and economic reproduction, and, in turn, dominance in Western society.

The politics of peace, in this regard, expresses transformation of Western relations between a governing elite and the governed, extending it to selected spaces outside the formalised areas of political representation. As such, the politics of peace is a technology of governing the masses who produce but are uninvolved in capital circulation.[85] In this context, the professionalisation of militaries trained in interventionist tactics such as counterinsurgency (COIN) rather than defence is no surprise. Its twin is the professionalisation of aid agencies designing their programmes to secure consent (or, rather, non-resistance) instead of fostering self-government and autonomous definitions of desirable, alternative ways of life. To stabilise existing orders, social technology is used to delegitimise alternative visions of peace which might go beyond state and capitalist orders. In the discursive environment of Western publics, peace 'experts' claim to know how peace can be achieved despite permanent failure of those concepts in practice.

Political discourse employs an impetus for reform, transformation and rebuilding, while practice is an exercise in stabilising and preserving the status quo. Everything has to change so that everything can remain the same (i.e. others have to change so that everything can remain the same for the West). In order to salvage its power and perpetuate its way of life and economy, adaptation is demanded from the multitude – domestically and abroad.[86] The class struggle from above relies on hermetic structures of governing and so social mobility must be limited and controlled. This has led to the military being reinstated to its historic role as a channel of upward social mobility for the lower classes; this is ironic for the same military personnel have to conduct, and die for, the politics of peace.

Instead of supplying sophisticated technologies of exacting interventionist policies, research ought to reconceptualise IR's understanding of 'international' relations. The world of states is too limited for analysing Western expansion. Different interests find themselves in antagonist, or at least conflictual, positions in world society in this process. Hence, peace studies should review capitalist relations and their influences on actors. The epistemology of peace requires the decisive questioning of liberal myths and narrative projections of future common goods. In other words, reflections on peace ought to focus on developing research designs that reflect on how to resurrect and integrate peace's emancipatory potential rather than downgrading peace to yet another technocratic exercise for stabilising existing patterns of domination.

Acknowledgements

I would like to thank Annette Jünemann, Berit Bliesemann de Guevara, Jana Hönke, Delf Rothe, Jesper Nielsen and the anonymous reviewers for helpful comments on this chapter. This is an amended version of Florian P. Kühn, 'The Peace-Prefix: Ambiguities of the Word "Peace"', *International Peacekeeping*, vol. 19, no. 4, 2012, pp. 396–409, Taylor & Francis Ltd, www.tandfonline.com, reprinted by permission of the publisher.

Notes

1 Dieter Lutz, 'Friedensforschung – Normativ, Interdisziplinär, Praxisorientiert' ['Peace Research – Normative, Interdisciplinary, Practical'], in Ulrich Eckern, Leonie Herwartz-Emden and Rainer-Olaf Schultze (eds), *Friedens- und Konfliktforschung in Deutschland* [*Peace and Conflict Research in Germany*], Wiesbaden: Verlag für Sozialwissenschaften, 2004, pp. 23–32.
2 Christopher J. Bickerton, Philip Cunliffe and Alexander Gourevitch, 'Politics without Sovereignty?', in Bickerton, Cunliffe and Gourevitch (eds), *Politics without Sovereignty*, London: University College London Press, 2007, pp. 20–38. Sovereignty is in itself highly ambiguous, as non-state actors will find it hard to be recognised as having legitimate demands unless they legitimise themselves by holding an official office or find powerful patrons.
3 For a sociological approach see John D. Brewer, *Peace Processes*, Cambridge: Polity, 2010. See also Stephan Nitz's seminal bibliography on the idea of peace, *Theorien des Friedens und des Krieges* [*Theories of Peace and War*], vol. 1, Baden-Baden: Nomos, 2010.
4 For an excellent account of the scholarly discussion see Oliver Richmond, *The Transformation of Peace*, Basingstoke: Palgrave Macmillan, 2005, pp. 1–19.
5 Karl W. Deutsch, Sidney A. Burrell, Robert A. Kann, Maurice Lee Jr., Martin Lichterman, Raymond E. Lindgren, Francis L. Loewenheim and Richard W. Van Wagenen, *Political Community in the North Atlantic Area – International Organization in the Light of Historical Experience*, New York: Greenwood, 1957.
6 Hans Joachim Gießmann, 'Terrorismus – Globales Problem und Herausforderung für "Weltinnenpolitik"' ['Terrorism – Global Problem and Challenge for "World Domestic Politics"'], in Dieter S. Lutz (ed.), *Globalisierung und nationale Souveränität* [*Globalisation and National Sovereignty*], Baden-Baden: Nomos, 2000, pp. 471–490. Gießmann warns that integrating security structures needs to be flanked by participatory mechanisms.
7 Berit Bliesemann de Guevara, 'Introduction: Statebuilding and state-formation', in Bliesemann de Guevara (ed.), *Statebuilding and State-formation*, London: Routledge, 2012, pp. 1–19.
8 Trevor Parfitt, *The End of Development? Modernity, Post-Modernity and Development*, London: Pluto, 2002, p.23.
9 On the so-called 'international community' and its function for political legitimisation see Berit Bliesemann de Guevara and Florian P. Kühn, '"The International Community Needs to Act": Loose Use and Empty Signalling of a Hackneyed Concept', *International Peacekeeping*, vol. 18, no. 2, 2011, pp. 135–151.
10 What Rasmussen calls the night-watch state (more commonly *night-watchman state*) is simply a regulating entity, as opposed to the creating and actively shaping welfare state; on the positive epistemology of peace after the second world war see Mikkel Vedby Rasmussen, *The West, Civil Society and the Construction of Peace*, Basingstoke: Palgrave Macmillan, 2003, pp. 106–126, 175.
11 Beate Jahn, *Liberal Internationalism. Theory, History, Practice*, Basingstoke: Palgrave Macmillan, 2013, p. 43.
12 John Gray, *Liberalism*, 2nd edn, Buckingham: Open University Press, 1995, p. 14.
13 John Locke, *Two Treatises of Government*, edited by Peter Laslett, Cambridge: Cambridge University Press, 1988, p. 350.
14 Andrew Williams, *Liberalism and War: The Victors and the Vanquished*, London: Routledge, 2006, p. 67.
15 Andrew Sartori, *Liberalism in Empire: An Alternative History*, Oakland, CA: University of California Press, 2014, pp. 203–204. Sartori argues that, in passing, the moral standpoint of 'subalternists' or 'leftists' criticising liberalism's discontents, is itself established by liberal categories.

16 David Keen, 'War and Peace: What's the Difference?', *International Peacekeeping*, vol. 7, no. 4, 2000, pp. 1–22.
17 Michael Howard, *The Invention of Peace and the Reinvention of War*, London: Profile, 2001, p. 3.
18 Jens Siegelberg, 'Staat und Internationales System – ein Strukturgeschichtlicher Überblick' ['State and International System: A Structural Historical Survey'], in Jens Siegelberg and Klaus Schlichte (eds), *Strukturwandel Internationaler Beziehungen* [*Structural Changes in International Relations*], Wiesbaden: Westdeutscher Verlag, 2000, pp. 11–56.
19 Kenneth Waltz, *Theory of International Politics*, Reading, MA: Addison-Wesley, 1979, p. 93.
20 Despite state-centrism being attributed to realist world views, state-centrism is likewise foundational for liberal conceptions of international politics; see Jahn (n. 11 above), p. 19.
21 Charles Tilly, *Coercion, Capital, and European States, AD 990–1992*, Oxford: Blackwell, 1992, pp. 67–95.
22 Jahn (note 11 above), pp. 67–8. According to Jahn, liberalism's international contradictions and ambiguities derive not from individual states but from the *relations* of political figurations liberal and non-liberal alike. This, however, begs the question if liberal states would not have to find it equally troubling accommodating with each other than with those outside their norms.
23 Murray Edelman, *Politik als Ritual: Die symbolische Funktion staatlicher Institutionen und politischen Handelns*, Frankfurt: Campus, 1976, quoted in Wolfgang Reinhard, *Lebensformen Europas* [*Life Forms of Europe*], Munich: C. H. Beck, 2004, p. 303 (author's paraphrasing).
24 Pierre Clastres, *Society Against the State*, New York: Zone Books, 1989, pp. 189–218. Quincy Wright distinguishes between 'primitive' and 'modern' societies, focusing on the economic base as a cause of aggressive or non-aggressive behaviour. Like Clastres, but to different conclusions, his distinction is about the extent to which social figurations are absorbed in a state and institutionalised domination, *A Study of War*, Chicago, IL: University of Chicago Press, 1965, pp. 51–100.
25 Tilly (note 21 above), p. 69.
26 Thomas Hobbes, *Leviathan*, English Works III, Aalen: Scientia, 1966, p. 113 (original emphasis). Although understood in IR as a realist conception of world politics, it seamlessly corresponds with liberal thought of the governed space within and the ungoverned, thus war-prone, space outside the state.
27 During East–West confrontation, interventionist practices such as in Iran, Egypt and Chile were not viewed as war, unless conducted by Soviet agents. 'Civil war' was understood to be conducted by civilians or, even more illustrative, in the German '*Bürgerkrieg*' ['War of Citizens'] indicates the, at least in principle, rights-based sphere this violence takes place in. If there is no rights-based citizenship individuals cannot be *Bürger*, hence, by definition, *Bürgerkrieg* would be impossible. *Bürger* violence is, if not illegitimate, in any case *illegal*.
28 Reinhard Meyers, 'Krieg und Frieden' ['War and Peace'], in Hans Joachim Gießmann and Bernhard Rinke (eds), *Handbuch Frieden* [*Peace Handbook*], Wiesbaden: VS, 2011, pp. 21–50.
29 Parfitt (note 8 above), p. 18.
30 Immanuel Kant, *Werke, Zweiter Band: Kritik der reinen Vernunft* [*Critique of Pure Reason*], Wiesbaden: Insel, 1956, pp. 371, 494–503.
31 Immanuel Kant, 'Zum Ewigen Frieden' ['Perpetual Peace'], in Kant, *Werke in sechs Bänden, Band VI: Schriften zur Anthropologie, Geschichtsphilosophie, Politik und Pädagogik* [*Writings on Anthropology, Philosophy, Politics and Pedagogy*], Darmstadt: Wissenschaftliche Buchgesellschaft, 1970, pp. 191–251.

32 John Stuart Mill, 'A Few Words on Non-Intervention', in John M. Robson (ed.), *John Stuart Mill: Essays on Equality, Law, and Education*, vol. 21, Toronto: University of Toronto Press, 1984, p. 118. Mill argues that nations apply rules in international behaviour when they can expect reciprocity; however, 'barbarians will not reciprocate'. Mill's idea about military relations between conquerors and conquered is notable: as the interveners are ridding local governments of military capacities, they are replacing indigenous ordering forces; this, in turn, gives local civilian rulers *carte blanche* to fall into desolation or become oppressive, as they need not think about and take precautions against internal rebellion or external threats (*ibid.*, pp. 118–122).

33 See William Clapton, 'Risk and Hierarchy in International Society', *Global Change, Peace and Security*, vol. 21, no. 1, 2009, pp. 19–35; Gerrit Gong, *The Standard of 'Civilization' in International Society*, Oxford: Clarendon, 1984; Deutsch (note 5 above); Amitai Etzioni, *Political Unification*, New York: Holt, Rinehart & Winston, 1965; Emmanuel Adler and Michael Barnett, *Security Communities*, Cambridge: Cambridge University Press, 1998; Alex J. Bellamy, *Security Communities and their Neighbours*, Basingstoke: Palgrave Macmillan, 2004.

34 Edward W. Saïd, *Orientalism*, New York: Pantheon, 1978.

35 Sartori (note 15 above), pp. 20–21.

36 David Campbell, *Writing Security*, Minneapolis, MN: University of Minnesota Press, 1998, pp. 17–23. Campbell's warning against reification of spatial markers remains valid: when criticising the national bounding of the politics of peace, this chapter runs the risk of a confirmation bias. State-driven politics, however, remain to be dominant for political economy as well as epistemology.

37 Regarding the liminal space which is the arena where such distinctions become empirical, see Lisa Smirl, 'Building the Other, Constructing Ourselves: Spatial Dimensions of International Humanitarian Response', *International Political Sociology*, vol. 2, no. 3, 2008, pp. 236–253. Of course, the notion of *intruding* into a society as if it was a secluded container is itself a naturalisation of states.

38 See Klaus Schlichte, *Der Staat in der Weltgesellschaft [The State in World Society]*, Frankfurt am Main: Campus, 2005, pp. 65–84.

39 Weber explains an ideal-type as an aspect of intellectual concepts carved out 'by the analytical accentuation of certain elements of reality. ... It is not a *description* of reality but it aims to give unambiguous means of expression to such a description. ... In its conceptual purity, this mental construct (*Gedankenbild*) cannot be found empirically anywhere in reality. It is a *utopia*.' *The Methodology of the Social Sciences*, New York: Free Press, 1949, p. 90 (original emphases).

40 See for example the Foreign Policy Index (at: www.foreignpolicy.com/ articles/2011/06/17/2011_failed_states_index_interactive_map_and_rankings). Its methodology illustrates how central a variable the state is: 'Q: What does "state failure" mean? A: A state that is failing has several attributes. One of the most common is the loss of physical control of its territory or a monopoly on the *legitimate use of force*. Other attributes of state failure include ... an inability to provide reasonable *public services*, and the inability to interact with other states as a *full member of the international community*' (italics added). For a general problematisation of analyses of state failure see Ken Menkhaus, 'State Failure and Ungoverned Spaces', in Mats Berdal and Achim Wennmann (eds), *Ending Wars, Consolidating Peace*, London: International Institute for Strategic Studies, 2010, pp. 171–188. Measuring the world with statistics is in itself modern practice.

41 Ulrich Schneckener (ed.), *Fragile Staatlichkeit [Fragile Statehood]*, Baden-Baden: Nomos Verlag, 2006.

42 From a world system perspective, weak states are those at the periphery of economic circulation. Immanuel Wallersteen, *World-System Analysis*, Durham,

NC: Duke University Press, 2004, pp. 29, 55. Ikenberry focuses on states' ability to transform and adapt socio-economically to exogenous changes; G. John Ikenberry, 'The Irony of State Strength: Comparative Responses to the Oil Shocks in the 1970s', *International Organization*, vol. 40, no. 1, 1986, pp. 105–137. Migdal's state is strong when it can mobilise capital, but also depends on symbolic orders, sources of legitimation, family structures, charisma or violence – strength derives from mutual networks of society and state; Joel S. Migdal, *State in Society*, Cambridge: Cambridge University Press, 2001.

43 See Erlend Grøner Krogstad, 'Local Ownership as Dependence Management: Inviting the Coloniser Back', *Journal of Intervention and Statebuilding*, vol. 8, nos. 2–3, 2014, pp. 105–125.

44 See Anna Geis, Lothar Brock and Harald Müller (eds), *Democratic Wars: Looking at the Dark Side of Democratic Peace*, Basingstoke: Palgrave Macmillan, 2006; Adam Ferguson, *An Essay on the History of Civil Society* (edited by Fania Oz-Salzberger), Cambridge: Cambridge University Press, 1995.

45 Kant (note 30 above), pp. 350–351.

46 Law became the guiding idea of the state, as expressed by Hegel 'The state is the realized ethical idea or ethical spirit', in *Philosophy of Right*, Kitchener: Batoche, 2001, p. 194. His notion of natural law leaves behind its nature as a given and establishes it as freely agreed upon. Arno Baruzzi, 'Hegel', in Hans Maier, Heinz Rausch and Horst Denzer (eds), *Klassiker des Politischen Denkens* [*Classics of Political Thought*], vol. 2, Munich: C. H. Beck, 1987, p. 167.

47 Michael Hardt and Antonio Negri, *Empire*, Cambridge, MA: Harvard University Press, 2001. Hardt and Negri lack a profound theoretical approach to explain political action. Rather, they focus on structures. For an analysis of the role of think tanks and research institutions in providing the intellectual underpinnings of neoliberal policy mainstreaming, see Dieter Plehwe and Bernhard Walpen, 'Buena Vista Neoliberal?', in Klaus Gerd Giesen (ed.), *Ideologien in der Weltpolitik* [*Ideologies in World Politics*], Wiesbaden: VS, 2004, pp. 49–88.

48 Rasmussen (note 10 above), pp. 127–173.

49 Florian P. Kühn, *Sicherheit und Entwicklung in der Weltgesellschaft* [*Security and Development in World Society*], Wiesbaden: VS, 2010, pp. 142–160.

50 Susan Strange, 'Towards a theory of Transnational Empire', in Werner Väth (ed.), *Political Regulation in the 'Great Crisis'*, Berlin: Edition Sigma, 1989, pp. 25–42; see also Robert O. Keohane, *After Hegemony. Cooperation and Discord in the World Political Economy*, Princeton, NJ: Princeton University Press, 1984/2005.

51 Rasmussen (note 10 above).

52 See for example Peter Burnell (ed.), *Democracy Assistance*, London: Frank Cass, 2000; also Annette Jünemann and Michèle Knodt (eds), *European External Democracy Promotion*, Baden-Baden: Nomos, 2007.

53 Rasmussen (note 10 above), p. 174.

54 For the cycles of cutting edge topics in development, see Arjan de Haan, *How the Aid Industry Works*, Sterling, VA: Kumarian, 2009, pp. 63–89.

55 Kühn (note 49 above), pp. 187–263.

56 Rasmussen (note 10 above), p. 175.

57 Florian P. Kühn and Jan Pospisil, 'The Resilient State: New Regulatory Modes in International Approaches to Statebuilding?', paper presented at 8th Pan-European Conference on International Relations, Warsaw, 20 September, 2013.

58 Bertin Martens, 'Why Do Aid Agencies Exist?', in William Easterly (ed.), *Reinventing Foreign Aid*, Cambridge, MA: MIT Press, 2008, pp. 285–310.

59 Mark Duffield, *Global Governance and the New Wars*, London: Zed, 2005; Mark Duffield, *Development, Security, and Unending War*, Cambridge: Polity, 2007; Bruno Charbonneau, 'The Security–Development Nexus. Reflections on International Interventions and the Purpose of Force', paper presented at International Studies

Association, Annual Convention, New Orleans, 17–20 February 2010; Kühn (note 49 above).
60 Berit Bliesemann de Guevara and Florian P. Kühn, *Illusion Statebuilding*, Hamburg: Edition Körberstiftung, 2010, p. 196.
61 Roger C. Riddell, *Does Foreign Aid Really Work?* Oxford: Oxford University Press, 2007, pp. 287–310.
62 Bliesemann de Guevara and Kühn (note 60 above), pp. 152–180.
63 Balakrishnan Rajagopal, *International Law from Below*, Cambridge: Cambridge University Press, 2003, p. 293. See also Shahar Hameiri, 'State Transformation, Territorial Politics and the Management of Transnational Risk', *International Relations*, vol. 25, no. 3, 2011, pp. 381–397.
64 Mark Duffield, *Global Governance and the New Wars* (note 59 above), p. 127; this reflects the merging of concepts (e.g. putting poverty and political rebellion in one category), instrumental for UN discourse since *An Agenda for Peace*, where violent conflict as war is causally connected to 'economic despair, social injustice'; *An Agenda for Peace: Preventive Diplomacy, Peacemaking and Peace-keeping*, Report of the Secretary-General pursuant to the statement adopted by the Summit Meeting of the Security Council on 31 January 1992, UN doc. A/47/277.
65 See Paul Collier and Anke Hoeffler, 'Greed and Grievance in Civil War', World Bank, 21 October 2001 (at: www-wds.worldbank.org/external/default/WDSContentServer/WDSP/IB/2004/03/10/000265513_20040310152555/Rendered/PDF/28126.pdf); Mats Berdal and David M. Malone (eds), *Greed and Grievance*, Boulder, CO: Lynne Rienner, 2000.
66 See Bethan K. Greener, 'The Rise of Policing in Peace Operations', *International Peacekeeping*, vol. 18, no. 2, 2011, pp. 183–195.
67 That the causes of the 2008 onwards financial crisis are being sought in individuals ('greedy investment bankers') rather than in a structural and systemic failure of capitalism illustrates the inherent liberal distrust of the individual. Conversely, political blame is deflected on to 'the markets' or anonymous rating agencies and so on. Delf Rothe brought this to my attention.
68 Luis Lobo-Guerrero, *Insuring Security*, Abingdon: Routledge, 2011, pp. 118–128.
69 Jens Siegelberg, *Kapitalismus und Krieg [Capitalism and War]*, Münster: Lit, 1994.
70 Dietrich Jung, 'The Political Sociology of World Society', *European Journal of International Relations*, vol. 7, no. 4, 2001, pp. 443–474.
71 *Ibid.*, p. 456, quoting Ernst Bloch, *Erbschaft dieser Zeit [Legacy of this Time]*, Frankfurt am Main: Suhrkamp, 1985 (orig. 1935).
72 Barry Buzan and Richard Little, 'Beyond Westphalia? Capitalism after the "Fall"', *Review of International Studies*, vol. 25, no. 5, 1999, pp. 89–104.
73 Kees van der Pijl, 'The Lockean Heartland and the International Political Economy', in Angus Cameron, Anastasia Nesvetailova and Ronen Palan (eds), *International Political Economy*, London: Sage, 2008, vol. 2, pp. 17–52.
74 Deutsch (note 5 above).
75 Tara McCormack, 'The Limits to Emancipation in the Human Security Framework', in David Chandler and Nik Hynek (eds), *Critical Perspectives on Human Security*, Abingdon, Routledge, 2011, pp. 99–113, here p. 109.
76 Duffield, *Development, Security, and Unending War* (note 59 above), p. 9.
77 Oliver Richmond, *Peace in International Relations*, London: Routledge, 2008, p. 40.
78 *Ibid.*, p. 52.
79 Hameiri (note 63 above), p. 386.
80 Barbara Tuchman, *The March of Folly*, New York: Ballantine, 1984, p. 383.
81 Mandy Turner, Neil Cooper and Michael Pugh, 'Institutionalised and Co-opted: Why Human Security Has Lost its Way', in Chandler and Hynek (note 75 above), pp. 83–96, here p. 87.
82 Rasmussen (note 10 above), p. 171.

83 Katrin Radtke, 'Die Entgrenzung der Solidarität: Hilfe in Einer Globalisierten Welt' ['Expanding Boundaries of Solidarity: Aid in a Globalised World'], *Aus Politik und Zeitgeschichte*, no. 21, 2008, pp. 27–32.
84 On risk see Shahar Hameiri and Florian P. Kühn, 'Introduction: Risk, Risk Management and International Relations', *International Relations*, vol. 25, no. 3, 2011, pp. 275–279; Florian P. Kühn, 'Securing Uncertainty: Sub-state Security Dilemma and the Risk of Intervention', *International Relations*, vol. 25, no. 3, 2011, pp. 363–380.
85 Thomas Piketty, *Capital in the Twenty-First Century*, Cambridge, MA: Belknap Press of Harvard University Press, 2013, pp. 252–260.
86 Hardt and Negri (note 47 above), pp. 60–63.

2 Geographies of reconstruction
Re-thinking post-war spaces

Scott Kirsch and Colin Flint

Post-conflict reconstruction has always been, among other things, a hegemonic strategy. It is a process of conflict and of militarised power, we argue in this chapter, more a war of position than something that clearly demarcates a post-war period of peace. We suggest that geographic approaches to 'post-conflict' can be effective in unsettling presumed boundaries between war and peace, allowing us to learn more about how processes, events and relations of war become integrated with (internal to) new spaces of reconstruction: new state forms and institutions, new landscapes and territories, and new maps and stories in which the terrain of conflict is itself being remade. By challenging the ontological distinctions between conflict and post-conflict, and in challenging presumed linear pathways from war to peace and reconstruction, our purpose in this chapter is to show how processes of war, and relations of power shaped through war, become embedded in relations of peace.

Post-conflict reconstruction has long been a powerful *idea*, a notion of rebuilding state, economy, culture and society in the wake of war, frequently conceived while war is ongoing, which draws its rhetorical power from an apparently neat demarcation, both spatially and temporally, between war and peace. The reality is, of course, more complex. Even as efforts to produce functioning, harmonious and regionally or globally integrated post-conflict spaces out of war zones continue to be defined through the language and institutions of reconstruction, conditions of peace and security can be difficult to disentangle from ongoing wars and other forms of political violence. War itself has been phrased as a process of reconstruction and renewal; so has genocide. Of course, we acknowledge that the activities conventionally associated with *reconstruction* – such as emergency relief (aimed at the amelioration of suffering), restoration of energy provision, distribution of healthcare and social services, creation or recreation of state institutions and legal systems, training of armed forces – are typically far less destructive than many forms of institutionalised violence. We similarly acknowledge the many different kinds of violence, and different scales of bloodshed, endemic in different conflicts. However, in identifying reconstruction as a site of conflict, our point is not to underemphasise the transformative effects of post-war reconstruction processes. Rather, we argue that projects culturally framed as reconstruction, recovery and renewal provide an important window onto the conflicts that rage around (and within) 'post-conflict' societies, allowing us to better understand the integration of wartime and post-war spaces.

To develop these arguments, in the following section we introduce the geographic concepts of place and site as an effective framework to identify and explore the false dichotomy of war and peace. The efficacy of the geographic approach is illustrated by examining some of the ways that scholars have conceptually integrated war and post-war geographies in critical studies of war and occupation; terrorism, state terror and the 'war on terrorism'; and other forms of political and structural violence.[1] Next, we trace the history of the idea of post-war reconstruction by exploring the language of reconstruction as a *keyword* for studying both material and symbolic cultural and political processes.[2] This approach allows us to explore the evolution of contemporary notions of reconstruction as they have articulated with concrete historical processes of conflict and political violence, from the (capital R) Reconstruction of the American South following the US Civil War, to the wartime construction of the World Bank in 1944 as the International Bank for Reconstruction and Development, up to more contemporary events. The overall intent of this brief introduction to the geography of post-war reconstruction is to expand on a range of concepts, and to expound on geographic frameworks of power and place, to argue for a conceptualisation of war as an ongoing, more or less 'permanent' process of militarised power and conflict, varying in intensity over space and time from banal occupation and low-level warfare to suddenly terrifying bombardments and displacements, but premised ideologically on a distinct horizon of peace, and the closure of war as a discrete event.

Integrating war and 'post-war' geographies

In this section, we argue that the value of exposing the false dichotomy of war and peace, and in resisting neat definitions of conflict, peace, and reconstruction in discrete stages, is in better understanding the continuity of violent power relations; or the existence of power, violence and marginalisation within the politics of peace. Such an understanding is enhanced by a focus on the geographic concepts of place and site, and depends on the relational sense of power embodied by critical geographic approaches to the study of war.

Power and place: zoning for conflict

To identify and interrogate the false dichotomy between war and peace, it is useful to consider places and political spaces, such as nation-states or 'war-zones', as socially constructed. Cities, regions and countries are constantly being shaped by the decisions of a variety of actors, but this very general sense of the process of social construction is contextualised to take on different forms in different settings. Historical-geographical context is simultaneously framed by and created through social action in a way that leads to an examination of how behaviour and outcomes vary across time and space.

In the study of conflict and post-conflict reconstruction, it is common to begin by thinking of war and peace as two forms of context that are distinct and are associated with particular forms of politics and other social activities. However, we argue that once it is recognised that politics and the social construction of place are inseparable and mutually constitutive, then the geographic approach *requires* a breakdown of the false dichotomy between the processes and zones of war and peace. The construction of places and spaces is continual and contested. Power relations are constantly being enacted to define access to particular places, rules and norms of behaviour, and spheres of jurisdiction. Sometimes these power relations will manifest in violence, and when it becomes organised and sustained it becomes defined as war. However, militarised power relations are very much evident in what is generally categorised as peace, perhaps most obviously in dedicated settings of Reconstruction. It is the perpetual process of power politics, often manifest violently, and the role it plays in continually reshaping places and spaces, that makes geography a very useful perspective in showing the continuities and legacies across war and post-war periods, and hence the false dichotomy of conflict and reconstruction.

To explore the false dichotomy, we can conceptualise periods of war as periods of construction. Materially, war has played a key role in creating new industries and related economic geographies of production and consumption,[3] requiring new 'domestic' spaces for training and billeting soldiers,[4] and new 'proving grounds'– sometimes framed as national sacrifice zones[5] – for developing the technologies of warfare.[6] Race, gender and class relations are often radically redefined as part of war-time mobilisation, especially in modern periods of 'total war' that require all aspects of state and society to be oriented towards the execution of war.[7] Minefields, missile silos, regions of 'scorched earth', vast areas made uninhabitable by nuclear tests and bombing ranges, demarcated areas made inaccessible through secrecy[8] or what is deemed military necessity such as the Korean Demilitarised Zone are all examples of how war creates distinctive landscapes on a variety of scales and transforms or reproduces associated social relations. Processes of war, in other words, construct places, spaces and social relations that extend far beyond the battlefield. Meanwhile, the US modern battlefield, wherein remote piloting of drone aircraft in extraterritorial engagements has become an emblematic practice, can itself now be said to circulate in real time through distant, military bases, spaces seemingly both at war and at peace.[9]

On the other hand, what is termed reconstruction is frequently a conflictual process, or may set the stage for subsequent violence. The Treaty of Versailles after World War I is infamously known as an act of grand politics that sowed the seeds of Nazism and World War II. The optimistic constructive belief among protagonists that World War I would end war between great powers was soon replaced by a process of international relations that was all about competition and excluding some from the decision-making process. Many a 'brave new world' has been claimed as the reason why wars are fought, but the racial politics of the US after the Civil War and World War II, or the politics of identity and region that all too often is manifest in bombing and shooting in Iraq,[10] are just a few cases from a pervasive set of examples that shows conflict, sometimes violent, continues in post-war, ostensibly 'peaceful' settings. Simply, a post-war context is a particular type of setting in which embedded power relations play out.

To fully investigate the processes fusing conflict/post-conflict settings, it is necessary to put power front and centre in a discussion of post-war reconstruction. Power is understood here in a relational sense;[11] as a process of interaction between social actors with different resources and structural positions, with outcomes partially determining the nature of new relations. Hence, a transition between a period of formal conflict and post-conflict is likely to redefine some sets of relationships and not others. Overall, the combination of all power relations is transformed by conflict, renegotiating some and cementing others. Thinking of power as relational and as a process thus identifies conflict/post-conflict as a false dichotomy in two ways. First, many of the social actors involved in conflict, if not most or all, are likely to remain post-conflict. For example, the de-Ba'athification of Iraq after the US invasion eliminated a formal political party and its role in government, but Ba'athist party members still played a political role, including in the subsequent insurgency. Second, conflict is likely to produce renegotiation but not complete transformation of the power relations between actors. For example, the 1985 Anglo-Irish Agreement and the relative decline of terrorist activity around the issue of Northern Ireland put former paramilitaries in formal political positions, situating the continuing sectarian tensions within a different arena of politics (though not completely, as some terrorist activity continued).

Along with the emphasis on the social construction of places and political spaces, the geographic approach emphasises the contextual 'coming together' of power relations. The actual manifestation and understanding of power relations is a product of place-specific histories and experiences, or 'entanglements of power'.[12] Power relations are continually renegotiated in place-specific contexts, a conceptualisation that makes it possible to see resistance to dominance, and, simultaneously, the politics of dominance continuing within the politics of resistance. For example, a social movement resisting imperialism may be imbued with gender and racial political inequities.

The conceptual power of place is enhanced through the term 'site'. The greater explanatory power of site lies in its recognition of the material and rhetorical components of place, and, most efficaciously, the situation – and positionality – of places within broader historical processes and geographic linkages that connect particular geographic locations and make them 'extra-local'.[13] The negotiation of power relations is rarely limited to a bounded geographical space (a town, region or state), but connected to global political, economic and cultural processes. For example, the 'reconstruction' of Afghanistan has been a global project that has connected Afghan towns with the homes of South Korean aid workers, the conference rooms in Washington DC and London within which policy is hashed out, and the hometowns of serving soldiers. Thus, a geographical approach utilises a relational sense of power to see relations of resistance and domination to be entangled or co-existent, and situated within particular geographic settings that are to be understood within broader historical processes and geographical connections.

Geographic approaches to the connections between war and peace

Reflecting the changes in warfare, and the pervading sense that the War on Terror is an ongoing concern, there has been growing interest in rethinking the dynamics of post-conflict. Though initiated by the War on Terror, the evolution of the military response of the US through drone warfare, domestic surveillance and changing border technologies has maintained academic interest in new forms of state-sponsored organised violence and its connection to rhetorical usages of 'peace'. Some of these works, though, are utilitarian, aimed at providing guidelines and feedback for NGO practitioners.[14] We turn instead to the ways that critical scholars have refuted the sense of a dichotomy between war and peace, and to the implications of these approaches for understanding the nature of 'post-war' spaces.

The sense of war-reconstruction-peace being different, and mutually constitutive, moments or angles upon a continual process of political competition has deep roots in literature from the Marxist tradition. Lenin's thesis on imperialism, published in 1916, politicised the understanding that war was an inevitable feature of monopoly capitalism.[15] The logic of this argument is that capitalism inevitably generates war in a search for markets. World-systems theory, building on Marxist theories of primitive accumulation, offers a somewhat different take, that wars created new zones of cheap labour. The work of Harvey expands on these traditions by noting that warfare is a means of 'accumulation through dispossession'.[16] War, in this sense, is a component of capitalism's need to create new regions or landscapes of accumulation to compensate for declining rates of profit. The deconstruction of swathes of physical infrastructure is a form of devaluation of assets that is necessary for a new round of investment and profit.[17] In this sense, the destructive process of warfare is a component of the capitalist cycle of disinvestment (or devaluation) and reinvestment that destroys and recreates landscapes.

Others have also made the argument that capitalism needs war. Emanating from the work of Baran and Sweezy, the identification of total war has led some to see arms production, and the need for new wars to stimulate new production, as a driving force behind military expeditions.[18] World War I has been noted as an important threshold in modern warfare for the mobilisation of the entire society and economy for the prosecution of war; a conclusion readily accepted by historians of all political hues.

Much contemporary scholarship leans on the polemical traditions of Baran and Sweezy, and argues for a linkage between neoliberal forms of accumulation and the 'contracting out' of warfare. Coined 'disaster capitalism' by Klein, landscapes of post-war reconstruction are identified as frontiers of capital.[19] Critical scholarship on post-war reconstruction has engaged this same issue by noting how post-war reconstruction has become a vehicle or opportunity for the establishment of neoliberal forms of governance.[20] In other words, post-war reconstruction is a process of establishing a certain set of social relations.

The themes of capitalism making and needing war are situated within broader social processes, and need not be looked at from a Marxist perspective. Kearns, for example, has reminded us of the deep connection between geopolitics, including the waging of war, and imperialism.[21] A specific linkage between the structural inequalities of the world-economy and conflict and violence has been made in a number of ways. The work of Watts promoted the term 'structural violence', first developed in the classic paper by Galtung, to examine the impact of the flow of profits from poor areas of the world to rich upon life expectancy, a 'silent violence' in which global and regional markets and institutions remain deeply implicated.[22] The expansion of capitalism and the role of imperial practices in reshaping the pattern of political economy led to the identification of different types of wars – including those facilitating colonial expansion[23] – which intersect with events and processes of structural violence to reinforce the idea, explicit in the Marxist perspective, that the processes of capitalism are seen to involve, or even require, violence for territorial expansion. Critical to this scholarship, then, is a sense that the 'constructive' aspects of the economy are inseparable from conquest and war.

The process of the territorial spread of capitalism from its European origins across the whole of the globe requires the establishment of institutions and social relations facilitating capital investment, infrastructure to extract resources, and the flow of profits back to the metropole.[24] In some cases this required the establishment of formal colonial control, but more recently it tends to have been maintained without actual political annexation or control, or through what is known as informal imperialism. However, both formal and informal imperialism are violent. Gregory's analysis of the 'colonial present', framing landscapes of war and security in Afghanistan, Palestine and Iraq in terms of long-term, asymmetrical colonial encounters, provides additional concepts for understanding the nature of 'post-conflict' geographies.[25] The persistence of extra-territorial control, that is of powerful countries exerting influence in other sovereign territories through direct and indirect violence, is thus another pervasive aspect of global politics; and one that denies a clear break between periods of war and periods of diplomacy or 'normal relations'.

The development of total war, the relationship between geopolitics and empire, and the relative permanence of structural colonial relationships have created another way in which any sense of clear lines between war and peace must be challenged. Following the work of Tilly and Mann on the formation and persistence of the modern state, it is wrong to think of any moment when politics was not connected to the violence of territorial control. The formation of the modern territorial state has involved territorial expansion and consolidation of state authority over diverse populations, which in turn has involved explicit or latent violence. In other words, politics has always been connected to force, coercion and violence. Hence, the term militarisation may be a misnomer, as it implies a time when the politics was separate from the norms and imperatives of the military.[26] Instead, we might also use the term securitisation to see how all aspects of society can be imbued with the language and practice of violence (prisons, immigration control) in particular contexts, while it is still appropriate to talk about militarisation when the specific institutions of the military are involved. Hence, modern society is largely imbued with intersecting ideologies of militarism and securitisation, as is evident in economics, politics and the construction of landscapes.[27]

One manifestation of this prevalent and, often, latent or banal militarism is the construction of everyday behaviours,[28] and the creation of subjects that internalise and practise militarism. Focusing upon the politics of citizenship, warfare is exposed as one of the driving forces in defining the institutions and practices of citizenship across historical and geographical contexts.[29] Provisions of state benefits to war veterans illustrate how the total war phenomenon has manifest itself in the development of what is commonly accepted as the domestic politics of peace time.[30] Hence, practices of securitisation and militarisation blend across ostensibly distinct spaces and periods of war and peace to create citizens and everyday behaviour that are always, to varying degrees, constructed by, and supportive of, the institutions and practices of war.

Theoretically, the study of war and citizenship has built upon the Foucauldian idea of biopolitics ('power over life'), the ways in which norms of behaviour are created by a variety of state and non-state institutions,[31] institutions which increasingly draw their legitimacy, in Foucault's terms, from 'the power to "make" live and "let" die'.[32] In this sense, militarisation is a pervasive process because it constantly attempts to create political subjects imbued, to varying degrees, with militaristic beliefs and practices. Building upon the idea of biopolitics, there has been a plethora of studies using Agamben's contribution to identify the process by which some segments of the population are deemed unworthy of protection from international law, and even basic understandings of morality;[33] Agamben's theory has thus been mobilised by geographers investigating the war on terror and related conflicts.[34] Such approaches also rest on the critique of long-standing practices and rhetoric of Orientalism developed by Said,[35] and have shown that structural imperatives of imperialism produce a connective tissue of othering and violence that cannot easily be separated into distinct zones and periods of peace and war.

Among geographers, a number of recent studies have been provoked and informed by the military responses to the terrorist attacks of 11 September 2001, or what has become known as the 'War on Terror'[36]; but this work has been diverse in focus.[37] The dominant theme of this body of work, however, is that overt military exercises cannot be separated from economic processes. For Cowen and Smith, the logic of geo-economics is one that is constantly global and exploitive and, often times, demanding military action.[38] We have thus, in some ways, come full circle, and are continuing to build upon Lenin's connections between monopoly capitalism and war to identify the ties between neoliberalism and war.[39] Alternatively, perhaps the deeper reason that Lenin's claims are being echoed is precisely that there are persistent structural causes of war; notably the continuing processes of exploitation in a capitalist world-economy, and the always incomplete, overlapping and conflicting projects of state-territorial politics.[40] Of course, this is not to say that nothing has changed in the past one hundred years or so, or in the last ten. The disturbing point is precisely that the idea of continual or constant war has become routine.

One clear outcome of these processes, then, is an impoverished sense of peace: even as the horizon of peace is mobilised to justify new conflicts (as well as new landscapes of reconstruction), the meaning of peace is often reduced to conditions of militarised security.[41] Efforts have been made to break away from the fixation with war and illustrate more effectively the work of peace and peacebuilding activities in the world. Hence, the call for a 'pacific geopolitics' shows how people actively make spaces of peace in place-specific contexts by creating institutions and everyday practices aimed at tolerance and mutual cooperation between different, and potentially antagonistic, social groups.[42] This approach is a fertile avenue to understanding how 'entanglements of power' in geographic sites may indeed produce geographies of peace. Although there is a danger that this approach may be misinterpreted and further the understanding of a war-peace binary through its emphasis on peaceful (non-conflictual) time-space context, a more accurate interpretation of the concept illustrates how everyday practices of peace provide an alternative to the power politics of state, transnational and capitalist institutions that we have identified as the primary agents of the war-reconstruction-contested peace continuum.[43] Everyday politics of peace, practiced within the complexity of interwoven and place-specific power relations, have the potential to challenge specific forms of the politics of reconstruction that we have interpreted as a continuation of war.

We have argued that geographic perspectives, emphasising the social construction of places and political spaces, and the positional, situated nature of social relations in post-conflict settings, are effective in resisting neat distinctions among the spaces and times of conflict, peace and reconstruction, allowing us to better understand the continuity of violent power relations. In the next section, we flesh out these concepts further through a situated history of the idea of reconstruction. A closer look at the heritage of reconstruction, including the specific historical and geographical contexts within which the language and material practices of reconstruction took shape, in this sense, allows us to appreciate the cultural and political work of reconstruction today.

Reconstruction as a keyword

Among the first traces of the term *reconstruction* in political discourse, according to the *Oxford English Dictionary*, was the reflection of one commentator who gazed from across the English Channel at Gallicæ, in the aftermath of revolution, and wondered 'whether, from its ruins, fragments were to be collected for re-construction of the political edifice'.[44] The sense that the political edifice could be rebuilt in a planned, rational, perhaps even improved manner, was nicely rendered in the grammar of *reconstruction*, and it was one that closely articulated with the currents of Enlightenment political thought. While the literal meaning of reconstruction (that is, the rebuilding of *anything*, whether natural, artificial, or abstract) has persisted, the *Oxford English Dictionary* also points to the emergence of a particular US-based meaning at the onset of the Civil War, gaining currency – and complexity – as northerners and unionists began to imagine the 'reconstruction' of a *post*-war Union. Reconstruction, the proper noun, would come to embody a temporality of simultaneous war and post-war, and an equally complex spatiality, as we discuss below. The centrality of Reconstruction as a defining term for political conditions after the American Civil War would, in turn, help to harden the semantic relationship, during the mid-twentieth century, between reconstruction as the rebuilding of an area devastated by warfare, and the restoration of political, social and economic stability to the region or locality. Indeed, the language of reconstruction embedded in post-World War II international institutions – notably the International Bank for Reconstruction and Development (World Bank) – suggests the extent to which reconstruction processes can serve as hegemonic strategies for newly-emerging international regimes. Notions of reconstruction, in this sense, have provided cultural and ideological resources for various historical actors, but in the process that language has itself been remade in the production and integration of war and post-war geographies.

Reconstruction in America

Already in 1861, shortly after the onset of the US Civil War, references to a *reconstruction of the Union* were in circulation in Washington. By 1863, when President Lincoln reported to Congress on the problem of the 'political framework of the states on *what is called* the reconstruction', *the* reconstruction was evidently an acceptable phraseology for imagining post-war futures, albeit one focused explicitly on the conditions and processes by which the seceding Confederate states were to be restored constitutionally to the federal government. In December of that year, Lincoln's Proclamation of Amnesty and Reconstruction, which was concerned with the restoration of citizenship rights to loyalist southern whites, reflected what had clearly become an official language. The idea that the South itself was to be *radically* reconstructed, however, describing a great social transformation centred on the abolition of slavery, appears to emerge only slightly later, and for some, as a terrain of contention in an emerging post-war politics. One abolitionist would insist, for instance, that 'what is commonly termed "reconstruction"' meant that it was 'the whole organism of southern society that must be reconstructed'.[45]

The 1867–1868 *Reconstruction Acts*, as they were known, organised much of the South into Union-occupied military districts, and made ultimate restoration of the ex-Confederate states to the Union dependent on their ratification of the Fourteenth Amendment, which (theoretically) promoted ex-slaves to full citizenship on the basis of due process and equal protection law. The notion of *Reconstruction* had thus gained widespread political and cultural currency, but the more narrow legal focus had coalesced with the broader sense of reconstruction as post-war social, political and economic transformation. Moreover, as the term was elevated through usage to a proper noun in the American parlance, it also quickly came to signify not only the (diverse) events and processes (laws, institutions, debates, etc.) of reconstruction, but also the historical *period* during which they took place. This shift in some ways marks generic notions of reconstruction that are mobilised today to demarcate clearly defined periods of post-war stabilisation and peace. A closer look at the actual historical-geographical transition from wartime to post-war relations of power in the South, however, allows us to better understand how Reconstruction was shaped and realised through interrelations between various social forces both internal and external to the state, and through new forms of organised political violence and terror.

Foner's trenchant and comprehensive history, *Reconstruction: America's Unfinished Revolution, 1863–1877*, offers a number of useful starting points for this mapping, both historically and conceptually.[46] It is not incidental that Foner dates Reconstruction from 1863, not 1865, positioning it as a process at least partly co-existing with war, articulated with it, rather than something that follows war in a linear fashion. For Foner, Reconstruction begins with Lincoln's Emancipation Proclamation, which constitutionally freed slaves from the Confederate states, but which also opened opportunities provided for blacks, including those from border states and elsewhere behind Union lines, to enlist in the US army. The army, attempting to meet voracious demands for labour, would ultimately enlist some 180,000 ex-slaves during the war, employing them primarily in the construction of fortifications and protection of supply lines. For many, military service presented a clear path to freedom.

Neither was Lincoln's Emancipation Proclamation a meaningless gesture in the Confederate states; it ensured that the Union army would henceforth be an army of liberation. It was also, increasingly, an occupying force, as the war was re-purposed as one of simultaneous destruction and reconstruction. Critically, Foner's narrative is not one that presumes a top-down sense of agency. Rather, he recalls the historical analysis of Du Bois, in *Black Reconstruction in America*, who argued that 'with perplexed and laggard steps, the United States followed in the footsteps of the black slave'.[47] So, while the Emancipation Proclamation plays a critical role in signposting the onset of the Reconstruction amidst ongoing war, we also see how this move was, in some ways, thrust upon Lincoln by footsteps on the ground, and the collapse of slavery from within well before formal emancipation – a highly uneven geographical process. Perhaps initially in regions characterised by the most brutal working conditions, like the Louisiana sugar plantations, widespread 'insubordination' and refusal of slaves to work coincided with diminished enforcement capacities among planters as the war began, and expanded, in Du Bois's terms, into a general strike.[48] More militant sacking of plantation houses when abandoned by planters or encompassed behind Union lines were taken as rites of freedom among emancipated slaves, along with destruction of cotton gins in areas such as the South Carolina Sea Islands. For Du Bois, drawing on Marx's labour theory of value, this reconfigured sense of agency made visible how 'the black worker won the war by a general strike which transferred his labour from the Confederate planter to the Northern invader, in whose army lines workers began to be organised as a new labour force'.[49]

Elsewhere, new geographies of war and liberation took shape as slaves escaped in mass to Union-held territory in coastal Virginia and South Carolina, and the plantation belt along the Mississippi River, particularly after a March 1862 decree which forbade the Army from returning the runaway slaves of the disloyal. To return them would have amounted to abetting the enemy, since the Confederate armies had impressed tens of thousands into labour, but even these conditions had enabled new opportunities to the slaves for escape behind Union lines. New enclaves of emancipated or runaway slaves were produced both in fixed locations, like New Orleans, and in mobile camps, following behind the Union army camps, reflecting changed social conditions across a devastated landscape, and anticipating the dramatic transformations expected to follow.

Army officers, meanwhile, found themselves in positions of authority under martial law at various settings along the South Atlantic coast and the Mississippi Valley, and in position – and in practical need – to experiment with a range of new models of governance and practical reconstruction as back-of-the-lines duty. This brought the army into contact and coalition with a set of interest groups seeking a stake in the project of Reconstruction during the war and its immediate aftermath, from abolitionist, reformist and missionary groups, to spokespeople for the northern black community, to the industrial bourgeoisie, to the Republican Party which, reflecting a highly sectionalised electorate, was effectively running a one-party state in Washington. Under these conditions, the national state had itself been reinvented during the war, made visible in Reconstruction in terms of:

> vastly expanded authority and a new set of purposes, including an unprecedented commitment to the ideal of a national citizenship whose equal rights belonged to all Americans regardless of race. Originating in wartime exigencies, the activist state (paralleled at the local level both North and South) came to embody the reforming impulse deeply rooted in post-war politics.[50]

But this history also shows that the reform impulses that shaped the post-war state could be undermined, or even violently opposed. Some new state institutions, like the Freedmen's Bureau, created with local offices throughout the South to facilitate the transition to free labour and provide educational and health programmes for millions of ex-slaves, would not survive even the formal Reconstruction period. Others, including formal and informal mechanisms integrating the state with financial and industrial capital, were far more enduring;[51] and as expected, the war of liberation had also generated conditions for what Harvey would call, in a more recent context, 'accumulation by dispossession'.[52]

For many, conditions of security and of everyday life and labour had, in fact, been far better during the war than after. In the Sea Islands, for instance, the arrival of the US Navy as early as 1861 had caused the planters to abandon their cotton fields and slaves, who in turn realised new freedoms by extending their own food crops, hunting, fishing and leisure activities under martial law. But even in this early rehearsal for Reconstruction, the arrival of missionaries, teachers, treasury agents and entrepreneurs, among others, produced troubling results, as the large plantations frequently fell into the hands of army officers, land speculators and cotton companies. Most disquieting were the campaigns of reactionary violence waged against the agents of Reconstruction, most brutally by the Ku Klux Klan and similar groups between 1868 and the end of the formal Reconstruction period in 1877; a settlement achieved, in large part, through organised violence and intimidation.

Indeed, the scale and geographical extent of political violence carried out by the Klan and other paramilitary groups during this period compels us to rethink Reconstruction as a moment of transformative warfare, albeit a new kind of war, a war of terror waged through institutional mechanisms as well as directed violence, to reconfigure power relations around the restoration of relations of white supremacy, 'redemption' of the planter class and control of the black labour force. Just as the Civil War was also a moment of reconstruction, in other words, the Reconstruction was itself a period of intensely violent social and political conflict.

Challenging the limited capacities of occupying troops to enforce federal civil and voting rights legislation, along with the political will behind them, the Klan's war for 'home rule' in the Southern states had elements of a 'total war' which intentionally blurred the boundaries between combatants, political figures and civilians. While Klan violence was typically organised and carried out by local groups, its aims intertwined closely with those of the Democratic Party in the South, forming in some ways a military wing of the party which threatened the survival of black and white Republican Party politicians, infrastructure, and even voters, seeking, as one veteran Confederate officer put it, 'to defy the reconstructed State Governments, to treat them with contempt, and show that they have no real existence'.[53] Violence, perpetrated by veterans, among others, sometimes employed military tactics and resembled small military strikes. A January 1871 attack on a county jail in South Carolina, for instance, was carried out by some 500 masked men, who took the jail and lynched eight black prisoners before whipping and terrorising blacks and white Republicans in the area. The following month, thousands of blacks were still being forced to run to the woods every night to escape continuing attacks. An armed standoff around Colfax, Louisiana, in anticipation of the 1872 election, saw whites armed with guns and a small cannon lay siege against armed freedmen, under the direction of black union veterans, who had entrenched themselves around the county seat. On Easter Sunday, 280 freedmen were killed, including 50 massacred after surrendering.

But the violence was also more diffuse, widespread and banal, mobilised as a mode of everyday social regulation. Churches and schools were frequent targets for Klan arson; in the city of Tuskegee, Alabama, for example, nearly every black church and school was burned during the fall of 1870. Storekeepers were publicly whipped for treating blacks too well, as were some landlords for renting rooms to northern teachers. One 'carpetbagger' judge recorded 12 murders, 9 rapes, 14 arson cases and an astonishing 700 beatings in his North Carolina judicial district. Blacks who sought redress against employers, or who sought to change employers, were also frequent targets of violence. Reconstruction, for many, was not 'post-war', it was permanent – and asymmetrical – warfare. It was thus a conflict carried out at a wide range of social sites; it was also a war of words, which worked through the construction and maintenance of particular cultural norms and understandings, and the creation of a climate in which violence and terror were accepted as a legitimate weapon and political strategy.[54] After bloody electoral campaigns in Mississippi in 1875, when President Grant, the former Civil War General, refused to send in troops to protect black voters or ensure fair elections across the South in 1876, the federal state's failure to protect its citizens was complete. The interlocking systems of hegemony, engendered through violent resistance to the Reconstruction state, would become deeply entrenched in the Southern landscape; it would be nearly a century before they were challenged again.

Reconstruction and development

Ideas and practices of reconstruction have persisted in US foreign policy as an ideology of progressive military occupation, one which, as with Foner's army of liberation, identified the invading state, through acts of emancipation, with the interests of local populations or with humanity in general.[55] US expansionists would develop and draw on this rhetoric in support of more cynical liberations – Cuba, Philippines, Panama. World War I also presented new contexts for speculating on the problem of the post-war as one of rebirth and renewal. For example, the political and intellectual climate of Britain in the years between the two world wars was one of both fear that 'civilisation' itself was threatened and widespread belief that new projects of eugenics, peace-making and utopian politics were necessary and possible.[56] Hence, the principal literal meaning of reconstruction as the rebuilding of an area devastated by warfare, and the presumed restoration of political, social and economic stability to the region or locality, achieved global imperative. In 1916, Arnold Toynbee, the British historian – and later delegate to the Paris Peace Conference – offered a slim volume on *The New Europe: Some Essays in Reconstruction*, a Great War exercise in imagining European post-war futures along particular national lines. Toynbee, who worked for the British Foreign Office during the war, would later add a study on Austrian reconstruction,[57] thus reflecting how *reconstruction* had come to be generalised, a peculiarly modern name for programmes of post-war recovery and renewal which worked by evoking a horizon of post-war peace that is distinct from periods of war.

A focus on reconstruction as a keyword compels us to recognise the role the US played in establishing post-war reconstruction as a formal geopolitical strategy, that is, as an enduring political category in the modern world, although we do not offer an account of the specific mechanisms through which this has been achieved.[58] Crucially, *reconstruction* has remained an essential political tool for the US, and a hegemonic strategy, as it moved beyond consolidating its domestic politics to exerting its power and presence across the globe. From establishing control over the Philippines, through the Marshall Plan, to contemporary Iraq and Afghanistan, projects of reconstruction have created new landscapes and political realities that have played a crucial role in shaping new geopolitical worlds. But this is not to restrict reconstruction to be solely a feature of US geopolitics. The ideology of Nazism rested on the idea that a new German nation and Reich was to be constructed in the wake of World War I. The Bolshevik revolution was also sparked by the catastrophes of the Great War, and blended visions of utopia with violent practice, both immediately in the civil war and in the construction of collective farms and successive political purges. The same can be said for Mao's revolution in China and the millions of lives that were taken in the name of counter-revolution and constructing a socialist society. The wave of decolonisation post-World War II was undertaken to construct new independent nation-states and included the horrific violence of Zionism and the partition of India, to name just two. As work by Tyner on Cambodia and Dean and Grundy-Warr on the Thai–Burma border illustrates, reconstruction and state violence can be interpreted as national projects as well as part of the ongoing geopolitics of post-colonisation.[59] Hence, though the US has played a central role in establishing and maintaining post-war reconstruction as a component of contemporary geopolitics, the idea and practices have become pervasive, with widespread roots in the political ideologies of nationalism as well as the totalitarianism that emerged with the utopian politics of the twentieth century.

From the impetus provided by the end of World War II, and the immediate political imperatives of political distrust and competition between the Soviet Union and the US, the language of reconstruction has emerged as a distinctly global phenomenon. As with the case of the US reconstruction, post-war reconstruction became institutionalised: most prominently through the rhetoric and practice of the International Bank for Reconstruction and Development (World Bank) and the United Nations. Ironically, two US politicians especially reviled for their role in the prosecution of war (Robert McNamara and Paul Wolfowitz) went on to serve as presidents of the World Bank, suggesting the extent of linkages between war and 'reconstruction and development'. The UN has fully integrated notions of reconstruction into its institutional vocabulary – and its raison d'être is based upon a tacit acknowledgement of the persistence and globality of conflict. Increasingly, post-conflict reconstruction is seen as a globalised project serving the neoliberal agenda enacted by a transnational class of elite actors.[60] But practices carried out under the umbrella of reconstruction today are widespread. That the efforts of, for example, US 'Provincial Reconstruction Teams' in Afghanistan and Iraq, Doctors without Borders (MSF) aid workers in South Sudan, and the massive NGO, armed forces and services sectors arising in post-conflict spaces across the world, can all be framed under the category of reconstruction is indicative of the concept's broad and enduring ideological currency, but also suggests that the idea of reconstruction will continue to evolve in diverse contexts.

Conclusion

We have approached the varied literatures discussed in this chapter with the goal of highlighting how the social processes of capital accumulation, imperialism, state formation and militarisation are intertwined and pervasive. The continual operation of these processes is the basis for our central claim: war and peace should not be seen as dichotomous periods and spaces. The multiple processes that enable the waging of war are constant features of society, and not just moments or historic events we can compartmentalise in a linear fashion as war, peace and reconstruction. Moreover, places, regions and landscapes, even states themselves, are persistently being destroyed and re-built by organised violence, or war. Hence, the continuity of processes across what are commonly termed conflict/post-conflict situations is a matter of the ongoing power relations that contest the way spaces and places are made, maintained and altered. Processes of war continue to *make* the worlds we live in, often long after the treaties are signed or the explosions have quietened down. In this sense, 'reconstruction' is a misnomer: what is being constructed is rarely an idea of how society was but how it should be.

Our geographic approach highlights the practice of the social construction of post-conflict spaces, and examines the manner in which these spaces may both reflect and help to reproduce hegemonic power relations in specific regional and historical contexts.[61] Hence, when we examine where war and peace 'take place', to take a common expression, we find that 'where' is already a relational and contextual position, which requires situating actors in spaces defined (and contested) through the intermingling of power relations established across multiple social and geographical sites. Learning more about the ways in which socially produced spaces and boundaries serve to perpetuate power relations and practices of violence across contexts usually defined simply as war or peace, in this sense, can provide a road-map for the important academic and practical task of creating a true 'pacific geopolitics'.[62]

Acknowledgements

This chapter is a re-working of our introductory chapter in *Reconstructing Conflict*, a volume of edited essays, written by geographers, that critiques the false dichotomy of war and peace through the lens of post-war reconstruction. We have made some additions and changes to that chapter, but much of the text is reproduced in this essay in revised form. Adapted by permission of the publishers from 'Introduction: Reconstruction and the Worlds that War Makes' in Scott Kirsch and Colin Flint, *Reconstructing Conflict: Integrating War and Post-War Geographies*, Farnham, UK, and Burlington, VT: Ashgate Publishing, 2011, pp. 3–28.

Notes

1 K. Hewitt, 'Place annihilation: Area Bombing and the Fate of Urban Places', *Annals of the Association of American Geographers*, vol. 73, no. 2, 1983, pp. 257–284; Michael Watts, *Silent Violence: Food, Famine, and Peasantry in Northern Nigeria*, Berkeley, CA: University of California Press, 1983; David Harvey, 'The Geopolitics of Capitalism', in D. Gregory and J. Urry (eds), *Social Relations and Spatial Structures*,

London: Macmillan, 1985, pp. 128–163; Nancy Lee Peluso and Michael Watts (eds), *Violent Environments*, Ithaca, NY: Cornell University Press, 2001; David Harvey, *The New Imperialism*, Oxford: Oxford University Press, 2003; Derek Gregory, *The Colonial Present: Afghanistan, Palestine, Iraq*, Oxford: Blackwell, 2004; Derek Gregory and Allan Pred (eds), *Violent Geographies: Fear, Terror, and Political Violence*, New York: Routledge, 2006; Deborah Cowen and Emily Gilbert (eds), *War, Citizenship, Territory*, New York: Routledge, 2008; C. Dahlman, 'Post-Conflict', in C. Gallaher, C. Dahlman, M. Gilmartin, A. Mountz, and P. Shirlow (eds), *Key Concepts in Political Geography*, Thousand Oaks, CA: Sage Publications, 2009, pp. 235–246; Alan Ingram and Klaus Dodds (eds), *Spaces of Security and Insecurity*, Farnham: Ashgate Publishing, 2009; Audrey Kobayashi, 'Geographies of Peace and Armed Conflict: Introduction', *Annals of the Association of American Geographers*, vol. 99, no. 5, 2009, pp. 819–826; Stephen Graham, *Cities Under Siege: The New Military Urbanism*, London: Verso, 2010; James A. Tyner, *Military Legacies: A World Made by War*, New York: Routledge, 2010; Derek Gregory, 'The Everywhere War', *The Geographical Journal*, vol. 177, no. 3, 2011, pp. 238–250.
2 Raymond Williams, *Keywords: A Vocabulary of Culture and Society*, revised edition, New York: Oxford University Press, 1983; Tony Bennett, Lawrence Grossberg, and Meaghan Morris, *New Keywords: A Revised Vocabulary of Culture and Society*, Malden, MA: Blackwell, 2005; David Harvey, 'Space as a Keyword', in Noel Castree and Derek Gregory (eds), *David Harvey: A Critical Reader*, Malden, MA: Blackwell Harvey, 2006, pp. 270–293.
3 Ann Markusen, Peter Hall, Scott Campbell and Sabina Deitrick, *The Rise of the Gunbelt: The Military Remapping of Industrial America*, New York: Oxford University Press, 1991.
4 Catherine Lutz, *Homefront: A Military City and the American Twentieth Century*, Boston, MA: Beacon Press, 2001; Rachel Woodward, *Military Geographies*, Malden, MA: Blackwell, 2004.
5 Mike Davis, 'Dead West: Ecocide in Marlboro Country', *New Left Review*, no. 200, July–August 1993, pp. 49–73.
6 A. Makhijani, H. Hu and K. Yih, *Nuclear Wastelands: A Global Guide to Nuclear Weapons Production and its Health and Environmental Effects*, Cambridge, MA: MIT Press and International Physicians for the Prevention of Nuclear War, 2000; Scott Kirsch, *Proving Grounds: Project Plowshare and the Unrealized Dream of Nuclear Earthmoving*, New Brunswick, NJ: Rutgers University Press, 2005, pp. 15–27.
7 R. Chickering, S. Förster and B. Greiner (eds), *A World at Total War: Global Conflict and the Politics of Destruction, 1937–1945*, Cambridge: Cambridge University Press, 2004.
8 Trevor Paglen, *Blank Spots on the Map: The Dark Geography of the Pentagon's Secret World*, New York: Dutton, 2009.
9 Scott Kirsch, 'War and Peace', in M. Goodwin, P. Cloke and P. Crang (eds), *Introducing Human Geographies*, London: Routledge, revised 3rd edition, 2014, pp. 542–555; see Stuart Elden, *Terror and Territory: The Spatial Extent of Sovereignty*, Minneapolis, MN: University of Minnesota Press, 2009; Gregory, 'Everywhere War' (note 1 above).
10 See Gregory, *Colonial Present* (note 1 above).
11 John Allen, *Lost Geographies of Power*, Malden, MA: Blackwell, 2003.
12 J. Sharp, P. Routledge, C. Philo and R. Paddison (eds), *Entanglements of Power: Geographies of Domination/Resistance*, New York: Routledge, 2000.
13 *Ibid.*; see also Doreen Massey, *For Space*, London: Sage, 2005.
14 W. I. Robinson, *Transnational Conflicts*, London: Verso, 2003.
15 V. I. Lenin, *Imperialism the Highest Stage of Capitalism*, London: Pluto Press, 1996.
16 Harvey, 'Geopolitics' and *New Imperialism* (both at note 1 above).
17 Harvey, 'Geopolitics' (note 1 above).

18 P. Baran and P. Sweezy, *Monopoly Capital: An Essay on the American Economic and Social Order*, New York: Monthly Review Press, 1966.
19 Naomi Klein, *The Shock Doctrine: The Rise of Disaster* Capitalism, New York: Penguin Books, 2007.
20 Robinson (note 14 above).
21 Gerry Kearns, *Geopolitics and Empire: The Legacy of Halford Mackinder*, Oxford: Oxford University Press, 2009.
22 Watts (note 1 above); J. Galtung, 'Violence, Peace, and Peace Research', *Journal of Peace Research*, vol. 6, 1969, pp. 167–191. Such structural violence, as the editors of this volume remind us, was itself easily rendered as 'peace', for some audiences at least, amidst a 'high noon' Cold War geopolitical context in which the mere absence of nuclear holocaust could be said to constitute peace. See also Peluso and Watts (n. 1 above); H. van der Wusten, 'Violence, Development, and Political Order', in C. Flint (ed.), *The Geography of War and Peace*, Oxford: Oxford University Press, 2005, pp. 61–84.
23 John O'Loughlin, 'The Political Geography of Conflict: Civil Wars in the Hegemonic Shadow', in C. Flint (ed.), *The Geography of War and Peace*, Oxford: Oxford University Press, 2005, pp. 85–110; John O'Loughlin and H. van der Wusten, 'Political Geography of War and Peace', in P. J. Taylor (ed.), *Political Geography of the Twentieth Century: A Global Analysis*, London: Belhaven Press, pp. 63–113.
24 Immanuel Wallerstein, *The Capitalist World-Economy*, Cambridge: Cambridge University Press, 1979; Watts (note 1 above); James Blaut, *The Colonizer's Model of the World: Geographical Diffusionism and Eurocentric History*, New York: Guilford Press, 1993.
25 Gregory, *Colonial Present* (note 1 above)
26 R. Bernazzoli and C. Flint, 'From Militarization to Securitization: Finding a Concept that Works', *Political Geography*, vol. 28, no. 8, 2009, pp. 449–450.
27 Cynthia Enloe, *The Curious Feminist: Searching for Women in a New Age of Empire*, Berkeley: University of California Press, 2004, p. 219; Woodward (note 4 above). We define militarism as an ideology privileging military culture, norms, practices and behaviour over those of civil society. See R. Bernazzoli and C. Flint, 'Embodying the Garrison State? Everyday Geographies of Militarization in American Society', *Political Geography*, vol. 29, no. 3, 2010, pp. 157–166; A. Vagts, *A History of Militarism*, New York: Meridian Books, 1959; Enloe (this note).
28 Bernazzoli and Flint (note 26 above).
29 Cowen and Gilbert (note 1 above).
30 T. Skocpol, *Protecting Soldiers and Mothers: The Political Origins of Social Policy in the United States*, Cambridge, MA: Belknap Press of Harvard University Press, 1992; M. Power, 'War Veterans, Disability, and Postcolonial Citizenship in Angola and Mozambique', in Cowen and Gilbert (note 1 above), pp. 177–198.
31 Power (note 31 above); Matthew G. Hannah, 'Spaces of Exception and Unexceptionability', in Cowen and Gilbert (note 1 above), pp. 57–73.
32 M. Foucault, *Society Must Be Defended: Lectures at the Collège de France, 1975–76*, translated by David Macey, New York: Picador, 2003.
33 G. Agamben, *Homo Sacer: Sovereign Power and Bare Life*, translated by D. Heller-Roazen, Stanford, CA: Stanford University Press, 1998.
34 Derek Gregory, *Colonial Present* (note 1 above); Matthew G. Hannah, 'Torture and the Ticking Bomb', *Annals of the Association of American Geographers*, vol. 96, no. 3, 2006, pp. 622–640; Hannah (note 31 above).
35 Edward Saïd, *Orientalism*, New York: Pantheon, 1978.
36 Among the many problems with the notion of a *war* on terror, as Elden (note 9 above), p. xxii observes, are 'that it suggests that war is something that is distinct from terror, and that war is the means of combating it'.

37 See Harvey, *New Imperialism* (note 1 above); Gregory, *Colonial Present* (note 1 above); Elden (note 9 above); Gregory and Pred (note 1 above); Cowen and Gilbert (note 1 above); Graham (note 1 above); Scott Kirsch and Colin Flint, *Reconstructing Conflict: Integrating War and Post-War Geographies*, Farnham: Ashgate Publishing, 2011.

38 Deborah Cowen and Neil Smith, 'After Geopolitics? From the Geopolitical Social to Geoeconomics', *Antipode*, vol. 41, no. 1, pp. 22–48. See also Neil Smith, *The Endgame of Globalization*, New York: Routledge, 2005; O. Richmond, *The Transformation of Peace*, Basingstoke: Palgrave Macmillan, 2007.

39 Ingram and Dodds (note 1 above); Klein (note 19 above).

40 C. Flint and S. Radil, 'Terrorism and Counter-Terrorism: Situating al Qaeda and the Global War on Terror within Geopolitical Trends and Structures', *Eurasian Geography and Economics*, vol. 50, no. 2, 2009, pp. 150–171.

41 F. Kühn, 'The Peace Prefix: Ambiguities of the Word 'Peace', *International Peacekeeping*, vol. 19, no. 4, 2012, pp. 396–409.

42 N. Megoran, 'Towards a Geography of Peace: Pacific Geopolitics and Evangelical Christian Crusade Apologies', *Transactions of the Institute of British Geographers*, vol. 35, no. 3, pp. 382–398; see also N. Megoran, 'War *and* Peace? An Agenda for Peace Research and Practice in Geography', *Political Geography*, vol. 30, no. 4, 2011, pp. 1–12; P. Williams and F. McConnell, 'Critical Geographies of Peace', *Antipode*, vol. 43, no. 4, 2011, pp. 927–931.

43 P. Williams, 'Hindu–Muslim Brotherhood: Exploring the Dynamics of Communal Relations in Varanasi, North India', *Journal of South Asian Development*, vol. 2, no. 2, 2007, pp. 153–176; P. Williams, 'Reproducing Everyday Peace in North India: Process, Politics, and Power', *Annals of the Association of American Geographers*, vol. 103, no. 1, 2013, pp. 230–250.

44 Mackintosh (writing in 1791) in *Oxford English Dictionary*, OED Online, Oxford: Oxford University Press, 2010.

45 Schurz (writing in 1865) in *Oxford English Dictionary*, ibid.

46 Eric Foner, *Reconstruction: America's Unfinished Revolution, 1863–1877*, New York: Harper & Row, 2005 (Parkman Prize edn). First published 1988.

47 Du Bois in Foner (*ibid.*), p. 4. Du Bois's analysis, published in 1935 but marginalised for decades by historians who had systematically 'ignored the testimony of the principal actor in the drama of Reconstruction – the emancipated slave', (in Foner, *ibid.*), p. xxi, radically re-interpreted US Southern Reconstruction as both a struggle for genuine democracy in an interracial society and a phase in the struggle between capital and labour. Du Bois thus offers students of the Reconstruction, and of reconstruction processes more generally, a reconfigured sense of human agency. This move not only contributes, as Foner shows, to more adequate historical analyses of US Reconstruction; it also portends a richer sense of global reconstruction processes, and the ideological construction of the 'post-war', as geographically differentiated phenomena which are shaped, like other political processes, through contested social relations, and structured by hierarchies of power. W. E. B. Du Bois, *Black Reconstruction in America: An Essay Toward a History of the Part which Black Folk Played in the Attempt to Reconstruct Democracy in America, 1860–1880*, New York: Oxford University Press, 2007.

48 *Ibid.*, pp. 44–67.

49 *Ibid.*, p.44.

50 Foner (note 46 above), p. xxvi.

51 R. F. Bensel, *Yankee Leviathan: The Origins of Central State Authority in America, 1859–1877*, Cambridge: Cambridge University Press, 1991; R.F. Bensel, *The Political Economy of American Industrialization, 1877–1900*, Cambridge: Cambridge University Press, 2000.

52 Harvey, *New Imperialism* (note 1 above).

58 *Scott Kirsch and Colin Flint*

53 In Foner (note 46 above), p. 444.
54 A. W. Trelease, *White Terror: The Ku Klux Klan Conspiracy and Southern Reconstruction*, Baton Rouge, LA: Louisiana State University Press, 1995.
55 Scott Kirsch, 'Object Lessons: War and American Democracy in the Philippines', in Kirsch and Flint (note 37 above), pp. 203–225.
56 R. Overy, *The Twilight Years: The Paradox of Britain Between the Wars*, New York: Viking Press, 2009.
57 Toynbee (writing in 1925) in *Oxford English Dictionary* (note 44 above).
58 However, for a more explicit consideration, from an international law standpoint, of the relations between twentieth century post-war institutions and Cold War and contemporary projects linking development, democracy, and securitisation, see B. Rajagopal, *International Law from Below: Development, Social Movements, and Third World Resistance*, Cambridge: Cambridge University Press, 2003.
59 James A. Tyner, 'Genocide as Reconstruction: The Political Geography of Democratic Kampuchea', in Kirsch and Flint (note 37 above), pp. 49–66; K. Dean and C. Grundy-Warr, 'Not Peace, Not War: The Myriad Spaces of Sovereignty, Peace and Conflict in Myanmar/Burma', in Kirsch and Flint (note 37 above), pp. 91–114.
60 Robinson (note 14 above).
61 We have illustrated this point with the assistance of the authors of the individual essays in our edited volume *Reconstructing Conflict* (note 37 above). This chapter is a re-working of our introduction to that book. Drawn from settings as diverse as Afghanistan, Indonesia, Cambodia, France, Iraq, Cyprus, Japan, Philippines and the US, the chapters in *Reconstructing Conflict* illustrate the ambiguity between spaces of conflict and spaces of reconstruction, and the complex intertwined geographies of *both* war and peace that emerge from them.
62 Megoran, 'Towards a Geography of Peace' (note 42 above).

3 Still the spectre at the feast

Comparisons between peacekeeping and imperialism in peacekeeping studies today

Philip Cunliffe

This chapter reassesses the discussion of imperialism in the literature on UN peacebuilding. In particular, it sets out to re-examine the various ways in which modern peacebuilding operations are differentiated from forms of neo-imperial rule.[1] The discussion proceeds by identifying the types of distinctions that are made between peacebuilding operations and imperialism within the scholarly literature. I examine the conceptual and logical integrity, and historical validity, of claims to the effect that modern peacebuilding operations possess certain distinctive attributes that raise peacebuilding above imperialism. These claims are unconvincing because they rely on under-theorised and historically impoverished understandings of empire. A more profound understanding of peacebuilding and peacekeeping can be gained by drawing more deeply on a rich tradition of imperialist theorising in the discipline of international relations.

The geographic extent of UN peacekeeping operations throughout the world, the transformative intent of peacebuilding and the political reach that peacebuilders extend in the course of their operations makes imperialism an obvious benchmark with which to gauge the role and place of peacebuilding in international affairs today. But while the question of whether or not peacekeeping/peacebuilding mirrors imperialism is often raised, it is also with ritualistic predictability equally often summarily dismissed. The question is important because it raises broad concerns about the purpose and rationale of peacekeeping in world order. Nor is the question merely abstract. The extent to which peacebuilding can be differentiated from imperialism is directly used to legitimate peacebuilding operations. Although there is a greater variety of voices in peacebuilding debates than ever before – extending to post-colonial, Foucauldian and critical theory perspectives – imperialism remains under-theorised and under-utilised in the study of peacekeeping. While much invoked as a concept, it is seldom systematically deployed in peacekeeping debates. Thus the spectre of imperialism that scholars of peacebuilding conjure with is more powerful than they realise and, as shown below, attempts to exorcise it to date have failed.

The focus of this chapter is on what Roland Paris termed 'post-settlement peacebuilding' (his definition is discussed below). At least since the US-led

60 *Philip Cunliffe*

invasion of Iraq in 2003, empire has returned to the core of debates in international relations. While imperial power is more easily identified in those peacebuilding operations that are directly tied to the political interests and military initiatives of a powerful state – such as with US operations in Iraq and Afghanistan – 'post-settlement peacebuilding' as opposed to 'post-conquest peacebuilding' is widely believed to possess attributes that distinguish it from outright imperialism or the more dubious and militarily robust 'post-conquest' operations.

While Paris concedes that 'all peacebuilding missions involve a measure of foreign intrusion in domestic affairs', he maintains that 'destroying a regime through external invasion is hardly equivalent, in degree or kind, to deploying a mission at the request of local parties with the goal of [implementing] a peace settlement'.[2] At the very least it can be said that questions of imperial power are more ambiguous when it comes to these cases of post-settlement peacebuilding. Simply put, post-settlement peacebuilding is the 'hard case' for questions of imperialism. Thus although not sharing Paris's confidence that post-settlement and post-conquest peacebuilding operations can be so easily distinguished, in this chapter I am not seeking to draw out these similarities but rather to scrutinise the case made for those supposedly redeeming features of post-settlement peacebuilding. I begin by providing some context for the discussion by briefly surveying how imperialism has been repeatedly invoked – often with surprising bluntness – in discussion of peacekeeping, and how this itself reflects changed attitudes to imperialism and its legacy. I identify the stakes involved in analysing peacebuilding by considering how such operations are legitimated in international politics. I then analyse in more detail the ways in which peacebuilding is believed to resemble imperialism, and the crucial factors seen to differentiate peacekeeping from imperialism.

The claims made for the redeemed character of post-settlement peacebuilding are clustered into arguments of two broad types: aims and modalities. In the first case, the aims of peacebuilding are held to be a-strategic and therefore non-imperial; while in the second case, the modalities of peacebuilding – that it is multilateral and consensual – make it incompatible with empire-building projects. I will show that the contemporary practices of peacebuilding are not only visible in the historical record of European imperialism, but are also consistent with neo-imperial theories of international order. The method therefore is that of immanent critique. Rather than semantic jugglery or attempts to force discussion of peacebuilding into pre-given definitions of empire, I expose the conceptual and historical shortcomings of those attempts to rescue peacebuilding from charges of imperialism.

Peacekeeping scholarship and the study of imperialism

One might expect that comparisons between modern-day peacebuilding operations and imperial rule, colonialism and empire, would be controversial and bitterly contested. Empire, after all, is widely seen to be a redundant and intrinsically illegitimate form of political rule, while peacekeeping and peacebuilding is an accepted and established international practice that has become ever more widespread since the end of the Cold War. Such an assumption would be wrong: discussion of empire in peacekeeping studies is open, and even frank, among the staunchest supporters of peacebuilding.

Discussion of 'liberal imperialism' is rife, albeit most commonly in reference to those operations and cases of intervention that, for whatever reason, have been more prominent in the policymaking of Western capitals, as indicated by the sub-title to Michael Ignatieff's *Empire Lite: Nation-building in Bosnia, Kosovo and Afghanistan*.[3] Even the viceroys of the new 'liberal imperialism' are unashamed about their role. 'What we have [in Bosnia] is near-imperialism', Lord Paddy Ashdown, former High Representative in Bosnia and Herzegovina, told a British journalist, adding that his job incorporated 'a Gilbert and Sullivan title and powers that should make a liberal blush' (although, as the reporter noted, Ashdown wasn't blushing).[4] According to Kimberly Marten, '[e]mpire and peacekeeping have become intertwined as never before'.[5] Indeed, it is possible to identify a broad consensus within the literature that peacebuilding is near-enough imperialism ... *nearly*, but not quite. What are the crucial ingredients of peacebuilding that distinguish it from imperialism?

First, let us consider in what way peacebuilding can be compared to imperialism. Roland Paris sketches out several issues: transformative peacebuilding represents the dissemination of a distinctive, Western-inspired model of liberal political and economic relations from the core to the periphery. This model was variously diffused or implanted through peace settlements crafted with international support and containing internationally sponsored provisions, alongside the supplying of expert advice and imposition of conditionalities and 'proxy governance' (where local functions and institutions of government are administered by outside actors).[6] According to Paris, this amounts to a new 'standard of civilisation' which states 'must accept in order to gain full rights and the recognition of the international community'.[7] The old *mission civilisatrice* empowered the European colonial states to impose their will on other territories; today, similar sentiments of benevolent reform drives peacebuilding, according to Paris.

Along similar lines, Marten says that 'squeamishness' about the imperial label should not blind us to the utility of the analytic comparison.[8] She compares what she calls 'complex peacekeeping' and colonialism – mostly based on the similarity of conflicts that early colonisers and today's peacekeepers face: '[t]he tasks performed by imperial soldiers in many ways match what is being asked of today's peacekeepers, and we should therefore not pretend that peacekeeping tasks are unprecedented or out of the realm of military competence'.[9] Michael Doyle and Nicholas Sambanis suggest that 'multidimensional peace operations entail' a 'quasi-colonial presence'.[10]

Simon Chesterman notes that the sheer scale of socio-political transformation embodied in peacebuilding operations leaves colonialism and the military occupations resulting out of the world wars as the only possible scale of comparison for the most ambitious of UN peacebuilding operations. 'Is it possible', he asks, 'to establish the conditions for legitimate and sustainable national governance through a period of benevolent foreign autocracy?'[11] Ignatieff has perhaps been most explicit of all with his idea of 'empire lite': an empire because US interventions abroad represent 'an attempt to permanently order the world of states and markets according to its national interests',[12] undertaken 'for imperial reasons: to consolidate its global hegemony, to assert and maintain its leadership and to ensure stability in those zones essential to the security of itself or its allies'.[13]

These views are representative rather than exhaustive. There are several striking aspects of this literature worth emphasising. First, peacebuilding is seen to be similar to imperialism in several respects, notably that it involves outsiders promoting a distinctive set of values, consonant with the reigning values of international order, transforming societies up to and including the use of force if necessary. Second, the aforementioned authors are all supportive of peacebuilding and international intervention, albeit to varying degrees and with varying recommendations. They do not represent radical opinion on the subject. It is this that, third, makes the frank comparison with imperialism and colonialism all the more striking. For the comparison between peacebuilding and imperialism is not a bitter concession made by these authors in the course of a struggle with their critics where they are forced to admit that peacebuilding is like the much-derided (and illegal under the terms of international law) practice of colonialism. Indeed, there is at least as much 'mainstream' literature that makes the comparison between imperialism and peacekeeping as there is critical literature.[14] This indicates that the character of peacebuilding today makes comparison with imperialism unavoidable.

Redeeming peacekeeping

Part of the reason that the comparison between imperialism and peacebuilding can be made so openly is because these varied analysts believe that peacekeeping is different from imperialism in crucial respects. The arguments against imperialism are marshalled along two axes – the aims of peacebuilding and its modalities. But in the effort to exorcise imperialism and thereby redeem peacekeeping, the defenders of peacekeeping summon a spectre more powerful than they realise. For all the assumptions that supposedly differentiate peacekeeping from imperialism can be challenged.

The aims of peacebuilding

Why are peacebuilding missions undertaken? Paris suggests that 'European colonialism was practised primarily to benefit the imperial states themselves', while 'the motivation behind recent peacebuilding operations is less mercenary'.[15] He cites a variety of factors at play – the absence of theories of racial superiority and the fact that operations are limited in time ('No imperialists have ever been so impatient for quick results' according to Ignatieff[16]). Paris even cites the great liberal anti-imperialist John Hobson in support of his arguments, the latter having supported the *mission civilisatrice* if it was to 'secure the safety and progress of ... the world, and not the special interests of the interfering nation. Such interference must be attended by an improvement and elevation of the character of the people who are brought under this control'.[17] The overriding assumption here is that selfish motivations are the key problem to be avoided or managed.

Yet to claim that peacekeeping is disinterested, while imperialism is self-interested, is perhaps the weakest of all ways to differentiate the two. For imperialism was frequently justified by altruistic claims of spreading the benefits of progress and modernity to backward peoples incapable of realising their own interests. So deeply engrained were the assumptions of imperial altruism that, for example, Lord Frederick Lugard, the British imperial administrator and theorist of colonialism, felt compelled to remind his readers that British colonialism was *not* 'based on motives of philanthropy only'.[18] In other words, Lugard assumed that his readers did not even consider the possibility that Britain was advancing its own interests through colonial expansion. Liberal imperialism, the idea that imperial rule is justified by the backwardness of its subjects, has been a powerful legitimating force for imperial expansion ever since the rise of modernity. To assert that it is possible to partition peacebuilding from imperialism on the basis that the former is altruistic and the latter self-interested would be to ignore the history of imperialism, and to lack objectivity, for the interests secured through peacebuilding operations seem close in their substance and rationale to justifications given for imperialism.

Among the many reasons powering imperial expansion was the need to consolidate regional security and the need to prevent local conflicts from spilling over into areas of imperial interest and influence. Such themes echo in peacekeeping today, which is often justified by the need generally to neutralise the 'externalities' associated with conflict on the periphery of the state system. The need to maintain global security and order that underpins the justification for UN peacekeeping would be familiar to imperial statesmen of yesteryear concerned with protecting global interests, even if such interests are of a lesser order than those more immediately tied to the direct use of military force associated with 'post-conquest' peacebuilding operations.

As regards the relationship between imperial political economy and peacekeeping/peacebuilding, it is a vast topic beyond the scope of this chapter. But some observations are possible about the character of the claims made regarding economic interests in peacekeeping and peacebuilding. Michael Gilligan and Stephen J. Steadman have averred that the geography of peacekeeping deployments does not correlate with an imperial geopolitics, whether or not for the purposes of ensuring outside access to supplies of raw materials and primary commodities. They also maintain that peacekeepers have penetrated spheres of influence that states had hitherto jealously defended against external penetration.[19] That peacekeepers have encroached on traditional great power spheres of influence – such as the US 'backyard' of Central America – is indeed noteworthy. To imagine that this nullifies imperialism would be to stretch credulity however, as it would be to assume that great powers cannot bend the UN to their will. Reading these interventions against the grain, it could be argued that UN legitimacy has been purposefully stretched by great powers in order to legitimate, and thereby buttress, their imperial interventions in their traditional spheres of influence, Haiti being a case in point.[20]

Considered against the backdrop of imperial history, the assumption that the absence of valuable raw materials disproves imperialism is an odd one. The fact that the European empires covered vast swathes of territory around the world, including virtually the entire continent of Africa, demonstrates that empire encompassed plenty of territory that held no valuable raw materials whatsoever. Moreover, there were other economic drivers of imperialism – such as capturing economic spheres of influence, establishing privileged trading zones from which one could exclude one's economic rivals, and taxing local populations. Nor should we discount indirect economic motivations that were folded into the strategic rationale for territorial expansion, such as controlling lines of communication and consolidating territorial buffer zones for colonies that were more economically valuable.

While peacekeeping and peacebuilding may not guarantee effective access to primary commodities, this is not to say that such operations have no economic value. The ordering functions of peacebuilding are widely understood to reduce the costs of war in terms of the blood and treasure lost to conflict, as well as the general disruption to regional trade, investment and commerce. The UN itself defends peacekeeping on this basis. If the global deployment of peacekeeping operations does not map precisely onto the known deposits of strategic or valuable raw materials around the world, it does not mean that there is no economic rationale for peacekeeping. In broad terms, peacebuilding operations help to reintegrate conflict-torn societies into the global economy as part of consolidating the wider 'liberal peace'. The imperial character of such efforts need not be restricted to extracting valuable raw materials, but could also reside in the fact that such operations restrict the range of economic policies and options available to post-conflict societies.[21]

The modalities of peacebuilding

Multilateralism is frequently cited in the literature as an attribute of peacebuilding operations that expunges any residual or lingering traces of imperialism. While the logic underpinning such claims often varies or is left unspecified, it

Still the spectre at the feast 65

appears that multilateralism is seen to provide a check on the pursuit of national self-interest in these operations. The assumption seems to be therefore that to count as imperialism, such operations have to be mounted in the exclusive interests of a single state. Multilateralism here designates not only the diverse range of countries that contribute to peacebuilding and peacekeeping operations, but also the diversity of institutions involved in peacebuilding operations at the global level. Doyle and Sambanis for example, argue that the UN's 'mere presence guarantees that partial national interests are not in control', and that the UN ethos of multilateral impartiality, state equality and universal human rights 'make the quasi-colonial presence that a multidimensional peace operation entails not only tolerable but effective'.[22] Marten strongly emphasises these claims: '[m]ultilateralism is the *one thing* that *removes any hint* of individual state gain from what might otherwise appear to be a colonial effort'.[23]

Yet the notion that multilateralism is incompatible with imperialism is not borne out by even the most cursory survey of imperial history. Eric Ouellet cites the suppression of the so-called 'Boxer Uprising' in China by the Eight-Nation Alliance at the turn of the twentieth century as an example of 'multilateral counter-insurgency' with lessons for Western-led multinational military expeditions today.[24] Indeed, such examples of imperial interventions and colonial policing are cited as historical precursors of peacekeeping in the leading textbook on the subject, without ostensibly being seen to call into question the validity or integrity of peacebuilding today.[25] There are other examples of 'multinational imperialism'. The Ottoman empire was often subject to such interventions as the great powers sought collectively to manage Turkish imperial decline.[26] Albania was collectively established by the great powers as an international protectorate in 1913, in order to help secure imperial interests in the Balkans (Erwin Schmidl even takes the Albanian protectorate as a model for international pacification in the Balkans today).[27]

One noteworthy aspect of the intervention in Shanghai was that the majority of 'British' troops sent to crush the Boxer rebellion were, in fact, from Britain's Indian army.[28] The army of the Raj often acted as Britain's imperial 'fire brigade' – a metaphor also used for UN peacekeeping – helping to buttress British rule from China to Africa.[29] Lord Salisbury called British India 'an English barrack in the Oriental Seas from which we may draw any number of troops without paying for them'.[30] It is no exaggeration to call the successor states of the Raj – India, Pakistan and Bangladesh – a UN barracks, given the extent to which South Asia contributes to current peacekeeping. Where does this leave questions of the multinational make-up of many peacebuilding operations? We shall return to this theme below.

Of course, today peacebuilding multilateralism is institutionalised through the UN rather than through episodic great power cooperation. But to assume that imperial interests cannot be secured through the machinery of the UN would be naïve. As Paris himself concedes, UN missions 'still reflect the interests of the world's most powerful countries'.[31] To all intents and purposes the Security Council controls UN peacekeeping operations in all their fundamental aspects, led in large measure by its permanent bloc of three Western states – the United States, UK and France. Furthermore, UN peacekeeping is overwhelmingly financed by Western states.[32] The lack of influence that poorer troop- and police-contributing countries hold over the direction and purpose of UN peacekeeping is repeatedly emphasised by these countries, as shown in an open debate on peacekeeping held in the Security Council in August 2011. In this debate, the representative of Guatemala likened peacekeeping to a 'great outsourcing exercise, in which developed countries contracted lower-cost troops from developing countries to do the hard and dangerous work'.[33]

Going further, in certain instances multilateralism is the *guarantee* that imperial interests can be secured. Consider the 1960–1964 UN Operation in Congo, known by its French acronym ONUC. If, on the one hand, the UN mission succeeded in preserving the territorial integrity of the Congolese state by suppressing those secessionists supported by European mining interests; on the other, it also helped deliver the Congo to US imperial influence during the Cold War. The United States recognised that in the circumstances of Third World anti-colonial revolt, direct intervention in Congo was politically impossible, and that stabilisation would have to be achieved through reliance on the proxy of UN peacekeepers. As detailed by Inis Claude Jr.,

> [t]he major theme [of official American commentary] was that ONUC served the interests of the whole world by helping the major powers avoid a collision in the Congo. But a significant counter-theme was woven into the composition: the United Nations action in the Congo was a means of giving the West a victory over the Soviet bloc that it might not have been able to win for itself.[34]

ONUC shows that if multilateralism contributes legitimacy to international military expeditions, it does not necessarily nullify their imperial character – multilateralism can justify imperialism. Yet if the range of states on which peacekeeping draws (particularly as the majority come from poor and developing countries) is taken as an argument against imperialism, this takes us back to the question of the national composition of peacebuilding missions. The fact that UN peacekeeping is not simply 're-hatting' the military deployments of rich and powerful states is taken as evidence that it is not imperialistic. According to Cynthia Enloe, 'the United Nations peacekeeping forces, drawn from the militaries of its member states, are being looked upon by the governments of many industrialised and Third World countries as offering the best hope for a genuinely post-Cold War, nonimperialist military'.[35]

In her survey of early post-Cold War peacekeeping, Laura Neack argues that one way to ensure that peacekeeping served the interests of the 'international community' rather than the self-interest of mandating states would be if peacekeeping was democratised and broadened beyond the Western powers and the narrow range of neutralist, middle powers that dominated peacekeeping during the Cold War.[36] Neack's injunction has since been realised, as Andrea Talentino points out: '[a]nother argument against imperialism derives from the fact that states of all types promote intervention, not simply the most powerful. Indeed, if intervention relied primarily on Western or American participation it would rarely happen at all'.[37] As the data on the UN peacekeeping website attest, peacekeepers are diverse, with the overwhelming majority coming from poor developing countries.

But why should this distinguish peacekeeping from imperialism? As the experience of the Raj suggests, historically imperialism has relied on multiracial and multinational soldiery serving imperial centres of power. All the major imperial powers recruited forces from their colonies, and during the world wars the British and French colonial forces grew into mass armies millions strong. Drawing on such forces expanded the pools of manpower available to imperial states in their rivalries with each other. It also helped to cement imperial rule in peacetime by allowing metropolitan powers to garrison their colonies with indigenous rather than foreign troops. Colonial armies could also be deployed to remote areas without the need to involve European soldiers in protracted conflicts that might induce war-weariness at home. As Lord Salisbury suggested, from the imperial vantage point one key advantage of colonial troops was their relative cheapness. Colonial armies could be paid less than white metropolitan soldiery and cost less to maintain. As they were most often only expected to fight against technologically inferior opponents in low intensity conflicts, they did not require modern weaponry. Each soldier in the British Indian Army cost one-quarter of what it took to maintain a British soldier. At the turn of the twentieth century, a *tirailleur sénègalais* in French West Africa cost less than half of what it took to maintain a white French marine infantryman.[38] But also, more simply, subaltern lives were less important to metropolitan power centres.

Such themes are strongly echoed in peacekeeping and peacebuilding today: one constant refrain in Western public discourse is that of a 'bargain'. According to Susan Rice, UN ambassador for the Obama administration, for every dollar the United States spends on unilateral stabilisation efforts the UN spends only 12 cents. 'That is a pretty good deal' she told the US Senate in her confirmation hearing.[39] Part of the reason that UN peacekeeping is cheaper is due to UN legitimacy: the nominally consensual character of UN peacekeeping means that international peacekeeping forces need not fight their way into countries or hold territory – activities that would require more manpower and larger outlays on weaponry as well as air supremacy and perhaps naval support. But the lower costs of UN peacekeeping and its intensified version, peacebuilding, can be attributed to the fact that its operations rely on the cheaper armed forces of poorer, often formerly colonised countries. According to Richard Gowan, a NATO soldier costs five times more to deploy than a UN peacekeeper.[40]

The diversity of nations involved in contemporary peacebuilding and peacekeeping only seems striking on the assumption that international relations is composed simply of the interaction of nation-states. If we broaden the scope of international history to include empires, then the unified coordination of large multinational armies around the globe from a single centre would appear a less novel and cosmopolitan phenomenon. As Darryl Li has pointed out, the regimental history of some armies of post-colonial states goes straight from recounting their participation in imperial campaigns to participation in UN peacekeeping operations as the forces of freshly independent states.[41] While today's peacekeepers represent independent states rather than empires, it need not follow that imperial power relations have been entirely superseded. As Tarak Barkawi and Mark Laffey argue: 'imperial states and empires typically constitute significant coercive power from colonized and client populations and that force is integral to processes of globalization'.[42] Determining the scope of imperial power is partly a question of control: who decides the key political and strategic questions of peacekeeping? As noted above, defenders of liberal peacebuilding themselves admit the degree of control Western states have over international institutions. Doyle notes the multilayered power relations of British imperial rule and its reliance on indigenous forces and local power structures for its perpetuation. He suggests these as models for military intervention and post-conflict reconstruction today:

> Over the longer run, indigenous forces such as the political zamindars and the King's Own African Rifles and other locally recruited military battalions (not metropolitan troops) were the forces that made imperial rule effective, that preserved a balance of local power in favour of metropolitan influence – and that kept it cheap.[43]

The practice of contemporary peacebuilding – particularly its emphasis on developmentalism and reconstruction – is also visible in the record of colonialism. Not unlike peacebuilding operations today, many multinational imperial interventions were not purely military. International administrations in Tangier and Shanghai enjoyed a multinational gendarmerie, complete with white police officers and reserve military units to enforce their rule. These expeditions also saw foreign-led administrative and judicial functions superimposed over local power structures.[44] Importantly, many of these interventions were decided through collective agreement and with extensive cooperation among the great powers. Alex J. Bellamy and Paul D. Williams cite the 1885 Congress of Berlin at which the great powers divided up Africa between them, as a precursor of UN transitional administrations today.[45]

Finally, one remaining significant attribute of peacebuilding that is held to distinguish it from imperialism is the former's consensual nature. Paris stresses that it is only rarely that peacekeepers deploy without the express consent of the host state or of belligerent parties.[46] They do not fight their way into countries or mount campaigns of conquest.

Two points can be made. First, how substantial is the consent offered in peacebuilding operations? With missions increasingly deployed under the terms of Chapter VII of the UN Charter – terms that empower peacekeepers with greater recourse to force – the meaning of consent has correspondingly narrowed. The mechanisms through which consent has been extracted have also been restructured. According to Eşref Aksu, the meaning of consent in UN peacekeeping has been crimped to a narrow, formalistic shell:

> In several cases, as in Central America and Mozambique, comprehensive peace plans and agreements ... extracted parties' consent not only for the initial UN deployment, but also for subsequent UN activities in the field. By carefully placing the peacekeeping mandate on peace accords, international actors increasingly downplayed the requirement of seeking consent at every stage of the operation.[47]

What does consent mean if it cannot be revoked, but is only extracted on a one-time basis? If consent is only extracted once, particularly in relation to a comprehensive peace agreement, it means that a greater range of externally driven changes can be mounted throughout a host country, without requiring the formal invocation of consent again.

The second point is the assumption that consent is incompatible with empire. As a type of political order, empire is rightly understood as the opposite of autonomy and self-determination, the bases on which consent can be offered. Yet consent can also be nominal, bogus, manipulated or exercised in such restricted conditions as to be effectively meaningless. Certainly neo-imperial theorists have little trouble accommodating voluntarism and varying degrees of circumscribed 'consent' into their visions of empire.

Former British diplomat and EU foreign policy envoy Robert Cooper speaks of a 'new liberal imperialism' that involves stratification of the international order. This order is crowned by enlightened, 'postmodern' states which have renounced instincts of conquest and are bound by international cooperation, contrasted with 'modern' states selfishly focused only on their own interests, and a morass of 'premodern' states with no stable authority structures. The last group needs order implanted into them by postmodern imperialists in order to prevent the spread of disorder. According to Cooper, this is 'an imperialism which, like all imperialism, aims to bring order and organisation but which rests today on the *voluntary* principle'.[48]

Ignatieff describes contemporary imperialism 'as an empire lite', a 'hegemony without colonies', a 'global sphere of influence without the burden of direct administration and the risks of daily policing'[49] Much like Cooper, Ignatieff sees the target of imperialism to be 'a vacuum of chaos and

70 *Philip Cunliffe*

massacre', emanating security threats that draw in reluctant outsiders to impose stability through imperial order.[50] Ignatieff too sees consent as integral to this project, harkening back to the experience of the British Empire: '[w]hat the history of the British Empire shows is that self-determination and imperial rule are *not* incompatible ... promising self-government has always served as a key instrument in maintaining control'.[51]

Ignatieff and Cooper largely restrict their discussion of modern imperialism to Western-led and 'post-conquest' peacebuilding efforts: Cooper is primarily concerned with EU nation-building efforts in the Balkans, while Ignatieff sees his 'humanitarian empire' in the mixture of peacebuilding initiatives in Bosnia and Herzegovina, Kosovo and Afghanistan. Yet by the criteria offered by Cooper and Ignatieff, UN post-settlement peacebuilding would offer the model of a more successful imperium, in so far as it has undertaken efforts in a wider variety of countries more consistently since the end of the Cold War. Much like the visions offered by Cooper and Ignatieff, UN peacebuilding operations have helped to produce 'sub-sovereign' states locked into international institutions that help to control remote zones of instability on the periphery of great powers' concerns.

Summary

Summarising the discussion so far, the first point to note is that the imperialism against which peacekeeping and peacebuilding are favourably compared is understood to be a historical rather than a contemporary phenomenon. Given that peacekeeping is an aspect of contemporary international affairs, one might assume that contemporary rather than historical discussions of imperialism would be the most useful resource from which to mount a comparison. Yet this is not the case: discussions about the dynamics of imperial power today are simply ignored in these discussions of peacebuilding, despite the extent and theoretical sophistication of many discussions of imperialism in the contemporary international relations literature. Indeed, no theories of imperialism – historical or contemporary – are engaged with in the peacekeeping and peacebuilding literature, nor is any of the complex historiography regarding the nature and purpose of imperial expansion. One could argue that the terms of the debate have been weighted in favour of peacebuilding because imperialism is understood to be something that belongs to history rather than being of the present.

But to go further, even by the standards of historical comparison, the discussion of imperialism in peacekeeping studies is remarkably limited. It could be said that each of the arguments discussed above sets up a caricature of imperialism, the easier to cut it down. Of all the claims made for peacekeeping, among the most important is that multilateralism signals the absence of selfish motivation. The absence of private benefits from peacebuilding operations monopolistically accruing to a single imperial state allows analysts to accept the universalistic rhetoric that accompanies peacebuilding operations.

Intention, then, seems to be the main measure of the legitimacy of peacebuilding. But why is intention the standpoint for assessing the legitimacy of a particular political practice? The legitimacy of the practice seems to be proved negatively: peacebuilding is legitimate not because of what it is, but because of what it is not (classical nineteenth century imperialism). Not only is this *not* a positive case for peacebuilding, it could be read as an evasion of the very question of standards of assessment.

Imperial peacebuilding

Peacebuilding can be seen as imperial in the way in which it restricts the range of options available to post-conflict societies. Paris, for example, is sensitive to the way in which the choices made by peacekeepers impose 'relatively narrow limits on the type of polity and economy that will be allowed to emerge' (though he is willing to countenance such authoritarianism).[52] It is true of course in the formal sense that, if the activities of national governments are absorbed by the UN, this will tend to 'crowd out' the room for 'indigenous' and 'participatory' activities by people in the host state. Any technical, externally imposed programme will tend to reduce the scope for innovation and political creativity in the work of building post-conflict institutions.

Yet in so far as imperialism and peacekeeping operations *are* historically distinct, it is not clear that these differences make peacebuilding a preferable form of international intervention. To be sure, peacekeepers are not deployed to annex territory to metropolitan states. Even in the most extreme instances of 'proxy governance', where UN viceroys have substituted for local rulers such as in Cambodia, Kosovo and East Timor, the aim has not been to snuff out the formal independence of these territories for good. But for that very reason, one could argue that peacebuilding operations constitute a more insidious exercise of imperial power. The old aspects of imperialism – colonies, mandates, trusteeship – were all based on the recognition that external rule and tutelage were incompatible with self-determination – hence the explicit revocation of self-determination put off as a glittering goal for a distant future. Peacebuilding by contrast is predicated on the notion that 'proxy governance' is compatible with substantive national independence, and that the machinery of government can be annexed by 'internationals' without prejudice to the practice of self-determination.

How are political structures of responsibility and accountability to be established under such circumstances? When it is more difficult to attribute political responsibility, then a situation arises that was eloquently described (appropriately enough) by the former UN Under Secretary-General for Peacekeeping Operations from 2000 to 2008, Jean-Marie Guéhenno, thus:

> There [is] not a statue ... to pull down from its pedestal, only the amorphous mass of a diffuse and imperceptible power. The new order makes policemen of us all, and there is no longer a police chief against whom

72 *Philip Cunliffe*

we may direct our revolt. We are deprived not of liberty, but of the idea of liberty.[53]

But the problem lies not only in the fact that peacebuilding is insinuated into the operation of nominally independent states, but also with the justification given for the political choices made in peacebuilding – the dissemination of pre-given techniques and standards. Guéhenno argues that '[t]here are no longer great decisions from which proceed lesser ones ... [and] traditional political debate, a debate about principles and general ideas, an ideological debate, a debate over how society is to be organised, fades away, or rather crumbles'.[54] Peacebuilding by its nature is based on the acceptance of a distinctive set of political institutions and values – those of the liberal peace.

Rather than facilitating mediation and resolution between competing political or national projects, the UN now facilitates conformity with one political order, the 'liberal peace': liberal government and market society. This consensus is taken to be beyond challenge: economic, legal and political models of governance that are all so well established and entrenched that they are assumed to be self-evidently good and enjoy universal support, thereby obviating the need for assent. In this way, decisions about political order and social organisation are assumed to be a given. As Guéhenno argues, 'It matters little whether a norm is imposed ... by a committee of bureaucrats. It is no longer the expression of a sovereignty, but simply something that reduces uncertainties, a means of lowering the costs of transactions, of increasing transparence [*sic.*]'.[55]

UN peacebuilding and modern imperialism

Empire remains, therefore, a remarkably under-utilised concept in the study of peacekeeping and peacebuilding. Although Michael Hardt and Antonio Negri see the UN as offering a conceptual bridge across which the imperialism of nation-states is scaled up into Empire, the nebulous categories of their thin theory do not easily meld with the reality of peacebuilding operations.[56] As Alejandro Colás points out, peacebuilding operations are focused on rearticulating a decentralised international order based around independent states, not dissolving states into a transnational political order.[57] Although David Chandler by contrast addresses statebuilding directly as a new type of imperial politics, he does not specifically differentiate between post-conquest and post-settlement peacebuilding, and focuses on state- and EU-led rather than UN-led peacebuilding operations.[58]

If we examine the scholarly literature on imperialism, the most obvious defining feature that recurs is the existence of a hierarchical relation between distinct political units, with asymmetric power relations that effectively restrict the autonomy of the subordinated society. This unequal relationship can be formally constituted via institutions that ensure the subordinate society is directly ruled by the political institutions of the imperial state, or via informal power relations – whereby the subordinate society is nominally independent but where crucial policy questions are determined in a sustained and systematic fashion by the imperial state.[59]

Empires may adopt inclusionary or exclusionary strategies in their relations with local elites. In his classic study of empire, Doyle stresses the varieties of imperial and informal political dependence as achieved variously through force, collaboration or non-political forms of dependence (economic, social or cultural).[60] Moreover, imperial power structures typically involve a variegated hierarchy, with imperial power centres enjoying heterogeneous relations with different types of subordinate societies, the better to disable collective action or self-organisation by the subordinated societies.[61]

UN peacebuilding fits both the visions of international order offered by neo-imperialist theorists and the broad characterisations of empire offered in the academic literature on the topic as synthesised. Empire is thus a fruitful device for understanding the dynamics of peacekeeping in international order today, and on the basis of the current literature, there is no reason not to read peacekeeping against the backdrop of empire and imperial history. A decade ago Paris argued that the study of peacekeeping would be enriched from being plugged into mainstream discussions of international relations and international relations theorising.[62] Today the study of peacekeeping and peacebuilding would benefit no less from drawing on the theoretical and historical discussion of imperial power in international affairs.

Conclusion

Almost by default, the expansion of peacebuilding in the contemporary world spontaneously conjures up the spectre of imperialism: peacekeepers are sent to pacify unruly but ultimately marginal territories, using deterrence and force, and propagating ideals and institutions that are consonant with the values espoused by the most powerful members of the international system. The similarities cannot be ignored. The purpose of this chapter was not to argue that peacebuilding and historical imperialism are perfectly symmetrical; rather that the existing attempts in the literature to differentiate peacebuilding from imperialism, and thereby legitimate the former, are weak and unconvincing.

That it is fairly straightforward to puncture the claims made for the supposedly post-imperial character of peacebuilding shows that the extant discussion in peacekeeping studies is not particularly rigorous or well-informed. It also suggests that if peacebuilding can indeed be conceptually assimilated to a long history of imperial practice in international politics, it also represents a refined form of imperialism, whereby extensive international influence over, and penetration of, domestic political systems is not seen as mutually exclusive of self-determination.

As we have seen, the use of the imperial analogy in peacekeeping studies deploys a crude construct as a stand-in for imperialism, ignoring the suppleness and versatility of imperial domination in world politics, as well as the broad range of theories used to study it. If peacebuilding would benefit from a more systematic and rigorous engagement with theories of empire, the converse is equally true: the study of peacebuilding would help broaden debates about contemporary imperialism, forcing scholars and students of modern empire to cast their gaze further than the machinations of US power, and to consider the rise of imperial multilateralism and the institutions it deploys. In so far as UN interventions and post-settlement peacebuilding initiatives still accrue greater legitimacy than unilateral interventions and post-conquest peacebuilding, it is high time that the former was subject to greater scrutiny.

Acknowledgements

I would particularly like to thank the following people for their feedback on earlier drafts of this chapter: Bruno Charbonneau, Alex Gourevitch, Roger Mac Ginty, Mandy Turner and Michael Pugh. This chapter first appeared in *International Peacekeeping*, vol. 19, no. 4, August 2012, Taylor & Francis Ltd, www.tandfonline.com, reprinted by permission of the publisher.

Notes

1 On definitional issues, see note 2 below.
2 Roland Paris, 'Saving Liberal Peacebuilding', *Review of International Studies*, vol. 35, no. 3, 2010, p. 348. I use this definition of post-settlement peacebuilding in here. Henceforward, unless specified otherwise, references to 'peacebuilding' can be assumed to refer to Paris' definition of post-settlement UN peacebuilding.
3 Michael Ignatieff, *Empire Lite: Nation-building in Bosnia, Kosovo and Afghanistan*, London: Vintage, 2003.
4 Julian Glover, 'King Paddy', *Guardian*, 11 October 2002 (at: www.guardian.co.uk/politics/2002/oct/11/foreignpolicy.uk).
5 Kimberly Marten, *Enforcing the Peace: Learning from the Imperial Past*, New York: Columbia University Press, 2004, p. 17.
6 Roland Paris, 'International Peacebuilding and the "Mission Civilisatrice"', *Review of International Studies*, vol. 28, no. 4, 2002, pp. 643–644.
7 *Ibid.*, p. 650.
8 Marten (note 5 above).
9 *Ibid.*
10 Michael W. Doyle and Nicolas Sambanis, *Making War and Building Peace: United Nations Peace Operations*, Princeton, NJ: Princeton University Press, 2006, p. 318.
11 Simon Chesterman, *You, the People: The United Nations, Transitional Administration and State-building*, Oxford: Oxford University Press, 2005, p. 1.
12 Ignatieff (note 3 above), p. 2.
13 *Ibid.*, p. 3.
14 The most notable examples are: David N. Gibbs, 'Is Peacekeeping a New Form of Imperialism?', *International Peacekeeping*, vol. 4, no. 1, 1997, pp. 122–128; Sharene H. Razack, *Dark Threats and White Knights: The Somalia Affair, Peacekeeping and the New Imperialism*, Toronto: University of Toronto Press, 2004.
15 Paris (note 6 above), p. 638.
16 Ignatieff (note 3 above), p. 115.
17 Hobson, cited in Paris (note 6 above), p. 651.

Still the spectre at the feast 75

18 See H. L. Wesseling, 'Editorial: Changing Views on Empire and Imperialism', *European Review*, vol. 12, no. 3, 2004, p. 268.
19 Michael Gilligan and Stephen J. Steadman, 'Where Do Peacekeepers Go?', *International Studies Review*, vol. 5, no. 4, 2003, pp. 37–54. The claim that peacekeeping has correlated with imperial interest in economic plunder has been made in relation to Somalia and Cold War-era UN activity in the Middle East. See Gibbs (note 14 above); Hirofumi Shimizu, 'An Economic Analysis of the UN Peacekeeping Assessment System', *Defence and Peace Economics*, vol. 16, no. 1, 2005, p. 2. John Pilger made a similar claim in respect of the British support to the UN operation in diamond-rich Sierra Leone. 'Britain is Recolonising Sierra Leone in an Attempt to Get Its Hands on the Country's Diamonds', *New Statesman*, 18 September 2000. Neither claim is particularly convincing in their original formulation.
20 See Mohammed Ayoob, 'Humanitarian Intervention and State Sovereignty', *International Journal of Human Rights*, vol. 6, no. 1, 2002, p. 87.
21 See Michael Pugh, 'The Political Economy of Peacebuilding: A Critical Theory Perspective', *International Journal of Peace Studies*, vol. 10, no. 2, 2005, pp. 23–42.
22 Doyle and Sambanis (note 10 above), p. 318.
23 Marten (note 5 above), p. 19 (emphasis added).
24 Eric Ouellet, 'Multinational Counterinsurgency: The Western Intervention in the Boxer Rebellion 1900–1901', *Small Wars and Insurgencies*, vol. 20, nos. 3–4, 2009, pp. 507–527.
25 See Alex J. Bellamy and Paul D. Williams with Stuart Griffin, *Understanding Peacekeeping*, 2nd edn, Cambridge: Polity, 2010, ch. 3.
26 Interestingly, some of these nineteenth century expeditions against the Ottoman empire are also cited as prototypes of humanitarian intervention. There are earlier examples from the nineteenth century too, such as military cooperation between the European powers against the Barbary pirates until 1830. Schmidl also covers the counterrevolutionary interventions of the Congress and Holy Alliance powers in Europe itself. Erwin Schmidl, 'The Evolution of Peace Operations since the Nineteenth Century', *Small Wars and Insurgencies*, vol. 10, no. 2, 1999, pp. 4–20.
27 Erwin Schmidl, 'The International Operation in Albania 1913–14', *International Peacekeeping*, vol. 6, no. 3, 1999, pp. 1–10.
28 David Killingray, 'Guardians of Empire', in David Killingray (ed.), *Guardians of Empire: The Armed Forces of the Colonial Powers, c. 1700–1964*, Manchester: Manchester University Press, 1999, p. 4.
29 *Ibid.*, p. 7.
30 Cited in Alex Callinicos, *Imperialism and Global Political Economy*, Cambridge: Polity, 2009, p. 194.
31 Paris (note 2 above), pp. 349–50.
32 See for example, Khrusav Gaibulloev, Todd Sandler and Hirofumi Shimizu, 'Demands for UN and Non-UN Peacekeeping: Nonvoluntary versus Voluntary Contributions to a Public Good', *Journal of Conflict Resolution*, vol. 53, no. 6, 2009, pp. 827–852.
33 UN Security Council, 'Security Council Commits to Strengthening Partnership with Troop, Police Contributors in Debate on United Nations Peacekeeping Operations', 26 August 2011, UN doc. SC/10368 (at: www.un.org/News/Press/docs/2011/sc10368.doc.htm).
34 Inis L. Claude, Jr., *Swords into Plowshares: The Problems and Progress of International Organization*, 4th edn, New York: Random House, 1971, pp. 329–330.
35 Cynthia Enloe, *The Morning After: Sexual Politics at the end of the Cold War*, Berkeley, CA: University of California Press, 1993, p. 30.
36 Laura Neack, 'UN Peace-keeping: In the Interest of Community or Self?', *Journal of Peace Research*, vol. 32, no. 2, 1995, pp. 181–196.

37 Andrea K. Talentino, *Military Intervention after the Cold War: The Evolution of Theory and Practice*, Athens, OH: Ohio University Press, 2005, p. 89. Andrew Blum argues on similar lines that while it is fairly easy to account for the conflict management activities of wealthy and powerful states, the activity of poorer peacekeeping countries is less obvious. See Andrew Blum, '"Blue Helmets from the South": Accounting for the Participation of Weaker States in United Nations Peacekeeping Operations', *Journal of Conflict Studies*, vol. 20, no. 1, 2000, p. 1.
38 Killingray (note 28), p. 7.
39 Neil Macfarquar, 'Gentle Questioning for U.N. Nominee', *New York Times*, 15 January 2009 (at: www.nytimes.com/2009/01/16/us/16webrice.html).
40 Richard Gowan, *UN Peace Operations: The Case for Strategic Investment*, Berlin: Center for International Peace Operations, p. 2 (at: www.zif-berlin.org/fileadmin/uploads/analyse/dokumente/veroeffentlichungen/Policy_Briefing_Richard_Gowan_Aug_2010_ENG.pdf).
41 Darryl Li, 'Peacekeepers and the Countries That Send Them', unpublished manuscript, 2003, p. 6.
42 Tarak Barkawi and Mark Laffey, 'The Imperial Peace: Democracy, Force and Globalization', *European Journal of International Relations*, vol. 5, no. 4, 1999, p. 414.
43 Michael Doyle, 'The New Interventionism', *Metaphilosophy*, vol. 32, nos. 1–2, 2001, p. 227.
44 Larry Fabian, *Soldiers without Enemies: Preparing the United Nations for Peacekeeping*, Washington, DC: The Brookings Institution, 1971, pp. 43–44. Fabian calls these early 'adumbrations' of peacekeeping.
45 Bellamy and Williams (note 25 above), p. 76.
46 Paris (note 6 above), p. 652.
47 Eşref Aksu, *The United Nations, Intra-state Peacekeeping and Normative Change*, Manchester: Manchester University Press, 2003, p. 92.
48 Robert Cooper, 'The New Liberal Imperialism', *Observer*, 7 April 2002 (emphasis added).
49 Ignatieff (note 3 above), pp. 2–3.
50 *Ibid.*, p. 21.
51 *Ibid.*, p. 114.
52 Roland Paris, 'Broadening the Study of Peace Operations', *International Studies Review*, vol. 2, no. 2, 2000, p. 43.
53 It should be noted that Guéhenno wrote those words in a previous capacity as French ambassador to the EU. From Guéhenno, *The End of the Nation-State*, trans. Victoria Elliott, Minneapolis, London: University of Minnesota Press, 1993, pp. 121–122.
54 *Ibid.*, pp. 19–20.
55 *Ibid.*, p. 56.
56 Michael Hardt and Antonio Negri, *Empire*, Cambridge, MA: Harvard University Press, 2000.
57 Alejandro Colás, *Empire*, London: Polity, 2007, p. 176.
58 David Chandler, *Empire in Denial: The Politics of State-building*, London: Pluto Press, 2006.
59 See further Yale H. Ferguson, 'Approaches to Defining "Empire" and Characterizing United States Influence in the Contemporary World', *International Studies Perspectives*, vol. 9, no. 3, 2008, p. 274.
60 Michael W. Doyle, *Empires*, Ithaca, NY: Cornell University Press, 1986, p.45.
61 Hendrik Spruyt, '"American Empire" as an Analytic Question or a Rhetorical Move?', *International Studies Perspectives*, vol. 9, no. 3, 2008, p. 293.
62 Paris (note 52 above), passim.

4 Lineages of aggressive peace

Michael Pugh

One of the political absurdities portrayed in Roman Polanski's 2010 film *The Ghost Writer* occurs when an author employed to write the memoirs of a Blairite politician keen on regime change wars encounters a peace protest. 'There's a crowd of pacifists out there trying to kill me', he exclaims. This may well be the reaction of societies comprehended as subjects of peace which may ultimately interpret the impacts of foreign 'peace' missions as not wholly benign, however well intentioned.[1]

The following discussion notes the importance of the UN as an instrument for the promotion of Western, Atlanticist interests, coded as 'civilisational values', and then focuses on two coercive developments in quests for peace: the militarisation of peace operations and the fostering of neoliberal economics. This is not to deny that interventions comprise elements of great complexity. Indeed, typologies that grade them according to degrees of top-down coercion hardly capture the mix of elements.[2] For example, the UN Office for the Coordination of Humanitarian Assistance has a high reputation in emergency relief, the UN pioneered international de-mining operations, the UN High Commission for Refugees has contributed to voluntary refugee returns and, as Mats Berdal notes, the UN's unmatched election monitoring experience has had war-torn societies queuing up for help with elections (rewarded by high turnouts in the aftermath of interventions).[3] Nor do the subjects of pacification ignore opportunities for cooperation, or adoption and adaptation. Sectors of society may internalise aspects of the values and ideologies of peace missions. But peace missions as conceived in the past twenty years also encompass asymmetries of power, resistances and agonistic struggles. Thus, for example, resistance to disruption of traditional political economies means that donors usually have to struggle to undermine local ways of doing things and counter any resistance to projects of transformation.

Other authors have analysed in depth the liberal peace crisis; critiques of that manifold project are familiar. It merges security and development, characterises inhabitants as victims or illiberal, builds hollow institutions, designs economic life to reproduce assertive capitalism, equates peace with statebuilding, and assumes the interveners have privileged knowledge.[4] On the other hand, some of the responses to such critiques seem to uphold liberal approaches as problem-solving management.[5] What, then, can be inscribed as 'aggressive' about the concept of intervention for peace? After all, designated subjects often welcome external involvement in their struggles, at least initially because they want military support to win a conflict or because it promises to provide greater physical security and assistance in everyday life. Two critical points are emphasised here: the militarisation and codification of violence as peace; and the platforms of aggressive political economy. They are linked because the one activity hastens progress towards the other.

The militarisation of peace

In addressing the foundational issue – the purpose of peace missions – it can hardly be overlooked that the vast majority of them have occurred in former territories of European empires, from Kashmir in 1948 to Libya in 2011. Historians of traditional peacekeeping argue that it functioned as a face-saving mechanism for imperial powers to facilitate withdrawal from territories that could no longer be held by force against independence movements amid increasing condemnation by the General Assembly, not least on human rights grounds.[6] The argument dovetails with Mark Mazower's contention that by inheriting the Eurocentrism of the League of Nations, the UN's founders worked hard to ensure the continued influence of empire in decolonised territories and the preservation of a Western civilised superiority.[7] At times, when the UN failed to uphold the interests and practices of liberal imperialism, whether of old imperial or informal US kinds, the institution could be ignored through unilateral action and self-serving interpretations of international law and human rights. This power base acquired three permanent NATO seats on the Security Council, influence over the appointment of Secretaries-General, sway over budgets and management practices, control of the Bretton Woods institutions, and an ability to provide or withhold diplomatic clout and material support in a crisis. The US State Department's Bureau of Conflict and Stabilization Operations (CSO) declared in 2011 that the benefits of 'stabilization' in war-torn societies is that it 'advances US national security by driving integrated, civilian-led efforts to prevent, respond to, and stabilize crises in priority states, setting conditions for long-term peace'.[8]

This is not to assume continual harmony among the NATO three and their allies in struggling to enforce world peace. The US undermined the UK and France at Suez; the UK refused to send military support to France and the US in Indo-China; the US rejected ground troops for the Balkan wars; and disarray emerged over the use of force in Kosovo, Iraq, Afghanistan and Syria. US administrations also regarded allies, as well as the UN, as targets for spying.[9] Nevertheless the NATO three and their allies constructed a sophistry of superior civilisational values, bolstered by the end of the Cold War. Within schools of liberal supremacy – including champions of the 'responsibility to protect' idea – John Ikenberry and Anne-Marie Slaughter argued for institutionalising a 'concert of democracies' under US leadership within a UN now more globally representative than envisaged by the organisation's imperial founders.[10] The Ikenberry–Slaughter disposition entertained US re-adherence to international law, less reliance on costly military solutions, and the conversion of unruly parts of the world into (albeit varied) mirror images of Western states. However, such a bloc – determining legalities, state failure and the diverse credentials of governments and rebel or separatist movements – would replicate contradictions of the post-Napoleonic Holy Alliance, such as the pragmatism of participants in backing some dictatorships and military coups but not others. Besides, the bloc already operated de facto, as evidenced by the *stasi* collusion between Western intelligence agencies and their symbiotic relationship with data gathering corporations. With such lineages and promoters, the militarisation of peace missions and by extension 'peace' is hardly surprising.

Uniformed peace missions of the UN still claim political disinterest in crisis outcomes. They are primarily disposed to supervise ceasefires, help transfer power by agreement or underpin peace accords, rather than trying to change or support a regime by force. Although such missions used force under Chapter VII, sometimes beyond self-defence (as in the Congo in the 1960s), the UN traditionally avoided operations likely to involve combat. So-called Chapter VI-and-a-half peacekeeping could interpose in situations where there was a peace to keep and host consent obtained.[11] As originally conceived, peacekeeping has been mandated for traditional functions in all but 22 of the 68 authorised operations by the end of 2013. But the 22 had the possibilities of enforcement in accordance with Chapter VII, though not necessarily directly authorised to use it.[12] Further, the UN had acquiesced in combat coalitions, such as the Korean Allied Force of 1950–1953 and the Multinational Force in Lebanon of 1982–1984. By the mid-1990s, backing for such combinations to act as mercenary-proxies in aggressive peace became a guiding principle of policy.

A quickening occurred in the light of painful experiences in Somalia, Rwanda, Haiti and Yugoslavia. In Somalia the US-led Unified Task Force of 1992 had a Security Council mandate (resolution 794) mainly to ensure security for relief aid but also had a military designation as an 'operation' ('Operation Restore Hope'). When the Somalia situation deteriorated and follow-on UN missions floundered (marked by the killing of 24 Pakistani peacekeepers), the UN secretariat and US ground forces moved towards enforcement policies. A Security Council mandate in June 1993 (resolution 837) facilitated aggression that culminated in July in a US missile attack on a Somali clan meeting, killing 50 and injuring 170 Somalis. Thereafter, the Security Council, UN secretariat and its Department of Peacekeeping Operations (DPKO) remained extremely reluctant to allow its blue helmet peacekeepers to be the risk takers. Unease about mixing peacekeeping and enforcement was also reflected in the ambiguous postures and multiple mandates for Yugoslavia.[13] The UN Protection Force (UNPROFOR) was just about capable of holding on to Sarajevo airport under a Chapter VII mandate issued in June 1992, but it could not protect civilians or so-called 'safe areas'. Moreover the Clinton Administration had no intention of risking help to the UN with ground forces (the CIA also wire-tapped UN officials and bugged General Rose's HQ next to the US Embassy in Sarajevo).[14] However, the US operated a 'lift and strike' policy to provide arms to Croatia and the Bosnian Army, and persuaded Kofi Annan, acting in Boutros-Ghali's absence at the UN, to overrule a UN veto on NATO air strikes against Bosnian Serb forces in 1994.[15] Discrimination about using force persisted over Rwanda when the P5 refused to refer to the crisis as genocidal or contribute troops to a UN intervention. On the other hand, the Security Council gave retrospective legitimacy under a Chapter VII mandate (resolution 929) to a French force crossing into Rwanda ostensibly to end the Hutu regime.[16] In contrast to the reluctance to boost UN forces in Rwanda, the UN Secretariat and Security Council agreed in July 1994 on a US military operation to end turmoil in Haiti (resolution 940) thereby staunching an influx of refugees to the US.[17] The operation fared little better than the Somalia episode, but it reinforced disquiet about UN commanders having responsibility for force.

These events persuaded Annan when he became UN Secretary-General to announce in July 1997 that without sufficient resources or political will to endow the UN with capabilities to act under Chapter VII, the most effective mechanism for enforcement missions would be to delegate to ad hoc coalitions of 'the willing'.[18] An expert panel on peace operations chaired by the Secretary-General's Special Representative and adviser, Lakhdar Brahimi, reinforced the policy in 2000. The future of enforcement would lie in hybrid operations, or contracting-out to regional organisations as in Bosnia and Herzegovina (where NATO led a 60,000 strong Implementation Force) and Kosovo where NATO took control of security.[19]

Until Operation Enduring Freedom, authorised by the Security Council against the Taliban in Afghanistan, the UN had previously authorised only two all-out wars (in Korea in 1950 and in Kuwait/Iraq in 1991). But whereas peacekeeping forces came largely from post-colonial states, notably from south Asia, the Brahimi report opened the way for an institutional blessing of mainly Atlantic coalitions to take risks in support of UN or other international mandates, and also to pursue their political and strategic interests in regime change through species of coercion and war usually under a humanitarian banner. The gambit paid off not merely because it seemed a practical solution to UN overstretch, but also because it enabled traditional peacekeeping contributors such as Canada to evade UN control in risky situations. A lesson learned by Canadian Major-General Lewis Mackenzie, whose peacekeeping experience stretched from Cyprus to the Balkans, concluded that international crisis management required leadership by the world's foremost military power which had refused to contribute ground forces in the Balkans until the fighting stopped.[20]

However, in place of this the US and its partners engaged in self-selected military campaigns to further national and alliance interests. Another former peacekeeper and student of imperial counterinsurgency, John Mackinlay, favoured peace support operations being adapted to help deal with what he called a global insurgency that had links to terrorism.[21] Peace operations and counterinsurgency were increasingly merged, deviating significantly from blue beret peacekeeping. Above all, aggressive peace could be delegated, condoned, retrospectively endorsed, tolerated or simply left unchecked by UN forums.

From Kosovo onwards, the pattern of regime-change wars, underwritten by UN resolutions or by the Secretary-General's own discourse or silence, echoed if not replicated nineteenth century imperial wars – with important differences, including the reshaping of language. A welter of alternatives arose: 'peace operations', 'humanitarian intervention', 'peace enforcement', 'stability operations', 'counterinsurgency' and the US preference, 'operations other than war'.[22] Significantly, too, the UN, national governments, and sections of global public opinion, clamoured for forceful intervention to protect civilians. This placed the UN in a quandary. The UN was not a war-fighting organisation. Nor, as Annan writes, was it a pacifist one.[23] Indeed on matters of threats to international security the UN was primarily an interstate diplomatic institution, and traditional peacekeeping a relatively inoffensive arm of diplomacy. But the turn to enforcement for civilian protection meant enlisting military establishments that preferred to operate outside UN command.

For the NATO three and allies, whose historical military cultures had not honoured UN career breaks very highly, this was more in tune with their traditions and their concern to limit risks in conflict. They postulated military engagements involving combat short of war. But lacking a strategic concept for supporting multilateral peace processes, they stressed 'escalation dominance' over parties to disputes. British Army doctrine noted that while use of force in peacekeeping could be limited to self-defence, it might be necessary 'in the conduct of any operation, to escalate to enforcement and war fighting'.[24]

Among Western militaries, national doctrines differed in detail and terminology. But in 2001 a NATO consensus led to a 'peace support operations' doctrine for addressing complex emergencies 'posed by collapsed or collapsing states in an uncertain and evolving strategic environment'. Peace support operations were to be conducted impartially, *normally* in support of an internationally-recognised organisation, such as the UN.[25] NATO doctrine assumed that peace support operations could be distinguished from 'enforcement action or war with a designated enemy, by specifying a desired political end-state rather than the achievement of military victory'.[26] Such operations would require extraordinary sophistication of military means, given that indicators of state failure are unreliable and state weakness is only meaningful in relation to an idealised Western norm. However, as evident in the UK's early doctrinal iterations and assumptions about escalation dominance, edges were blurred and overlaps incorporated. In 2008, Anglo-American–French concepts absorbed by military and civilian advisers to the DPKO led to 'principles and guidelines' for UN peacekeeping. Although this had no doctrinal status it was elevated by the American inscription 'Capstone doctrine'. It distinguished between robust tactical force (with host consent) and enforcement. But rather than linear movement from one to the other (and back) it envisaged peace operations of all kinds as mutually reinforcing, an implication that UN peacekeeping and proxy enforcement could coexist.[27]

Predicaments arose. Robustness and enforcement leads to a preoccupation with force protection and a fortress culture that reinforces alienation from the population. Common interpretations of rules of engagement in multinational operations are crucial but more difficult to achieve. It compromises humanitarian activities and can raise false expectations of protection among local civilians. Nor is it clear that local militias and civilians distinguish between various purposes of a mission or understand the niceties of its military doctrine. Moreover, as Mats Berdal acutely observes:

> the idea that a 'peace enforcement' or 'peace restoring' operation can clinically apply force to manipulate the behaviour of various parties on the ground *without* designating an enemy, while simultaneously assuming that such action will not influence the political dynamics of the conflict is to seriously underestimate the impact of outside military action on the balance of military, political and economic interests in ... complex intrastate conflicts.[28]

The conundrum clearly encompasses civilian protection and political decisions about the parties to a dispute, such as which 'rebels' have legitimacy among civilians for instance.

However, the Security Council appeared to act on the logic and for the first time in peacekeeping embraced counterinsurgency in resolution 2036 (2012) to designate a specific enemy in its mandate for the African Union Mission in Somalia.[29] The UN's Principles and Guidelines noted that 'peace enforcement may involve the use of force at the strategic or international level, which is normally prohibited for Member States under Article 2 (4) of the Charter unless authorized by the Security Council' (para. 72), and that the Council 'may utilize, where appropriate, regional organizations and agencies for enforcement action under its authority' (para. 25).[30] How deep that authority extends once delegation has occurred is open to question, but a lack of UN control over these proxy forces and the decay in the UN's legitimising function has been marked by manipulation of the first resort of scoundrels – 'the international community'.

Usually assumed to mean UN approval and a Security Council or General Assembly resolution, Berit Bliesemann de Guevara and Florian Kühn show that the term 'international community' has been a useful ambiguity constructed by interveners to suit particular contexts.[31] What constituted the 'international community' for legitimising aggressive activities became more specific in 2005 when the Under Secretary-General for Peacekeeping, Jean-Marie Guéhenno, fostered a five-year plan, 'Peace Operations 2010',[32] predicated on support from other security organisations. NATO received particular mention in Guéhenno's plan. In 2008 the UN signed a cooperation declaration with NATO, which had begun missions beyond Europe to reinforce its prolongation after the Cold War. The cooperation aimed to 'contribute significantly to addressing the threats and challenges to which the international community is called upon to respond'.[33] The privileged relationship was not only partial but diminished UN pretensions to distinguish between UN and NATO interests in, for example, the course of operational coordination and support.

Promoting peace in pursuit of political interests required NATO to act as arbiter of what constituted humanitarianism, responsibility to protect, last resort, legitimacy, and other codifications of military action.[34] In total as of 2014, regional or coalition contractors, including non-NATO bodies such as the African Union, supported eight UN peacekeeping missions in which such components were authorised; another eight missions had authorisation mandated only for the partners; and five were authorised to act independently of UN peacekeeping. Only five separate UN peacekeeping missions were directly authorised to use 'all necessary means' (ONUB, UNAMSIL, UNMIS, MONUSCO and UNISFA). Most missions with enforcement potential did not rely solely on blue beret peacekeepers. Apart from its dubious political purposes, such an increasingly common but disorderly practice raises a regulatory issue because enforcement cannot presume a legal basis derived from traditional peacekeeping.[35]

Moreover the Security Council was sometimes bypassed under the rubric of the 'international community' and 'humanitarianism' – as with NATO's bombing of Serbia in 1999 and the EU's Council authorising naval helicopters to bomb Somali coastal villagers in May 2012 to protect maritime commerce. Moreover, a Security Council resolution was interpreted as an opportunity for removing the Qaddafi regime from Libya in 2011. It was precisely to forestall a replay of NATO's war option that China and Russia vetoed Security Council resolutions on Syria in October 2011 and February 2012 that sought to condemn the Assad government rather than all belligerents.[36] Ironically, in 2014 the Obama and Assad governments had a common interest in attacking the jihadist 'Islamic State' in parts of Syria and Iraq.

Economic liberalisation

The second aspect of critique unravels the framing of peacebuilding to meet threats produced by others, often pathologised as 'failed states' that lack the harmony detectable in liberal democracies.[37] Peace missions are also burdened with addressing the root causes of violence, a concern uttered by many academics and practitioners. For example, the Security Council tasked the UN Integrated Office in Sierra Leone with building local capacity to address root causes of conflict.[38] This raises conundrums. Can there be agreement about identifying root causes that legitimise interventions, and could ameliorative actions be based on them? An academic literature locates causation in broad global contexts, including the structural violence inherent in hierarchies of power and global capital accumulation. For example, Susan Woodward has argued that in the case of Yugoslavia the International Monetary Fund also played a role from the 1980s that hardly had neutral consequences for the country's stability.[39] However, dominant discourses and practices tend to justify interventionism by emphasising domestic mal-dispositions such as ethnicity.

In political economy, neoliberals sought to transform political economies into an aggressive order of deregulation, privatisation, marketisation and international competition.[40] In the diplomacy of peace agreements, for example, US neoliberalism was reflected in the draft constitutions of Bosnia and Herzegovina, Kosovo and Iraq, requiring a replication of open capitalist economies. Further, where interventionists have had administrative and military control, the tenets could be attempted directly and incorporated into law reform projects.[41]

International financial institutions (IFIs) are more interested in debt repayment than peace processes per se. But directly and indirectly the IFIs and the World Trade Organization (WTO) affect the social and political foundations of peace through knowledge production and post-conflict aid conditionalities. The World Bank organises donor conferences and drives reconstruction processes. Impacts certainly vary between situations but local authorities are often subsequently unable to manage the tensions consequent on structural adjustments. The intruding bodies do not act with unanimity (nor are all field-workers and foreign administrators steeped in a neoliberal ideology), otherwise the UN would not have to make efforts to establish 'integrated missions'. The UN and other international organisations tend to react to crises, and there are spaces to contest agendas. However, as Susan Woodward points out, the hierarchies of power and influence mean that donors operate the culture of conditionality even in the absence of negotiated agreement with the IFIs.[42] Thus although the UN Development Programme (UNDP) and the UN Conference on Trade and Development tend to promote policies of social inclusion and protection, they have more limited resources and the former tends to operate within World Bank frameworks while the latter's countervailing contentions are deliberately squashed by the rich countries.[43]

A prime post-conflict reconstruction formula of the IFIs and large aid donors is the creation of a favourable business environment. Hardly conforming to pure neoliberal economic theory, business is favoured with support for enterprise zones, small and medium-sized enterprises, and micro-credit initiatives, together with tax breaks, subsidies and profit repatriation for foreign firms with investment capital. The main purpose has been to expand capital accumulation and bring business models into the art of government. Notably, as Toby Dodge demonstrates (in Chapter 10 of this book), the post-war plan for Iraq was to turn it into a model 'neoliberal' state.

It is also in the practice of subsidising business that hidden power and unaccountable authorities arguably employ disguise, and facilitate corruption. A camouflage of 'local empowerment' occurred in the hand-over by the euphemistically entitled Kosovo Trust Agency (KTA) – an EU-run body for privatising state and social assets – to the locally run Privatisation Agency of Kosovo (PAK). According to a PAK official report of August 2008, the new director accompanied by Kosovo police found office equipment gone, traces of burnt documents in the yard, some of them stamped 'confidential', all files of the former KTA Board of Directors missing, safe boxes for confidential evaluations of privatised socially-owned enterprises emptied, and five regional offices devoid of records.[44] In particular, privatisation of public enterprises and state assets has rewarded corrupt cronies of interim administrations and victorious war elites. Such groups generate a common cause with the dispensers of 'free market' policies, as evident in Iraq, Afghanistan and the Balkans (the Mostar aluminium works a prime example).[45]

Paradoxically, societies emerging from conflict are sometimes partly shielded from financial sector excesses. In capitalist cores a favourable business environment has meant that enormous riches are concentrated in the hands of a few, while at the same time private, market-derived debts are transferred to governments which then introduce pro-cyclical austerity for citizens in order to pay off debts. But societies vulnerable to regime change either have weak financial sectors with localised risks or operate their own forms of business protection. Consequently, so-called 'failed states' may have widespread corruption and financial chicanery. But their macroeconomic dysfunction also derives from toxic debts inherited from previous regimes, from attempts to introduce neoliberalism, from the indirect impacts of global trading conditions such as commodity price increases and falls in demand for exports, and from economic manipulation elsewhere. Local authorities then have to confront the tensions that arise as a consequence of the imposition of aggressive free trade. Required by donors to abandon forms of economic protectionism and import substitution that secludes socially significant, albeit inefficient, local production, host governments encounter trade imbalances, destruction of productive capacity and high unemployment (at 50 per cent among youth in Kosovo and Bosnia and Herzegovina) that global integration brings for countries with little comparative advantage. From a critical perspective it seems doubtful that the institutions of advanced capitalism can be reformed in order to facilitate future peacebuilding in spite of indications that donors take domestic customs and traditions increasingly seriously.[46]

To interveners it seems far more relevant to reform internal state structures. Indeed there appears to be no clear distinction between peacebuilding and statebuilding, though as Oliver Richmond argues state institutions do not necessarily hold the key to social contracts for many peoples.[47] Inevitably that means interference in internal politics and forging relationships with favoured rebel or government elites (evident in the UN Mission in the Democratic Republic of Congo's support to the government's armed forces and the EU Force–Chad support to the Déby regime in Chad).[48] Critics can point to tensions and contradictions between the state as guarantor of security and the non-state allegiances of some populations; between institutionalism and organic roots of ownership; between restructuring a state after regime change and denying statehood to others. For non-UN coalitions, strategic and geopolitical concerns are more likely to determine the approach to statebuilding, supporting it for Albanian Kosovars but denying it to Palestinians. Such partiality became apparent when the US withdrew funding for UNESCO when Palestine joined that body in October 2011. The UN Secretary-General, Ban Ki-moon, schooled in the diplomacy of a US client state, chose to ignore principles of international law, human rights and self-determination to express concern about possible damage to UN institutions if the Palestinian Authority pressed ahead with a quest for statehood.[49] Clearly, one of the penalties of the 'capacity to pay' principle for assessing both the UN's general and peacekeeping budgets has long been the UN's over-dependence on a single economic source. The United States pays 22 per cent for the former and 25 per cent for the latter, as well as about a third of voluntary contributions to various programmes that it favours.[50] As the capacities of the United States and EU diminish relative to the BRICs (Brazil, Russian, India, China and South Africa), as well as on political grounds, it is perhaps time to revisit the notion that no state should contribute more than 10 per cent of the general budget.

On the one hand, agencies in the UN family have attempted to engage 'stakeholders', encompass traditional justice systems and pay greater attention to everyday welfare in peace processes. There have been changes to peace discourse and frameworks of action.[51] However, regime change missions cannot but echo, if not replicate, imperial processes – whether through modern versions of gunboat diplomacy or working through supposed 'local empowerment'.[52] Discourses of good governance, law and order, stakeholding, participation, local ownership, empowerment, and trouncing spoilers, naturalise structures of global inequality and exploitation produced by imperialism.[53] The power to implement restructuring is also disguised by evasions of responsibility on all sides and resistance on the part of inhabitants.[54] Aggressive peace conducted by drivers of liberalisation with or without the UN is one of many influences on outcomes.

Conclusion

Peace missions have been pursued through militarisation and liberalisation. This does not imply that the upholders of liberalisation themselves conform to liberal values, adhere to international law or practise meaningful democracy at home, and nor is it to imagine a conspiracy. Rather, the path identified follows views about human security and human rights, intervention, democracy and peace fostered by 'liberal' states. One can trace, for example, the militarisation of peace operations to humanitarian emergencies and 'spectrum of force' doctrines for peacekeeping devised in the mid-1990s by the UK and French militaries and adopted by the US and NATO. Although military and civilian operations are distinctive in crucial ways, their spheres intersect because the presence of uniformed personnel offers reassurance to multinational operations as a whole, and provides security for transition to occur. The security apparatus of an intervention protects the political economy preferred by institutions with power, and interlocked by close partnership between the DPKO, NATO, the UN Peacebuilding Commission and the World Bank. As Annan recalled: 'It was vital that we integrate development, security, military, and political activity in our interventions in our war-torn countries.'[55]

The moment of bipolar collapse opened the world to alignment with a triumphant social, political and economic system more to convert than protect. Western democracies could attempt to monopolise discourses on intervention, peacebuilding and development, and pursue a vision of a global order. Perhaps the speed at which the Soviet Union dismantled and at which global financial capitalism ascended produced its own kind of shock and awe. It may have offered Western economic and foreign policy communities aspiration for protecting and transforming strangers. Setbacks, including domestic revolts, as well as a sense of relative Western incapacities, could be partly masked, by encouragement to rebels, as in Syria, or by supposedly smart violence from the air as in Kosovo.

Nevertheless, a crisis of moral purpose as well as poor long-run results for regime change operations may make it increasingly difficult for the Western bloc, beset by the iniquities of financial crisis and competition in the international system, to command authority as role models and purveyors of good order. The Syrian crisis exposed the dangers of identifying rebels as ideologically reliable, and the Crimean and Ukrainian crises of 2014 tattered the EU's expansionist aspirations which in regard to accession of new members, popular majorities in most EU states opposed anyway.[56]

In light of this critique, several avenues might command further attention in researching peace. First, the extent to which the UN has ideological authority on peace issues merits further investigation. It has always been circumvented by states and dependent on horse-trading between them. Assemblages of subcontracted governance, only vaguely accountable, include for instance the 'Peace Implementation Council' for Bosnia and Herzegovina, the 'Quint' in Kosovo, and the 'Quartet' in the Middle East. NATO members are privileged in all of these. Another bias occurs in the deals for top UN and agency positions so that, for example, since 1997 the Under Secretary-General for Peacekeeping has had a French military career.[57]

A post-Cold War genealogy of militarised and liberalised peace should also encompass the predispositions of bureaucracies and special advisers. For example, a move to reconfigure the UN as a corporate business led to the appointment of Joseph E. Connor (former Chair of Price Waterhouse, one of world's largest financial services corporations) who virtually ran the UN Secretariat from 1994 to 2002, enlisting some of his former corporate associates to help.[58] UN Secretaries-General, the Security Council and UN departments receive counsel from academics and other experts selected by an obscure process. Drawn from a range of backgrounds they contribute significantly to debates. However, many prominent advisers on peace and conflict have been US-based, often illustrious Ivy League academics, their services sometimes paid for by USAID. Liberal multilateralists who became special advisers to Secretaries-General have included:

- Michael Doyle (Columbia and other Ivy League universities: democratic peace, strategic planning, UN–corporate relations and UN–US relations);
- Jeffrey Sachs (Columbia University: development);
- Charles Call (American University: peacebuilding);
- Edward Luck (International Peace Institute: responsibility to protect);
- Francis Deng (Sudanese based at the US Institute for Peace: prevention of genocide);
- John Ruggie (Canadian with US citizenship Columbia, California and Harvard universities: the 'Global Compact');
- Bill Durch (Stimson Center: Brahimi report); and
- Stephen J. Steadman (Stanford University: strengthening collective security, peacebuilding, counter-terrorism).[59]

Pertinent questions arise: what values do the advisers impart and how do they impact on policy formation?

Equally notable are institutions within comfortable distances of the UN's headquarters in New York and Geneva. A glance at the websites of the International Peace Institute, US Institute for Peace, the Stimson Center and the Geneva Centre for Security Policy, among others, reveals a blizzard of seminars, conferences, training courses, receptions and publications (to which this author has contributed). While the UN and other authorities may make strong efforts to encompass alterity – and NATO members have no majority on the Peacebuilding Commission for instance – the genealogy of concentrated knowledge-power invites exploration, for which a fine excavation of the International Crisis Group think-tank stands as a model.[60]

This does not imply a homogeneous framing of knowledge. In the UN system for example, resistance to narrow, elitist conceptions of legitimate interventionism exist as an undercurrent among many recruits who reveal and act upon a variety of stimuli. Accordingly the backgrounds and world views of agency field workers (already undertaken for Kosovo) merit investigation.[61] The UN Development Programme has also sponsored research that features such slogans as 'nurturing indigenous drivers' and 'enabling local ingenuity' to foster liberation from top-down peacebuilding on the grounds that '[i]ndigenous drivers provide the most viable platform on which to base post-war recovery efforts.[62]

Second, a political economy critique of peace missions requires analysts to assess resistance in societies opened up to neoliberal peace. Policies of intruders are constantly adopted, adapted or resisted in multiple ways. Resistance in local communities may include a quest for authority to set economic priorities – including protection from the deleterious effects of global integration. In this respect it is crucial to engage with political economy debates. The everyday workings of labour markets and employment conditions clearly animate populations; on the other hand foreign direct investment (FDI) is regarded as a peacebuilding panacea by aid donors, local elites and the IFIs. How does FDI work out in practice; are investors net extractors rather than benefactors? What are the functions of economies usually dismissed as 'black', 'grey' or 'informal', of bartering, remittances and smuggling in borderlands? Analyses can also embrace socio-economic rights manifest in the emergence of movements for welfare distribution, economic empowerment, and the protection of public, socially owned and community property from dispossession by private accumulation. Such enquiries would allow for the historically and spatially-contingent transformation and the 'economies of power' in varied war-torn societies.[63] From a critical perspective the institutional and elite drivers of policy that enshrine the norms of rational individualism and market forces idealised by corporate capitalism fails to provide economic justice. Accordingly, the *in situ* investigations cannot be divorced from the potential for far-reaching change in the global economic and political environments and structures that also constitute 'the limits of potential' for life. Aggressive peace operations reveal a contradiction in liberalism: tolerance limited to principles that are exclusionary. The oversight, guidance, control and conditionalities exercised by international agencies morph into the aggressive pursuit of permanent integration into global capitalist structures.

At the end of 'The Ghost Writer' the hero is bumped off, not by the 'peace protesters' but by a 'liberal' elite protecting its power from accountability. A waning of popular support and the lack of success in foreign ventures may resolve to 'hit and run' strategies in the Western bloc. And the impact of debt-driven capitalism on risky militarism is also uncertain. But as Karl Marx observed of economic evolution, '[e]conomists express the relations of bourgeois production, the division of labour, credit, money, and so on, as fixed, immutable, eternal categories ... These categories are as little eternal as the relations they express'.[64] In the process of understanding this, policy-makers and implementers can recognise the importance of fluid economic structures for understanding the interactions and negotiations that are produced when engagement occurs – and to raise such fundamental questions as 'what is peace?' and 'whose peace?'.

Acknowledgements

I am grateful to the Leverhulme Trust for its Emeritus Fellowship and suggestions by Florian Kühn, Oliver Richmond and Mandy Turner. Responsibility for the essay is mine alone. This chapter is an updated and extended version of 'Reflections on Aggressive Peace', *International Peacekeeping*, vol. 19, no. 4, August 2012, Taylor & Francis Ltd, www.tandfonline.com, reprinted by permission of the publisher.

Notes

1 See, e.g., Béatrice Pouligny, *Peacekeeping Seen From Below*, London: Hurst, 2006; Paul Higate and Marsha Henry, *Insecure Spaces: Peacekeeping, Performance and Power in Haiti, Kosovo and Liberia*, London: Zed Books, 2009.
2 See, e.g., Oliver P. Richmond, *The Transformation of Peace*, Basingstoke: Palgrave, 2005.
3 Mats R. Berdal, 'The UN's Unnecessary Crisis', *Survival*, vol. 47, no. 3, 2005, pp. 7–23.
4 See, e.g., Mark Duffield, *Global Governance and the New Wars*, London: Zed Books, 2007; Neil Cooper, 'On the crisis in the liberal peace', *Conflict, Security and Development*, vol. 7, no. 4, 2007, pp. 605–616; David Chandler, *Empire in Denial: The Politics of State-building*, London: Pluto, 2006; Mark Duffield, *Development, Security and Unending War*, Cambridge: Polity, 2008; Oliver P. Richmond, *A Post-Liberal Peace*, London: Routledge, 2011; Shahrbanou Tadjbakhsh (ed.), *Rethinking the Liberal Peace*, London: Routledge, 2011.
5 Roland Paris, 'Saving Liberal Peacebuilding', *Review of International Studies*, vol. 36, no. 2, 2010, pp. 337–365; Charles T. Call and Vanessa Wyeth (eds), *Building States to Build Peace*, Boulder, CO: Lynne Rienner, 2008. See also, Neil Cooper, Mandy Turner and Michael Pugh, 'The End of History and the Last Liberal Peacebuilder: A Reply to Roland Paris', *Review of International Studies*, vol. 37, no. 4, pp. 1995–2007.
6 Alan James, *Peacekeeping and International Politics*, Basingstoke: Macmillan/IISS, 1990.
7 Mark Mazower, *No Enchanted Palace: The End of Empire and the Ideological Origins of the United Nations*, Princeton, NJ: Princeton University Press, 2013. See also, Michael Pugh, *Liberal Internationalism: The Interwar Movement for Peace in Britain*, Basingstoke: Palgrave Macmillan, 2012; Beate Jahn, 'The Tragedy of Liberal Diplomacy: Democratization, Intervention, Statebuilding (Part II)', *Journal of Intervention and Statebuilding*, vol. 1, no. 2, 2007, pp. 211–229.
8 Bureau of Conflict and Stabilization Operations website (at: www.state.gov/g/cso/).
9 As ordered by Hillary Clinton, US Secretary of State, in 2009. Robert Booth and Julian Borger, 'US Diplomats Spied on UN Leadership', *The Guardian*, 10 November 2010. See also, James Bamford, *The Puzzle Palace. A Report on NSA, America's Most Secret Agency*, London: Penguin 1983.
10 G. John Ikenberry and Anne-Marie Slaughter (directors), *Forging A World Of Liberty Under Law: US National Security in the 21st Century*, Final Report of the Princeton Project on National Security, 27 September 2006.
11 For further analysis see: Michael Pugh (ed.), *The UN Peace and Force*, London: Cass, 2001; Trevor Findlay, *The Use of Force in UN Peace Operations*, Stockholm: SIPRI, 2002.
12 Júlia Gifra Durall, 'United Nations Peacekeeping Operations under Chapter VII: Exception or Widespread Practice?', *Revista del Instituto Español de Estudios Estratégicos*, no. 2, 2013.

13 See Marrack Goulding, *Peacemonger*, London: John Murray, 2002, pp. 317–319.
14 'Allies and Lies', *Correspondent*, BBC2, broadcast 24 June 2001 (transcript at: http://news.bbc.co.uk/1/hi/programmes/correspondent/1390536.stm).
15 Richard Holbrooke, Clinton's special envoy to the Balkans, claimed that this gained US support for Annan's subsequent election as UN Secretary-General. The US blocked Boutros-Ghali's reappointment; Richard Holbrooke, *To End a War*, New York: Random House, 1998, p. 103.
16 Roméo A. Dellaire, *Shake Hands with the Devil: The Failure of Humanity in Rwanda*, Toronto: Random House, 2003. But France had a special relationship with the Hutu government and its forces made little effort to protect Tutsis and moderate Hutus; Philip Gourevitch, *We Wish to Inform You That Tomorrow We Will Be Killed With Our Families: Stories from Rwanda*, London: Picador, 1998.
17 Pouligny (note 1 above), pp. 19–20.
18 Kofi Annan, 'Renewing the United Nations: A Programme for Reform', United Nations, New York, UN doc. A51/1950, 31 October 1997 (at: http://daccess-dds-ny.un.org/doc/UNDOC/GEN/N97/302/22/PDF/N9730222.pdf?OpenElement).
19 'Report of the Panel on United Nations Peace Operations' (Brahimi Report), UN doc. A/55/305–S/2000/809, 21 August 2000 (at: www.un.org/peace/reports/peace_operations).
20 Lewis Mackenzie, *Peacekeeper: The Road to Sarajevo*, Vancouver: Douglas & McIntyre, 1993.
21 John MacKinlay, *The Insurgent Archipelago*, London: Hurst, 2009.
22 See US Army, 'FM 100–20/AFP 3–20: Military Operations in Low Intensity Conflicts', Departments of the Army and Air Force, Washington, DC, 5 December 1990; Wesley K. Clark, *Waging Modern War: Bosnia, Kosovo, and the Future of Conflict*, New York: Public Affairs, 2002. Clark concluded, also, that ground operations were highly problematic compared to Kosovo-style air campaigns, a strategy revisited for Libya in 2011.
23 Kofi Annan with Nader Mousavizadeh, *Interventions: A Life in War and Peace*, London: Penguin, 2013, p. 97.
24 Draft Army Field Manual, 'Peace Support Operations', 1996/97, ch. 7, p. 12; Michael Pugh, 'From Mission Cringe to Mission Creep? Implications of New Peace Support Operations Doctrine', *Defence Studies* no. 2, Oslo: Institute for Defence Studies, 1997; Henning A. Frantzen, *NATO and Peace Support Operations, 1991–1999: Policies and Doctrines*, London: Routledge, 2006; Theo Farrell, 'Sliding into War: The Somalia Imbroglio and US Army Peace Operations Doctrine', *International Peacekeeping*, vol. 2, no. 2, 1995, pp. 194–214.
25 Author's emphasis. NATO, *AJP-3.4.1: Peace Support Operations*, July 2001 (at: www.osrh.hr/smvo/Library/ajp-3.4.1.pdf).
26 *Ibid.*, para. 0204.
27 UN Department for Peacekeeping Operations (DPKO), 'United Nations Peacekeeping Operations: Principles and Guidelines', 2008, para. 29 (at: http://pbpu.unlb.org/pbps/library/Capstone_Doctrine_ENG.pdf).
28 Mats Berdal, 'Lessons Not Learned: The Use of Force in Peace Operations in the 1990s', in Adekeye Adebajo and Chandra Lekha Sriram (eds), *Managing Armed Conflicts in the 21st Century*, London: Cass, 2001, p. 67.
29 The resolution specified the Islamic force, al-Shabab. 'Security Council Requests African Union to Increase Troop Level of Somalia Mission to 17,700, Establish Expanded Presence in Keeping with Strategic Concept. Resolution 2036 (2012) Adopted Unanimously. Also Expands Support Package', UN doc. SC/10550, 22 February 2012.
30 DPKO (note 26 above).
31 On the protean attributes of 'international community', see Berit Bliesemann de Guevara and Florian P. Kühn, '"The International Community Needs to

Act": Loose Use and Empty Signalling of a Hackneyed Concept', *International Peacekeeping*, vol. 18, no. 2, 2011, pp. 135–151.
32 Jean-Marie Guéhenno, 'Peace Operations 2010', letter to all DPKO and mission staff, New York, 30 November 2005.
33 'Joint Declaration on UN/NATO Secretariat Cooperation', 23 September 2008, NATO doc. Annex to DSG (2008)0714 (INV) (at: www.nato.int/docu/update/2007/01-january/e0124a.html).
34 Noam Chomsky, *The New Military Humanism: Lessons from Kosovo*, London: Polity Press, 1999.
35 Durall (note 12 above), p. 19.
36 '"NATO Hijacking UN Powers" – Putin', *Russia Today* (Moscow), 27 February 2012 (at: http://rt.com/politics/putin-nato-us-elections-2012-265/); 'China, Russia veto UN draft resolution on Syria', *Xinhua News* (Beijing), 5 February 2012 (at: http://news.xinhuanet.com/english/video/2012-02/05/c_131392174.htm).
37 See Kai Koddenbrock, 'Recipes for Intervention: Western Policy Papers Imagine the Congo', *International Peacekeeping*, vol. 19, no. 4, 2012, pp. 549–564.
38 'Security Council Establishes UN Integrated Office in Sierra Leone to Further Address Root Causes of Conflict', SC res. 1620, 31 August 2005 (at: www.un.org/News/Press/docs/2005/sc8487.doc.htm).
39 Susan Woodward, *Balkan Tragedy Chaos and Dissolution after the Cold War*, Washington, DC: Brookings Institution, 1995. The literature includes such diverse critiques as: Johan Galtung, 'Three Approaches to Peace: Peacekeeping, Peacemaking, and Peacebuilding', in Johan Galtung, *Peace, War and Defense: Essays in Peace Research*, vol. II, Copenhagen: Christian Eljers, 1976, pp. 297–304; Frances Stewart and Valpy FitzGerald (eds), *War and Underdevelopment*, 2 vols, Oxford: Oxford University Press, 2001; David Harvey, *Spaces of Global Capitalism: Towards a Theory of Uneven Geographical Development*, London: Verso, 2006.
40 Michael Pugh, 'Normative Values and Economic Deficits in Postconflict Transformation', *International Journal*, vol. 62, no. 3, 2007, pp. 479–493.
41 See, e.g., Cornelius Friesendorf and Susan E. Penksa, 'Militarized Law Enforcement in Peace Operations: EUFOR in Bosnia and Herzegovina', *International Peacekeeping*, vol. 15, no. 5, pp. 677–694.
42 Susan L. Woodward, 'The IFIs and Post-conflict Political Economy', in Mats Berdal and Dominik Zaum (eds), *Political Economy of Statebuilding: Power after Peace*, Oxford: Oxford University Press, 2012, pp. 140–157.
43 See Heiner Flassbeck on The Real News.com, 28 July 2014 (at: www.youtube.com/watch?feature=player_embedded&v=GWednAjxWdQ); *Die Marktwirtschaft des 21. Jahrhunderts*, Frankfurt: Westend, 2010.
44 'PAK Official Work Report, 2008–09', Prishtina, 2009 (at: www.pak-ks.org/repository/docs/090904-English_Ver.pdf).
45 See Michael Pugh and Neil Cooper with Jonathan Goodhand, *War Economies in a Regional Context*, Boulder, CO: Lynne Rienner, 2004.
46 See Roger Mac Ginty, 'Indigenous Peace-Making Versus the Liberal Peace', *Cooperation and Conflict*, vol. 43, no. 2, 2008, pp. 690–708.
47 Richmond (note 4 above), pp. 46–50.
48 See Adekeye Adebajo, *UN Peacekeeping in Africa: From the Suez Crisis to the Sudan Conflicts*, Boulder, CO: Lynne Rienner, 2011, pp. 208–209; Stephan Hensell and Felix Gerdes, 'Elites and International Actors in Post-War Societies: The Limits of Intervention', *International Peacekeeping*, vol. 19, no. 2, 2012, pp. 154–169.
49 David Ravid, 'UN Chief to *Haaretz*: Palestinians Will Only Get a State through Negotiations', *Haaretz*, 3 February 2012 (at: www.haaretz.com/print-edition/news/un-chief-to-haaretz-palestinians-will-only-get-a-state-through-negotiations-1.410687). I am grateful to Mandy Turner for pointing this out.
50 Phillis Bennis, *Calling the Shots: How Washington Dominates Today's UN*, New York: Olive Branch Press, 2000.

Lineages of aggressive peace 93

51 E.g. *World Development Report 2004, Making Services Work for the Poor*, Washington, DC: World Bank, 2003.
52 On the Balkans specifically, see Susan Woodward, 'The Long Intervention: Continuity in the Balkan Theatre', *Review of International Studies*, vol. 39, no. 5, 2013, pp. 1169–1187. See also Philip Cunliffe in Chapter 3 of this volume.
53 See Branwyn Gruyffed Jones (ed.), *Decolonising International Relations*, Lanham, MD: Rowman & Littlefield, 2006, pp. 9–10; Chandler (note 4 above).
54 Chandler (note 4 above).
55 Annan with Mousavizadeh (note 23 above), p. 220.
56 European Stability Initiative, *Waiting for Godot: Vladimir and Estragon in Skopje*, report of 17 July 2014 (at: www.esiweb.org/index.php?lang=en&id=156&document_ID=152).
57 'Head of UN Peacekeeping to Resign in June', UN Elections.Org, no. 53, 21 March 2008 (at: www.unelections.org/?q=node/572).
58 UN Forum, 'Joseph E. Connor Managed the U.N. for Eight Years', 15 June 2009 (at: www.unforum.com/UNheadlines575.htm). However, UN budget committees have the clout to resist neoliberal policies.
59 In addition: James S. Sutterlin (US Foreign Service: 13 years in the Secretariat, 'An Agenda for Peace', subsequently Yale University); Michael Sheehan (formerly US Army and counter-terrorism expert in Latin America and US State Department Counter-terrorism Coordinator: Assistant Secretary-General, DPKO, 2001–2003); Robert C. Orr (Harvard and Council on Foreign Relations: Assistant Secretary-General for Policy Coordination and Strategic Planning in the Secretary-General's Executive Office).
60 Berit Bliesemann de Guevara (ed.), 'Knowledge Production in Conflict: The International Crisis Group', special issue, *Third World Quarterly*, vol. 35, no. 4, 2014.
61 Catherine Goetz and Berit Bliesemann de Guevara, 'The "Statebuilding Habitus": UN Staff and the Cultural Dimension of Liberal Intervention in Kosovo', in Berit Bliesemann de Guevara (ed.), *Statebuilding and State-Formation: The Political Sociology of Intervention*, London: Routledge, 2012, pp. 198–213.
62 UNDP, *Post-Conflict Economic Recovery: Enabling Local Ingenuity*, New York: Bureau for Crisis Prevention and Recovery, 2008, p. xvii. See also, Zoë Marriage, *Not Breaking the Rules, Not playing the game. International Assistance to Countries at War*, London: Hurst, 2002; Simon Chesterman, *You the People: The United Nations, Transitional Administration and State-Building*, Oxford: Oxford University Press, 2004.
63 For instance, the discourse of crime and corruption dovetails into neoliberalism in El Salvador, in which the individual is responsible for 'attracting' and coping with crime, which is thereby disconnected from the structural tensions that facilitate it. Ellen Moodie, *El Salvador in the Aftermath of Peace: Crime, Uncertainty and the Transition to Democracy*, Philadelphia PA: University of Pennsylvania Press, 2010; Michael Pugh, Neil Cooper and Mandy Turner (eds), *Whose Peace? Critical Perspectives on the Political Economy of Peacebuilding*, Basingstoke: Palgrave, 2008; Carlos Chagas Vianna Braga, Maíra Siman Gomes and Marta Fernández Moreno, 'Trapped Between Many Worlds: A Post-colonial Perspective on the UN Mission in Haiti (MINUSTAH)', *International Peacekeeping*, vol. 19, no. 3, 2012, pp. 377–392.
64 Karl Marx, 'The Poverty of Philosophy', in Karl Marx and Friedrich Engels, *Collected Works*, London: Lawrence & Wishart, vol. 6, 1976, pp. 165–166.

5 A double-edged sword of peace?
Reflections on the tension between representation and protection in gendering liberal peacebuilding

Heidi Hudson

Towards unravelling the myths of a gendered spring

In the wake of the 'Arab Spring' of 2011 women have been depicted as change agents through their leading role in protests in Tunisia, Egypt, Syria and Yemen.[1] Likewise, the 'Arab Spring' is touted as opening up 'unprecedented opportunities for women to participate in the public life of their country'.[2] However, apart from these public developments, no woman was included in the committee for changing the constitution prior to the elections in Egypt. Instead, a committee was created 'that deals with the advancement of women'.[3] In many post-conflict states, tension also emerges between the public gains of women and huge protection concerns at the private level. In this regard, Kathleen Carter provides a detailed discussion of the extent of rape as a weapon against women in, for example, Bosnia and Herzegovina, Rwanda, the Democratic Republic of Congo (DRC) and Darfur, and against men in the DRC.[4] While huge progress in awareness about sexual and gender-based violence (SGBV) has been made, implementation has not produced results where it counts – in the lives of ordinary men and women.[5]

While some argue that norms take time to evolve, others remain cynical in the wake of how gender discourses have been manifested in Afghanistan and in Libya since the beginning of 2011. Critiques of the liberal peace have grown, but the mutually formative relationship between the liberal peace and a type of peace that might be described as liberal-feminist has been largely overlooked in both mainstream and critical literature.[6] The liberal peace project uses gender discourses as a tool to help enforce its norms. And herein also lies a paradox: gender is a much neglected topic in the central documents and debates on the 'responsibility to protect' (R2P) principle and only implied through reference to SGBV on the list of atrocity crimes.[7] Yet, ironically, the protection of women was invoked to partially justify the intervention and regime change in Libya.[8]

Peacebuilding and regime change are not one and the same. Galtung's conflict triangle distinguishes peacebuilding from other interventions such as peacekeeping and peacemaking, which address direct (behavioural) and cultural (attitudinal) violence, respectively. Peacebuilding seeks to address structural contradictions or root causes.[9] Within this broad framework, the focus here is on 'liberal' peacebuilding efforts (interventions that are mainly orchestrated from the top down by Western donors and international organisations). Although regime change practices have certainly helped to demonise all liberal peacebuilding efforts, individual programmes may produce emancipatory results. Nevertheless, peacebuilding executed under the liberal banner after conquest (military intervention), ceasefires or consent lies on a continuum mainly stretching along levels of commitment to the neoliberal wisdom of good governance and the free market.[10]

Drawing on Gayatri Spivak's seminal essay, 'Can the Subaltern Speak?', this chapter offers a postcolonial-feminist framework for explaining the way in which gender is framed in security discourses and peace operations.[11] A postcolonial-feminist lens serves to make the operations of discursive power visible by revealing how security discourse (to paraphrase Jeff Huysmans) 'positions people in their relations to [their gendered selves] ... and to other [gendered] human beings within a particular symbolic [gender] order'.[12] I argue that the way in which gender is framed in security discourses and peace operations is symptomatic of the hegemonic way in which the dominant liberal peace discourses and practices are naturalised and institutionalised. Gendered power relations are shaped and reproduced through the discourses and practices of peacebuilding actors such as the UN and key Western powers. As the discourses shape meaning, they eventually produce representational 'truths' about the strange ('them') in relation to the familiar ('us'), and exert significant power in determining the gendered path of post-conflict peace and reconstruction processes. For example, there has been lack of insight regarding the notion of the 'unintended consequences' associated with external intervention. When liberal peace discourses use such euphemisms and are blind to the way in which the 'other' is represented, they risk *re*producing or *re*institutionalising gendered relations of domination, subordination and insecurity in a phase that, theoretically, is intended to produce a new beginning. But as Julietta Hua and Holly Nigorizawa emphasise, the act of representation is never transparent: 'even when the "other" speaks to represent herself, the solution of speech neither eradicates nor addresses the privileging of colonial and orientalist logics producing what and who counts in women's human rights discourse'.[13] From a critical postcolonial-feminist perspective this analysis thus seeks to better understand the gendered inner workings of international organisations as they relate to peace operations. How does the adoption of liberal feminist language and mainstreaming policies by international agencies function to produce certain exclusionary outcomes in peace processes?

The first aim of this contribution is to examine the manifestation of liberal-feminist assumptions, with specific reference to the tension between representation and protection in peace processes. The term 'representation' is used here to suggest 'speaking for', as in public decision-making structures, but more importantly, also to 'representations' of women and girls' agency in international discourses.[14] The politics of representation/exclusion and the politics of protection are intertwined. Keeping women out, or SGBV off the table, often serves a pragmatic and deeply depoliticising purpose – ensuring that the peace agreement between elites proceeds unhindered. Including women by using 'gender protection' issues to justify intervention, as in Afghanistan, represents the other side of the coin. Following this, the second aim is to discuss how a postcolonial-feminist approach could enhance a critical feminist understanding of how and why international institutions, among others, 'do gender' in such a way.

The chapter begins by outlining the key conceptual pillars of a postcolonial-feminist approach and then analyses the tenets of liberal peace hegemony through its politics of 'othering' and the types of violence that it generates. The next section focuses on liberal-feminist discourses and practices and how the preoccupation with problem-solving, gender-mainstreaming narrows the scope for radical change within gendered institutions. This is followed by analysis of the tension between the representation and protection of women. I explore layers of agency; problematise the contradictions emanating from the politics of inclusion/exclusion; and illustrate the disempowering effects of international discourses on SGBV. The penultimate section offers a postcolonial-feminist alternative that navigates the regions of co-option, multiple identities, global inequalities and everyday resistance.

Gender and liberal peacebuilding – the art of 'othering'

The liberal peace thesis rests on two pillars: that effective liberal states are a bulwark against international instability; and that failing or conflict-prone states represent a threat to international security. Consequently, the liberal peace project is a statebuilding project, but also a gender project in the making. Both the epistemic and empirical violence of the liberal peace are brought to the surface when viewed through a gender lens. Seemingly benign features such as the acknowledgement of context, multilateralism, a combination of top-down and bottom-up processes, rule of law and democracy mask the fact that liberal peacebuilding disempowers whole populations (especially women) in conflict and post-conflict states through a complex process of security governance.

The violence is manifest in the tacit meta-consensus on neoliberal interdependence of the post-Cold War in the UN, international financial institutions, powerful states such as the United States, the UK and France, as well as NGOs. The assumption that free markets would address social and economic inequalities that are believed to drive conflicts in many parts of the underdeveloped world is often at odds with local interests, which may support economic well-being, but not necessarily free market solutions.[15]

Structural adjustment programmes in Ghana, Uganda and Tanzania, for instance, have produced widespread hardship among the poor in the context of a skewed global political economy.[16] Such neoliberal dogmatism is also incompatible with the economic realities of many women in the developing world where, paradoxically, their disadvantaged position in the formal employment sector forces them into a rather precarious informal sector characterised by a complex relationship between informality, gendered relations of power and poverty.[17] This situation is exacerbated by the fact that conflicts in the developing world impact on the 'feminisation of poverty' and the burden of female-headed households.[18] These examples underline the power of international consensus when key assumptions, policies and structurally violent effects become intertwined. Such manifestations further reinforce the multiplying potential of gendered power imbalances.

The liberal peace project is also violent, because it manipulates moral imperatives to justify intervention. It is presented as a human project or 'a war that has the element of humanity as its central organizing principle'.[19] An intrinsic part of this project is the Responsibility to Protect (R2P) principle, adopted at the UN World Summit in 2005. The International Commission on Intervention and State Sovereignty (ICISS) Report (2001) recast sovereignty as derived from how the state treats its citizens.[20] Accordingly, if the state fails the test of accountability in the face of actual or threatened mass atrocity against its population, the 'international community' must intervene to ensure the accountability of the state. Feminist critiques of the war in Afghanistan have highlighted how the struggle for the emancipation of women has been used as part of the justification of R2P.[21] Although George W. Bush's 'war on terror' was not justified in gender terms or gender invoked as a reason for regime change in Iraq and Afghanistan, a gender narrative certainly drove the 'demonisation' of the Ba'athists and Taliban in the late 1990s. The appropriation of feminist language and the banner of oppressed women fed into the overall discourse, albeit as a secondary argument. However, with such indirect justification for R2P also come violent consequences – propping up patriarchy and perpetuating women's inability to speak for themselves.

But as much as intervention in itself can do harm, paradoxically, as the West begins to lose interest in Afghanistan with the gradual withdrawal of troops, activists fear that backsliding on women's rights is on the rise. Since the fall of the Taliban, women have made substantial gains in government. The Afghan Constitution stipulates that the Wolesi Jirga (lower house) must be at least 28 per cent female (68 seats of a total of 249), and in the parliamentary elections of 18 September 2010, 69 women (one more than the quota) were elected.[22] However, in the face of reactionary backlash, strong official (insider) as well as donor voices were needed. According to Franz-Michael Mellbin, EU ambassador to Afghanistan, Hamid Karzai's government failed to end the prosecution of rape victims and other abused women for so-called 'moral crimes'. Although maternal mortality decreased and the number of girls in schools increased to 42 per cent (4.4 million girls), in 2013, 'a landmark law to prevent violence against women was pushed out of parliament, the quota of seats for women on provincial councils was cut [from 20 to 25 per cent], and a proposal to reintroduce stoning as a punishment for adultery – used more against women than men – was put forward by the justice ministry'.[23] In 2014, there was also an attempt by parliament to pass a law gagging victims of domestic violence by preventing relatives testifying against each other.[24] During the campaign for presidential and provincial council elections, the picture was also mixed: three presidential candidates chose women as vice-presidential 'running mates' and a relatively high number of women voters participated on election day (5 April 2014); whereas some female candidates were marginalised on the basis of having lower educational status and intimidation against female candidates was reported.[25] Public representation of women is thus a double-edged sword: although it offers women visibility, the transformative potential is limited, perhaps concealing the continuation of other forms of gender inequality. The Afghanistan case illustrates that fast-tracking gender equality through procedural (technocratic) democracy can easily become the flip side of reinforcing the notion that 'gender inequality is somehow inherent in Afghan culture'.[26]

Because of the political nature of such representational dilemmas, a postcolonial-feminist challenge to liberal peacebuilding is committed to those 'subaltern' women (and men) who wage daily struggles in a post-conflict world. Western (liberal) feminists are criticised for presenting women of the global South as homogeneously different, namely as passive, victimised, in need of protection by their Western 'sisters', and ultimately inferior. In this way, according to Spivak, 'the emergent perspective of feminist criticism reproduces the axioms of imperialism'.[27] Instead, postcolonial feminists are sensitive to the complexity of power relations that emanate from overlapping identity constructions of race, gender, class and culture in specific historical and geographical contexts.[28] Rather than being a simple relationship of domination versus subordination, all these relations embody a connectedness between power, discourse and political institutions and practices, thus allowing a deeper understanding 'of how past and present relations of inequality are constructed and maintained'.[29] This approach therefore firmly connects global gender inequalities and gendered everyday practices to their collective production of insecurities during peacebuilding and post-conflict reconstruction.

A postcolonial-feminist perspective is critical of an understanding of political identity that uses a universalised Western notion as benchmark, and which only allows self-governance if it is based on the universalist principles of democracy and statebuilding. The agency of the 'illiberal other' is therefore circumscribed by the 'responsibility' of the West to uphold international norms. Peace as war thus becomes part of the simplistic assumption that action reflecting the will of the 'international community' is inherently 'good', though held by critics to create 'exclusivity and construct[s] in-group/out-group divisions'.[30]

The dominant reasoning not only further disempowers those who are to be protected, but also depoliticises the act of intervention. It obscures understanding of issues truly at stake in the intervention process, making it difficult to contest. Since the causes of conflict, state fragility or underdevelopment are constructed as a domestic problem and not sought in an unjust global political economy or specific historical context, intervention is stripped of its political underpinnings. Also, because security is the overriding imperative, it closes off political expression. This point is particularly relevant to the mixed success that women in Afghanistan have experienced: in the haste to secure and stabilise society, the complex connection between global and local (gendered) power imbalances are glossed over. Intervention, in this context, is understood as a purely moral act by the Western 'self' to protect 'illiberal others' from themselves.[31] For women particularly, intervention distils into the 'dispossession of agency, the capacity to determine what constitutes political identity'.[32]

The non-political way in which agency is framed in these liberal discourses makes it possible for peacebuilders to escape accountability for the so-called 'unintended consequences' of intervention. Chiyuki Aoi, Cedric De Coning and Ramesh Thakur contend that unintended consequences should be viewed as a 'natural' result of 'the dynamic character of complex systems'.[33] Significantly, while conceding that the effectiveness of some missions was hindered by, for instance, sexual exploitation by peacekeepers, they argue that some unintended consequences may be only vaguely connected to the peace operation itself. There is also a tendency to sensationalise the position of women under oppressive regimes for the purpose of strengthening the argument that the intervention was justified. However, a proper contextual analysis would reveal a much more complex image of, for instance, Iraqi women's deteriorating human rights situation after the invasion.[34] Members of the international community, in particular NATO and partners, are complicit in backlashes against women not only when they ignore or marginalise gender issues in the post-conflict period, but also in their selective use of gender (e.g. the threat of gender-based violence) to justify forceful intervention. This lack of accountability has profound political consequences, especially considering that subaltern women are not invisible and do speak but, as in Afghanistan, not on their own terms. In specific contexts increased representation within a gender equality framework, as propagated by international actors, could therefore be an indirect form of silencing.

Liberal feminism and gender equality – going nowhere slowly?

The narrow focus of liberal feminism on gender equality through gender mainstreaming as the path to emancipation is problematic, because it lacks nuance and contains a number of 'traps'. First, an exclusive focus on gender equality can lead to easy slippage between gender and women, especially since women often point out these inequalities. A liberal-feminist analysis overlooks the complexities of the link between gender and power and does not theorise much about gender identities or how they overlap with other identities such as race, class, sexuality and ethnicity. In a peacebuilding context, liberal-feminist approaches to gender would therefore not view gender as a product of, and productive of, security practices, linking 'these practices to patriarchal conduct outside war, and interpret[ing] security politics as a politics of gender'.[35] Second, the embedding of liberalism within mainstream discourses about gender and peacebuilding practices makes it all the more difficult to challenge. Contesting this means going against the tide of 'common sense assumptions' about gender mainstreaming, which has been widely advocated for almost two decades by international organisations such as the UN and the EU. Yet gender mainstreaming has increasingly come under fire for failing to address 'the material and discursive constructions of masculinity and femininity that shape and are shaped by organisational systems, work practices, norms and identities'.[36] Teresa Rees criticises the so-called 'tinkering and tailoring' approaches, a short-term agenda focused on individual rights, legal remedies and women's special needs.[37] Subsequently, these 'tools' become depoliticised through institutionalisation, as the latter involves unavoidable processes of co-option and adaptation of gender equality objectives to fit within taken-for-granted regulatory frameworks that are still largely defined by male standards. This explains why quotas often fail to prevent women from being relegated to the margins of security institutions. For instance, in Sierra Leone, female police officers often functioned only as cooks for male police officers.[38] What is needed is transformation – a long-term agenda for structural change that transcends masculinity and femininity and creates new standards for everyone.

The problem-solving approaches are reflected in the rapidly expanding international Women, Peace and Security (WPS) normative framework, such as the UN Security Council Resolution (UNSCR) 1325 on 'Women, Peace and Security' (2000) and UNSCR 1820 to 'End Sexual Violence against Civilians in Armed Conflict' (2008).[39] UNSCR 1325 makes the case for the protection of and participation (agency) of women by emphasising how conflict impacts on men and women differently, and that women have a positive role in peacebuilding. UNSCR 1820 recognises rape and other forms of sexual violence as crimes against humanity. In addition UN agencies firmly guide the drafting of national action plans in such countries as Liberia, Uganda, Sierra Leone and Côte d'Ivoire with increasing emphasis on indicators and other sophisticated measuring instruments.

The representation–protection dilemma of UNSCR 1325 (and its offspring) is complex. Caught between the radical anti-militarist feminist intent driving the birth of UNSCR 1325 and a world that reifies the notion of soldiers dying for the societies sending them, the Resolution represents trade-offs for women 'between influence and co-optation, and between changing international law and changing the situation of women'.[40] While the adoption of these resolutions on the one hand constitutes an unprecedented promise of visibility (representation) and an important development in norm diffusion at the global level, feminist scholars have also criticised such instruments for not challenging structural inequities, thus making them little more than blunt tools of protection.[41] The perceived global norm diffusion remains tenuous. The reasons are two-fold: first, essentialist claims that women are inherently good peacebuilders are increasingly refuted by evidence of their direct and indirect involvement in violence. With regard to the latter, the case of the Hakammas in Darfur comes to mind. Here women instigate violent male behaviour through shaming men in public places, singing songs about their cowardice.[42] Second, and perhaps more importantly, 'masculine' traits of honour and bravery continue to be valorised – not only within military institutions but also in broader society – and this seems to be world-wide. Beyond the military necessity, the kind of unfulfilled homoerotic camaraderie that drives soldiers to die for each other (as described by Sebastian Junger) can be extrapolated to explain the societal glorification of soldiers' sacrifice of life and limb.[43] Two more recent examples flowing from Israel's 'Operation Protective Edge' launched on 8 July 2014 against Palestinians in the Gaza Strip further support the entanglement of gender and militarisation. Following this violence, several websites promoted women showing their breasts in support of the Israel Defense Force. The implication is that the valorisation of the military is so strong that women would literally get naked for them (i.e. risk objectification for the military cause). There was also a notable increase in Israeli women asking to have the sperm donations of soldiers for their pregnancies.[44] Such powerful affirmation of militarism leads to a rather ambivalent situation, where inherently male military structures have opened their doors to women, but with less than benign consequences. In this respect one can cite the way in which NATO has mainstreamed women (not gender), peace and security awareness as illustrating how a resolution as the product of radical anti-militarist intent has been co-opted into the mainstream of military institutions. NATO Secretary-General, Anders Fogh Rasmussen, can therefore confidently pronounce that, in Afghanistan, the WPS policy has facilitated 'our protection of the civilian population; and the protection of our own forces'.[45] This example indicates the pervasive acceptance of masculine/militarised norms and how international organisations collude in rewarding and reinforcing such values.

The fact that the UN and other institutions extend the gender equality principle to include equal participation in ending wars does nothing to address war as an institution in itself. Nor does allowing women to participate in peace processes challenge the dominant rules and practices of international institutions.[46] While not discounting the benefits that may accrue from women's participation in decision-making, it is ironic that the integration of women into military institutions has become such a priority, particularly as UNSCR 1325 did not advocate that.

The politics of women's representation and protection

This section takes the critique further and focuses on three interrelated manifestations: the protectionist constructions of agency; the contradictions emanating from the politics of inclusion or representation; and the production of SGBV discourses and their effects.

Representations of 'good' victims and 'bad' agents

A critical interrogation of gender and agency reveals how global discourses determine who is assigned or denied agency at the grassroots level. Agency is framed hegemonically in terms that are set by international discourses, such as UNSCR 1325. The resolution is criticised for insufficiently conceptualising the range of spaces (and women's various conflicting roles within those contexts) in which peace has to be negotiated.[47] This results in the depiction of unproblematised gender roles and uncritical, utopian assumptions that a female presence will result in positive change.[48] The overemphasis on essentialist, stereotypical notions of women as victims or mothers underplays the role of women as political agents in conflict, and conversely masks the victimhood of men and boys.[49] While UNSCR 1325 attempts to establish women's agency – albeit a thin version – in peacebuilding processes, the narrow focus of UNSCR 1820 may vitiate UNSCR 1325, reinforce women's victimhood, and largely exclude SGBV against men and boys.[50] But this critique has further implications for how one connects agency and violence. Since agency is a relational concept, and liberal discourses work with a binary of femininity versus masculinity, it follows that if women are cast as victims, the immediate effect is that the positive masculinity (protector) and negative masculinity (perpetrator) of men are reinforced. That would mean, implicitly, that women have more agency where they can force others to accept theirs – thereby challenging assumptions about women's roles as peacemakers.

Partly as a consequence of the power of these international discourses, we continue to witness the general neglect of the needs and roles of civil society actors in conflict and in the planning and execution of peace reconstruction efforts. Feminist scholars have played an important role in exposing these flaws, but a substantial body of work in the donor and policy world still describes women's agency roles in homogenised and essentialised terms, for example, as 'natural' peacebuilders.[51] For instance, there is a general acceptance that women bring a specific skill set to peacekeeping in terms of searching and interrogation of women, and building trust in the system. Due to innate qualities, women are also considered to be better equipped to deal with SGBV.[52] In the case of security sector reform (SSR) – for the sake of operational efficiency – intervening states and local/national authorities therefore acknowledge women's agency as security providers.[53] However, ironically, as soon as women begin to question government action, they are labelled as troublemakers ('bad' agents), who are either sidelined or co-opted to be 'governed' and to help 'govern' other troublemakers. Field research in Cambodia in 2008 revealed the difficulty of women's organisations such as Silaka in having an impact on political reform and democratisation, and yet remaining impartial.[54]

But why is the role of women's organisations as service providers in the peacebuilding process different from the normal contestation between government and civil society actors? In order to answer this question, one should consider the unique characteristics of the postcolonial forms of governance that shape contemporary peacebuilding. Women's organisations as security providers in many African states must operate in contexts in which indigenous brotherhood networks determine the authoritative allocation of resources. Such networks consist of customary law institutions, traditional societal structures (extended families, clans, tribes), traditional authorities (such as village elders, headmen, clan chiefs), secret societies, businessmen, the military and warlords.[55] They stand in a neopatrimonial relationship with male-dominated governments. And since conventional wisdom in the development community has it that indigenous, non-state, security networks are often more 'accountable' and therefore 'indispensable for the ... distribution and delivery of justice and safety',[56] they tend to lose sight of their deeply patriarchal nature. Women are largely excluded from these authority structures, and this makes their engagement with the state not only different but also quite precarious. In the process of being the object of contention for both traditional and 'imperial' authorities (strong states, donors and international agencies), subaltern women are cast even more deeply in shadow. It therefore becomes a case of local and international 'agents' colluding to narrowly circumscribe women's agency in the security sector and limit it to the non-political sphere.

This illustration of 'thin' agency underlines, in the first instance, the need not to accept the increased acknowledgement of women's agency at face value. Making rationalist modes of masculinity and femininity the mouthpiece of subaltern women or men does not leave room for 'other' versions of masculinity and femininity. In the second place, this example drives home the importance of considering gender in context, as it relates to other identities.

The politics of inclusion/exclusion and its protectionist conundrum

Conflict creates many opportunities for women to increase their representation, politically as well as in business or as heads of households. Aili Tripp, Isabel Casimiro, Joy Kwesiga and Alice Mungwa indicate that in African countries where conflicts ended after 1985, women hold on average 24 per cent of legislative seats compared with countries that did not experience conflict, where women account for only 13 per cent of the legislative seats.[57]

Ironically the former also tend to have better representation than many of the intervener states. However, discourses on inclusion or exclusion exhibit several puzzles.

First, liberal peacebuilding is preoccupied with the inclusion of women, yet displays a rather simplistic understanding of the reasons why inclusion is important. Simple additive approaches cannot deal with the ambiguities emanating from complex contexts. It would be equally oversimplified to establish a connection between democratisation and the adoption of women-friendly policies.[58] Many non-democratic African countries such as Ethiopia, Rwanda, Uganda and Zimbabwe have adopted women's rights policies, but the test for inclusion lies in the implementation of such policies.[59] In Uganda, the 30 per cent quota system for women consists of special 'add on' seats, thus implying secondary citizenship and the pervasiveness of patriarchy and patronage politics.[60] The evidence thus defies the conventional belief that higher rates of female representation ensue because democratisation promotes a change in cultural perceptions about women's leadership potential.

A second contradiction emerges from the assumptions informing the inclusion of women in security institutions. Conventional discourses maintain simplistically that the integration of a gender perspective will contribute to making the security forces more accountable, professional, respectful of human rights, and thereby helping to decrease levels of violence. The inclusion of women automatically means strengthening the local ownership and oversight of the security sector.[61] The discourse thus assumes that women in security institutions not only change the cultural environment of the organisation (a 'pacifying presence') but also make them more democratic.[62] Yet this is an argument that is at once based on stereotypes and anecdotal evidence. More women as peacekeepers will not necessarily make the institution sensitive to gender.[63] Even if it did, it would not (as with capitalism) change the structural impediments of statebuilding as a policy regime. There is very little evidence that women in the military have actually succeeded in breaking down masculinist militarist cultures. The conviction of Lynndie England in connection with the torture and prisoner abuse at Abu Ghraib prison in Baghdad is a case in point. We should also not underestimate the power of mechanisms such as institutional culture and habit within the military which at times overwrite normative codes about gender sensitivity. Usually, it is more a case of women having to 'out-male' their colleagues in order to succeed in spite of male networks and expectations. Increased attention to gender within UN operations has raised some awareness, but, as Sandra Whitworth contends, '[g]ender critiques have been forced to fit into the UN's "way of doing business" without transforming how that business is done'.[64] Furthermore, we can no longer view the representation and protection of women in security discourses as grounded in a singular logic of masculinity versus femininity. Empirical evidence shows that we cannot make a simple causal link between expressions of violent hypermasculinity and the effects of military masculine socialisation. In this regard, Paul Higate warns that an overreliance on militarised masculinities as explanation for the sexual exploits of peacekeepers not only strips male peacekeepers of their agency, but also presents masculinity as homogenised.[65] In the same way that some women in the military may also benefit from the unequal gender arrangements as long as they do not challenge entrenched male power, not all masculinities benefit from a heterosexual reification of physical ability and courage. And, would women in the security sector necessarily benefit from replacing militarised masculinities with 'pastoral' masculinities that seek to protect?[66]

Third, liberal peacebuilding views inclusion and/or exclusion in rather instrumentalist terms. Based on liberal notions of public representation, inclusion of women in peace processes is then simplistically equated with peace – and exclusion of women with conflict. Women's representation in post-conflict Rwanda is often cited as a success story for gender mainstreaming. In 2003, Rwanda achieved the world's highest representation of women in parliament with women constituting 48.8 per cent of parliamentarians. Yet the 'representative' role of women in politics is 'represented' as based on their innate role as peacemakers and mothers. Inclusion therefore does not mean that needs will necessarily be met. Under conditions of growing authoritarianism, the gender project is also harmed, as overlapping identity constructions of race, culture and gender, as well as their political implications are not interrogated. This creates a paradoxical situation where – despite 'representation' – violent discourses that sustained the conflict in the first place are allowed to smoulder.[67] Another paradox has to do with the fact that women's exclusion may not be the result of a lack of sensitivity or insight, but rather a strategic choice, because the inclusion of women's issues may make it more difficult for parties to 'make peace'.[68]

Finally, contradictions related to the participation–protection nexus need examining. The case of the sexually-based atrocities against women in Côte d'Ivoire demonstrates that participation and protection are fundamentally linked.[69] Women's absence at the peace table during the Ouagadougou Agreement (2007) can be directly linked to the failure to protect. Women were not consulted in the international decision to dismantle the buffer zone, which led to a rise in crime and sexual violence. While women were subjected to systematic rape and sexual violence by both rebel and government forces, they had no recourse to either customary or formal law. Impunity thus reigned, making it difficult for Ivorian women to exercise agency (and participate).

The gendered logic of Western protectionism against SGBV

The discourse around SGBV has become quite robust and made sexual violence a matter of international security. At one level, the adoption of UNSCR 1820 is a positive development. It has broken the silence about crimes such as rape. However, UN rape discourses unwittingly perpetuate the protector–protected power relationship, keeping vulnerable women at the mercy of their male protectors. The reasons are as follows: UN advocacy has revolved around exposing the crime, urging governments to condemn sexual violence, and demanding and offering justice for victims (but all within the realm of the resolution as a non-political instrument). Consequently, the failure to acknowledge the incidence of SGBV (breaking the silence) is treated as the main cause for its prevalence.[70] Awareness-raising has therefore become a goal in itself. In this problem-solving framework, there is little room for considering the contextual dimensions of a complex problem. In all of this, how culture is treated by the international community is often the deciding factor: a fine line therefore has to be trodden between two extremes, namely liberal-feminist treatment of non-Western women as homogenised victims of a 'backward' society or viewing sexual violence as a stand-alone issue with little connection to pre-existing gender, other power relations, and the culture of violence that often permeates the social fabric of post-conflict countries.[71]

Both extremes are equally problematic, as sexual violence is intimately connected to the economic, political, social and cultural structures of patriarchy that existed before the conflict broke out. Sustained by hegemonic masculinist institutions, these skewed gender relations also give rise to the subordination of women in both the productive and reproductive spheres of the global economy. Since the public focus on the prevalence of sexual violence is centred on women and girls' victimhood, it might direct 'attention away from the effects of economic exploitation under neoliberal globalisation and how sexual violence in armed conflict serves economic interests'.[72] Meredeth Turshen's analysis of rape as a form of political and economic violence is instructive in this regard. She shows how, in Mozambique and Rwanda, systematic rape is used to strip women of their productive and reproductive labour power, as well as their possessions and access to land and livestock.[73] In a sense one could call this – following David Harvey's conception – a form of 'gendered accumulation by dispossession'.[74] In addition, more nuanced contextualised explanations are beginning to unravel the gendered dimensions of sexual violence against men and boys. Chris Dolan's work in the DRC points to multiple interlinked causes of the violence post-conflict, with not only economic inequality and weak governance but also changing gender relations as key factors. With 'men becoming like women' and 'women becoming like men', the violent consequences of shifts in the private–public gender dichotomy are highlighted.[75]

In view of the inadequacy of universalist tools to address complexities at the ground level, it could thus be argued that the motivation for UNSCR 1820 was pragmatic – to give a mandate for action to peacekeepers, law enforcement agencies and the justice system. Commentators should be realistic about what provisions against sexual violence can achieve. These tools are not geared for addressing root causes such as patriarchy, hypermasculinity and the motives feeding the political economy of war. The fact that provisions in the 2002 Sun City peace accord for the DRC did not help to end SGBV is therefore no surprise.[76] This agreement established a transitional government of national unity to end the conflict and pave the way for democratic elections. However, the Inter-Congolese Dialogues that preceded the agreement allowed very little room for women's voices to be heard. In the 2006 elections, the number of women elected to government was, unsurprisingly, very low. The fact that the peace negotiations failed to address entrenched gender hierarchies and discrimination against women provided fertile ground for continued gender violence in the aftermath of the conflict.[77]

International instruments devised to address SGBV also fall short when powerful states, acting in the name of the 'international community', use gender as a tool to frame the discourse of intervention – protecting women by military means. In the 2011 intervention in Libya, the prevalence (and threat) of sexual violence was not the predominant reason for the intervention, but it fed into the overall discourse against the Qaddafi regime.[78] 'International' discourses that use gender language to frame a crisis thus capitalise on the general assumption that rape is an early warning sign of a disintegrating social order. With international attention squarely focused on the so-called domestic disintegration, it becomes an issue of protection, stripped of the political connotations associated with how victims of SGBV are represented, and for what purpose. International discourses may therefore unwittingly further victimise or silence by devising ill-conceived solutions.[79]

This analysis highlights a strange discursive disconnect between international codes and policy making, and the dynamics of local/national politics and resistance. As this postcolonial-feminist critique has shown, there are many layers of assumption about agency, representation and protection that permeate liberal thinking on gender. Although these solutions are not meant to be deliberately supportive of the dominant order, liberal-feminist practice is complicit in the imperial peacebuilding project. Can radical, anti-imperialist feminisms offer a way out?

Is there life after liberal peacebuilding and feminist co-option?

Can feminists who are critical of the liberal underpinnings of the WPS system afford not to be part of the system? What form should resistance take? Jacqui True offers a nuanced answer, namely that the concern is not avoiding co-option, but rather 'whether we can afford not to engage with such institutions, when the application of gender analysis in their policymaking is clearly having political effects'.[80] There are no easy answers to this question, but postcolonial-feminist perspectives can be valuable in illustrating how they have balanced the difficult task of pointing out the oppressiveness of conventional practices, also recognising that these can be used to provide agency, albeit in a limited way. Resistance in this context is not pure opposition, but involves moving away from a binary of domination versus opposition, operating 'instead inside a structure of power that it both challenges and helps to sustain'.[81] A postcolonial-feminist alternative is therefore not pure counter-hegemonic politics seeking to build consensus around an emancipatory project. Postcolonial-feminist politics must disrupt and not reproduce the terms of domination. Anti-hegemonic or non-hegemonic feminisms work according to a different logic and require a kind of elasticity. They are sceptical of any attempt to construct general interest, to build unity, consensus, or coordinated political advocacy.[82] Elasticity occurs in many forms. First, such an approach celebrates a politics of plurality and multiplicity of locations and subjectivities; that is, rooted in context, constructed and contingent with sensitivity for overlapping identities. This stands in sharp contrast to the neoliberal understanding of context as the mere site for the execution of liberal peace frameworks. Second, a non-hegemonic postcolonial approach engages with the everyday. It reminds us that daily life is political and is both shaped and can shape international organisations. Local, everyday oppressions interact with the masculinist underpinnings of the global political system. Third, out of the constant interaction between agents and structures, hybrids emerge that have the potential to (re)connect pre-conflict political orders with post-conflict efforts at reconstituting norms, practices and institutions.

Conceptualised in this way, postcolonial feminism mutates into an outsider–insider perspective, with the potential to offer a different way of looking at peacebuilding. As an outsider rooting for the underdog, it critiques the liberal-feminist focus on affirmative politics of representation in peace processes and argues for deep agency that considers multiple overlapping identities. As an insider that engages and co-exists with other feminisms, it helps us to better grasp why and how the gendered inner workings and liberal language of international organisations entrench women's insecurity. Its hybrid identity therefore enables it to recognise the need for integrating a politics of recognition/representation with a (non-paternalistic) material politics of distribution (empowerment, protection).[83] Instead of applying global norms to local contexts, it compels us to study the politics of the everyday – the place where difference and disadvantage, as well as compliance and resistance meet.

Conclusion

The aim of this chapter was to focus on what happens in the liminal space between feminist production of security knowledge and its (re)production in the mainstream world of liberal peacebuilding. How and why does the adoption of liberal-feminist language within international institutions produce or reinforce exclusionary outcomes in peace processes? I therefore examined the connections between the assumptions of liberal peacebuilding and their manifestations at the gender level. I discussed how powerful discourses (such as WPS resolutions) and their indicators strip agency of its political connotations.

Peacebuilders are required to measure the success of international legal tools against the extent to which these instruments ensure protection of women and girls; increase women's participation in peace processes; increase general public awareness; improve cooperation and coordination at regional and intrastate levels; build capacity of those tasked to implement the plan; and improve coordinated data collection, analysis and reporting.

Such technical tasks in the name of gender equality have done little to achieve protection and participation in everyday lives. The gender strategies of the UN peacebuilding agenda do not address the needs of, for instance, women's movements in the developing world, whose overriding concern is global capitalism or neocolonialism. As an alternative to liberal-feminist complicity in the overall hegemonic project of liberal peacebuilding, the chapter offers a more nuanced and contextualised feminist alternative based on an intrinsic resistance against universalist conceptions of women, gender and self. The task to overcome liberal-feminist conventional wisdom is indeed huge, but more empirical evidence of women's and men's everyday contestations within liberal peacebuilding could shed light on the bridge-building qualities that a postcolonial-feminist frame brings to peacebuilding.

Acknowledgements

This chapter is partly based upon research conducted while the author was a Peace Studies research fellow at the Consortium for Peace Studies, University of Calgary, Canada, in 2010. This chapter is a slightly altered version of the article of the same name that appeared in *International Peacekeeping*, vol. 19, no. 4, August 2012, Taylor & Francis Ltd, www.tandfonline.com, reprinted by permission of the publisher.

Notes

1 Kathleen Kuehnast, 'President Obama's Speech and Gender', US Institute of Peace, 20 May 2011 (at: www.usip.org/publications/president-obamas-speech-and-gender).
2 Mary Hope Schwoebel, 'Women and the Arab Spring', US Institute of Peace, 5 May 2011 (at: www.usip.org/publications/women-and-the-arab-spring).
3 Kuehnast (note 1 above).
4 Kathleen R. Carter, 'Should International Relations Consider Rape a Weapon of War?', *Politics and Gender*, vol. 6, no. 3, 2010, pp. 356–360.
5 Sanam Anderlini, 'Translating Global Agreement into National and Local Commitments', in Kathleen Kuehnast, Chantal de Jonge Oudraat and Helga Hernes (eds), *Women and War. Power and Protection in the 21st Century*, Washington, DC: US Institute of Peace Press, 2011, pp. 23–24.
6 See for instance Mark Duffield, *Global Governance and the New Wars: The Merging of Development and Security*, London: Zed Books, 2001; Oliver P. Richmond, 'The Problem of Peace: Understanding the "Liberal Peace"', *Conflict, Security and Development*, vol. 6, no. 3, 2006, pp. 291–314; Richmond, *Peace in International Relations*, London: Routledge, 2008; Vivienne Jabri, 'War, Government, Politics: A Critical Response to the Hegemony of the Liberal Peace', in Richmond (ed.)

Palgrave Advances in Peacebuilding. Critical Developments and Approaches, New York: Palgrave Macmillan, 2010, pp. 41–57. Relatively speaking, far fewer texts offer a gender critique of peacebuilding. See for instance Vivienne Jabri, 'Feminist Ethics and Hegemonic Global Politics', *Alternatives*, vol. 29, 2004, pp. 265–284; Tarja Väyrynen, 'Gender and UN Peace Operations: The Confines of Modernity', *International Peacekeeping*, vol. 11, no. 1, 2004, pp. 125–142; Väyrynen, 'Gender and Peacebuilding', in Richmond (ed.), *Palgrave Advances*, pp. 137–153.

7 Eli Stamnes, *The Responsibility to Protect: Integrating Gender Perspectives into Policies and Practices*, report no. 8, Oslo: Norwegian Institute of International Affairs, 2010, pp. 5, 11.

8 The UN Special Envoy for Libya, Abdul Elah al-Khatib, warned that the grave humanitarian conditions following Qaddafi's threat of violence against the demonstrators included 'significant' protection concerns over gender-based violence. See UNifeed, 'UN/Libya', 4 April 2011 (at: www.unmultimedia.org/tv/unifeed/d/17361.html). US Ambassador to the UN, Susan Rice, also told the Security Council that evidence (referring to the allegations that Libyan government soldiers had been issued Viagra to increase their potential to perform mass rapes) did indeed exist of widespread raping of women within the opposition by Libyan forces. Gordon Lubold, 'Libyan Forces Use Rape as Weapon of War, Experts Say', US Institute of Peace, 9 June 2011 (at: www.usip.org/publications/libyan-forces-use-rape-weapon-war).

9 Johann Galtung, *Peace by Peaceful Means: Peace and Conflict, Development and Civilization*, London: Sage, 1996, p. 112.

10 See Neil Cooper, Mandy Turner and Michael Pugh, 'The End of History and the Last Liberal Peacebuilder: A Reply to Roland Paris', *Review of International Studies*, vol. 37, no. 4, 2011, pp. 1995–2007.

11 Gayatri Chakravorty Spivak, 'Can the Subaltern Speak?', in Cary Nelson and Larry Grossberg (eds), *Marxism and the Interpretation of Culture*, Basingstoke: Macmillan, 1988, pp. 271–313, reprinted in Patrick Williams and Laura Chrisman (eds) *Colonial Discourse and Post-Colonial Theory: A Reader*, New York: Harvester Wheatsheaf, 1994, pp. 66–111.

12 See Jeff Huysmans, cited in Benjamin Sovacool and Saul Halfon, 'Reconstructing Iraq: Merging Discourses of Security and Development', *Review of International Studies*, vol. 33, no. 2, 2007, p. 228.

13 Julietta Hua and Holly Nigorizawa, 'US Sex Trafficking, Women's Human Rights and the Politics of Representation', *International Feminist Journal of Politics*, vol. 12, nos. 3–4, 2010, pp. 416–417.

14 As in Spivak (note 11 above), p. 70.

15 Mandy Turner and Michael Pugh, 'Towards a New Agenda for Transforming War Economies', *Conflict, Security and Development*, vol. 6, no. 3, 2006, pp. 471–479; Oliver P. Richmond, 'A Genealogy of Peace and Conflict Theory', in Richmond, *Palgrave Advances* (note 6 above), p. 22.

16 Roger Southall, 'Africa in the Contemporary World', in Patrick J. McGowan, Scarlett Cornelissen and Philip Nel (eds), *Power, Wealth and Global Equity. An International Relations Textbook for Africa*, 3rd edn, Cape Town: University of Cape Town Press, 2006, p. 230.

17 Sylvia Chant and Carolyn Pedwell, *Women, Gender and the Informal Economy: An Assessment of ILO Research and Suggested Ways Forward*, Geneva: International Labour Office, 2008, p. 1.

18 Caroline O. N. Moser, 'Gender Planning in the Third World: Meeting Practical and Strategic Needs', in Rebecca Grant and Kathleen Newland (eds), *Gender and International Relations*, Bloomington, IN: Indiana University Press, 1991, p. 87.

19 Jabri, 'War, Government, Politics' (note 6 above), p. 42.

20 *Ibid.* Also, Francis M. Deng, 'Reconciling Sovereignty with Responsibility: A Basis for International Humanitarian Action', in John W. Harbeson and Donald Rothchild (eds), *Africa in World Politics: Reforming Political Order*, 4th edn, Boulder, CO: Westview Press, 2009, pp. 345–383.
21 Alyson M. Cole, 'The Other V-Word: The Politics of Victimhood Fueling George W. Bush's War Machine', in Robin L. Riley, Chandra Talpade Mohanty and Minnie Bruce Pratt (eds), *Feminism and War: Confronting US Imperialism*, London: Zed Books, 2008, pp. 117–130.
22 Kenneth Katzman, *Afghanistan: Politics, Elections, and Government Performance*, Washington, DC: Congressional Research Service, 2012 (at: www.fas.org/sgp/crs/row/RS21922.pdf), pp. 53, 56.
23 Franz-Michael Mellbin, 'Afghanistan Still One of the Worst Places to be a Woman, Says EU Ambassador', *The Guardian*, 7 March 2014 (at: www.theguardian.com/world/2014/mar/07/hamid-karzai-afghanistan-women-eu-mellbin).
24 *Ibid.*
25 National Democratic Institute for International Affairs, *Preliminary Statement of the National Democratic Institute's Election Mission for Afghanistan's 2014 Presidential and Provincial Council Elections*, 7 April 2014, Kabul/Washington, DC: National Democratic Institute for International Affairs (at: www.ndi.org/files/NDI-Afghanistan-2014-Election-Mission-Preliminary-Statement-4.7.2014.pdf).
26 Torunn Wimpelmann, *Leaving Them to It? Women's Rights in Transitioning Afghanistan*, Asia Programme, May 2014, Afghanistan: Opportunity in Crisis Series no. 5 (at: www.chathamhouse.org/sites/files/chathamhouse/field/field_document/20140522Women'sRightsAfghanistanWimpelmann.pdf).
27 Gayatri Chakravorty Spivak, 'Three Women's Texts and a Critique of Imperialism', *Critical Inquiry*, vol. 12, no. 1, 1985, p. 243.
28 Anna M. Agathangelou and Lily H. M. Ling, 'Power, Borders, Security, Wealth: Lessons of Violence and Desire from September 11', *International Studies Quarterly*, vol. 48, no. 3, 2004, p. 518.
29 Rita Abrahamsen, 'African Studies and the Postcolonial Challenge', *African Affairs*, vol. 102, no. 407, 2003, p. 190.
30 Berit Bliesemann de Guevara and Florian P. Kühn, '"The International Community Needs to Act": Loose Use and Empty Signalling of a Hackneyed Concept', *International Peacekeeping*, vol. 18, no. 2, 2011, p. 137.
31 Jorg Meyer, 'The Concealed Violence of Modern Peace(-Making)', *Millennium – Journal of International Studies*, vol. 36, no. 3, 2008, p. 555.
32 Jabri, 'War, Government, Politics' (note 6 above), p. 42.
33 Chiyuki Aoi, Cedric De Coning and Ramesh Thakur, 'Unintended Consequences, Complex Peace Operations and Peacebuilding Systems', in Chiyuki Aoi, Cedric De Coning and Ramesh Thakur (eds), *Unintended Consequences of Peacekeeping Operations*, New York: UN University Press, 2007, p. 7.
34 Shahnaz Khan, 'Afghan Women: The Limits of Colonial Rescue', in Riley *et al.* (note 21 above), pp. 173–174.
35 Elisabeth Prügl, 'Feminist International Relations', *Politics and Gender*, vol. 7, no. 1, 2011, p. 112.
36 Yvonne Benschop and Mieke Verloo, 'Sisyphus' Sisters: Can Gender Mainstreaming Escape the Genderedness of Organizations?', *Journal of Gender Studies*, vol. 15, no. 1, 2006, p. 19.
37 Teresa Rees, 'Reflections on the Uneven Development of Gender Mainstreaming in Europe', *International Feminist Journal of Politics*, vol. 7, no. 4, 2005, pp. 555–574.
38 Megan Bastick, *Integrating Gender in Post-Conflict Security Sector Reform*, Policy Paper 29, Geneva: Centre for the Democratic Control of Armed Forces (DCAF), 2008, p. 16.

39 UN Security Council Resolution 1325, 31 October 2000 (at: www.un.org/events/res_1325e.pdf); UN Security Council Resolution 1820, 19 June 2008 (at: www.peacewomen.org/assets/file/BasicWPSDocs/scr1820english.pdf). Since then follow-up resolutions have been adopted to facilitate implementation: 1888 (2009), 1889 (2009) and 1960 (2010).
40 Christine Bell and Catherine O'Rourke, 'Peace Agreements or Pieces of Paper? The Impact of UNSC Resolution 1325 on Peace Processes and Their Agreements', *International and Comparative Law Quarterly*, vol. 59, October 2010, p. 945.
41 For a positive interpretation see Torunn L. Tryggestad, 'Trick or Treat? The UN and Implementation of Security Council Resolution 1325 on Women, Peace, and Security', *Global Governance*, vol. 15, 2009, pp. 539–557; Laura J. Shepherd, 'Sex, Security and Superhero(in)es: From 1325 to 1820 and Beyond', *International Feminist Journal of Politics*, vol. 13, no. 4, 2011, pp. 504–521. For a less optimistic view see, Carol Cohn, 'Mainstreaming Gender in UN Security Policy: A Path to Political Transformation?', in Shirin M. Rai and Georgina Waylen (eds), *Global Governance. Feminist Perspectives*, New York: Palgrave Macmillan, 2008, pp. 186–191.
42 Laura Sjoberg and Caron E. Gentry, *Mothers, Monsters, Whores: Women's Violence in Global Politics*, London: Zed Books, 2007; Azzain Mohamed, 'From Instigating Violence to Building Peace: The Changing Role of Women in Darfur Region of Western Sudan', *African Journal on Conflict Resolution*, vol. 4, no. 1, 2004, pp. 11–26.
43 Sebastian Junger, *War*, New York: Twelve, 2010.
44 Jenny Kutner, 'Israeli Women are Showing Support for the IDF (Israel Defense Forces) – by Showing Their Boobs', *Salon*, 24 July 2014 (at: www.salon.com/2014/07/24/israeli_women_are_showing_support_for_the_idf_by_showing_their_boobs/); Stuart Winer, 'Israeli Soldiers' Sperm in Hot Demand', *The Times of Israel*, 10 August 2014 (at: www.timesofisrael.com/israeli-soldiers-sperm-in-hot-demand/).
45 Cynthia Cockburn, 'Snagged On The Contradiction: NATO, UNSC Resolution 1325, and Feminist Responses', No to War – No to NATO Annual Meeting, Dublin, 15–17 April 2011 (at: www.wloe.org/fileadmin/Files-EN/PDF/no_to_nato/women_nato_2011/NATO1325.pdf).
46 Cohn (note 41 above), pp. 197–198.
47 Nicola Pratt and Sophie Richter-Devroe, 'Critically Examining UNSCR 1325 on Women, Peace and Security', *International Feminist Journal of Politics*, vol. 13, no. 4, 2011, p. 494.
48 Fionnuala Ní Aoláin and Eilish Rooney, 'Underenforcement and Intersectionality: Gendered Aspects of Transition for Women', *The International Journal of Transitional Justice*, vol. 1, no. 3, 2007, pp. 349–350.
49 Bell and O'Rourke (note 40 above), p. 945.
50 Anderlini (note 5 above), p. 21; Carter (note 4 above), p. 346; Amy Barrow, 'UN Security Council Resolutions 1325 and 1820: Constructing Gender in Armed Conflict and International Humanitarian Law', *International Review of the Red Cross*, vol. 92, no. 877, 2010, p. 234.
51 See for instance, Sjoberg and Gentry (note 42 above), as opposed to Megan Bastick and Kristin Valasek (eds), *Gender and Security Sector Reform Toolkit*, Geneva: DCAF, OSCE/ODIHR, UN-INSTRAW, 2008; Margaret Verwijk, *Developing the Security Sector: Security for Whom, by Whom?*, The Hague: Ministry of Foreign Affairs, 2007.
52 Bastick (note 38 above), pp. 13–14; Olivera Simić, 'Does the Presence of Women Really Matter? Towards Combating Male Sexual Violence in Peacekeeping Operations', *International Peacekeeping*, vol. 17, no. 2, 2010, p. 194.
53 Kristin Valasek, 'Security Sector Reform and Gender', in Bastick and Valasek (note 51 above), pp. 6–8.
54 Interview with Thida Khus, *Silaka*, Phnom Penh, July 2008.

55 Eric Scheye, *State-Provided Service, Contracting out, and Non-state Networks: Justice and Security as Public and Private Goods and Services*, Paris: Organisation for Economic Co-operation and Development, 2009 (at: www.oecd.org/dataoecd/43/8/43599221.pdf), pp. 6–7.
56 *Ibid.*, p. 8.
57 Aili Mari Tripp, Isabel Casimiro, Joy Kwesiga and Alice Mungwa, *African Women's Movements: Changing Political Landscape*, Cambridge: Cambridge University Press, 2009, pp. 195–196.
58 Ronald Inglehart, Pippa Norris and Christian Welzel, 'Gender Equality and Democracy', *Comparative Sociology*, vol. 1, nos. 3–4, 2002, pp. 321–345.
59 Tripp *et al.* (note 57 above), pp. 8–9.
60 Josephine Ahikire, *Women's Engagement with Political Parties in Contemporary Africa: Reflections on Uganda's Experience*, Policy Brief 65, Johannesburg: Centre for Policy Studies, 2009 (at: www.peacewomen.org/assets/file/Resources/Academic/part_womensengagementpoliticalpartiesafricauganda_ahikire_2010.pdf).
61 Valasek (note 53 above), pp. 4–5.
62 Simić (note 52 above), p. 189.
63 *Ibid.*, p. 194.
64 Sandra Whitworth, *Men, Militarism and UN Peacekeeping: A Gendered Analysis*, London: Lynne Rienner, 2004, p. 17.
65 Paul Higate, 'Peacekeepers, Masculinities, and Sexual Exploitation', *Men and Masculinities*, vol. 10, no. 1, 2007, pp. 99–119.
66 Iris Marion Young, 'The Logic of Masculinist Protection: Reflections on the Current Security State', *Signs*, vol. 29, no. 1, 2003, p. 6.
67 Jennie E. Burnet, 'Gender Balance and the Meanings of Women in Governance in Post-conflict Rwanda', *African Affairs*, vol. 107, no. 427, 2008, pp. 361–386.
68 Bell and O'Rourke (note 40 above), p. 976.
69 Amnesty International, 'Côte d'Ivoire: Targeting Women: The Forgotten Victims of the Conflict', Washington, DC, 15 March 2007 (at: www.refworld.org/docid/45ffa4dd2.html).
70 Eve Ayiera, 'Sexual Violence in Conflict: A Problematic International Discourse', *Feminist Africa*, no. 14, 2010, pp. 10–11.
71 *Ibid.*, pp. 14–15.
72 Janie L. Leatherman, *Sexual Violence and Armed Conflict*, Cambridge: Polity, 2011. p. 12.
73 Meredeth Turshen, 'The Political Economy of Rape. An Analysis of Systematic Rape and Sexual Abuse of Women During Armed Conflict in Africa', in Caroline O. N. Moser and Fiona C. Clark (eds) *Victims, Perpetrators or Actors? Gender, Armed Conflict and Political Violence*, London: Zed Books, 2001, pp. 55–68.
74 The term 'accumulation by dispossession' refers to neoliberal capitalist policies such as privatisation that have led to a centralisation of wealth and power in the hands of a few; David Harvey, *The New Imperialism*, Oxford: Oxford University Press, 2005; Ellen Meiksins Wood, *Empire of Capital*, London: Verso, 2003.
75 Chris Dolan, *'War is Not Yet Over': Community Perceptions of Sexual Violence and its Underpinnings in Eastern DRC*, London: International Alert, November 2010 (at: www.international-alert.org/resources/publications/war-not-yet-over).
76 Robert Jenkins and Anne-Marie Goetz, 'Addressing Sexual Violence in Internationally Mediated Peace Negotiations', *International Peacekeeping*, vol. 17, no. 2, 2010, pp. 263, 275.
77 V-Day, 'Violence in the DRC: Background' (at: www.vday.org/drcongo/background).
78 RFI English, 'Kadhafi Used Rape as Weapon of War, Moreno-Ocampo Claims', 9 June 2011 (at: http://allafrica.com/stories/201106090579.html).

79 See Niels Nagelhus Schia and Benjamin De Carvalho, *'Nobody Gets Justice Here! Addressing Sexual and Gender-Based Violence and the Rule of Law in Liberia*, Security in Practice 5, Working Paper 761, Oslo: NUPI, 2009. The report contends that in Liberia the establishment of Women and Children Protection Sections (WACPS) next to police stations in urban areas alone is a quick fix by the international community to address SGBV without taking cognisance of the broader framework of the reconstruction of both statutory and customary rule of law institutions.
80 True, cited in Cohn (note 41 above), p. 205.
81 Abrahamsen (note 29 above), p. 209.
82 William K. Carroll, 'Hegemony, Counter-Hegemony, Anti-Hegemony', *Socialist Studies*, vol. 2, no. 2, 2006, p. 30.
83 Nancy Fraser, 'Reframing Justice in a Globalizing World', *New Left Review*, vol. 36, 2005, p. 73.

PART II
Imposing peace

6 UNTAC, peace and violence in Cambodia

Caroline Hughes

Described as one of the United Nation's first efforts at a complex peacebuilding mandate, the United Nations Transitional Authority in Cambodia (UNTAC) combined traditional peacekeeping duties such as monitoring a ceasefire with tasks that, at the time, were regarded as innovative and ambitious aspects of a 'peacebuilding' agenda. These included supervising the incumbent administration, monitoring human rights and establishing local human rights organisations, and creating a neutral political environment for free and fair elections. However, UNTAC was not entrusted with a peace enforcement mission, and the failure to maintain the ceasefire and end the war in Cambodia was widely attributed to this limitation. UNTAC's deputy military commander Jean-Michel Loridon resigned after his proposal to use military force to compel Khmer Rouge cooperation was rejected by the UN. According to some contemporary observers, including diplomats and some within the mission, the failure of UNTAC to interpret its mandate more robustly was to blame for the fact that the election result was only partially respected.[1] In other words, much discussion during the mid-1990s blamed UNTAC for using too little violence, rather than too much. Some observers had regarded the high turn-out of Cambodian voters on election day as evidence of the population's high hopes for democracy, despite the fact that in some cases local officials forced individuals to go and vote. For these observers, UNTAC's failure to act more forcefully was a betrayal of popular Cambodian democratic aspirations.[2]

With hindsight, however, this debate misses the point. UNTAC, perhaps like most peace missions, contained a number of different factions promoting different conceptions of peace. These ranged from: a temporary ceasefire sufficient to allow external actors to disengage; to a full-fledged, thoroughly embedded liberal peace; to a stable neoliberal market. Cambodian actors, similarly, had different goals, and different actors nationally and locally subscribed to different aspects of this agenda and sought international alliances to pursue them.

Consequently, the 'peacebuilding' aspects of UNTAC's mandate represented an awkward amalgam of realpolitik, liberal triumphalism, and economic and political opportunism from the start, which continued over the subsequent two decades of international aid and diplomacy. A range of international actors have veered haphazardly between ideological conviction and opportunism in response to their own interests, to the changing international environment and to perceptions of distributions of political power within Cambodia. The result has been neither a consistent and concerted effort to promote a 'liberal peace' in Cambodia, although elements of this have been attempted; nor has the Cambodian government been permitted entirely free rein to reconstruct authoritarianism. Rather, Cambodia's political trajectory, like all political contexts, has been contingent upon shifting concatenations of interest and power – involving domestic, regional and international players.

What has become evident over the 20 years since UNTAC's departure from Cambodia is that the most powerful alliances were those that successfully united Cambodian elites with international investors in a form of predatory capitalism that has been brutal and rapacious. At the same time, the engagement of international actors, including bilateral and multilateral donors, in promoting a liberal politics in Cambodia during and since UNTAC's deployment has not helped to create a hospitable environment for grassroots actors struggling from below for social justice and more equal distributions of power. A large variety of such movements have sprung up over the past two decades, protesting land-grabbing, privatisation of natural resources, poor conditions in factories and destruction of forests. These movements have consistently been the target of violent repression by an increasingly authoritarian government; and liberal peacebuilders have not only failed to prevent this, but have also at times acted in ways that made repression easier and more likely.

International actors with a remit to promote post-conflict reconstruction and liberal peacebuilding in Cambodia have actively engaged emerging political movements of the poor in Cambodia in ways which have undermined their chances of securing meaningful concessions from Cambodia's elite. In line with neoliberal orthodoxy, Cambodia's 'development partners' post-UNTAC regarded the key task to be the establishment of a well-functioning regime of property rights and labour relations to facilitate free market activity. This has been regarded as a matter of institution- and capacity-building rather than a political struggle over distributions of resources and power. In attempting to steer societal activism into avenues that are non-threatening to potential investors, international interveners have significantly inhibited the ability of Cambodian social movements to make empowered claims to a stake in the post-war economic and political order.

In part, this outcome is due to the legacy of the deep disruption of both traditional and class-based social movements in Cambodia during the war. Superpower intervention in Cambodia in the 1960s and 1970s was extraordinarily violent even by Cold War standards. Between 1965 and 1975 more bombs were dropped on Cambodia than were dropped by all the Allied forces anywhere in the world during the whole of World War Two, costing up to 1.5 million lives.[3] Subsequently, under the radical communist Khmer Rouge regime of 1975 to 1979, a further 1.8 million people – 21 per cent of the population – died, and virtually the whole nation was forcibly displaced in an attempt to destroy connections between people and birthplaces. The Khmer Rouge set out deliberately to dismantle societal structures down to the family level. Although some of these structures recovered under the Vietnamese-backed regime that governed most of the country from the capital Phnom Penh in the 1980s, repression and civil war prevented the emergence of class-based organisations with the power to defend or contest the interests of particular economic groups.

Part of the liberal peacebuilding agenda since UNTAC has been explicitly to foster and support Cambodian civil society groups. However, civil society was understood not to mean class-based social movements that could articulate and defend collective interests in the context of rapid economic change, but rather a set of professionalised organisations that could scrutinise and critique state policy, when this deviated from international norms. International engagement with local organisations in Cambodia has been didactic and relatively unsympathetic to local conceptions of customary rights and obligations.

Consequently, protest movements have found it difficult to find useful political allies, not only within the Cambodian elite, but also via transnational or international affiliations. This chapter will show that international prescriptions for 'civil society' from UNTAC onwards have in fact undermined the struggles of workers and the poor in Cambodia to claim a share of the peace dividend. This occurred because funding, training and guidance for emergent local activist groups by international organisations has been uniformly based upon anodyne conceptions of a liberal politics that takes no account of existing structures of power in Cambodia and how these might be tackled. International involvement in Cambodia, in consequence, has at best failed to assist the poor in their struggles with an emerging class of predatory capitalists, and has at worst rendered them more vulnerable to violent suppression by the Cambodian government and its allies in the military and business. The latter outcome has been particularly prominent in cases where local activism interfered with the establishment of neoliberal regimes for controlling labour and property rights. Although the civil war is over in Cambodia, the new order that UNTAC ushered in, and which subsequent aid donors, foreign investors and diplomatic missions have viewed with overall approval, continues to be based upon violence, associated in particular with a wave of enclosures of natural resources that have dispossessed the Cambodian poor.

Twenty-five years after UNTAC's departure, a violent peace prevails in Cambodia, in which a populist authoritarian government allied with a predatory capitalist class habitually resorts to violence to police a new economic order based on primitive accumulation. In the decades since private ownership of land was legally recognised in 1989, Cambodia's development strategy has to a significant extent focused on the award by the state of tracts of land to private business for the purposes of logging and/or establishing plantations or mines. This has entailed the expropriation of large areas of land and fresh water that were previously used as common resources for grazing, hunting and gathering, fishing and sometimes agricultural cultivation. The efforts devoted to human rights training and 'civil society' promotion by international agencies have failed to grapple with the fundamental cleavage in Cambodian society between those who profited from the transition to free markets by using political power to obtain economic resources, and those who found their access to land and other resources inexorably constrained. International intervention has focused on attempting to impose models of liberal citizenship and property ownership that are highly vulnerable in a context of violent expropriation. In the context of a weak post-conflict society faced with entrenched transnational networks of natural resource extraction that have long implicated the Cambodian state, liberal forms of citizenship and ownership have offered no protection to the poor, but have rather been complicit in their (continued) dispossession. At the same time, international interveners have ignored or even undermined local attempts to defend livelihoods through a rhetoric of customary rights that could have been more successful in extracting concessions from the elite.

This chapter explores this process, beginning with an examination of UNTAC's approach to the liberal peace, and its conception of civil society in Cambodia. The role of international actors in cultivating particular forms of activism, while ignoring or suppressing others, is linked to the failure of any social forces in Cambodia to successfully protest the rampant expropriation of land and forests over the twenty years after UNTAC. The chapter concludes with an account of contemporary fault lines in the Cambodian political order and the current nature of Cambodia's violent peace.

UNTAC and the liberal peace

UNTAC's mandate was negotiated in 1991 as part of the Paris Peace Accords signed within months of the collapse of the Soviet Union and the end of the Cold War. It was pioneering in that it envisaged a comprehensive political settlement to the conflict, going beyond traditional activities such as overseeing ceasefires and demobilising armies to incorporate the institution of a new political system. The Paris Peace Agreements included provisions for multi-party elections to produce a constitutional assembly that would draft a new constitution. Certain provisions of that constitution were stipulated in advance by the Peace Accords; for example, that the constitution would contain human rights safeguards 'consistent with the provisions of the Universal Declaration of Human Rights and other relevant international instruments'. The accords also stipulated, 'The constitution will state that Cambodia will follow a system of liberal democracy, on the basis of pluralism.'[4]

In June the following year, as UNTAC troops struggled to maintain a ceasefire on the ground in Cambodia, representatives from Southeast Asian countries, bilateral donors and multilateral donor agencies met in Tokyo to form the 'International Committee on the Reconstruction of Cambodia'. This was a donor club formed to coordinate international aid to Cambodia following the peace process. Its founding document, the Tokyo Declaration on the Rehabilitation and Reconstruction of Cambodia, included the observation that 'International financial institutions stressed the importance of market-based reforms in Cambodia to increasing output in major sectors of the economy', and commented on remaining 'fundamental institutional and policy-related constraints to further economic progress which must be addressed promptly'. Members of the committee committed themselves to providing technical and other assistance for 'appropriate approaches that ensure and strengthen Cambodia's own capacity to sustain its development' as well as offering an avenue for Cambodia 'to be integrated into the dynamic economic development of the Asia-Pacific region and of the world'.[5] These provisions, written into the basic documents determining international engagement in post-conflict Cambodia, suggest that the liberal nature of the Cambodian peace was decreed from the outset, by external actors.

The prominent incorporation of liberal provisions in the Paris Agreements fulfilled a tactical role. The embrace of free market economics was uncontroversial among signatories to the Agreements. The Phnom Penh regime, heir to the Vietnamese invasion of Cambodia in 1979, had abandoned collectivisation and embarked on its first reforms in the late 1980s, taking initial steps towards land privatisation in 1989. Economic reforms in China and Vietnam were a powerful motivator for improved relations between the two countries, to which the issue of Cambodia was a significant obstacle. And on the crest of an economic boom, capital-rich Thai businesses saw Cambodia as an investment opportunity.[6] The disastrous experience of all the Asian communist countries with collectivisation, and eagerness among faltering communist regimes to grasp a share of the 'East Asian miracle', made the move to a free market an uncontroversial choice.

Provisions regarding liberal democracy and respect for human rights were designed to sanitise an agreement which ran the risk of bringing the infamous Khmer Rouge back into government. The Khmer Rouge regime of 1975–1979 had implemented brutal policies of forced collectivisation, producing conditions of virtual slave labour in which up to a million Cambodians died. Although defeated by an invading Vietnamese army in 1979, following defection of a group of Khmer Rouge provincial commanders, the Khmer Rouge had fled to the Thai border where they were resuscitated by support from regional and international actors, particularly the Thai military and China. The Khmer Rouge's political vehicle, the Party of Democratic

Kampuchea, participated with republican and royalist movements in a Coalition Government of Democratic Kampuchea (CGDK) which claimed throughout the 1980s to be the rightful government of Cambodia. In the context of the Cold War, the CGDK continued to occupy Cambodia's seat at the United Nations.

As contemporary analysts pointed out, the Cambodian stalemate of the 1980s had suited regional players well. ASEAN benefited from Vietnam's preoccupation with Cambodia; Thailand used the issue to gain military support from the US; and the issue offered China an opportunity to improve relations with ASEAN members, particularly Thailand.[7] However, as the Cold War came to an end, the Vietnamese army withdrew and aid from the Soviet Bloc to the Phnom Penh government dried up, the Khmer Rouge appeared as a renewed threat to the stability of the region. A successful offensive by the movement's armed forces, the National Army of Democratic Kampuchea, in September 1989 led to fears for the collapse of the Phnom Penh government.

This led to some alarm in Western circles – in the US, for example, Congressional pressure prompted the administration of George H. W. Bush to end US support for CGDK occupation of Cambodia's seat in the UN in 1990 because of the Khmer Rouge's participation in the coalition. The inclusion of the Khmer Rouge in the peace negotiations was also internationally controversial. According to one observer, the plan to incorporate elections into the peace process was conceived as 'the surest way to prevent a return to power by the Khmer Rouge. According to this rather optimistic scenario, the Khmer Rouge, because of its past record of brutality, will certainly lose any free elections and China would then use the result as its face-saving excuse for cutting off the arms flow to its Khmer Rouge allies.'[8]

Liberal human rights provisions were incorporated into the agreements with the explicit aim of ensuring that the elections were, indeed, fair, and that any government elected – even if it did ultimately end up including the Khmer Rouge or some faction of them – could not return to 'the policies and practices of the past' without thereby attracting further external intervention. External signatories to the Paris Peace Accords, including the Permanent Five members of the Security Council, all the countries that were then members of ASEAN as well as Cambodia's neighbours, Vietnam and the Lao People's Democratic Republic, undertook to promote and encourage respect for and observance of human rights and fundamental freedoms in Cambodia as embodied in the relevant international instruments and the relevant resolutions of the United Nations General Assembly, in order, in particular, to prevent the recurrence of human rights abuses.[9]

UNTAC was charged with responsibility 'during the transitional period for fostering an environment in which respect for human rights shall be ensured'.[10] Following the transitional period, the Agreements stipulated that the UN Commission on Human Rights should 'continue to monitor closely the human rights situation in Cambodia, including, if necessary, by the

UNTAC, peace and violence in Cambodia 123

appointment of a Special Rapporteur who would report his findings annually to the Commission and to the General Assembly'.[11] Because of the specific nature of these human rights commitments, UNTAC became the first peacekeeping operation to include a dedicated Human Rights Component. The Component was supposed to oversee human rights during the transitional period, educate the population about human rights and investigate specific cases of abuse, taking appropriate remedial action.[12]

UN Secretary-General Boutros Boutros-Ghali, in his report on the implementation of the Paris Accords, referred to human rights education as the 'cornerstone' of UN human rights promotion.[13] He stated, 'The Cambodians themselves... clearly have the obligation to promote and protect human rights and fundamental freedoms in Cambodia',[14] and that, consequently, 'Cambodians must fully understand both the content and significance of those rights and freedoms in order to be in a position to know when and how to protect them properly.'[15] UNTAC was also mandated to 'encourage the establishment of indigenous human rights associations',[16] who could gradually take over the UN's human rights education programme. Civic education regarding the electoral process and voting was also initiated on a grand scale, along with a dedicated team for delivering information and education to the population, including through a UN radio station.

Liberal provisions were thus incorporated in the Paris Agreements in large part because of concerns by international players to avoid backlash from liberal constituencies at home if further atrocities occurred in Cambodia, or if the Khmer Rouge were strengthened as a result of the peace process. However, the negotiation of the terms of the peace accords coincided with a wave of interest in the promotion of liberal cosmopolitanism, in the wake of the Cold War's end. Cambodia therefore became an early test case for liberal idealism, and attempts to promote human rights in Cambodia during UNTAC and after its departure represent a fascinating illustration of how promotion of the liberal peace was attempted. Yet UNTAC's own treatment of human rights issues – in particular, its lacklustre performance in investigating abuses and arresting and prosecuting abusers – was highly ambivalent, reflecting a tension between tactical and idealistic approaches to human rights promotion.

This tension was evident in two dimensions. First, UNTAC itself was a divided mission. It incorporated some actors for whom the primary concern of the mission was to accomplish a transfer of power to a government with an acceptable level of control and leave with the UN's reputation and organisational interests intact. Other actors, recruited from outside the UN, from universities and NGOs, and including many who spoke Khmer well and had extensive experience in border refugee camps or among refugee communities abroad, had broader and more liberal ambitions. Debate within the mission over human rights promotion exemplified the different perspectives of these camps. For example, the Human Rights Component argued that 'attention ... had to be focused, from the very start of the mission, on the post-transitional period, on ways and means to ensure future human rights protection and continued international involvement. The Component saw its work as being only the beginning of a long term process tied in part to a successful transition to democratic government.'[17] Other sections of the UN were reluctant to accept such an open-ended engagement.[18] The differences between these two groups was exemplified by the dissenting final report circulated by the Human Rights Component at the end of the mission, which complained bitterly about the lack of support among senior managers of the mission for firm action against abusers.

Second, and perhaps more interestingly, there was ambivalence over how human rights policy should be implemented among the more liberal actors within the mission, and within the UN agencies subsequently charged with protecting human rights in Cambodia on an ongoing basis after UNTAC departed. The UN had stipulated in its initial planning that human rights promotion needed to be 'culturally sensitive' and 'generally accessible' to Cambodians.[19] However, it was unclear whether this was to be understood in instrumental terms as advancing the ability of UNTAC to work effectively to protect Cambodians, rather than in political terms as opening space for Cambodians to debate the terms of their own emancipation.

UNTAC's Human Rights Component struggled throughout the transitional process with the tension between the dictates of ideas of liberal peace, on the one hand, and the idea of cultural relevance on the other. It was asserted early on that 'the message to be disseminated would be consonant with concepts and principles of Cambodian society today'.[20] This formulation opened the prospect for a potentially empowering, locally negotiated alliance between international human rights activists and local Cambodian reformers. However, input from Cambodian 'concepts and principles' was in practice very limited, as the Human Rights Component focused on promoting a strongly liberal version of human rights in which Cambodian engagement was limited to those considered 'ready' to take part. However, it is important to note also that within Cambodia, there were no organised groups or constituencies with the power or status to effectively articulate any particular statement of what Cambodian 'concepts and principles' might be. The legacy of the extraordinary violence and repression suffered over the previous thirty years, at the hands of external interveners and home-grown despots, was that there were no actors with sufficient authority to proclaim an authentic 'Cambodian' position on human rights.

Non-governmental organisations in Cambodia: UNTAC's children?

UNTAC's response to this legacy was to treat it essentially as a lack of capacity rather than a lack of power, creating a didactic form of interactions between international agencies and Cambodian NGOs that arguably persisted for more than a decade. Assessments of Cambodia's reform prospects in the early 1990s focused heavily on the low level of education and the relative absence of a professional or intellectual class rather than on the sharp contrast between the deeply disorganised condition of Cambodian society in comparison to the very well-organised threat of violence posed by the highly militarised post-UNTAC state. Thus the weakness of civil society could be blamed on the policies of the Pol Pot regime of the 1970s, which had targeted intellectuals and professionals for extermination, rather than on the contemporaneous failure of UNTAC to disarm the ruling parties. Rebuilding of the education system in the 1980s had taken place, but against a backdrop of famine, civil war and Western embargo. Consequently, illiteracy was widespread in the countryside. The urban intellectual class, filling the ranks of the civil service and the faculty of the University of Phnom Penh, had largely been trained in the Soviet Union or other Eastern Bloc countries and thus lacked the acculturation to Western legal and political traditions that would have made them useful as partners of the UN in human rights promotion. Furthermore, the Human Rights Component commented, 'the deep psychological scars of the recent past were readily apparent.'[21] Lack of education, lack of acculturation to Western values and the legacy of trauma allowed a focus on capacity rather than on the real threat of violence posed by the parties with whom UNTAC was working to create a new Cambodian state. It also entailed that, for the Human Rights Component, the lack of 'viable local partners', as they put it, entailed that the United Nations would have to take on the role of human rights protection itself.[22]

As a consequence of these assumptions, local space for discussion of rights issues remained dominated by international agencies. In the early 1990s, international agencies were suspicious of Cambodian public attitudes. Dennis McNamara, head of the Human Rights Component, commented that 'The basic structures and institutions for [the institution of rule of law] are lacking in Cambodia as is the availability of qualified Cambodians able *or willing* to assist.'[23] Human Rights Component personnel referred to:

- 'a need to reform official *and popular* attitudes, as well as to provide the technical and other expertise and training needed to restore good governance';[24]
- 'to increase participants' understanding, acceptance and observance of human rights; and to encourage authorities and those in positions of influence to respect those rights, and ordinary people to be more active in exercising them';[25]
- 'to promote a psychological and attitudinal change in officials *and the population at large* through investigations, training and education';[26] and
- 'to establish a human rights culture in Cambodia'.[27]

This conceptualisation of the task at hand framed the population as the problem as well as the abusive state. At the close of UNTAC's mission, the newly-appointed Special Representative for Human Rights in Cambodia,

Michael Kirby, commented that the prevalence of fear in Cambodia had prompted 'resistance to concepts of human rights amongst some members of the public'.[28]

Even local human rights NGOs established under UNTAC's auspices were viewed as lacking in certain respects. They were referred to in a statement by Kirby as 'the children of the UN'. Former UN staffers Steve Heder and Judy Ledgerwood described these organisations as 'fledgling facsimiles of archetypical bodies of civil society', which, under UNTAC's protection, 'play[ed] a disproportionate and precocious role'.[29] A UN official at the UN Centre for Human Rights in Cambodia – the agency established to oversee human rights issues in Cambodia after UNTAC's departure – commented in 1996:

> during UNTAC the approach was a mixture of supportive and patronizing. On the one hand they realised that building civil society through NGOs was critical, but also they were established under the UN umbrella, so there was a patronising attitude: they are children, they can't stand on their own feet, they don't know what they are doing.[30]

There was a certain degree of scepticism over the motivations of such human rights NGOs among UNTAC and international NGO workers also. One international NGO worker commented:

> NGO work in Cambodia generally is a good job for young, bright people. Foreign aid is coming in – it has prospects and a good salary… A lot of hopeful, mildly idealistic youngsters join because they get foreign aid. They do care, but enthusiasm for human rights is complex. It's perceived as a growth area.[31]

Another former UNTAC official similarly commented that Cambodian human rights workers 'didn't go in as human rights activists. They mainly went in for the salary. Or for the card. But gradually they began to believe in them.'[32]

The question of Cambodian culture gave rise to further ambivalence (i.e. regarding Cambodian culture as a potential obstacle to human rights promotion would undermine assertions as to the universality of human rights across cultures). However, the conviction of the Human Rights Component that there was something lacking in Cambodian psychology and society which affected Cambodian attitudes to human rights promotion made an essentialist explanation focused on the supposed nature of Cambodian culture very attractive. At an international symposium on human rights in Cambodia organised by UNTAC, it was reported,

> Given Cambodia's tragic past, it is easy to assume that human rights are 'alien' to Cambodia. The Symposium was unwilling to accept this, even

though many speakers agreed that structures and attitudes had evolved that were inimical to human rights.[33]

Cambodian 'willingness to assist', however, needs to be understood in the context of the profound transition it was undergoing at the time. For international actors, the key transitions that the peace process ushered in were from war to peace and from communism to liberal democracy. Consequently, human rights efforts were framed by these broader concerns. UNTAC's approach to human rights focused overwhelmingly on the issue of civil and political rights, since this was necessary for the use of 'free and fair elections' as a device for ending the conflict and external engagement in it, and for producing a new, more stable and rights-respecting political regime.

From the perspective of ordinary Cambodians, however, another key transformation of the early 1990s was arguably of equal or greater immediate concern, namely the transformation of regimes of resource governance and landholding, which demanded attention to economic and social rights. UNTAC treated these as being of lesser significance. Tackling such issues would have required a far more imaginative and better informed understanding of Cambodian society and livelihoods than UNTAC had at its disposal, given the instrumental approach to human rights that drove its mandate. By far the largest number of complaints about rights abuses that UNTAC's Human Rights Component received from ordinary Cambodians related to land conflicts; yet UNTAC did not regard these issues as properly within its mandate and consequently did not respond to them. Where UNTAC did deal with such issues – for example, in allocating land and other livelihood resources to returning refugees – it quickly fell foul of the complexities of customary regimes of ownership and access, as well as the difficult of dealing with social and economic matters in an impoverished and war-torn environment where there simply wasn't enough to go around. The initial plan to allocate land plots to returning refugees had to be abandoned due to failure to identify sufficient land that was uncontested and free of landmines.[34] There were subsequently concerns that many refugees who had been allocated land had found it unusable for agriculture, and had therefore abandoned it and drifted into shanty towns in Phnom Penh.[35]

Idealists within UNTAC focused on political liberalism and the installation of a democratic regime as a means by which to provide Cambodians with the procedures and capacities to resolve these problems peacefully. However, the practice of international intervention, the pervasive distrust of Cambodian agency within international organisations, and the resources and effort expended in attempting to promote specifically liberal ways of understanding rights issues arguably delayed the emergence of organisations that dealt with Cambodian conflicts in ways that were locally pertinent.

International frustration at the apparent difficulty of cultivating liberal attitudes in Cambodia's hostile climate was compounded by a military battle in Phnom Penh in 1997 which facilitated the extra-constitutional return to de facto power by the Cambodian People's Party – the party of the Phnom Penh regime of the 1980s. This presaged new elections which the CPP won through blatant cheating and manipulation, and a drift back to authoritarianism and single party dominance. A resurgent CPP moved quickly to consolidate control over the rural population through populist policies of mass patronage combined with intensive surveillance, and this was successful in isolating NGOs further from any kind of rural base.

Many bilateral donors and diplomats in Phnom Penh regarded the collapse of the fragile proto-liberal peace as an inevitable consequence of Cambodia's lack of liberal democratic potential, and the liberal democratic agenda in Cambodia was largely abandoned by Cambodia's donors from 1997 in favour of a 'good governance' agenda that focused much more on promoting investor-friendly economic governance than on democratisation. This stance was confirmed in 2001, when concerns about a 'second front in the war on terror' in Southeast Asia made Cambodia's ruling party suddenly appear a rather stalwart ally of Western governments. Political space narrowed dramatically from 2001, as the CPP-led government began to ban demonstrations and harass opposition politicians, forcing the main leaders of Cambodia's popular opposition parties into exile for much of the next decade. In this context, liberal civil society organisations in Cambodia appeared more isolated than ever, and the future of a liberal agenda in Cambodia consequently appeared to be bleak.

From liberal peace to predatory capital

With hindsight, it is clear that issues to do with land distribution and the governance of natural resources have been the fundamental political contests that have informed Cambodia's post-war political trajectory. Despite the lack of success of UNTAC's faltering efforts at introducing political liberalism to Cambodia, it succeeded extraordinarily well in producing an environment in which capitalist development could flourish. Cambodia's GDP growth averaged around 5 per cent per year in the 1990s and then rose to 8 per cent per year in the 2000s. In a four-year period between 2004 and 2007, Cambodia's GDP growth exceeded 10 per cent per year, making it one of the most rapidly developing countries in the world, albeit from a low base, comparable with China's performance over the same period.[36]

However, the nature of Cambodia's economic development has been predatory and brutal. Elite groups and foreign investors associated with the military and the state have stripped Cambodia of its natural resources, dispossessing swathes of the population by violent means, backed by state security forces, and devastating a huge proportion of Cambodia's previously pristine old-growth forests. Environmental campaigners have been beaten and murdered by agents of the Cambodian government, with few repercussions for the legitimacy of that government internationally.[37] Violence is routinely used to evict households from lands earmarked for 'development'. Foreign and domestic elites have presided over a mass expropriation of land, causing a rapid widening of inequality, particularly in rural Cambodia, since 1993.[38] In the smaller manufacturing sector, there has been a high degree of contestation over wages, recognition of unions and conditions of work. While there have been some successes in raising pay and improving conditions as a result of strikes, there has also been a history of violent policing on picket lines, intimidation of union activists, and political assassination of union leaders.

These issues have been more highly politically charged than those pertaining to democratic representation or freedom of choice, and it is over these issues that Cambodian villagers have been prepared to defy security forces and face violence and social exclusion. From the mid-1990s onwards, these issues prompted significant although sporadic and ad hoc mobilisations of the population in the form of protests, demonstrations, and claims against political leaders. The privatisation of water resources and forests, issues of access to common land and forest products, rights of tenure to various types of urban and rural land, and the treatment of workers have dominated post-war Cambodian politics. Political claims made by poor, marginalised and dispossessed groups on these issues combine appeals to customary rights and to ideas about obligations owed by leaders to loyal followers, as well as to liberal conceptions of rights. Consequently, in Cambodia in the 1990s, the spectacle of groups of poor and dispossessed people travelling to Phnom Penh to petition the royal palace over land grabbing was commonplace. Meanwhile forest dwellers and squatters facing eviction attempted to occupy land they regarded as theirs by common right, even in the face of armed police, soldiers and bulldozers.

These mobilisations have frequently occurred independently of professional or organised NGOs, and have often used conceptions of rights which differ from those associated with the liberal peace.[39] Indeed, civil and political rights per se have come into focus largely in the context of popular mobilisations over these issues, when demonstrators or strikers are threatened or beaten, or when leaders of these movements are threatened, arrested or killed.

The NGO movement that emerged under UNTAC and afterwards was slow to link up with groups contesting these kinds of issues. This movement was weakened by a combination of factors, principally because of the continued selective resort to political violence and intimidation by the Cambodian government, declining pressure from diplomatic missions and bilateral donors on human rights issues, and paternalist attitudes of liberal peacebuilders. These combined pressures limited the ability of NGOs to take an assertive role in Cambodian politics. Rather, it encouraged a lengthy period of dependence, for protection and disciplinary guidance, on their foreign funders. This guidance translated into heavy-handed intrusion into the affairs of NGOs competing for dwindling international funding. In order to attract international support, NGOs focused their efforts on their own professionalisation, spending much of their time studying the English language, the use of Excel spreadsheets and the mysteries of logframe construction, and spending relatively little time engaging with potential constituents. A survey of Cambodian NGOs conducted by a Cambodian organisation in 1999 found that respondents listed as strengths their ability to plan and strategise, work with donors and government, comply with donor auditing requirements, stage forums and seminars, engage in self-education and capacity building, and collaborate among themselves. Weaknesses cited by respondents included 'lack of understanding of the real needs and interests of people ... too few NGO programmes in the rural areas, donor dependency'.[40] Similar concerns were noted on a review of the nature of NGO–donor engagement by an international practitioner ten years later in 2009.[41]

The outcome of this was a range of organisations that were closely aligned with international human rights issues, but poorly embedded in local struggles. This enabled the Cambodian government to pursue a political strategy of divide and rule with respect to NGOs. Those civil society organisations that avoided any kind of critical commentary on issues of politics or governance, confining themselves to service delivery and development work, were awarded political space to work. NGOs that began in the mid-2000s to advocate on issues to do with predatory capitalism by government-aligned companies – namely environmental and human rights NGOs – were regularly intimidated, denigrated and presented as creatures of foreign intervention, seeking to impose a Western agenda upon Cambodia. This argument was all the easier to make, since the NGOs had done little to embed themselves in rural society in the 1990s.

Fifteen years after UNTAC's departure, the World Bank conducted an assessment of Cambodian 'civil society'. Although the report did not define 'civil society', its authors offered 'an overview of civil society organisations in Cambodia' dividing these into five main types: a small number of 'traditional associations', such as pagoda committees and savings cooperatives; a large number of village development committees established in conjunction with state or international donor development projects; approximately 700 active non-governmental organisations; almost 400 trade unions; and youth and student organisations.[42] However, the assessment found that these organisations and associations were not only heavily dependent upon either the government or external donors, but also sharply divided between two types of organisation. The most common type of organisation took the form of apolitical service delivery vehicles, focused on providing education about sanitation, volunteers to work on development projects and so on. The less common type was the professional advocacy NGO: a product of the liberal peacebuilding promoted by UNTAC that had belatedly linked to the economic and social rights agenda, and attracted the deep hostility of the government as a result, but which had relatively poor connections to grassroots actors.⁴³ Consequently, ad hoc struggles emerging on the ground over issues of land grabbing or resource privatisation found it difficult to form positive alliances with effective advocates. Linking with advocacy NGOs was difficult, since such NGOs were neither well embedded in local communities nor influential vis-à-vis the government, and even potentially made the struggle more dangerous. Meanwhile, service delivery NGOs generally avoided direct involvement in such movements. Consequently, resistance to predatory practices of business tycoons close to the Cambodian People's Party has tended to remain sporadic, localised and fragmented, and therefore rather weak.

International assessments of the record of Cambodian NGOs in assisting the poor have generally applied a framework which avoids recognition of the predatory nature of Cambodian development. Although international agencies are critical of the Cambodian government's record on corruption and its failure to act on judicial reform, they have generally understood the problems in forestry and land through a legal lens, rather than as an issue of distributions of power between rich and poor. Consequently, much emphasis in these areas has focused on technical issues and on strengthening formal rights and processes as part of a good governance agenda, rather than on strengthening the ability of ordinary people to resist dispossession. This has fed into approaches within Cambodian NGOs also, through the kinds of funding and training given by international organisations to local counterparts. This kind of approach has been welcomed by the Cambodian government because it preoccupies the NGO movement with activities that are relatively unthreatening to the political economy of power.

This tendency is illustrated by a scheme launched by the World Bank to promote the use of social accountability practices to improve governance in Cambodia. Following on from their 2009 assessment of Cambodian civil society, the World Bank launched a grant scheme whereby any Cambodian NGO could apply for a grant to implement social accountability projects – participatory planning, citizen report cards, establishment of user groups and so on – in various sectors. The project was intended to boost civil society influence in reforming governance, through providing a means by which NGOs could engage constructively and effectively with the state on service delivery, financial management and development planning. It was considered by the World Bank to provide a third way for NGO activism – going beyond the quiescent service provision of the majority of the sector while falling short of the confrontational stance of advocacy NGOs.

The scheme was viewed with suspicion by Cambodian NGOs. For one thing, it incorporated the controversial requirement that NGOs apply jointly for the funding with the state agencies they planned to hold to account. World Bank officials played down the significance of this provision, contending that it merely boiled down to the condition that 'someone in government knows what you are planning to do and is prepared to listen – otherwise what is the point in doing it?'⁴⁴ However, for the Ministry of Interior official responsible for the scheme, the provision had greater significance: 'We have a principle of constructive engagement – it is clear that those that are not supporting the government will not be funded.' The official noted that only a few NGOs, working in areas of human rights and corruption, fell into this category and had an 'attitude of unconstructive engagement', but commented that these NGOs would be excluded from the programme on the basis that they were disruptive to orderly development: 'we can't afford to have fighting with each other – democracy is not mature yet' in Cambodia.[45]

From the perspective of the Cambodian government, the scheme represented a means by which relatively tame NGOs could be further co-opted, while advocacy NGOs were further excluded and restricted, with a stamp of legitimacy from the most influential donor in Cambodia. NGOs who participated in the scheme were strongly aware of the potential for this outcome, and sceptical of the ability of social accountability to make much of a difference in the context of the power relations prevailing in Cambodia. One interviewee from a Cambodian NGO compared the conditions for social accountability in Cambodia unfavourably with those he observed in India, during a World Bank-organised study visit: 'The Indian government is very democratic: because of full democracy, the level of threat is almost zero. People can say what they want to say.'[46] In Cambodia, by contrast, the only NGOs brave enough to delve seriously into the realm of social accountability were those with which the government would refuse to work. The main attraction of the scheme for most NGOs was that receipt of World Bank funding was 'CV-building' for them with respect to their relations with international donors. This scheme illustrates the ways in which plans for governance reform in Cambodia have occupied considerable time and energy on the part of donors and NGOs, but have signally failed to address the fundamental problem of highly unequal power relations and conflicting interests between government officials, external interveners and poor recipients of state services in Cambodia.

Similar dynamics are observable in international involvement with the emergent trade union movement. Here, too, international schemes to promote constructive engagement between civil society organisations and government have had the effect of reinforcing unequal relations by isolating and undermining potentially transformative movements. Trade unions emerged in Cambodia in the mid-1990s, as a garment industry began to develop around Phnom Penh. Garments remain the mainstay of Cambodian manufacturing, employing around 500,000 workers, and accounting for 80 per cent of exports. Investment in the garment industry has largely been by regional players from East and Southeast Asia. These companies initially built plants for garment assembly in Cambodia to take advantage of its privileged export quotas to the US and Europe under the Multi-Fibre Arrangement that ended in 2004.

From an early stage, garment workers' unions were extraordinarily militant, in comparison to other sectors of Cambodian civil society. Spontaneous walk-outs and demonstrations by workers, protesting not only low wages and poor conditions but also ill-treatment and violence perpetrated by supervisors, preceded formal unionisation. Once trade unions became better established, industry-wide strikes in 1996, 1997 and 2000 were successful in increasing wages from US$27 a month in 1996 to US$45 a month by 2000, and gaining some initial improvements in terms and conditions. These early strikes were led by the Free Trade Union of Workers of the Kingdom of Cambodia (FTUWKC), an organisation which had close links to the opposition Sam Rainsy Party (SRP). The Garment Manufacturers' Association of Cambodia, on the other hand, enjoys close links with the Cambodian People's Party and Prime Minister Hun Sen. The relationship between the FTUWKC and the SRP offered mutual benefits. The SRP was an effective vehicle for raising funds and international profile, and could supply organising resources to factory workers. FTUWKC organisers linked to the SRP expanded the union's membership base by showing up at ad hoc protests at factories around Phnom Penh, addressing the crowd through loudspeakers promising support for their cause, and recruiting members on the spot. For the SRP, open advocacy of the cause of labour awarded them immense political support in electoral constituencies around Phnom Penh and provided bodies that could be turned out for political rallies and protests.

For the FTUWKC, and its militant leader Chea Vichea, strike action was a means by which fundamental inequalities of power between rich and poor in Cambodia could be directly challenged. Thus Vichea commented in an interview in 2000:

> If we have a strike, I go to the factory, I take a megaphone. I tell them, if we are afraid every day, they will pay a small salary and use us very hard. But if we start to fight we can have better conditions ... The employers and the government have a good alliance – one has money and the other has power. They co-operate and abuse the poor ... So we must break the alliance, by paying dues to the trade union and organising a strike.[47]

The view of strikes as a specifically political weapon to be used not merely to achieve a particular concession but to fundamentally rebalance the relationship between rich and poor in Cambodia represented a radical approach that was not paralleled anywhere else in the Cambodian civil society sector at the time.

The government's response to the emergence of unions was initially repressive. A grenade attack, apparently perpetrated by a member of the Prime Minister's bodyguard unit, on a rally at which garment union leaders appeared on a platform with SRP leader Sam Rainsy in 1997 killed 20 and injured 100 people. The attack made international headlines and brought international attention to the trade union movement in Cambodia. Subsequently, labour organisations from the US and France as well as the

International Labour Organization became actively involved in providing training and finance for Cambodian unions, and big brand buyers such as Disney, Nike, H&M and Gap began to make monitoring visits to Cambodian factories to ensure compliance with particular codes of conduct.

The Cambodian government responded to this attention by establishing unions of its own to compete with the FTUWKC. These unions discouraged strikes and protests while providing gifts and benefits to workers. This resulted in a fluctuating membership pattern in which workers joined government unions for the perquisites when industrial relations were going smoothly, then shifted back to the FTUWKC when relations broke down.[48] In 2004, the FTUWKC suffered a further blow when Chea Vichea was assassinated in Phnom Penh.[49] The perpetrators of this killing have never been brought to justice.[50]

In contrast to the FTUWKC's approach of setting industrial relations in the context of broader class struggles within Cambodia, international organisations who have become engaged in the labour movement in Cambodia have arguably privileged a superficial harmony in industrial relations over questions of distributions of power between rich and poor. This approach is illustrated by the ILO's engagement with unions and industry in Cambodia. A bilateral trade treaty negotiated between the US and Cambodia in 1999 linked export quotas from Cambodia to the US to the establishment of an ILO regulated regime to govern industrial relations and working conditions in Cambodian factories.

The ILO's engagement led to the emergence of a new governance regime for Cambodian industrial relations which has frequently been praised as a model for ensuring ethical conduct. However, this regime has severed the connection drawn by the FTUWKC between industrial relations on the one hand and the broader political economy of class relations on the other. The ILO took a strong line against the FTUWKC's relationship with the SRP, insisting that the ties between the union and party be cut in order that the union could become a 'real, independent, democratic, free trade union'.[51] However, the severing of this relationship significantly weakened both parties. The SRP, Cambodia's only significant opposition party, subsequently suffered years of harassment, and Sam Rainsy himself spent most of the decade from 2003 to 2013 outside of Cambodia due to threat of imprisonment on a series of trumped up libel charges brought by members of the government.

Meanwhile the FTUWKC was drawn into an ILO-sponsored process of labour bargaining that was focused on defusing workers' struggles. In 1999, the existing Labour Advisory Committee in the Ministry of Social Affairs, Labour, Veterans and Youth was transformed into a tripartite committee to be used as a venue for peaceful negotiation over labour relations issues. The Committee comprised five trade union representatives, one of which was the FTUWKC, and ten representatives of government and employers groups. Given that other trade unions were themselves pro-government, the committee was clearly heavily stacked in favour of government-aligned groups, and the most militant sections of labour, represented at the time by the FTUWKC, was far outnumbered. In 2002, an Arbitration Council was established to provide arbitration services for industrial disputes, which had the same tripartite structure. In both cases, removing struggles over wages and conditions away from the workers and the shop floor and confining it to the forum of bureaucratically constituted bargaining space to which participants were invited significantly reduced the democratic import of union organisation, by taking decisions far away from any space in which workers themselves were likely to appear.

Furthermore, specific provisions promoted by the ILO, such as the implementation of a seven-day cooling off period between an issue arising and the calling of a strike, significantly weakens the ability of workers to make demands. In a context like Cambodia, where intimidation, threats and even violence against union activists are commonplace in factories, such provisions have an intensely chilling effect on activism. ILO conceptions of professionalism, ostensibly aimed at promoting better relations between workers and employers in fact combine with heavy-handed authoritarianism on the part of the Cambodian government to demobilise activist sections of the community. This approach does little to facilitate effective demands for serious redistributions of power in Cambodia emerging from below.

Conclusion: no justice, no peace?

In 2014, post-election protests against electoral fraud by the ruling party, continued violence across the country in response to evictions and land-grabbing, and a general strike that saw workers killed in confrontations with police are evidence that Cambodia is not enjoying much peace, liberal or otherwise. Rather, the country is politically polarised along fault lines that reflect the co-optation of certain constituencies by a ruling elite comprised of close-knit networks of political, bureaucratic, business and military power-holders, and the exclusion and exploitation of the poor. Although there has been no return to insurgency, nevertheless authoritarian policing and violence are routinely used to repress the struggles of the poor to improve their position.

Liberal organisations engaged in Cambodia from UNTAC onwards have failed to recognise that the key to a more genuine peace is a recalibration of power relations and redistribution of resources currently tightly in the grip of a ruling class of predatory capitalists. External liberal peacebuilders have employed a paternalistic approach in which the key problem is regarded as lack of capacity for resolving disputes, rather than genuine conflicts of interest emerging from patterns of capitalist expropriation. Consequently, liberal peacebuilders have used the promise of funding and support to attract activists into a world of capacity-building, grant proposal writing and networking that has little to do with tackling the exploitative political economy of power in Cambodia. Rather, these activities bind activists into projects and frameworks that promote a superficial conception of social harmony in the midst of conditions of growing inequality. This conception often corresponds rather well to the ruling party's notion of peace as the use of violence and intimidation, combined with dispensation of patronage, to maintain public order and facilitate strategies of primitive accumulation. Meanwhile, Western pension schemes join Chinese and regional firms investing in the emergence of a new plantation economy built over the top of the customary rights of rural Cambodians.

Notes

1 See discussions in United States General Accounting Office, *UN Peacekeeping: Lessons Learned in Managing Recent Missions*, Report to Congressional Requesters, Washington, DC: US GAO, 1993, p. 58; Benny Widyono, *Dancing in Shadows: Sihanouk, the Khmer Rouge and the United Nations in Cambodia*, Lanham, MD: Rowman & Littlefield, 2008, pp. 119–131; Brad Adams, 'PM's History of Electoral Manipulation, Intimidation and Violence Show that He Has No Desire to Cede Power to Democracy', *Bangkok Post*, 20 August 2013 (at: www.hrw.org/news/2013/08/20/pm-s-history-electoral-manipulation-intimidation-and-violence-shows-he-has-no-desire).
2 For example, David Chandler, *Facing the Cambodian Past*, Chiang Mai: Silkworm, 1996, p. 323.
3 According to analysis of data released by the US government in 2000, 2,756,941 tonnes were dropped on Cambodia between 1965 and 1973, compared with just over 2 million tonnes dropped by the Allies in the whole of World War 2. Taylor Owen and Ben Kiernan, 'Bombs over Cambodia', *The Walrus*, October 2006 (at: www.yale.edu/cgp/Walrus_CambodiaBombing_OCT06.pdf).
4 Principles for a New Constitution for Cambodia, 'Agreement on a Comprehensive Political Settlement of the Cambodia Conflict', annex 5, UN doc. A/46/608-S/23177, Paris, 30 October 1991, paragraphs 2 and 4.
5 'Tokyo Declaration on the Rehabilitation and Reconstruction of Cambodia', issued at the conclusion of the Ministerial Conference on the Rehabilitation and Reconstruction of Cambodia on 22 June 1992, UN doc. A/47/285-S/24183, 25 June 1992, annex II.
6 Surin Maisrikrod, 'Thailand's Policy Dilemmas Towards Indochina', *Contemporary Southeast Asia*, vol. 14, no. 3, 1992, p.296.
7 Chang Pao-min, 'Kampuchean Conflict: the Continuing Stalemate', *Asian Survey*, vol. 17, no. 7, 1987, pp. 756–759.
8 Keith Richburg, 'Back to Vietnam', *Foreign Affairs*, vol. 70, no. 4, 1991, p. 125.
9 'Agreement on a Comprehensive Political Settlement of the Cambodia Conflict', art. 15, para. 2.
10 *Ibid.*, art. 16
11 *Ibid.*, art. 17.
12 *Ibid.*, annex 1, section E.
13 Report of the Secretary-General on Cambodia containing his proposed implementation plan for UNTAC, including administrative and financial aspects, UN doc. S/23613, 19 February 1992, para. 12.
14 *Ibid.*, para. 9.
15 *Ibid.*, para. 12.
16 *Ibid.*, para. 13.

17 UNTAC Human Rights Component, 'Final Report', unpublished report, Phnom Penh: UNTAC, 1993, p. 9.
18 Steve Heder and Judy Ledgerwood, 'The Politics of Violence: An Introduction', in Steve Heder and Judy Ledgerwood (eds), *Propaganda, Politics and Violence in Cambodia, Democratic Transition under United Nations Peace-Keeping*', London: M. E. Sharpe, 1996, p. 15.
19 Report of the Secretary-General on Cambodia (note 13 above), para. 13.
20 UNTAC Human Rights Component (note 17 above), p. 58.
21 For a comparative account of how international peacekeepers and peacebuilders 'psychologised' Cambodia, see Caroline Hughes and Vanessa Pupavac, 'Psychologising Post Conflict Societies, Cambodia and Bosnia Compared', *Third World Quarterly*, vol. 26, no. 6, 2005, pp. 873–889.
22 UNTAC Human Rights Component (note 17 above), p. 10.
23 Emphasis added. Dennis McNamara, 'Opening Statement by Dennis McNamara, Director, UNTAC Human Rights Component', in *Report on the International Symposium on Human Rights in Cambodia (30 November–2 December 1992)*, Economic and Social Council, Commission on Human Rights, UN doc. E/CN.4/1993/19/Add. 1, 14 January 1993, annex 2 (at: www.unhchr.ch/html/menu2/7/a/mcam.htm).
24 Emphasis added. UNTAC Human Rights Component (note 17 above), p. 3.
25 Dennis McNamara, 'UN Peacekeeping and Human Rights in Cambodia: A Critical Evaluation', unpublished paper prepared for a meeting on UN Peacekeeping and Human Rights, Geneva, August 1994, p. 14.
26 McNamara (note 23 above).
27 McNamara (note 25 above), p. 18.
28 Report of the Special Representative of the Secretary-General, Mr Michael Kirby, on the situation of human rights in Cambodia submitted pursuant to Commission on Human Rights Resolution 1993/6, UN doc. E/CN.4/1994/73/Add.1, 21 February 1994, para. 3(g).
29 Heder and Ledgerwood (note 18 above), p. 18.
30 Christophe Peschoux, Director, UN Centre for Human Rights in Cambodia, interview with the author, Phnom Penh, 20 January 1996.
31 International NGO activist (name withheld upon request), interview with the author, 22 August 1995, Washington, DC.
32 Former UNTAC Human Rights Component staffer and International NGO activist (name withheld upon request), interview with the author, 24 August 1995, Washington, DC.
33 *Report on the International Symposium on Human Rights in Cambodia* (note 23 above), para. 30.
34 See Asia Watch, *Political Control, Human Rights and the UN Mission in Cambodia*, Washington, DC: Asia Watch, September 1992 (at: www.hrw.org/sites/default/files/reports/CAMBODIA929.PDF).
35 Michelle Legge and Thor Savoeun, *Nine Years On: Displaced People in Cambodia*, Phnom Penh: Ockenden International, 2004.
36 Council for the Development of Cambodia, *Cambodia Investment Guidebook*, Phnom Penh: CDC and JICA, 2012, ch. 2. The average GDP growth rate for Low Income Countries over the period from 2004 to 2007 was 6–7 per cent; see World Bank, 'GDP Growth Data' (at: http://data.worldbank.org/indicator/NY.GDP.MKTP.KD.ZG/countries/XM?display=graph).
37 Activists belonging to the international NGO Global Witness have been beaten and harassed in Cambodia. In 2012, environmental activist Chut Wutty was murdered while investigating illegal logging, and an investigative journalist working on logging issues was also killed; Licadho, 'Attacks and Threats Against Human Rights Defenders in Cambodia 2010–2012', Phnom Penh: Licadho, 2012 (at: www.licadho-cambodia.org/collection/15/attack_hrd_2010_2012).

38 World Bank, *Cambodia: Sharing Growth: Equity and Development in Cambodia*, Equity Report, Phnom Penh: World Bank, 2007, p. v. Relative inequality increased over the period of Cambodia's boom from 2003 to 2007. In 2003, the richest fifth of the population consumed five times as much as the poorest fifth. By 2007 this had increased to more than six times as much. Since then relative inequality has narrowed somewhat – to around four times as much in 2011. However, since the consumption of the poorest fifth has grown at the same time, the absolute difference in the amount consumed has increased unabated over the whole period. See World Bank, *Where Have All the Poor Gone? Cambodia Poverty Assessment 2013*, Phnom Penh: World Bank, 2013.
39 See Caroline Hughes, *The Political Economy of Cambodia's Transition 1991–2001*, London: Routledge, 2003, pp. 173–213. The Cambodian human rights organisation Licadho has coined the phrase 'human rights defender' to describe any 'social actors who, individually or as part of a group, work to uphold and protect fundamental human rights through peaceful means'; Licadho (note 37 above), p. 4. In identifying these individuals, however, it is the organisation that supplies the human rights framing for the rights at issue. The organisation also notes that human rights defenders 'are identified primarily by their actions, not their profession' and are drawn from many walks of life (*ibid.*).
40 Kao Kim Hourn, *Grass Roots Democracy in Cambodia: Opportunities, Challenges and Prospects*, Phnom Penh: Cambodia Institute for Cooperation and Peace and Forum Syd, 1999, pp. 51–52.
41 Roger Henke, 'NGOs, People's Movements and Natural Resources in Cambodia', in Caroline Hughes and Kheang Un (eds), *Cambodia's Economic Transformation*, Copenhagen: NIAS Press, 2011, pp. 317–338.
42 Carmen Malena and Kristina Chhim, *Linking Citizens and the State: An Assessment of Civil Society Contributions to Good Governance in Cambodia*, Phnom Penh: World Bank, 2009, pp. 8–9.
43 *Ibid.*
44 Vinay Bhargava, interview with the author, Phnom Penh, 20 July 2009.
45 Ngy Chanphal, interview with the author, Phnom Penh, 22 July 2009.
46 Soeung Saroeun, interview with the author, Phnom Penh, 23 July 2009.
47 Chea Vichea, FTUWKC president, interview with the author, Phnom Penh, 21 July 2000.
48 *Ibid.*
49 Cambodian Human Rights Action Committee, 'CHRAC Condemns Assassination of Chea Vichea', statement, Phnom Penh, 22 January 2004.
50 Two men were arrested and jailed for the murder in 2005, following trials that were internationally condemned as ignoring key evidence and abusing due process. After a long campaign by human rights organisations, the men were provisionally released by the Supreme Court in 2008. However, they were convicted again and sent back to jail in December 2012, before their convictions were finally quashed by the Cambodian Supreme Court in 2013. Nobody else has been arrested for the crime.
51 Nuon Ritthy, ILO official, interview with the author, Phnom Penh, 10 August 2001.

7 Securing and stabilising
Peacebuilding as counterinsurgency in the occupied Palestinian territory

Mandy Turner

Since the signing of the Oslo Peace Accord between Israel and the Palestine Liberation Organization (PLO) in 1993, the occupied Palestinian territory (oPt) has been the site of extensive Western donor peacebuilding policies and practices. As one of the first extensive post-Cold War Western peacebuilding interventions in a non-sovereign context (but which did not involve full UN control), many innovations were introduced that became part of Western practice in other war-torn societies. However, it was also subject to and driven by many assumptions that underpin other Western peacebuilding missions that were particularly problematic for the oPt – a situation which is neither post-conflict nor post-colonial. Indeed, for these and many more reasons, Western peacebuilding in the oPt has been subjected to extensive and frequent criticisms, particularly that there is a contradiction in promoting Palestinian institutions, governance structures and economic development in preparation for sovereignty in the context of Israel's occupation and colonial practices.[1] It stands further accused of failing to deliver peace.[2] However, despite writing pieces myself that argue this,[3] I am no longer convinced there is a contradiction. My argument here is that if Western donor-led peacebuilding is understood as a form of counterinsurgency whose goal is to secure a population, then the contradictions vanish, and we see that peacebuilding has not failed – in fact, quite the contrary, it has largely succeeded. Explicitly relabelling peacebuilding as counterinsurgency in the oPt provides us with a 'deep grammar' to comprehend policies and processes that on first glance appear contradictory when viewed through the self-proclaimed benign peacebuilding lens, but are not when looked at through the lens of counterinsurgency with its unashamed focus on stabilisation. Modern counterinsurgency doctrine (COIN) is based on the idea that successfully securing a population and immunising it against unrest requires serious and extensive strategies in the realm of governance, development and security. Western donor-led peacebuilding activities also focus on these spheres – albeit with the self-proclaimed benign goal of developing mechanisms to avoid and/or reduce violent conflict and build a sustainable peace. The commonalities in the philosophical underpinnings of, and policy developments in, counterinsurgency doctrine and Western conceptions of peacebuilding are stark. This chapter therefore unpacks these commonalities and reconstructs how they play out in the case of the oPt.

This analysis of Western peacebuilding in the oPt takes as its starting point that the Israel-Palestine conflict is fundamentally a struggle over land which pits a powerful state against a stateless people, and which has created a vicious cycle of insurgency and counterinsurgency. Israel's counterinsurgency strategies against the Palestinians involve the use of 'kinetic' techniques (i.e. 'killing power')[4] that covers direct military intervention;[5] extensive repression through mass incarceration, detention without trial, torture and house demolitions[6] as well as targeted assassinations and collective punishment.[7] Israel has also developed sophisticated pacification techniques that involve methods of population control such as 'stratified citizenship' and restrictions on movement, marriage and residency;[8] a closure regime of checkpoints, barriers and the Separation Wall[9]; and the use of local proxies and collaborators.[10] And it is within this context that the usual activities in the peacebuilding toolbox – statebuilding, security sector reform, democracy promotion, private sector economic promotion and civil society support – have been pursued. The central argument of this chapter is that Western peacebuilding practices – which have as their underlying structural goal to stabilise the situation – have operated as another layer of pacification techniques that have complimented and meshed with Israel's structures of domination and repression.

In order to expand this thesis, the chapter is split into three sections. The first section outlines what I mean by peacebuilding as counterinsurgency by exploring the symbiosis in the philosophy and methods of COIN and peacebuilding. It shows how they have a shared ontology on the causes, consequences and techniques of dealing with societal violence. The second section outlines the context for Western peacebuilding in the oPt – a situation subjected to Israel's colonial practices, the insurgency and resistance this provokes from Palestinians, and Israel's counterinsurgency strategies. It argues that understanding this context is essential in order to analyse the implementation and impact of Western peacebuilding strategies and the particular type of 'peace' being built. The third section develops the thesis of peacebuilding as counterinsurgency through an analysis of development assistance, governance strategies and security coordination in the oPt, and shows how these operate as a further layer of pacification techniques that have meshed with Israel's methods of control in subtle but crucial ways. The chapter concludes by arguing that Western peacebuilding interventions have therefore helped to create a political economy that stabilises *from the inside* – and so have played a key role in the creation and preservation of a violent colonial peace.

Securing the population: understanding peacebuilding as counterinsurgency

Until relatively recently, discussions of counterinsurgency operations and doctrine were limited to military strategists and historians. However, it is now 'fashionable again', as noted by David Kilcullen, an influential theorist of counterinsurgency and from 2005–2006 chief strategist in the US State Department's Office of the Coordinator for Counterterrorism. Kilcullen argues that 'classical counterinsurgency focuses on securing the population rather than destroying the enemy'.[11] The underlying rationale is to instil acquiescence and ensure control. Counterinsurgency techniques have a long and extensive history as a method of control. The colonial powers used them in an attempt to crush anti-colonial movements within their empires, and the US utilised them during the Cold War to control and defeat nationalist and socialist movements that challenged its economic and strategic interests. In the now post-Cold War and (largely) post-colonial world, they have remained central to the global control strategies pursued by the US and its allies – but have been further enhanced and developed. Overt codifications of the doctrine distil lessons from past counterinsurgency interventions remodelled for the twenty-first century conflict environment largely defined by strategic defence documents (which elaborate on the use of other forms of power in addition to military intervention).[12] The objective is 'to manage the tempo of activity, the level of violence, and the degree of stability in the environment'.[13] This is not to suggest, however, that intense levels of violence are not a logical and necessary corollary of modern COIN operations because direct violence still plays a crucial role if and when structural methods of stabilisation fail.[14]

The key goal of the counterinsurgent is not to impose order but to achieve 'collaboration towards a set of shared objectives'.[15] The 2009 *US Government Counterinsurgency Guide* therefore argues for the primacy of non-military means: 'COIN is a complex effort that integrates the full range of civilian and military agencies. It is often more population-centric (focused on securing and controlling a given population or populations) than enemy-centric (focused on defeating a particular enemy group).'[16] Modern COIN doctrine thus seeks to successfully immunise countries against uprisings by ensuring control over the economic, political and military spheres through development aid, supporting sympathetic elites, and military assistance.

This coheres with the concepts and practices of peacebuilding strategy as expressed through documents such as *An Agenda for Peace* (1992), *A More Secure World: Our Shared Responsibility* (2004) and *In Larger Freedom* (2005) – and as implemented through the gamut of peacebuilding activities undertaken by Western donors and international organisations.[17] From the late 1990s, the relationship between military force and peacebuilding activities was overtly codified through their fusion in peace support operations (PSOs) in the pursuit of what Michael Pugh has labelled 'an aggressive peace'.[18] Indeed, the *US Government Counterinsurgency Guide* posits that 'The capabilities required for COIN may be very similar to those required for peacekeeping operations, humanitarian assistance, stabilization operations, and development assistance missions.'[19] In constructing the 'three pillars of counterinsurgency' – defined as security, political, economic – Kilcullen incorporates best practices from all these examples and compares the process of developing the 'pillars' as akin to conducting a USAID conflict assessment.[20] Pugh also notes that John Mackinlay, researcher of UK imperial counterinsurgency (and one of the authors of the RAND counterinsurgency study, referred to above), favoured PSOs being modified and implemented to defeat what he regarded as a 'global insurgency that had links to terrorism'.[21] These all indicate a 'deeply entrenched and necessary articulation between globalised militarised practices and transnational neoliberal governance'.[22]

To posit that there is a structural symbiosis between the principles and goals of peacebuilding and counterinsurgency should not be controversial; many Western states openly express that their international development strategies (particularly in what is commonly referred to in donor parlance as 'fragile states') are working to advance counterinsurgency. And we can trace the echoes of such ideas to imperial power in the early twentieth century as encapsulated in the British Colonial Development Act of 1929.[23] In response to a tsunami of anti-colonial insurgencies against imperial rule, the British developed a strategy designed to restrict independence and ensure continued British control.[24] Britain's manipulation of Egyptian and Iraqi politics from the 1920s to 1950s, for instance, was designed to prevent economic and foreign policies that would threaten Britain's interests in the region.[25] In the case of the US, development assistance was explicitly regarded as playing a key role in its global counterinsurgency anti-Communist strategies and this was solidified through the creation of inter-agency country teams in the 1950s and codified in its first interagency counterinsurgency manual produced in 1962.[26] The Provincial Reconstruction Teams in Afghanistan in the 2000s, therefore, merely provide another, more recent, example of such coordination and priorities.[27] And in the political and security realms, the US has long believed in, and practiced, the principle of propping up 'friendly governments' and training militaries to suppress insurgencies, particularly in its own 'back yard' of Latin America.[28]

The crucial interrelationship between US military, development and foreign policy interests was again more recently signalled in the 2009 *US Government Counterinsurgency Guide*, which was co-signed by the Department of State, Department of Defense and USAID, and whose chief author was David Kilcullen (discussed earlier).[29] This interconnected organisational and goals-oriented relationship is also reflected in the UK's practice. The UK's development agency, the Department for International Development (DFID), has its origins in various precursors connecting (and sometimes within) the Foreign and Commonwealth Office (FCO) and the various offices that dealt with the British colonies. Fast forward to 2001 when the UK established the Global Conflict Prevention Pool (GCPP) as a joint FCO, Ministry of Defence (MOD) and DFID mechanism for funding and managing the UK's contribution towards violent conflict prevention and reduction – and we can see just how essential are these interconnections.[30] Similar histories of the symbiosis of defence, foreign policy and development can be traced with all the major Organisation for Economic Cooperation and Development (OECD) donors.

But, of course, counterinsurgency is not the language used by the development and peacebuilding community: the preferred labels in this lexicon are the so-called 'security/development nexus'[31] and the concept of 'human security' – both of which have played a central role – in the West's analysis of how to promote violence reduction, particularly in conflict zones and 'fragile states'.[32] And yet the symbiosis of the two strategies is obvious.[33] US General David Petraeus – who, in effect, wrote the counterinsurgency 'bible', the 2006 *US Army/Marine Corps Counterinsurgency Field Manual* (FM-324), and is one of the key people behind the highly visible re-emergence of the doctrine (which has sometimes even been referred to as the 'Petraeus Doctrine') – proposed to Mary Kaldor (one of the major proponents of human security[34]) that the two concepts of counterinsurgency and human security had the same principles and goals.[35] Initially regarded as offering a radical alternative to the dominant discourse of international security based on state security and the threat of inter-state conflict, the concept of human security, which emerged in the brave new optimistic post-Cold War world of the 1990s, promoted the idea that insecurity causes poverty and that civil wars were *the* major cause of insecurity. Its entry into the international lexicon was announced in the 1992 UN document, *An Agenda for Peace*, which is, in fact, the same document that the concept of peacebuilding made its first appearance. Both concepts captured the *zeitgeist* of debates in academic and policy communities; and their subsequent integration into mainstream policymaking spawned a dizzying array of definitions, matrices and toolboxes[36] as well as a plethora of networks and institutions, such as the UN Peacebuilding Commission, the EU Peacebuilding Partnership, the UN Trust Fund for Human Security and the Human Security Network.[37]

This institutionalisation curiously resulted in both a broadening and a narrowing of the application of human security and peacebuilding. The broadening took place in policy documents which, on occasion, read like a wish-list for the 'good society'.[38] The narrowing took place in their application whereby statebuilding, security sector reform and rule of law programmes have been prioritised. In the clash between the two versions of human security – broad (freedom from want) and narrow (freedom from fear) – the latter has been privileged.[39] Donor-led peacebuilding has, therefore, since the early 2000s, prioritised statebuilding and security over other aspects of peacebuilding.[40] These shifts were visible in the recommendation of the UN High Level Panel on Threats, Challenges and Change in 2004 that peacebuilding should focus on statebuilding, which reinforced the 2000 Brahimi Report's emphasis on civilian security and rule of law.[41] So while the 'security-development nexus' promotes the popular donor tautology that 'development requires security and security requires development', securing the population is prioritised and is seen as an essential precondition to improving the economic environment.[42] Critics argue that such conclusions merely justify greater donor involvement – as in order to secure populations more intervention is required.[43] Thus more and more programmes directed at 'capacity building', 'rule of law', 'security sector reform', 'statebuilding' and 'good governance' are implemented in countries deemed to require securing. And elites who try to resist these policies are either to be co-opted or marginalised. Indeed the common thread that runs through both COIN and peacebuilding – in their language *and* application – is control, which tells us something fundamental about the global structures of power and the emptiness of claims regarding freedom and autonomy.[44] The shared ontologies of peacebuilding and counterinsurgency on the causes, consequences and techniques of dealing with societal violence are therefore palpable. And in their application they share the same aim: stabilisation. Nowhere is this more visible than in the oPt where Israel's techniques of counterinsurgency, implemented to suppress opposition to resource appropriation and population transfer, have been supplemented since 1993 with Western donor-led peacebuilding policies and practices which have assisted in securing the population and ensuring acquiescence in the face of violent dispossession.

The context for peacebuilding: Israel's colonial and counterinsurgency practices in the oPt

Israel's aims of creating and expanding its state, and securing dominance over the land and resources of historic Palestine, creates a structural imperative of control and displacement – but carefully refracted through the discourse of 'security'. Israel has generally been regarded as a prime example of a vulnerable state where security concerns are given primacy in both domestic and foreign policy – indeed it has been labelled as constituting a 'nation in arms'.[45] It has a large national army that has a prominent place in Israeli society and politics due to its mandatory military and reserve service (not, of course, for Palestinians in Israel, although they can volunteer[46]), which is required for access to certain jobs and state benefits. There is a very strong connection between the state and the military with high office in the Israel Defense Forces (IDF) being an almost automatic stepping stone into politics as indicated by the fact that by 2005 only three of the 16 men who had served as IDF General Chiefs of Staff had *not* entered politics. Several former senior generals, for example Yitzhak Rabin and Ariel Sharon, became prime ministers, and former IDF Chiefs of Staff, such as Ehud Barak and Moshe Dayan, became defence ministers.[47] It is therefore unsurprising that the military receives huge amounts of government funding; in fact Israel's military expenditure is the fifth highest per capita in the world.[48]

Israel justifies most of its actions towards the Palestinians on the grounds of traditional state security concerns. But an exploration of Israel's actions and elite-level debates indicates that these security priorities expand well beyond what is generally perceived as traditional state security concerns.

Debates about how to preserve the Jewish character of the state in the face of a 'demographic threat' (provided by the 20 per cent of the Israeli population that are of Palestinian heritage and therefore are Muslim and Christian) show that the concept of security being applied is much more broad and complex. Indeed, the first Herzliyah conference, the annual gathering of Israel's political and security elite, addressed this as a key issue for Israel and it is frequently on the agenda as highlighted by the amount of policy papers and keynote speeches discussing the issue.[49] This emphasis on demographics is a product of the logic of Zionism whose goal is not just about securing a Jewish majority in Israel but is about ensuring that Israel is a home for *any* Jewish person in the world to come at any time and instantly be given citizenship. As Israeli sociologist Baruch Kimmerling explains: 'The state is not defined as belonging to its citizens, but to the entire Jewish people.'[50] This was shown by an October 2013 Israeli Supreme Court judgement against people identifying themselves as 'Israeli' rather than 'Jewish', as this, so it ruled, would pose a danger to the foundations of Israel as a Jewish state for the Jewish people.[51] Land must therefore be kept under the control of the state (93 per cent is owned by the state and quasi-state entities), and this requires differential rights for Jews and non-Jews to ensure this.[52] It also helps explain why the demand, since 2009, that Palestinians recognise Israel as a Jewish state[53] (a demand made to no other signatory to a peace treaty with Israel) has a hidden depth and meaning largely ignored by the mainstream media and academics.

The language of security is dominant in the 1993 Oslo Accord and subsequent agreements between Israel and the PLO. This has been understood by third party actors as encapsulating the reasonable demand that violence should cease during negotiations, but what it has meant in reality is that the Palestinian leadership has been continually forced to prove that it can deliver security to Israel *before* the withdrawal of occupation forces and during the continuation of land expropriation, settlement expansion and military violence. And yet history shows us that occupiers never withdraw willingly or easily – particularly if it is territory that is coveted; a fact that multiplies when, as in this case, it is tied up with religious mythology.[54] Israel's actions show that its security concerns expand to the protection of an illegal extra-territorial population in the West Bank (including East Jerusalem) which, by 2014, had doubled since the signing of the Oslo Accord to between 500,000 and 650,000.[55] Indeed, ironically, during periods of 'peacebuilding' Israel managed to transfer more settlers to the oPt.[56]

Israel's strategy has one main aim: to gain and retain control over as much of the land and resources (particularly water[57]) of historic Palestine with the least number of Palestinians on it while provoking minimal, or at least manageable, amounts of international condemnation. This process of modern colonisation implemented through the creation of 'facts on the ground' in which the tiny fragmented remains of historic Palestine are being rapidly absorbed into an expanding Israeli state was sharply exposed in

August 2013 by Israel's refusal to include in agreements with the EU a territorial clause that required it to acknowledge that its sovereignty does not extend beyond the 1967 'Green Line'.[58] The settlers in the West Bank are therefore regarded to be an integral part of the Israeli body politic, and they enjoy access to all Israeli services, they vote in the national elections, they are subject to Israeli law, and they are protected by the IDF.

Palestinian responses to their experiences of dispossession and occupation include different forms of resistance, collaboration, acquiescence and migration – and these have not necessarily been mutually exclusive. The everyday lives of Palestinians and their resistance strategies have been conditioned by the shifting geography and political-economy of Israel's control and counterinsurgency practices. Two main strategies have been followed by Israel: 'integration' (1967 until the early 1990s) followed by 'skewed integration and separation' (early 1990s until the present day).[59] In the initial period after the Six-Day War, Israel's policy was to directly rule the oPt and integrate it into the Israeli economy, but in a way that benefited Israeli businesses, therefore instituting a process that Sara Roy has referred to as 'de-development'.[60] These policies turned the oPt into Israel's largest export market and a source of cheap migrant labour. Thus effective strategies of mass civil disobedience in the first intifada (1987–1993) encompassed both street confrontations between Palestinians and the Israeli army *and* an 'economic war' designed to strike at the heart of the Israeli economy through boycotting Israeli goods and jobs and refusing to pay taxes. The cost to Israel was huge: in the first three months alone, government revenues dropped by 30 per cent (compared to the same period the previous year) and exports to the oPt declined by 40 per cent.[61] Furthermore, the withdrawal of Palestinian workers from their jobs in Israel, estimated to lie anywhere between 20–40 per cent, led Israel's Minister of Finance to conclude that 'ending the uprising is one of the top priorities for the Israeli economy'.[62] In response, everyday life for Palestinians was disrupted (and suspended for those jailed) as Israel sought to crush the resistance by curfews, arrests and direct military violence.[63]

In order to contain and insulate it from such mass-based insurgency, Israel thereafter adopted a strategy of 'skewed integration and separation' in the early 1990s. This involved restricting the numbers of Palestinian workers in Israel, encouraging Israeli companies to subcontract to Palestinian firms, and 'outsourcing' responsibility for the population of the oPt to a Palestinian-run administrative entity without sovereignty – namely the Palestinian Authority (PA) – established as part of the Oslo Accords and discussed in further detail in the following section. The institution of the 'closure regime' and the classification of Palestinians as either residents of Jerusalem, Gaza or the West Bank (and *within* the West Bank between Areas A, B and C, with Israel retaining control over 70 per cent of it), created a political economy that transformed the relationship between space, power and resistance. These policies of 'skewed integration' were codified in the Paris Economic Protocol (the economic counterpart to the Oslo Peace Accord that governed economic relations between Israel and the PA), which tied the Israeli and Palestinian economies together, but to the benefit of the former and detriment to the latter. The 'separation' aspect of the strategy was imposed through the closure regime which dramatically reduced the ability of Palestinians to negatively affect the Israeli economy. And it masked the source of real control in that the economic framework created financial hardship but strikes no longer impacted on the Israeli economy (only the PA's budget). The territorial, economic, social and political fragmentation of the Palestinian body politic reduced the ability of Palestinians to resurrect the types of community action witnessed in the first intifada.[64] Actions thereafter took place in defined geographical spaces: on the fringes of 'autonomous' Palestinian zones (Area A) and Israeli settlements (Area C), and at army checkpoints (into and out of Areas A, B and C). In addition to everyday resistance to the occupation, i.e. refusing to leave land and homes (referred to by Palestinians as *sumud*) despite Israel's methods of direct and structural violence to do so, resistance strategies in the post-second intifada period have taken four main forms: popular resistance committees, attacks on settlers, the Boycott, Divestment and Sanctions (BDS) movement and (specific to Gaza) the firing of rockets into Israel. Popular resistance committees (re)emerged after 2004 in villages in the West Bank affected by the route of the Separation Barrier being built by Israel – and they have held weekly demonstrations which are often violently suppressed by the IDF. Attacks on settlers and soldiers take place on a regular basis, but they are usually random rather than planned, due to the level of control and surveillance in the West Bank. Recognising the asymmetries of power and the reduced ability to harm Israeli interests through local actions, the BDS movement directs the boycott mechanism as a tool of resistance to be applied to Israel by international actors (including civil society, governments, international organisations and businesses).[65] Insurgency strategies in Gaza, however, given the blockade, have largely taken the form of the firing of rockets into Israel. Because of the asymmetric nature of the conflict, raising and keeping the Palestinian issue in the international media has been the key aim of these resistance strategies.

As outlined in the previous section, Western counterinsurgency techniques have developed from attempts at outright suppression to 'winning hearts and minds' to a shared ontology with the goals and principles of human security and peacebuilding. In comparison with these advances in COIN theory and practice, Israel has tended to rely on 'deterrence by punishment' and disproportionate violence, designed to make the population believe that resistance is futile.[66] This has involved policies of mass incarceration: between the beginning of the occupation in 1967 and the middle of 2009, approximately 700,000 Palestinian men, women and children had been detained by Israel.[67] And from 2000 until September 2013, Israel issued 700 life sentences against Palestinians, with 430 sentenced during the second intifada alone.[68] As of October 2014, there were 6,500 Palestinian political prisoners in Israeli jails, including 500 administrative detainees (detention without trial).[69] It is therefore rare to meet a Palestinian who has not had a family member imprisoned.

Israel has also followed a strategy of assassinating the political leaders and cadre of Palestinian resistance groups. From September 2000 until 30 June 2008, for instance, the IDF carried out 348 extra-judicial executions that killed 521 Palestinian activists (as well as 233 bystanders including 71 children and 20 women).[70] Intense levels of direct violence have been supplemented by the structural violence of collective punishment techniques such as curfews and blockades. The Gaza Strip, for instance, is completely encircled by a perimeter electric fence with patrol roads and observation towers for the IDF, while the sea is patrolled by the Israeli Navy. Israel controls the movement of goods and people in and out of the area despite its 'disengagement' in September 2005.[71] After a split in the PA in June 2007 that left Hamas governing the Gaza Strip and Fateh governing the West Bank, Israel's blockade has restricted fuel and electricity supplies and has dramatically decreased humanitarian aid and commercial exchange.[72] On frequent occasions, Western donors have warned that the Gaza Strip is on the brink of economic collapse,[73] which is a deliberate policy of Israel's as exposed by Wikileaks in 2011.[74] The small impoverished enclave was further devastated in two military campaigns by Israel: *Operation Cast Lead* that ran from 27 December 2008 to 18 January 2009 (which killed 1,500 Palestinians and wounded 5,300,[75] inflicted property damage estimated between US$1.6 billion and $1.9 billion, and made over 10,000 people homeless[76]) and *Operation Protective Edge* that ran from 8 July to 26 August 2014 (which killed nearly 1,500 Palestinians and wounded 5,300, inflicted property damage estimated between US$1.6 billion and $1.9 billion, and made over 10,000 people homeless;[77] the reconstruction, relief and recovery was estimated at US$4 billion[78]). The widespread destruction of physical infrastructure and public and private property has been a key feature of Israel's counterinsurgency tactics. Operation Defensive Shield (28 March–21 April 2002), for instance, which was Israel's largest military operation in the West Bank since its occupation in 1967, is estimated to have inflicted damage worth US$3.5 billion.[79] Much of this infrastructure has been built (and rebuilt) with donor aid.

In addition to these 'kinetic' and 'enemy-centric' counterinsurgency strategies,[80] Israel has, on occasion, tried to foster acquiescence through other more benign methods, which had more success when taken up by Western donors and repackaged as peacebuilding. In the economic arena, for instance, in 1989, in response to the first intifada, Israel considered a development plan that focused on creating sealed industrial zones linked to the Israeli economy, and which would absorb Palestinian workers. This policy re-emerged after 1993 under the tutelage of the World Bank.[81] And in the political sphere, Israel tried to foster sympathetic elites and governance structures in the oPt, such as the Village Leagues introduced in the late

1970s.[82] Some critics argue that the creation of the PA is the result of the implementation of a more sophisticated form of this type of policy.[83] Israel's counterinsurgency techniques applied to the Palestinian population are mostly based on direct violence. But this has been inherently unstable and has twice been challenged by full-blown insurgencies i.e. the first and second intifadas, which were deeply damaging to Israel's international image as it used huge military force to crush them. The more subtle methods of counterinsurgency that have eluded Israel – the ones designed to immunise a population against unrest through instituting a form of self-policing – have been more successfully applied by Western peacebuilding agencies, as they are not directly involved in the processes of dispossession that spark opposition and insurgency. These are explored in the following section.

Peacebuilding as counterinsurgency in the oPt

In essence, Western peacebuilding policies pursue a modern version of the *mission civilisatrice* by attempting to implant Western socio-political and economic forms (or, rather, an idealised version) while ensuring security and control.[84] This has echoes in colonial practice in which the goal was not merely about extracting goods and wealth, but was also about restructuring economies and polities to tie them into a capitalist world economy and an international society of legally-sovereign states. Historically, political sovereignty was constructed as a relationship of power connecting citizens with the state – and for third world, post-colonial states this involved embracing a 'developmentalist social contract' (rather than a liberal democratic social contract model). Sovereignty in the neoliberal era, on the other hand, has been constructed as a relationship of power where states promote 'the social relations of the market and the participation of citizenry in that project'[85] in the context of a powerful international architecture of regulation that was built on the ashes of the period of Bandung and the campaign for a New International Economic Order (NIEO). Until the 1980s, development was defined as a state-centred process requiring a high degree of government intervention dominated by protectionist and corporatist policies.[86] After the 'neoliberal turn', the type of policies that states could follow became increasingly circumscribed as the transformation of the global political economy proceeded apace – and this has been enshrined in the architecture of global governance and imperial multilateralism.[87] The policies developed for wartorn societies are no different in this regard. Indeed, the 'overall framing of peace by external agencies reinforces neoliberal prescriptions, particularly in the realm of political economy, that neither take account of local needs and agency, nor reflect on the role of global capitalism and structural adjustment policies as drivers of conflict'.[88]

Despite the one-size-fits-all nature of Western peacebuilding policies, the way in which they interact with local political economies creates different kinds of peace,[89] or 'hybridities'.[90] Peacebuilding therefore takes place in concrete socio-economic and political settings, and interacts and affects these political economies in crucial ways. The ways in which peacebuilding practices have intertwined with Israel's methods of control has therefore created a particular form of 'colonial present'[91] in the oPt which has interacted with and assisted in the emergence of a Palestinian elite who are policing their own people and mediating between them and the occupier. This has created a subtle and more legitimate form of securing the Palestinian population and ensured some level of stability. But peacebuilding as counterinsurgency takes time to implement and implant because it is about establishing pacification techniques deeply embedded in recipient societal structures; it is about creating a particular form of political economy that stabilises *from the inside* in collaboration with local elites who benefit from its implementation. And yet the position of the Palestinian elite is also unstable and contradictory (dependent as it is on the Oslo peace framework); so the counterinsurgency circle is not completely sealed.

After the signing of the Oslo Accords, the PLO returned to the West Bank and Gaza Strip, and its cadre became the elite staffing the institutional structures of the PA with Yasser Arafat as first president.[92] Palestinian diaspora capitalists also returned, and were prioritised by the PA over local capitalists therefore giving them influence in determining PA economic plans and access to privileged monopolies that had to be coordinated with Israel and through Israeli companies.[93] Into this context, and indeed providing the essential support for these processes given the dire state of the oPt's political economy after 26 years of occupation and six years of intifada, came a huge expansion of Western aid and donor involvement. The rationale was to 'mobilise resources to make the agreement [i.e. Oslo] work'.[94] Western donors have therefore continually committed significant resources towards supporting the Oslo process, as shown by the level of overseas development assistance which rose from US$39.24 million in 1993 to $1.752 billion in 2013. In this same time period, total aid from OECD donors and multilateral agencies has constituted over US$15 billion.[95] To coordinate this aid and supervise the Palestinians in their institution-building, an elaborate layer of oversight committees was formed by the Western donors, which reflects common donor practice in other developing and war-torn societies.[96] However, the PA was created to govern in a context that was not post-conflict but one of continued occupation and colonisation – it has neither sovereignty nor control over its resources, and it has no defined borders. The only body that holds sovereignty over the land and resources of the oPt and controls the borders is Israel – which has continued to pursue a process of colonisation and strategies of counterinsurgency as outlined in the previous section. This situation has necessitated large and continuing amounts of aid to mitigate and manage the economic and social problems created by Israel's policies of skewed integration and separation (as outlined in the previous section), and the destruction of infrastructure through military violence. Donors are therefore indeed subsidising Israel's occupation, as charged by their critics.[97] This is not an unintended consequence, however, but a necessary corollary of peacebuilding as counterinsurgency in the context of a colonisation process.

The large numbers of donors (over 40) and multilateral agencies (over 20) involved in the oPt, necessitated the creation of an 'aid politburo' of the dominant players: the US, the EU, the World Bank and the UN.[98] Despite the key roles played by the UN, the World Bank and the EU, the most important third party actor is the US. Ultimately, the relations and roles of these main actors reflect global structures of power as they manifest themselves in the region. US support for Israel is the result of historical and cultural but mostly strategic reasons.[99] The US's dominant role is accepted by both Israel and the PLO/PA – and all other donors have tended not to publicly challenge US positions for self-interested policy reasons. For the US, ensuring stability and Western dominance in the region is a central foreign policy objective as indicated by the huge amount of military bases in the region, and the sheer number of aggressive military actions taken by the US in the Greater Middle East since 1980.[100]

The donor governance structures created to support the various peace agreements has ensured that Israel's security paradigm (discussed in the previous section) is prioritised, that budget support to the PA continues and that it progressively adopts neoliberal economic and good governance policies, and that humanitarian aid is provided – because the alternative is regarded to be much worse (i.e. the emergence of a Palestinian political movement with widespread support that is opposed to the Oslo process, and/or extreme poverty and political instability). The priority is stabilisation – and that is the structural prerogative underlying all the apparent twists and turns in donor policy. Indeed, since their inception in 1994, donor peacebuilding policies have altered on occasion to ensure that the Oslo peace framework continues, often in the face of threatened breakdown, while the PA has been persuaded to progressively embrace liberal peacebuilding policies in a context of colonisation. To date, there have been three phases – the 'interim' period (1993–1999), the 'Roadmap' period (2002–2006) and the 'West Bank first' period (2006–present day), which I analyse elsewhere in depth.[101] However, for reasons of space, this chapter merely outlines the main contours of the policy and practices in the realms of governance, development and security: the proposed core aspects of peacebuilding as counterinsurgency.

Donor policies in the oPt have followed general peacebuilding principles as applied in other war-torn societies, but they have manifested themselves in particular ways and with certain impacts. In the realms of governance, Western strategies have focused on supporting 'sympathetic' Palestinian elites and embedding their power in opposition to those who reject the vision of peace on offer. Using aid to prop up preferred 'peace partners' is common in peace processes where international donors confer legitimacy on some actors and withhold it from others. But in this context, 'sympathetic elites' are defined as those with which Israel will negotiate and who are acceptable to the donors, particularly those with the most power to decide and exclude (i.e. in this case the US).[102] I have labelled this the 'partners for peace' discursive framework (because of the constant use of this phrase), which has underpinned and provided the ideological rationale for two separate instances of changes in PA personnel insisted on by Israel and the donors. The first instance was during the second intifada: PA president Yasser Arafat was forced by the Roadmap to agree to reforms that diluted his power through for example the creation of the post of prime minister. The second instance was after the election of Hamas in 2006, where a boycott by the main peacebuilding actors and Israel created the conditions for Hamas to be forced out of office and restricted to the Gaza Strip. The continual operation of the 'partners for peace' paradigm has also meant Western donors have made the possibility of political reconciliation between Fateh and Hamas and thus the administrative reconciliation of the West Bank and Gaza Strip, extremely difficult if not impossible. This means that this most recent example of the fragmentation of the Palestinian body politic is underpinned and supported by Western donor practices.

In the realms of economic development, Western strategies have focused on supporting the development of infrastructure, a more open economy tied into the world market, and a Palestinian business elite with vested interests in ensuring stability (albeit one that they wish would lead to statehood). Opening up countries to the world market is a common donor prescription, and in this context it had a broader strategy of tying the oPt into a regional economic system designed to normalise relations with Israel and the Arab states, and which also has had the effect of intensifying Palestinian economic dependence on Israel. The West Bank is a captive market for Israel – and local companies find it impossible to compete with cheap imported goods. Monopolies, however, are still in existence and are often controlled by those connected to the PA, and so the form of crony capitalism created under Arafat has continued, albeit in a slightly different format. While the Western peacebuilding industry has a preference for neoliberal economic and good governance policies, their adoption in the oPt has been gradual and patchy – and has been the outcome of struggles and changes *within* the Palestinian elite, assisted and facilitated by changes in the policies of Israel and pressure from Western donors. And so despite billions of dollars of peacebuilding assistance over the past two decades, the strictures of the PEP, the restrictions of Israel's occupation, and neoliberal policies have all combined to create an economic climate in the oPt which is marked by weak GDP growth, high unemployment (particularly among the youth) and pressure on wages, a massive growth in private consumer debt, and a struggling private sector.[103] The Palestinian economy is therefore 'trapped on a path of low growth, economic dependence on Israel and reliance on foreign aid'.[104] Because of this, the PA has large and growing arrears to private suppliers and Palestinian banks (as well as recurring shortfalls in donor aid); by March 2014, the PA's debt stood at US$4.8 billion.[105] The Oslo framework and Western donor policies have helped to facilitate the skewed development of the oPt economy.

In the security realm, peacebuilding strategies have continually focused on the creation and enhancement of a Palestinian security force capable of ensuring stability. But in this context, this has meant promoting Israel's security first through a counter-terrorism strategy which required a tight regulation of security coordination between the PA and Israel under the auspices of US control. Under conditions of Israel's continued occupation and in a context where the Palestinians lack democratic governance, critics charge that the conditions have been created for authoritarianism and the construction of a police state.[106] In 2014, the Palestinian security services employed more than 70,000 across the West Bank and Gaza[107] – that is around one for every 57 Palestinians in the oPt, which by any comparisons is a high figure.[108] The involvement of Palestinian security personnel in the second intifada does not change these facts, it merely goes to prove that the PA itself is in a contradictory position, and its elites (and the military forces that protect them and the Oslo framework) continually have to make decisions to participate in this process.

And so a picture emerges of a political economy that is the outcome of the policies and practices of Israel, the donors, and different sections of the Palestinian elite under the auspices of liberal peacebuilding as structured by the Oslo Accords. In the first, interim period (1994–1999), the interaction of these three actors facilitated the emergence of a neo-patrimonial state which used nepotism and violence to suppress opposition, created trading monopolies and unaudited accounts, and instituted a proliferation of security institutions under the direct control of the PA president not the parliament. This period ended with the outbreak of the second intifada, during which security coordination disintegrated, the institutions of the PA were destroyed, and there was mass destruction of physical infrastructure. In the second, Roadmap period (2003–2006), peacebuilding strategies focused on rebuilding the PA but removing Arafat through democratic reform, reducing monopolies and corruption through good governance strategies, and rebuilding the security sector but this time more streamlined and more securely under the control of the US. This period ended with the election of Hamas, a party that rejects the Oslo framework, in January 2006 – an event that ushered in another period of instability and an internal Palestinian struggle for control which culminated in the administrative division between the West Bank and Gaza Strip. The third, West Bank first, phase (2007–present), signifies the coming to fruition of the policies introduced under the Roadmap and thus the adoption and internalisation of Western peacebuilding priorities. Codified in the 2008–2010 Palestinian Reform and Development Plan and subsequent national development plans, these document the PA's focus on building institutions within the framework of Oslo, promotion of a private sector focused on services and export-oriented activities, and good governance (rather than democracy).[109] The twists and turns of donor policies in the past 20 years has meant that democracy, human rights and even economic development have been downgraded, or ignored, if and when they have been an obstacle, or not been essential, to the survival of the Oslo framework. Western aid and donor practices have therefore become intricately intertwined and embedded within the processes of colonisation and fragmentation taking place in the oPt, while at the same time purporting to reduce (or manage) its impacts. The Oslo framework and the peacebuilding interventions have been a successful method of stabilisation because they have operated as another layer of counterinsurgency strategies designed to create an acquiescent Palestinian population.

The outcome of this meant that by 2015, there was an isolated and blockaded Gaza, an East Jerusalem increasingly integrated (but in a skewed and unequal manner) into Israel, and a West Bank with widely varying political economies (between middle class and prosperous towns such as Ramallah to desperately poor refugee camps and rural villages) living side-by-side with wealthy Jewish settlements integrated into Israel via an extensive road network system while enjoying political representation in the Knesset (Israel's parliament) and the protection of Israel's military and legal system. And yet there is a glaring contradiction that lies at the heart of these interlocking methods of control that could blow the whole edifice apart. Ensuring stability and acquiescence while an occupying state implements policies that are, in effect, a form of colonisation and primitive accumulation is inherently destabilising. Taking land and resources from people will always provoke opposition. What is more difficult to predict, however, is how, when and in what form this opposition will emerge. Western peacebuilding agencies, unfortunately do not have a 'Plan B' for this eventuality.[110]

Conclusion: complicit with a colonial peace

The Palestinian struggle for self-determination is hugely significant in the history of insurgency and counterinsurgency.[111] In fact the authors of an extensive RAND study in 2008 argue that Palestine continues to play a key role in global insurgency as a powerful recruiting tool for Jihadist groups.[112] This fact might possibly lead one to the common-sense conclusion that if this is indeed the case, then to resolve this issue would be in the interests of those who seek global stability. But this is only true if one believes that the global stability being sought is to be underpinned by justice, equality and self-determination, and there is nothing to suggest that this is the case. In fact, the polar opposite is true – strategies are designed to manage and suppress the instability that results from manifestations of inequality and repression, to control it not resolve it – because to do so would require a reconfiguration of global power to allow local populations to decide their own developmental and political futures.[113] This is a solution that is denied, particularly in the case of the oPt where even the most basic aid principles and agendas applied elsewhere (e.g. the Paris Declaration on Aid Effectiveness) are sidelined in favour of a highly securitised discourse. Indeed one senior academic with much experience of researching security issues in war-torn societies, told me that it was impossible to get interviews 'on the record' about security sector reform and security coordination in the oPt, which is a problem that she had not experienced before, even in Afghanistan and Iraq.[114]

People who argue that Palestine is but one example in an unstable, unequal and repressive world, that gets far too much academic and media coverage, miss the point. The Palestinian situation is internationally significant because it constitutes a struggle by its people for self-determination in a period regarded as post-colonial, against a state which has the support of the world's last remaining superpower and which invokes a moral rationale based on the long history of oppression suffered by the Jewish people. For this reason the competing narratives of suffering and quest for self-determination can often displace and replace a structural analysis; this chapter, however, posits the case for the necessity of the latter over a focus on the former.

The argument advanced made three key points. First, that there is a deep structural symbiosis in the philosophy and methods of counterinsurgency and peacebuilding that lie in securing the population against unrest through the implementation of governance, development and security strategies that instil acquiescence and ensure control. The second argument advanced was that the Israel-Palestine conflict is fundamentally a colonial struggle over land and resources that pits a powerful state against a stateless people, and which has created a vicious cycle of insurgency and counterinsurgency. Israel's counterinsurgency techniques against the Palestinians involve both direct violence and more subtle methods of population control to ensure acquiescence to the process of colonisation which is progressively disenfranchising, dispossessing and disarticulating the Palestinian body politic. And it is in this context that Western peacebuilding strategies of governance, security coordination and neoliberal economics have been pursued. This has constituted a further layer of pacification techniques through the pursuit of a political economy that stabilises *from the inside* in collaboration with a section of Palestinian elites. The political economy of the oPt has thus undergone a radical transformation since 1993 which has created an internal constituency also keen on stability. The third argument advanced, therefore, was that peacebuilding as counterinsurgency has complemented and meshed with the structures of domination and repression created by Israel in subtle but crucial ways that are not always visible, are often difficult to detect, and appear benign. The politics of international intervention in this case has played a crucial role in creating and sustaining a violent colonial peace.

Acknowledgements

Key parts of this chapter are based on an article that appeared in *Review of International Studies*, vol. 41, no. 1, January 2015, with the title of 'Peacebuilding as Counterinsurgency in the Occupied Palestinian Territory'. I would like to thank Cambridge University Press for permission to reproduce parts of it here. I would also like to thank the British Academy, the Council for British Research in the Levant, and the Leverhulme Trust for grants which made this research possible. Last, but definitely not least, I would like to thank Michael Pugh, Alaa Tartir and Roger Mac Ginty for insightful comments made on an earlier draft – all of which went towards creating a tighter, more coherent argument. But any errors are, of course, my own.

Notes

1 Anne Le More, *International Assistance to the Palestinians After Oslo: Political Guilt, Wasted Money*, Abingdon: Routledge, 2008; Mushtaq H. Khan, George Giacaman and Inge Amundsen (eds), *State Formation in Palestine: Viability and Governance During a Social Transformation*, Abingdon: Routledge Curzon, 2004; Sara Roy, *Failing Peace: Gaza and the Palestinian–Israeli Conflict*, London: Pluto Press, 2007; Sahar Taghdisi-Rad, *The Political Economy of Aid in Palestine: Relief from Development or Development Delayed?*, London: Routledge, 2011.
2 Roy (note 1 above).
3 For example, Mandy Turner, 'The Power of "Shock and Awe": The Palestinian Authority and the Road to Reform', *International Peacekeeping*, vol. 16, no. 4, 2009, pp. 562–577; Mandy Turner, 'Creating "Partners for Peace": The Palestinian Authority and the International Statebuilding Agenda', *Journal of Intervention and Statebuilding*, vol. 4, no. 1, 2011, pp. 1–21; Mandy Turner, 'Statebuilding in Palestine: Caught Between Occupation, Realpolitik and the Liberal Peace', in David Chandler and Timothy D. Sisk (eds), *Routledge Handbook of International Statebuilding*, Abingdon: Routledge, 2013.
4 Laleh Khalili, *Time in the Shadows: Confinement in Counterinsurgencies*, Stanford, CA: Stanford University Press, 2012, p. 58.
5 Journal of Palestine Studies, 'Israel's Military Operations Against Gaza, 2000–2008', *Journal of Palestine Studies*, vol. 38, no. 3, 2009, pp. 122–138; Human Rights Watch, *White Flag Deaths: Killing of Palestinian Civilians During Operation Cast Lead*, New York: HRW, 13 August 2009; Journal of Palestine Studies, 'Damage to Palestinian People and Property During Operation Cast Lead', *Journal of Palestine Studies*, vol. 38, no. 3, 2009, pp. 210–212.
6 B'Tselem, *Take No Prisoners: the Fatal Shooting of Palestinians by Israeli Security Forces During 'Arrest Operations'*, Jerusalem: B'Tselem, May 2005 (at: www.btselem.org/publications/summaries/200505_take_no_prisoners); Amnesty International, *Starved of Justice: Palestinians Detailed without Trial by Israel*, London: Amnesty, 2012; B'Tselem and Hamoked, *Absolute Prohibition: The Torture and Ill-Treatment of Palestinian Detainees*, Jerusalem: B'Tselem, May 2007.
7 Gal Luft, 'The Logic of Israel's Targeted Killing', *Middle East Quarterly*, Winter 2003, pp. 3–13; Palestinian Centre for Human Rights, *Extra-Judicial Executions as Israeli Government Policy: Extra-Judicial Executions Committed by the Israeli Occupation Forces August 2006–June 2008*, Gaza: PCHR, 2008; B'Tselem, *Act of Vengeance: Israeli's Bombing of the Gaza Power Plant and Its Effects*, Jerusalem: B'Tselem, September 2006.

8 Yoav Peled, 'The Evolution of Israeli Citizenship: An Overview', *Citizenship Studies*, vol. 12, no. 3, 2008, pp. 335–345; Human Rights Watch, *Separate and Unequal: Israel's Discriminatory Treatment of the Palestinians in the Occupied Palestinian Territories*, New York: HRW, December 2010; Human Rights Watch, *Forget About Him, He's Not Here: Israel's Control of Palestinian Residency in the West Bank and Gaza*, New York: HRW, February 2012.

9 B'Tselem, *Under the Guise of Security: Routing the Separation Barrier to Enable the Expansion of Israeli Settlements in the West Bank*, Jerusalem: B'Tselem, December 2005; International Court of Justice, 'Legal Consequences of the Construction of a Wall in the Occupied Palestinian Territory: Advisory Opinion', 9 July 2004 (at: www.icj-cij.org/docket/index.php?pr=71&code=mwp&p1=3&p2=4&p3=6&case =131&k=5a); Office for the Coordination of Humanitarian Affairs (UNOCHA), *The Humanitarian Impact on Palestinians of Israeli Settlements and Other Infrastructure in the West Bank*, New York: UNOCHA, July 2007; B'Tselem, *One Big Prison: Freedom of Movement To and From the Gaza Strip on the Eve of the Disengagement*, Jerusalem: B'Tselem, Jerusalem, 2005, p. 5.

10 Hillel Cohen and Ron Dudai, 'Human Rights Dilemmas in Using Informants to Combat Terrorism: The Israel-Palestine Case', *Terrorism and Political Violence*, vol. 17, no. 1, pp. 229–243; Neve Gordon, *Israel's Occupation*, Berkeley, CA: University of California Press, 2008.

11 David Kilcullen, 'Counterinsurgency Redux', *Survival*, vol. 48, no. 4, winter 2006–2007, pp. 111–130, here p. 121.

12 US Department of Defense, *Sustaining US Global Leadership: Priorities for 21st Century Defense*, Washington, DC: US Department of Defense, January 2012; UK Government, *Securing Britain in an Age of Uncertainty: The Strategic Defence and Security Review*, London: UK Government, October 2010.

13 David Kilcullen, *Three Pillars of Counterinsurgency*, Remarks delivered at the U.S. Government Counterinsurgency Conference, Washington, DC, 28 September 2006, p. 6 (at: www.au.af.mil/au/awc/awcgate/uscoin/3pillars_of_ counterinsurgency.pdf).

14 Khalili (note 4 above).

15 Kilcullen (note 13 above), p. 3.

16 US Government, *US Government Counterinsurgency Guide*, Washington, DC: United States Government Interagency Counterinsurgency Initiative, January 2009, p. 12.

17 Boutros Boutros-Ghalis, 'An Agenda for Peace: Preventive Diplomacy, Peacemaking and Peacekeeping', UN doc. A/47/277, S/24111, 17 June 1992 (at: www.unrol.org/files/A_47_277.pdf); UN Secretary-General High Level Panel on Threats, Challenges and Change, 'A More Secure World: Our Shared Responsibility', 2 December 2004 (at: www.un.org/secureworld); Kofi Annan, 'In Larger Freedom: Towards Security, Development and Human Rights for All', 21 March 2005 (at: www.un.org/largerfreedom/contents.htm).

18 Michael Pugh, 'Reflections on Aggressive Peace', *International Peacekeeping*, vol. 19, no. 4, 2012, pp. 410–425.

19 US Government (note 16 above), p. 12.

20 Kilcullen (note 13 above), pp. 4–5.

21 Pugh (note 18 above), p. 413.

22 Bruno Charbonneau, 'The Imperial Legacy of International Peacebuilding: The Case of Francophone Africa', *Review of International Studies*, vol. 40, no. 3, 2014, pp. 607–630.

23 Arturo Escobar, *Encountering Development: The Making and Unmaking of the Third World*, Princeton, NJ: Princeton University Press, 1995, p. 27.

24 Benjamin Grob-Fitzgibbon, *Imperial Endgame: Britain's Dirty Wars and the End of Empire*, Basingstoke: Palgrave Macmillan, 2011.

25 Raymond Hinnebusch, 'Europe and the Middle East: From Imperialism to Liberal Peace?' *Review of European Studies*, vol. 4, no. 3, July 2012, pp. 18–31.
26 Mark Moyar, *Development in Afghanistan's Counterinsurgency: A New Guide*, Washington, DC: Orbis Operations, March 2011, p. 12; Kilcullen (note 13 above).
27 Jaroslav Petrik, 'Development in Counterinsurgency: Marrying Theory to Practice', Paper presented at the International Studies Association annual convention, New Orleans, 17–20 February 2010.
28 Ruth Blakeley 'Still Training to Torture? US Training of Latin American Military Forces', *Third World Quarterly*, vol. 27, no. 8, 2006, pp. 1439–1461; David F. Schmitz, *The United States and Right-Wing Dictatorships, 1965–1989*, New York: Cambridge University Press, 2006.
29 US Government (note 16 above).
30 DFID, FCO and MOD, *The Global Conflict Prevention Pool: A Joint UK Government Approach to Reducing Conflict*, London: DFID/FCO/MOD, 2001.
31 For some expressions of how this has manifested, see Agnes Hurwitz and Gordon Peake, *Strengthening the Security-Development Nexus: Assessing International Policy and Practice since the 1990s*, Conference Report April 2004, New York: International Peace Academy, 2004; Necla Tschirgi, *Peacebuilding as the Link between Security and Development: Is the Window of Opportunity Closing?*, New York: International Peace Academy, December 2003.
32 There are too many policy documents proposing the human security perspective to list them all here. However, the United Nations Trust Fund for Human Security lists many of the UN documents that have outlined and expanded on the term and its potential uses in policy and practice (at: www.unocha.org/humansecurity/resources/publications-and-products).
33 Solomon Major, 'Sharpening Our Plowshares: Applying the Lessons of Counterinsurgency to Development and Humanitarian Aid', American Political Science Association 2010 Annual Meeting Paper (at: http://ssrn.com/abstract=1657482); Markus Kienscherf, 'A Programme of Global Pacification: US Counterinsurgency Doctrine and the Biopolitics of Human (In)security', *Security Dialogue*, vol. 42, no. 6, 2011, pp. 517–535.
34 Mary Kaldor, *Human Security: Reflections on Globalisation and Intervention*, Cambridge: Polity, 2007; Marlies Glasius and Mary Kaldor, *A Human Security Doctrine for Europe: Projects, Principles, Practicalities*, London: Routledge, 2008; Yale Journal of International Affairs, 'Putting People First: The Growing Influence of "Human Security"; an Interview with Mary Kaldor', *Yale Journal of International Affairs*, vol. 5, no. 2, Summer 2010, pp. 17–22.
35 Mary Kaldor and Shannon D. Beebe, *The Ultimate Weapon is No Weapon: Human Security and the New Rules of War and Peace*, New York: Public Affairs, 2010, p. 68.
36 World Bank, *Post-Conflict Reconstruction: The Role of the World Bank*, Washington, DC: World Bank, 1998; OECD–DAC, *The DAC Guidelines: Helping Prevent Violent Conflict*, Paris: OECD, 2001; Department for International Development, *Why We Need to Work More Effectively in Fragile States*, London: DFID, 2005.
37 Mandy Turner, Neil Cooper and Michael Pugh, 'Institutionalised and Coopted: Why Human Security has Lost its Way', in David Chandler and Niklas Hynek (eds), *Critical Perspectives on Human Security: Discourses of Emancipation and Regimes of Power*, Abingdon: Routledge, 2010, pp. 83–96, here p. 86.
38 Roland Paris, 'Human Security: Paradigm Shift or Hot Air?', *International Security*, vol. 26, no. 2, 2001, pp. 87–102.
39 Biljana Vankovska, 'The Human Security Doctrine for Europe: A View from Below', *International Peacekeeping*, vol. 14, no. 2, 2007, pp. 264–281.
40 Roland Paris and Timothy D. Sisk, 'Introduction: Understanding the Contradictions of Postwar Statebuilding', in Roland Paris and Timothy D. Sisk (eds),

The Dilemma of Statebuilding: Confronting the Contradictions of Postwar Peace Operations, London: Routledge, 2009, pp. 1–20.
41 UN, *A More Secure World: Our Shared Responsibility*, Report of the Secretary-General's High Level Panel on Threats, Challenges and Change, New York: UN, December 2004; UN, *Report of the Panel on United Nations Peace Operations* (the 'Brahimi Report'), New York: UN, August 2000.
42 World Bank, *World Development Report 2011: Conflict, Security and Development*, Washington, DC: World Bank, April 2011.
43 Mark Duffield, *Development, Security and Unending War: Governing the World of Peoples*, Cambridge: Policy, 2007.
44 I am thankful to Roger Mac Ginty for this point.
45 Yoram Peri, *Generals in the Cabinet Room: How the Military Shapes Israeli Policy*, Washington, DC: United States Institute for Peace, 2006, pp. 17–32.
46 International Crisis Group, *Back to Basics: Israel's Arab Minority and the Israel–Palestine Conflict*, Middle East Report no. 119, Jerusalem: ICG, 14 March 2012, p. 37, footnote 306. Although, of course, the Druze have been subject to compulsory military service since 1956, in contrast to Christian and Muslim Arabs.
47 Peri (note 45 above).
48 *The Economist*, 'The Israel Defense Forces: Taking Wing', 10 August 2013 (at: www.economist.com/news/middle-east-and-africa/21583317-israels-armed-forces-are-shifting-emphasis-mechanised-warfare-toward-air-and?frsc=dg|b).
49 Papers and keynotes speeches can be downloaded from its website (at: www.herzliyaconference.org/eng/?CategoryID=31&ArticleID=1892).
50 Baruch Kimmerling, 'Religion, Nationalism and Democracy in Israel', *Constellations*, vol. 6, no. 3, 1999, p. 340.
51 Associated Press, 'Israeli Court Rejects Israeli Nationality, Arguing it Could Undermine Jewish Character', 4 October 2013 (at: www.foxnews.com/world/2013/10/04/israeli-court-rejects-israeli-nationality-saying-it-could-undermine-jewish/).
52 Mushtaq H. Khan, 'Learning the Lessons of Olso: Statebuilding and Freedoms in Palestine', in Mandy Turner and Omar Shweiki (eds), *Decolonizing Palestinian Political Economy: De-development and Beyond*, Basingstoke: Palgrave Macmillan, 2014.
53 Amos Harel, Avi Issacharoff, News Agencies and Akiva Eldar, 'Netanyahu Demands Palestinians Recognize "Jewish" State', *Haaretz*, 16 April 2009 (at: www.haaretz.com/news/netanyahu-demands-palestinians-recognize-jewish-state-1.274207).
54 Nur Masalha, *The Bible and Zionism: Invented Traditions, Archaeology and Post-colonialism in Palestine–Israel*, London: Zed, 2007.
55 UN Secretary-General, 'Human rights situation in the Occupied Palestinian Territory, including East Jerusalem', A/HRC/28/45, 5 March 2015.
56 Neve Gordon and Yinon Cohen, 'Western Interests, Israeli Unilateralism, and the Two-State Solution', *Journal of Palestine Studies*, vol. 41, no. 3, 2012, pp. 6–18, here pp. 11–12.
57 Clemens Messerschmid, 'Hydro-apartheid and Water Access in Israel-Palestine: Challenging the Myths of Cooperation and Scarcity', in Turner and Shweiki (eds), *Decolonizing Palestinian Political Economy*, Basingstoke: Palgrave Macmillan, 2014.
58 Barakat Ravid, 'Israel to Tell EU: We Won't Sign Agreements Based on Settlement Guidelines', 8 August 2013 (at: www.haaretz.com/news/diplomacy-defense/.premium-1.540522).
59 Raja Khalidi and Sahar Taghdisi-Rad, *The Economic Dimensions of Prolonged Occupation: Continuity and Change in Israeli Policy towards the Palestinian Economy*, New York: UNCTAD, August 2009.

60 Roy (note 1 above), p. 33.
61 Mazim B. Qumsiyeh, *Popular Resistance in Palestine: A History of Hope and Empowerment*, London: Pluto Press, 2011, p. 157.
62 Quoted in Khalidi and Taghdisi-Rad (note 59 above), p. 7.
63 Gordon (note 10 above), pp. 154–164.
64 Jamil Hilal, 'The Polarisation of the Palestinian Political Field', *Journal of Palestine Studies*, vol. 36, no. 3, 2010, pp. 24–39.
65 Omar Barghouti, *Boycott, Divestment and Sanctions: The Global Struggle for Palestinian Rights*, Chicago, IL: Haymarket, 2011.
66 Or Honig, 'The End of Israeli Military Restraint: Out with the New, in with the Old', *Middle East Quarterly*, 2007, pp. 63–74.
67 Human Rights Council, *Human Rights in Palestine and Other Occupied Arab Territories*, Report of the United Nations Fact Finding Mission on the Gaza Conflict, ('The Goldstone Report'), Human Rights Council doc. A/HRC/12/48, 15 September 2009, paragraph 86.
68 Middle East Monitor, 'Israel Issues 700 Life Sentences against Palestinians in 13 Years', 30 September 2013 (at: www.middleeastmonitor.com/news/middle-east/7593-israel-issues-700-life-sentences-against-palestinians-in-13-years).
69 Addameer, 'Addameer Monthly Detention Report', 1 October 2014 (at: www.addameer.org/etemplate.php?id=729).
70 Palestinian Centre for Human Rights, *Extra-Judicial Executions as Israeli Government Policy: Extra-Judicial Executions Committed by the Israeli Occupation Forces August 2006–June 2008*, Gaza: PCHR, 2008, p. 7 (at: www.pchrgaza.org/files/Reports/English/pdf_killing/killing%20report9.pdf).
71 B'Tselem, *One Big Prison* (note 9 above), p. 5.
72 International Crisis Group, *Gaza's Unfinished Business*, Middle East Report, no. 85, Brussels: ICG, 23 April 2009.
73 Toni O'Loughlin, 'Gaza Near to Collapse as Israel Tightens Grip, Says Bank', *The Guardian*, 22 December 2008 (at: www.guardian.co.uk/world/2008/dec/22/israel-palestinians-middle-east).
74 Reuters, 'Wikileaks: Israel Aimed to Keep Gaza Economy on Brink of Collapse', *Haaretz*, 5 January 2011 (at: www.haaretz.com/news/diplomacy-defense/wikileaks-israel-aimed-to-keep-gaza-economy-on-brink-of-collapse-1.335354).
75 International Crisis Group (note 72 above), p. 1.
76 Journal of Palestine Studies, 'Damage to Palestinian People and Property' (note 5 above).
77 UNOCHA, *Gaza Crisis Appeal: September 2014 Update*, New York: UNOCHA, September 2014 (at: www.ochaopt.org/documents/gaza_crisis_appeal_9_september.pdf).
78 Association of International Development Agencies, *Reconstructing Gaza: Five Principles for Transformative Change*, Jerusalem: Association of International Development Agencies, 3 October 2014 (at: www.diakonia.se/globalassets/blocks-ihl-site/ihl---rightside-boxes/reconstructing-gaza-five-principles-for-transformative-change.pdf).
79 UN Conference on Trade and Development, *The Palestinian War-Torn Economy: Aid, Development and State Formation*, Geneva: UNCTAD, 2006, p. 8.
80 Khalili (note 4 above), p. 58.
81 Peter Lagerquist, 'Privatizing the Occupation: The Political Economy of an Oslo Development Plan', *Journal of Palestine Studies*, vol. 32, no. 2, 2003, pp. 5–20.
82 Gordon (note 10 above), pp. 96–115.
83 Edward Saïd, *From Oslo to Iraq and the Roadmap*, Bloomsbury: London, 2004; Gordon (note 10 above).

84 Mandy Turner, 'Completing the Circle: Peacebuilding as Colonial Practice in the Occupied Palestinian Territory', *International Peacekeeping*, vol. 19, no. 5, 2012, pp. 492–507.
85 Graham Harrison, *Neoliberal Africa: The Impact of Global Social Engineering*, London: Zed Books, 2010, p. 91.
86 Ha Joon-Chang, *Bad Samaritans: The Guilty Secrets of Rich Nations and the Threat to Global Prosperity*, London: Random House, 2008, pp. 26–28.
87 Mark T. Berger, 'From Nation-Building to State-Building: The Geopolitics of Development, the Nation-State System and the Changing Global Order', *Third World Quarterly*, vol. 27, no. 1, 2006, pp. 5–25.
88 Neil Cooper, Mandy Turner and Michael Pugh, 'The End of History and the Last Liberal Peacebuilder: A Reply to Roland Paris', *Review of International Studies*, vol. 37, no. 4, 2011, pp. 1995–2007, here p. 2001.
89 Neil Cooper, 'Picking Out the Pieces of the Liberal Peaces: Representations of Conflict Economies and the Implications for Policy', *Security Dialogue*, vol. 36, no. 4, 2005, pp. 463–478.
90 For instance, Roger Mac Ginty and Gurchathen Sanghera, 'Hybridity in Peacebuilding and Development', Special issue of *Journal of Peacebuilding and Development*, vol. 7, no. 2, 2012; Robert Egnell and Peter Halden (eds), *New Agendas in Statebuilding: Hybridity, Contingency and History*, Abingdon: Routledge, 2013; Oliver P. Richmond and Audra Mitchell (eds), *Hybrid Forms of Peace: From Everyday Agency to Post-Liberalism*, Basingstoke: Palgrave Macmillan, 2011.
91 Derek Gregory, *The Colonial Present: Afghanistan, Palestine, Iraq*, Oxford: Blackwell, 2004.
92 Nigel Parsons, *The Politics of the Palestinian Authority: From Oslo to al-Aqsa*, Abingdon: Routledge, 2005, p. 10.
93 Khalil Nakhleh, *Globalised Palestine: the National Sell-out of a Homeland*, Lawrenceville, NJ: Red Sea Press, 2012, pp. 37-129.
94 US Secretary of State Warren Christopher, 1993, quoted in Rex Brynen, *A Very Political Economy: Peacebuilding and Foreign Aid in the West Bank and Gaza*, Washington, DC: USIP, 2000, p. 73.
95 OECD aid database. These figures are for disbursements, *not pledges*, from OECD donors and multilateral agencies. Arab donors are not assessed here for two reasons: (i) it is difficult to get accurate statistics on Arab aid to the oPt and PA; and (ii) Arab donors have different rationales for giving aid to those of the Western donors, as indicated by preliminary interviews.
96 Richard Caplan, *International Governance of War-Torn Territories*, Oxford: Oxford University Press, 2005; Graham Harrison, *The World Bank and Africa: The Construction of Governance States*, London: Routledge, 2004.
97 Le More (note 1 above); Roy (note 1 above).
98 Rex Brynen quoted in Le More (note 1 above), p. 37.
99 Ilan Pappe, 'Clusters of History: US Involvement in the Palestine Question', *Race and Class*, vol. 48, no. 3, 2007, pp. 1–28.
100 David Vine, 'The Bases of War in the Middle East', *The Nation*, 13 November 2014 (at: www.thenation.com/article/190561/bases-war-middle-east#).
101 Mandy Turner, 'Peacebuilding as Counterinsurgency in the Occupied Palestinian Territory', *Review of International Studies*, vol. 41, no. 1, 2015, pp. 73–98.
102 Turner, 'Creating "Partners for Peace"' (note 3 above).
103 U. Kock (head of the IMF West Bank and Gaza office), 'Between a Rock and a Hard Place: Recent Economic Developments in the Palestinian Economy', lecture at the Palestine Economic Policy Research Institute, (MAS), 19 February 2014; UNCTAD, *Report on UNCTAD Assistance to the Palestinian*

people: Developments in the Economy of the Occupied Palestinian Territory, Geneva: UNCTAD, 13 July 2012, p. 3; World Bank, *Stagnation or Revival: Palestinian Economic Prospects*, Report to the Ad Hoc Liaison Committee, Washington, DC: World Bank, 21 March 2012.
104 UNCTAD, *Policy Alternatives for Sustained Palestinian Development and State Formation*, Geneva: UNCTAD, 2009.
105 YNet, 'IMF: Fund Palestinian Unity Government', *YNet*, 4 July 2014 (at: www.ynetnews.com/articles/0,7340,L-4537882,00.html).
106 Yezid Sayigh, *Policing the People, Building the State: Authoritarian Transformation in the West Bank and Gaza Strip*, Carnegie Papers, Washington, DC: Carnegie Endowment for International Peace, 2011; Tzvi Ben Gedalyahu, 'US Trained Armed Forces Turning PA into Police State', *Arutz Sheva*, 23 November 2011 (at: www.israelnationalnews.com/News/News.aspx/140787#.U6wqtbHvKSo).
107 Middle East Monitor, 'Security Agencies Consume Palestinian Authority Budget', 4 May 2014 (at: www.middleeastmonitor.com/news/middle-east/11264-security-agencies-consume-palestinian-authority-budget.#sthash.BofpXxWi.dpuf).
108 It is obviously problematic with what statistics to compare the Palestinian security services, as they expand beyond 'police' but they are certainly not an 'army', and all are stationed domestically. If we look at the UN figures published in 2010 for police officers, these show the world median for police officers was 300 to 100,000 inhabitants. The Palestinian figures translate into 1754 for every 100,000 Palestinian inhabitants in the oPt. S. Harrendorf, M. Heiskanen and S. Malby, *International Statistics on Crime and Justice*, Heuni Publications no. 64, Helsinki: European Institute for Crime Convention and Control, affiliated with the United Nations and United National Office on Drugs and Crime, 2010.
109 Palestinian National Authority, *The Palestinian Reform and Development Plan, 2008–2010*, Ramallah: Palestinian National Authority, *Ending the Occupation, Establishing the State: Programme of the 13th Government*, Ramallah: Palestinian National Authority.
110 Author interviews conducted with all major Western donor agencies in Jerusalem and Ramallah, October–November 2014.
111 John Mackinlay and Alison Al-Baddawy, *Rethinking Counterinsurgency*, Santa Monica, CA: RAND, 2008; Laleh Khalili, 'The Location of Palestine in Global Counterinsurgency', *International Journal of Middle East Studies*, vol. 42, 2010, pp. 413–433.
112 Mackinlay and Baddaway (*ibid.*), pp. 13–20.
113 Michael Pugh, Neil Cooper and Mandy Turner, 'Conclusion: The Political Economy of Peacebuilding – Whose Peace, Where Next?', in Michael Pugh, Neil Cooper and Mandy Turner (eds), *Whose Peace? Critical Perspectives on the Political Economy of Peacebuilding*, Basingstoke: Palgrave Macmillan, 2008.
114 Personal conversation with Professor Kimberly Marten, Jerusalem, May 2012.

8 Waging war and building peace in Afghanistan

Astri Suhrke

The international intervention in Afghanistan after 2001 was driven by two main forces – the US globalised 'War on Terror' and UN-centred efforts to create a less violent world. Visions of peace were thus from the very beginning built into the intervention next to the instruments of violence. The relationship between violence and peace was not a simple means–ends affair but a complex interaction whereby the two sustained as well as grated on each other. Most obviously, the peacebuilding aspect provided a measure of legitimacy that helped sustain political support for the military operations; on the other hand, the violence that soon spiralled into a war undermined the peacebuilding agenda. By the end of the decade, there was greater recognition in NATO (which had assumed command over the international forces in 2003) and the donor community that the costs of war were huge and the prospect of winning was elusive. The stage was thus set for a scaling back of the international military presence and its transformation into a training, advice and assistance mission. In this phase, a new pattern of interaction between military objectives and the peacebuilding agenda emerged. Normative visions of an Afghan peace articulated by the rights and peacebuilding communities thereafter warned against a precipitate NATO military withdrawal and negotiations with the Taliban.

This chapter examines four phases of interaction: the initial mission, the expansion of the International Security Assistance Force (ISAF), the growing tempo of engagement for both war and peace, and the scaling back.

The initial mission

Antecedents

UN-led peacebuilding activities in Afghanistan did not start in December 2001. Throughout the 1990s, the UN as well as national donor agencies and several international NGOs sought to build peace in Afghanistan through two main channels: diplomatic efforts to work out a political settlement between the warring Afghan factions, and provision of aid in ways that would encourage community-based structures and initiatives for peace.

The two tracks of intervention did not always cohere, nor did the various aid actors always agree. After the Taliban came to power in the mid-1990s and UN-authorised international sanctions were imposed, the need to coordinate humanitarian assistance and other aid with political action appeared more pressing. The UN took the initiative to create what became a code of conduct, called the Strategic Framework Agreement for Afghanistan. Established in 1998, the Agreement set out principles for delivering aid, and all aid actors were asked to sign up.

Proponents of the Agreement argued that the intention was 'not to subordinate humanitarian and human rights concerns under the political banner'.[1] Yet some aid organisations, notably Médecins Sans Frontières, considered the 'principled engagement' called for by the Agreement an attempt to do precisely that, and refused to join. A subsequent evaluation of the Agreement by Mark Duffield, Nicholas Leader and Patricia Gossman found that the Agreement's underlying political premise and specific principles served to restrict assistance.[2] The Agreement labelled Afghanistan as a 'failed state' without a legitimate government, and referred to the Taliban regime – which at that time controlled most of the country's territory - as a 'presumptive state authority' that did not adhere to international norms and savagely repressed its population. This 'definitional representation' of the situation, the evaluation pointed out, was 'the soil from which institutional arrangements and policy prescriptions' grew.[3]

The policy prescriptions of the Strategic Framework Agreement were condensed into seven main principles. The first three paraphrased long-standing principles of humanitarian assistance (aid should be provided on the basis of universality, neutrality, impartiality and neutrality); principle 4 stressed that aid should not benefit any of the Afghan warring parties, and the seventh called for high standards of transparency and accountability in aid programmes. The critical principles and those which caused most controversy – both within the aid community and in its relations with the Taliban – were the remaining two.

Principle 5 effectively banned any form of aid for institutional development and capacity-building that could benefit the Taliban state. Only institutional and capacity-building activities that advanced human rights were permitted, and the recipient authority had to adhere to UN laws and principles. That sharply circumscribed the list of potential local partners. Nevertheless, to give agencies some room to contribute to peace and longer-term development, principle 6 allowed for assistance activities that would increase 'indigenous ownership' at the village, community and national levels. As Duffield and his associates pointed out, this principle encouraged aid actors to circumvent state authorities that were unpalatable to the international donor community and engage on the local level. Several actors, including the United Nations Development Programme (UNDP), did precisely that by establishing projects of institution-building and capacity-creation at the local level, but keeping the Taliban authorities at arm's length.

The UNDP projects raised a broader issue of principle, as the evaluation noted: 'Promoting a community governance programme in what is effectively a totalitarian political space means that the UN aid mission now straddles a fine line between promoting local constituencies and fomenting a political opposition.'[4] The political core of the programme was wrapped in the language of peacebuilding – the projects were run under the acronym of PEACE (Poverty Eradication and Community Empowerment) – and provoked critics to remark that if UNDP was serious about peace, the agency should supply arms as well.[5]

The suggestion did not seem that far-fetched. At the time, the UN was recognising the Afghan government in opposition, which controlled only a small strip of territory in the north. The US had launched missile strikes against the eastern border region in 1998 to punish al-Qaeda after the attacks on its embassies in Kenya and Tanzania. The Taliban regime had itself been stigmatised as an international outcast and condemned in repeated UN Security Council resolutions for its support to international terrorists, repression of women, and involvement in the illegal opium economy upon which UN sanctions were imposed in 1999 and tightened in 2000.[6] The Strategic Framework Agreement was part of this front of hostility by harnessing 'aid as peacebuilding' to further isolate the regime. The attacks on the United States on 11 September 2001 dramatically altered the situation. Afghanistan thereafter became the scene for an ambitious project of social transformation that increasingly, however, became mired in violence.

The early years after Bonn

The Bonn Agreement of 5 December 2001 outlined a grand transformative project for social justice, rights and democracy. In the early post-invasion years there seemed to be little contradiction between this agenda and the military strategy pursued by the US-led coalition forces in Operation Enduring Freedom (OEF). There was a near-consensus among the governments and organisations engaged in Afghanistan that defeating the Taliban was necessary to create the security that the transformative peacebuilding project required.[7] The invasion itself caused significant civilian casualties, involved probable violations of the laws of war, and generated major displacements of Pashtuns in the northern provinces.[8] For the next two to three years, the costs to the Afghans of creating the foundational security of the new order seemed relatively low. The US-led forces mostly operated in remote border areas to eliminate retreating members of Taliban and al-Qaeda, and flush out their sympathisers. There were some grievous cases of unintended civilian casualties of US airstrikes, but these were rare events. Security concerns on the local level were mostly related to the return of former 'warlords', often flush with US dollars provided by the CIA and invasion force, who now were vying for power.

Meanwhile, the UN and the aid community launched large-scale humanitarian assistance and reconstruction programmes, the Afghan Independent Human Rights Commissioned was established, and the first steps in the political transition designed to move the country from war to peace were taken. The UN-authorised peacekeeping force, the International Security Assistance Force (ISAF), was deployed in Kabul in January 2002. The force was warmly welcomed by the Kabulis, who celebrated their newly-won freedoms and the prospect of peace and prosperity. The prominent journalist Ahmed Rashid wrote in March 2002 that British ISAF soldiers were so popular in Kabul that they caused an 'instant traffic jam. Hordes of well-wishers – including blue *burqa* clad women and laughing children – crowd around them'.[9]

Rashid's happy picture seemed to confirm the dominant international narrative that had framed the response to Afghanistan in 2001.[10] In this perspective, the Western governments and the UN had abandoned Afghanistan after the Soviet military withdrawal in 1988–1989. Left to itself, the country had descended into internal strife that brought enormous suffering to its people, paved the way for the Taliban regime and enabled international terrorists to use the country as a base for attack on the United States. From this narrative flowed several policy prescriptions. First, the 'international community' – which soon became a short-hand term for the US-led and UN supported coalition of states and organisations – must not again walk away from Afghanistan. Second, this 'international community' had both a security interest and a moral obligation to help Afghanistan recover from the last nearly three decades of strife and its 'failed state' condition. And, third, there was no fundamental contradiction between the military intervention, represented by OEF, and the UN peacebuilding agenda.

The US military intervention was widely seen in the UN system as a just war, and regime change was considered necessary for reconstruction, nation-building and peacebuilding. The UN had, after all, orchestrated and given institutional expression to the growing international hostility towards the Taliban in the second half of the 1990s. It was all part of the trend of the times of how to solve 'the frontier problem in international society', as James Mayall put it, and explicitly justified as such.[11]

The only early, visible crack in the consensus developed over the expansion of ISAF. Most of the civilians engaged in peacebuilding, as broadly defined, called for a large international stabilisation force to be deployed throughout the country. The military establishments, however, were initially quite hesitant.

Expansion

The expansion of ISAF started in October 2003 when the Security Council authorised force expansion to 'areas of Afghanistan outside of Kabul' (Security Council Resolution 1510). In retrospect, this was a watershed in the international involvement in the country and a major factor in the evolving conflict.[12] ISAF, it will be recalled, was originally conceived as an entity quite separate from the US combat forces under OEF. Variously called a stabilisation or peacekeeping force, ISAF was designed to assist the transitional government in Kabul to establish a secure environment for reconstruction. No sooner had the first ISAF contingent landed in Kabul, however, than a veritable campaign was launched in New York and Washington to expand its mandate and enlarge its area of operation beyond the capital.[13]

The campaign succeeded beyond expectations. Already by mid-decade, ISAF forces were deployed throughout the country and NATO's website started producing maps of Afghanistan bedecked with a bewildering variety of national flags. By the end of the decade, 46 countries plus the United States had troops under ISAF command. ISAF and OEF forces had by then come under a common NATO–ISAF command (although some US Special Forces remained outside it). There had also been a merger of functions. ISAF units that had originally been sent on what some contributing governments described as close to peacekeeping were involved in combat operations, while combat units sponsored reconstruction and development projects in line with NATO's 'comprehensive approach' to defeat the insurgency. The merger of military and aid functions was institutionalised in the concept of the civil-military Provincial Reconstruction Team (PRT), a controversial innovation in NATO's inventory of tools for dealing with unconventional conflicts. For civilians in the rights, aid and diplomatic communities who had advocated ISAF expansion in order to strengthen peacebuilding it was an unexpected (and, to many, troubling) outcome.

The case for expanding ISAF was nestled in a larger international discourse on post-conflict reconstruction and peacebuilding. In this perspective, security was a foundational requirement for the post-war agenda of statebuilding, economic development, democracy, the rule of law and human rights. The core task of building (or re-building) the state entailed establishing a monopoly of legitimate force; in the Afghan context, this meant that ISAF must expand beyond Kabul to do throughout the country what it had done for the capital.

A main argument for expansion was ISAF's success in executing its original mandate to make Kabul a safe and politically neutral place. ISAF's presence helped create sufficient safety and order in Kabul to permit the newly-established government and its international partners to start rebuilding the city, aid returning refugees, provide humanitarian assistance, and reopen schools and the university. There certainly was crime, abuse and insecurity, but a sense of normality prevailed that permitted commercial and political activities to resume.

The contingent that carried out these diverse and demanding tasks, the Kabul Multinational Brigade, was less than 5,000 strong. That it achieved a significant measure of success reflects three main factors: adroit demonstration of presence, a credible link to US air power, and the willingness of the principal Afghan factions with capacity to shape the security situation in Kabul at this time to 'buy into' the Bonn Agreement that had catapulted them into unprecedented positions of state power.

In the provinces, the situation was different. Local strongmen were much less inclined to welcome a stabilisation/peacekeeping force that had a formal mandate to help extend the power of the central government, as the UN Security Council resolution that authorised force expansion pointedly declared (Resolution 1510). ISAF units outside Kabul would therefore face a dilemma: they could accommodate local strongmen and warlords who did not accept the writ of the central government and its formal rights-and-democracy agenda, thereby compromising their mandate, or follow the mandate and risk violent conflict by confronting them.

The advocates of ISAF expansion clearly assumed the latter. Among the more influential voices was the UN Special Representative of the Secretary General, Lakhdar Brahimi. In November–December 2001, Brahimi expressed some scepticism towards sending a multinational force at all, warning that the Afghans were a proud people who did not like to be ordered around by foreigners in uniform.[14] As ISAF deployed in Kabul without meeting resistance and was warmly welcomed by the city's population, his apprehensions seemed to melt away. Already in January 2002, when international donors met in Tokyo, Brahimi called for expanding ISAF beyond the city: 'People up and down the country are calling for the force to be deployed in other regions of Afghanistan.'[15] He subsequently made the case for expansion to the Security Council in increasingly urgent tones.[16]

Brahimi rested his case on the weakness of the Afghan state and its lack of a monopoly of force. In the north, armed factions were fighting among themselves and Pashtun minorities were subjected to systematic harassment and violence. In the east, some governors appointed by the central authority were violently rejected by the local communities. In the south, attacks by militants were reported. Throughout the country, violence by local strongmen and general insecurity was a problem for both the local population and international aid workers.

Other powerful voices joined in. The UN High Commissioner for Human Rights, Mary Robinson, returned from a trip to Afghanistan in early 2002 to call for deployment of ISAF outside Kabul, citing the impossibility of rebuilding society and securing human rights 'if you have violence, if you have killings, if you have robberies, if you have looting, if you have women terrified'.[17] Human rights organisations carried a similar message. Human Rights Watch cited widespread violence against Pashtun minorities in the north to recommend immediate ISAF deployment to that region.[18] Aid agencies and NGOs that were poised to address the enormous need for assistance and chafing under security restrictions wanted ISAF to protect movement of personnel and materiel throughout the country. US analysts argued that US failure to support expansion would be read as a sign of US disengagement and a defeat in the front line of the 'War on Terror'.[19]

Experts, crisis management groups and think tanks joined the lobby. The International Crisis Group advocated an increase from the initial deployment of 4,500 to 25,000. All were cited in a major hearing in the US Senate in June 2002 that addressed the situation in Afghanistan.[20]

The appeals for a larger international military role in Afghanistan were overwhelmingly wrapped in the mantle of humanitarian action and peacebuilding. While persuasive to many, it did not move the Bush administration. When the administration later did authorise expansion, as we shall see, it was in response to resource assessments in the Iraqi theatre of war as well as the deteriorating security situation in Afghanistan.

Meanwhile, on the Afghan side, Hamid Karzai, then chairman of the transitional government, was a vociferous advocate for ISAF expansion. Given its mandate, and the fact that Karzai himself did not have a military force on which he could rely, ISAF was a surrogate army of the central state over which he presided. Other Afghan leaders concurred, but for different reasons. The powerful leader of the Northern Alliance forces that had taken Kabul, Marshal Fahim, had, at the Bonn meeting, already wanted the planned stabilisation/peacekeeping force to be deployed beyond Kabul. At the time, his own armies were in Kabul, and a multinational force in the capital would constrain Fahim while rival military strongmen in the north and the west would go scot free. Expansion of ISAF would neutralise this advantage.[21]

The US military had, in 2001 and well into 2002, strongly opposed the establishment of a multinational stabilisation/peacekeeping force outside Kabul, fearing that the force would impinge on the priority task of defeating the Taliban and al-Qaeda. US refusal to assist such a force with logistics or other matters, including extracting the contingent if necessary, effectively vetoed efforts by US and UK diplomats at the Bonn meeting in December 2001 to get agreement on ISAF deployment beyond Kabul.[22] Continued opposition from the military blocked attempts to expand the force in 2002, and the civilian leadership of the Pentagon firmly concurred, although for other reasons: US support for ISAF was regarded as a diversion from the forthcoming invasion of Iraq, set for early 2003.[23]

The protracted violence in Iraq triggered by the US invasion meant that even more US troops were needed there, and Washington changed to actively solicit allied troops for Afghanistan. An expanded ISAF was the main vehicle for contributions. The situation in parts of the country remained unsettled and in some ways had worsened. Already in mid-2003, US military intelligence in Afghanistan concluded that the Taliban were on their way back.[24] From then and onwards until the end of the decade, demands for more allied troop contributions to defeat the Afghan insurgency and demonstrate NATO solidarity became a steady drumbeat out of Washington.

Allied militaries had initially been hesitant towards the very concept of ISAF, even when deployed only in Kabul, wearily eyeing the ambiguous but potentially ambitious mandate of providing 'security assistance' to a weak, central government. The British defence chief reportedly threatened to resign rather than accept British leadership of the first ISAF contingent in Kabul. He only relented when assured that the mission would be short-lived (three months), and on the express condition that US military forces provided 'essential enabling support'.[25]

While ambiguity in mandate worried the military, it proved an advantage to the many civilian advocates for expansion who could make their case on multiple grounds. Some saw ISAF as an essential tool of statebuilding or, alternatively, a symbolic exercise of power to maintain the post-Bonn momentum; others wanted the international military forces to secure relief supplies and development projects, or to protect women and ordinary Afghans against abuse, or for standing down armed factions in the provinces, protecting minorities, and so on. While diverse in organisational and policy terms, the many human rights activists, aid organisations, UN officials, and analysts and national politicians that engaged on this issue, shared the conviction that an international military force was required to provide security for the multiple state-building and peacebuilding tasks ahead.

Waging war and building peace

Reality soon proved more complex. Rather than bringing security, the growing international military presence was an important factor that fuelled the insurgency in the second half of the decade.[26] As the violence escalated, the dividing line between a stabilisation mandate and combat mission became increasingly blurred, and was eventually recognised in the merger of the ISAF and OEF commands completed in 2009. Already by mid-decade, international forces and the insurgents were locked in a fierce conflict that turned large parts of the south and the east into a war zone. By the end of the decade, the violence had engulfed much of the west and the north as well, while the capital was rocked by suicide blasts and other forms of attack.[27] To a growing number of Afghans, the international militaries appeared as an occupation force that supported self-serving Afghan elites and failed to end a costly war that claimed civilian lives and destroyed property.[28]

The mounting violence exposed the underlying contradictions inherent in the task of building peace while waging war. The war, it became clear, had a corrosive effect on the entire peacebuilding project. It skewed policy priorities of the international project in favour of short-term military objectives. When faced with conflicting priorities between peacebuilding tasks, such as promoting justice and good governance, on the one hand, and working with violent or corrupt local authorities that facilitated the pursuit of the war and created short-term stability, on the other, the United States and its main allies generally chose the latter. Hopes that ISAF units deployed beyond Kabul would restrain local strongmen proved wrong; in most cases the accommodating presence of ISAF empowered them, and when these on occasion were removed (as the Dutch demanded in Uruzgan and the British in Helmand), greater instability seemed to follow.[29] The demands of war trumped the needs of peacebuilding to shape a preference for short-term benefits across a range of policy areas, manifested in the failure to institute transitional justice mechanisms and weak human rights policies,[30] the superficial commitment to develop parliamentary democracy,[31] tolerance of the narcotics economy and the rents it offered the state,[32] and unwillingness to combat corruption and other crimes or injustices committed by high officials and self-appointed power holders who represented short-term stability.[33]

There were also signs that the international military presence had negative effects that reduced the initial, popular support for the post-Taliban order. Repeated coalition offensives – with their civilian casualties, detested night raids, arbitrary detentions and the practice of some US forces of bulldozing villages to create 'safe zones' around their forward bases – caused deep resentment among the Afghans.[34] Possibly the costs would have been easier to live with if the rest of the international project had delivered economic benefits and protection from arbitrary exercise of power. As it was, the benefits from the aid-and-war economy were extremely unevenly distributed, the state administration was mired in corruption, and its legal system rarely offered redress of injustices experienced.

The escalating war ratcheted up the demand for rapid and visible results, both within Afghanistan and from domestic audiences in the contributing countries. To deliver quick and visible results, the interveners adopted measures that undermined basic precepts of statebuilding, and by extension its contribution to peacebuilding. To rapidly create Afghan military capacity, for example, the international forces started rearming the militias.[35] This, of course, weakened the possibility for establishing a monopoly of legitimate force controlled by the Afghan state. It was also a potential source of local conflict and violence, especially in ethnically mixed areas.[36] The massive expansion of the Afghan army and the national police in the second half of the decade created problems of fiscal sustainability and quality control, arguably two central objectives of both state- and peacebuilding. The equally massive infusions of aid – amounting to nearly 90 per cent of total official expenditures early in the decade and remaining almost steady throughout – produced a rentier state financed by international official transfers.[37] The creation of a rentier state was itself a pre-eminent example of how assistance modalities had been adjusted to suit wartime imperatives even though they violated all sound principles of promoting sustainable development and accountable government. Predictably, the rentier state also spawned corrupt and opportunistic elites, which the United States and its allies were unable to reform and reluctant to remove lest this should endanger the war effort.

The state's visible dependence on foreign support also contributed to the government's legitimacy deficit. Afghan rulers have traditionally invoked religion, tribal lineage and nationalism to legitimise their rule. A government visibly and heavily dependent on Western aid and military forces had to develop an alternative legitimising ideology. Hence the government, but especially its international supporters, looked to 'good governance' to legitimise the post-Taliban order. Unlike religion and nationalism, however, 'good governance' exerts no influence simply by virtue of its ideational existence; it has to actually deliver goods and services. In this case, it did not do so quickly and equitably, with corrosive consequences for the peacebuilding efforts.

As the contradictions between the peacebuilding venture and the war sharpened, the relationship between the respective policy agents became tense as well. Expressed most clearly in the interaction between parts of the international aid community and ISAF, the tension played out in several fields. In part, it was a conflict over knowledge and its use, as exemplified by the controversial practice of the US military to integrate civilian anthropologists and similar experts into combat teams, the so-called 'human terrain teams'. It was a conflict over aid resources as well. When ISAF adopted a counterinsurgency (COIN) strategy towards the end of the decade, national military contingents came to control substantial funds for discretionary spending to 'win hearts and minds' among the Afghans. US forces, in particular, were allocated large amounts of funds (estimated at US$1.5 billion for 2010–2011 alone). Civilian critics argued that this spending was at best ineffective, at worst counterproductive by creating conflict, and at any rate unsustainable.[38]

The underlying contest over who should control resources – civilian aid organisations or the military – extended to definitions of space. As the international military forces moved into development and humanitarian assistance as part of their COIN strategy, civilian aid actors became divided. Some chose to work closely with the military,[39] while many warned that aid was being dangerously militarised, jeopardising the neutral 'humanitarian space' fundamental to both international humanitarian law and assistance. Aid voices that had earlier argued for ISAF expansion now turned on ISAF's provincial reconstruction teams – the joint civil–military units that had been one of the principal expressions of force expansion – with bitter criticism.[40] When NATO's Secretary-General in 2010 said that the NGOs represented the 'soft power' of the foreign intervention in Afghanistan, the umbrella organisation of the major NGOs working in Afghanistan (ACBAR) responded with a forceful denial.[41] Failure to draw a strict line between military and humanitarian functions, ACBAR emphasised, would put the lives of the beneficiaries at risk as well as those delivering assistance. Humanitarian principles of humanity, neutrality and impartiality were invoked to cover the vast NGO aid community and mark its distance from the military. The possibility that the international military presence itself was undermining the peacebuilding project in which humanitarian and development assistance had a prominent role was not addressed.

Scaling back

The costs of the war and failure to gain strategic victories, led the principal international actors involved to reconsider both the war and the peace it was meant to bring. As the principal military actor, the US government led the way in defining a scaling-back process that set 2014 as the target date for withdrawal of international combat forces. The change was framed by a narrative that emphasised the distinction between the Taliban and al-Qaeda. In this narrative, gains could be made by splitting the two by negotiating with the Taliban and related militants who had exclusively Afghan political ambitions, while pursuing those identified as 'international terrorists' with military means.

Washington's strategy beyond 2014 was reflected in a framework agreement with Afghanistan signed on 2 May 2012.[42] The agreement committed the US to provide military and economic assistance to Afghanistan in return for use of bases and other military facilities on Afghan soil and conferred on Afghanistan the status of a Major Non-NATO Ally (MNNA) of the United States. This would enable the US to maintain a much lower-cost, lower-profile military presence, probably around 10,000 up to 2016, built around a training mission to assist Afghan forces as well as US Special Forces and drone crews to fight 'terrorists' in the region. The presence would also serve a larger strategic calculus to project US military power in the region, particularly vis-à-vis China in line with the Obama Administration's 'pivot to Asia' policy.

To activate the Agreement, the parties had to sign another agreement within a year that would regulate the status of American forces in Afghanistan and related matters. This proved difficult. A draft Bilateral Status Agreement (BSA) was prepared on time, but Karzai refused to sign. He held out even after outstanding issues were settled, relating to US insistence on exclusive legal jurisdiction over its forces in Afghanistan (granted), and Afghan demand for a security guarantee against aggression from Pakistan (not granted). In his last term as president, Karzai possibly wanted to go down in history as a nationalist leader who stood up against powerful allies as well as enemies and leave the signing to the next president. That the BSA eventually would be signed seemed probable. An assembly of notables (*loya jirga*) called by Karzai in November 2013 to assess the draft BSA, supported the agreement, as did both principal candidates in the 2014 presidential elections. The Agreement was also a *de facto* precondition for the planned NATO successor mission to ISAF, a training and assistance mission called Resolute Support which would be a keystone of the country's future relationship with Western powers.

On the political side, the grand transformative project launched in 2001 had, by the end of the decade, been qualified by 'good enough'. The enormous difficulties of building peace in a devastated land in a contested region had become increasingly recognised, and the timeline and scope of the agenda had been scaled back in fact, if not formally. The language of a second Bonn meeting that took place in December 2011 remained firm and upbeat. The concluding statement of the 85 countries and 16 international organisations present affirmed their commitment to 'a stable, democratic and prosperous future' for Afghanistan, and to uphold all international human rights obligations, in particular the rights of women, and support 'a thriving and free civil society'.[43] At the same time, the prospect of negotiations with the Taliban through third parties in Qatar, pursued as the diplomatic counterpart of the military scaling back, led to a discursive re-emphasis on the core values that had framed the initial peacebuilding agenda and were enshrined in the 2004 Constitution – human rights, the rights of women, liberal political democracy and a market economy. Respect for human rights and the rights of women were specifically included in the Bonn 2011 declaration as guidelines for future negotiations and possible 'reconciliation' with the insurgents.

No visible signs of sustained progress in talks with the Taliban were evident by the time of the presidential elections in 2014. The elections themselves appeared to mock the hopes for political democracy expressed at the second Bonn conference. Preceded by widespread expectations of fraud as a normal feature of Afghan electoral politics,[44] the polling was marred by fraud that was possibly greater than in the 2009 presidential elections, and on such a scale that the candidate who trailed after the second, run-off election, Abdullah Abdullah, demanded that the result be voided. A total recount of some 7 million ballots, supervised by 700 international observers flown in for the event, still did not settle the issue. Attempts by the US Secretary of State, John Kerry, to mediate by crafting a power-sharing bargain between Abdullah and his opponent, Ashraf Ghani, held out some promise for a resolution. Nevertheless, a post-election bargain of this kind would violate and hence undermine formal-rule democratic processes.

In the huge NGO sector, numbering around 2000 organisations, aid actors were preparing for an uncertain future. Many expected a tighter resource situation with donors gradually scaling back on assistance programmes. Spin-offs from the war-and-aid economy would likely be reduced as well. Some feared that the sector as a whole had become associated with the international military presence and confused with for-profit commercial companies, leading to a loss of good-will among the Afghan people that would make future work more difficult.[45] Deteriorating security conditions in some areas – mainly due to the short-term effects of international military withdrawal – and Taliban gains in other areas had led some organisations to conclude de facto agreements with the militants to continue to work in their areas.[46] Intensified competition for resources deepened concerns that NGOs would defect from the Code of Conduct established by ACBAR in 2007. To contain such tendencies, a group of mainly international NGOs started working on a set of Principles of Access to ensure that aid

War and peacebuilding in Afghanistan 175

would be based exclusively on need and delivered in a neutral and impartial fashion. By early 2014, almost 20 organisations had signed up.

Unlike the Strategic Framework Agreement of 1998, the language of coordination this time did not seek to streamline aid with diplomacy by favouring some power holders rather than others. The purpose was more modestly to protect humanitarian assistance and establish the right to provide such assistance anywhere it was needed. As such, the Principles of Access sharpened the conventional distinction between aid as palliative, humanitarian assistance and aid designed to change the social structures and political economy that affected peace, in a word, peacebuilding. Aid for local peacebuilding initiatives continued under other auspices, including a UN-supported civil society initiative that developed provincial roadmaps for addressing local conflict and human rights issues.[47]

Conclusions

The future of peacebuilding in Afghanistan depends on so many factors – local, regional and international – that uncertainty seems to be the overarching theme. Withdrawal of most of the international forces – which at its peak reached almost 150,000 – would take much wind out of the ideological sails of the insurgency, just as it did when the Soviet troops withdrew in 1988–1989. The present war could be transformed into a series of localised conflicts, possibly with regional international support for rival Afghan factions.[48] In a worst case scenario, the 1990s would be repeated, with limited space for international assistance. In a best-case scenario, foreign withdrawal would be accompanied by a political settlement that would facilitate reconstruction and peacebuilding on more genuinely Afghan terms.

Continued US warfare based on drones raises special issues for a peacebuilding agenda. The use of drones is deeply problematic in relation to international human rights law, international humanitarian law and transparency about their use and impact. However, drone warfare in Afghanistan is likely to be limited (by target and geography), and by its nature is less likely to stir the kind of political sensitivities associated with a massive foreign troop presence, its detested night-raids, large kill-or-capture operations, bulldozing of orchards, and civilian casualties caused by close air support for combat operations. This alone may lessen the systemic tensions of building peace while waging war observed during the past decade and enlarge the room for broader peacebuilding activities, spearheaded by Afghans with appropriate international support.

More than ten years of intervention in Afghanistan has demonstrated the complexity of the interaction between those engaged in 'peacebuilding' writ large, and the military. In the initial phases of the intervention, there was a near-consensus in the aid and peacebuilding communities that an expanded international military force was necessary to create the security required for peace and development. This turned out not to be the case. The past decade of international assistance in Afghanistan has also demonstrated the limitations on external assistance in creating the kind of legitimate government that is necessary for sustained peacebuilding. Admittedly, the local context was difficult and Afghanistan's location in a 'bad neighbourhood' certainly did not help. Yet the numerous evaluations and discursive analysis of the reasons for the shortcoming have paid insufficient attention to the internal contradictions in the ambitious, transformative project that was launched in 2001. These tensions stemmed in large part from policies pursued by foreign governments and organisations in two main areas: (i) deploying a large international combat force while simultaneously trying to build peace; and (ii) financing a rentier state depended on, and to that extent mostly accountable to, foreign donors, while simultaneously promoting a system of political democracy where the government would be accountability to its own people. A lessened international presence in the future will at least reduce these tensions, although probably accompanied by a slower pace of social transformation as well.

Acknowledgements

I am grateful to Susanne Schmeidl for comments on an earlier version of this chapter. This chapter is an updated version of the article of the same name that appeared in *International Peacekeeping*, vol. 19, no. 4, August 2012, Taylor & Francis Ltd, www.tandfonline.com, reprinted by permission of the publisher.

Notes

1 Antonio Donini, 'An Elusive Quest: Integration in the Response to the Afghan Crisis', *Ethics and International Affairs*, vol. 18, no. 2, 2004, p. 23.
2 Mark Duffield, Patricia Gossman and Nicholas Leader, *Review of the Strategic Framework for Afghanistan*, Kabul: Afghanistan Research and Evaluation Unit (AREU), 2002.
3 *Ibid.*, p. 13.
4 *Ibid.*
5 *Ibid.*
6 David Cortright and George A. Lopez with Linda Gerber, *Sanctions and the Search for Security*, Boulder, CO: Lynne Rienner, 2002.
7 Some analysts then and later questioned whether a policy of defeating and excluding the Taliban, rather than negotiating and including them in some post-war role, was wise. See Chris Johnson and Jolyon Leslie, *Afghanistan. The Mirage of Peace*, 2nd edn, London: Zed, 2008. Possibilities for negotiations at the local level are detailed in a study from Kandahar: Anand Gopal, *The Battle for Afghanistan. Militancy and Conflict in Kandahar*, Washington, DC: New America Foundation, 2010.
8 Aziz Hakimi and Astri Suhrke, 'A Poisonous Chalice. The Struggle for Human Rights and Accountability in Afghanistan', *Nordic Journal of Human Rights*, 2013, vol. 31, no. 2, pp. 201–223.
9 Ahmed Rashid, 'Security Concerns Mount in Afghanistan as Country Enters Critical Reconstruction Phase', Eurasianet.org, 13 March 2002 (at: www.eurasianet.org/departments/insight/articles/eav031402.shtml).

10 Jonathan Steele, *Ghosts of Afghanistan*, London: Portobello Books, 2011.
11 James Mayall, 'The European Empires and International Order', in James Mayall and Ricardo Soares de Oliveira (eds), *The New Protectorates. International Tutelage and the Making of Liberal States*, New York: Columbia University Press, 2011, p. 53.
12 Astri Suhrke, *When More Is Less. The International Project in Afghanistan*, London: Hurst, 2011, pp. 73–88.
13 Renata Dwan, Thomas Papworth and Sharon Wiharta, 'Multilateral Peace Missions, 2001', in *SIPRI Yearbook 2002*, Stockholm: Stockholm International Peace Research Institute, 2002, p. 126.
14 Todd Diamond, 'UN Representative Urges Focus on Humanitarian Efforts in Afghanistan', Eurasianet.org, 18 October 2001 (at: www.eurasianet.org/departments/insight/articles/eav101901.shtml).
15 Lakhdar Brahimi, 'Speech to the International Conference on Reconstruction Assistance to Afghanistan', Tokyo, 21 January 2002 (copy on file with author).
16 United Nations, *The Situation in Afghanistan and its Implications for International Peace and Security*, Report of the Secretary-General, UN doc. S/2002/278, 18 March 2002; United Nations, *The Situation in Afghanistan and its Implications for International Peace and Security*, Report of the Secretary-General, UN doc. S/2002/737, 11 July 2002.
17 Cited in Human Rights Watch, *Paying for the Taliban's Crimes*, New York: Human Rights Watch, April 2002, p. 49.
18 *Ibid.*
19 US Senate, Committee on Foreign Relations, *Afghanistan: Building Stability. Avoiding Chaos*, Washington, DC: GPO, June 2002, p. 16.
20 *Ibid.*
21 James Dobbins, *After the Taliban: Nation-Building in Afghanistan*. Washington, DC: Potomac Books, 2008, p. 128.
22 *Ibid.*, p. 88.
23 Seth G. Jones, *In the Graveyard of Empires: America's War in Afghanistan*, New York: Norton, 2009, pp. 114–115.
24 Douglas Jehl, 'Afghan Front Heats Up, and Rumsfeld Urges Patience', *New York Times*, 8 September 2003.
25 Dobbins (note 21 above), p. 88.
26 Suhrke (note 12 above), pp. 37–71.
27 Antonio Giustozzi, *Empires of Mud*, London: Hurst, 2008; Antonio Giustozzi (ed.), *Decoding the New Taliban: Insights from the Afghan Field*, New York: Columbia University Press, 2009.
28 After mid-decade, the militants caused many more civilian deaths than those attributed to the government international forces. The 'collateral damage' caused by international forces nevertheless created particular resentment because they were seen as having come to help the people and establish peace. Niamatullah Ibrahimi, 'When Few Means Many: The Consequences of Civilian Casualties for Civil–Military Relations in Afghanistan', in William Maley and Susanne Schmeidl (eds), *Reconstructing Afghanistan*, London: Routledge, 2014, pp. 165–177.
29 Suhrke (note 12 above), pp. 102–114.
30 Ahmad Nader Nadery, 'Peace or Justice? Transitional Justice in Afghanistan', *International Journal of Transitional Justice*, vol. 1, no. 1, 2007, pp. 173–179; Emily Winterbotham, *The State of Transitional Justice in Afghanistan*, Kabul: AREU, 2010.
31 Amin Saikal, 'The UN and Afghanistan: Contentions in Democratization and State-Building', *International Peacekeeping*, vol. 9, no. 2, 2012, pp. 217–234.
32 Mark Shaw, 'Drug Trafficking and the Development of Organised Crime in Post Taliban Afghanistan', in William Byrd and D. Buddenberg (eds), *Afghanistan's Drug Industry: Structure, Function, Dynamics and Implications for Counter-Narcotics Policy*, New York: UN Office of Drugs and Crime and World Bank, 2006; Florian P. Kühn,

'Aid, Opium and the State of Rents in Afghanistan: Competition, Cooperation, or Cohabitation?', *Journal of Intervention and Statebuilding*, vol. 2, no. 3, 2008, pp. 309–327.
33 Michael E. Hartmann, 'Casualties of Myopia', in Whit Mason (ed.), *The Rule of Law in Afghanistan*, Cambridge: Cambridge University Press, 2011.
34 *Strangers at the Door: Night Raids by International Forces Lose Hearts and Minds of Afghans*, Kabul: The Open Society Institute and The Liaison Office, February 2010.
35 Aziz Hakimi, 'Getting Savages to Fight Barbarians: Counterinsurgency and the Remaking of Afghanistan', *Central Asian Survey*, vol. 32, no. 3, 2013. pp. 388–405.
36 Thomas Ruttig, *Another Militia Creation Gone Wrong*, Kabul: Afghanistan Analysts Network, 18 October 2010.
37 Suhrke (note 12 above), ch. 5; World Bank, *Transition in Afghanistan: Looking Beyond 2014*, Washington, DC: World Bank, 2011 (at: http://siteresources.worldbank.org/INTAFGHANISTAN/Resources/AFBeyond2014.pdf).
38 Paul Fishstein and Andrew Wilder, *Winning Hearts and Minds? Examining the Relationship between Aid and Security in Afghanistan*, Boston, MA: Feinstein International Center, 2012; US Senate, *Evaluating US Foreign Assistance to Afghanistan: A Majority Staff Report Prepared for the Use of the Committee on Foreign Relations*, Washington, DC: GPO, 2011.
39 APPRO, *Transition and Non-Governmental Organizations in Afghanistan: An Assessment and Prospects*, Kabul: Afghanistan Public Policy Research Organization, 2014, p. 7.
40 Barbara J. Stapleton, 'A Means to What End? Why PRTs Are Peripheral to the Bigger Political Challenges in Afghanistan', *Journal of Military and Strategic Studies*, vol. 10, no. 1, 2007, pp. 1–49 (at: www.jmss.org/jmss/index.php/jmss/article/view/38/36); Kristian Berg Harpviken, *A Peace Nation Takes up Arms: The Norwegian Engagement in Afghanistan*, Paper 211, Oslo: PRIO (at: www.prio.no/Research-and-Publications/Publication/?oid=2216694).
41 APPRO (note 39 above), pp. 7–8.
42 *Enduring Strategic Partnership Agreement between Afghanistan and the United States*, 2 May 2012 (at: www.whitehouse.gov/sites/default/files/2012.06.01u.s.-afghanistanspasignedtext.pdf).
43 Bonn Conference, 'Afghanistan and the International Community: From Transition to the Transformation Decade', Conclusions of the International Afghanistan Conference in Bonn, 5 December 2011 (at: http://reliefweb.int/node/463139).
44 Carina Perelli and Scott Smith, *Anticipating and Responding to Fraud in the 2014 Afghan Elections*, Briefing Paper, London: Chatham House, February 2014 (at: www.chathamhouse.org/publications/papers/view/197727).
45 APPRO (note 39 above), p. 7.
46 Ashley Jackson and Antonio Giustozzi, *Talking to the Other Side: Humanitarian Engagement with the Taliban in Afghanistan*, Working Paper, London: Humanitarian Policy Group, ODI, 2012.
47 Called the Afghan People's Dialogue for Peace, the initiative had by 2014 finalized strategies for 30 of the country's 34 provinces. UN, *Report of the Secretary-General on the Situation in Afghanistan and its Implications for International Peace and Security*, UN doc. A/68/910-S/2014/420, New York: United Nations, 18 June 2014, p. 5.
48 Jonathan Goodhand, *Contested Transitions: International Drawdown and the Future State in Afghanistan*, Oslo: NOREF, 2012 (at www.peacebuilding.no/Themes/Global-trends/Fragile-states-and-peacebuilding-in-the-new-global-context/Publications/Contested-transitions-International-drawdown-and-the-future-state-in-Afghanistan).

9 War and peace in Côte d'Ivoire

Violence, agency and the local/international line

Bruno Charbonneau

This chapter examines the issue of violence in the context of international interventions for peace in Côte d'Ivoire. A long Ivorian episode ended on 11 April 2011, with the capture of President Laurent Gbagbo by the forces loyal to President-elect Alassane Ouattara. After months of intense negotiations between Ivorian actors, diverse foreign governments (especially African), the UN, the African Union (AU), and the Economic Community of West African States (ECOWAS), this conclusion to an election crisis in November 2010 generated polarised debates. The end was dramatic in the violence deployed by Ivorian belligerents against their adversaries and civilian populations, in the international actions taken to impose both peace and election results, and ultimately in the direct military involvement of France, the ex-colonial power. French military actions were indeed a key to turning the tide of the war in Abidjan by supporting a UN force in destroying heavy weapons and thus creating the tactical conditions that led to the capture of Gbagbo by forces loyal to Ouattara. This French and UN use of force raises numerous questions about the legitimacy and necessity of what was a 'robust' and 'regime change' international intervention.

It is common to distinguish the violence associated with war from the violence associated with international 'peace' interventions. The latter is rarely discussed as violence per se, but as peace interventions to subdue the violence associated with the conflict. This chapter problematises the relationship between these two kinds of violence, emphasises how they can be intertwined, and shows how they affect agency. The case of Côte d'Ivoire suggests how the use of violence and its representations are intimately tied to competing claims about legitimate force, legitimate agency and legitimate authority – thus about the legitimate forms that 'peace' can take. In exploring this question, 'local' agency is problematised and integrated into the analysis of international peace interventions in Côte d'Ivoire, particularly given that the issue of 'local' agency has been the subject of many peacebuilding debates.[1] Instead of the commonly assumed 'local/international' dichotomy found in the literature, it is argued here that the questions of violence and regime change were very much about negotiating or imposing this very line between 'local' and 'international'; a line that suggests where the constitutive effects of violence on agency can be found. The first section of this chapter elaborates briefly on violence and peace operations. The last two sections analyse the international politics of peace interventionism in Côte d'Ivoire.

Violence and peace operations

International peace interventions involve a paradox: they reflect and appeal to humanitarian-universal and to hegemonic-particular practices. In the context of the UN's early involvement in the process of decolonisation, Ali Mazrui argued that the new organisation was involved 'in two paradoxical capacities – in the capacity of a collective "imperialist" with "trusteeship" responsibilities of its "own" and in the capacity of the grand critic of imperialism at large'.[2] Mark Mazower goes further, arguing that the UN was in fact a product of empire that partly sought to sustain the supremacy of its founding members. Only later, notably with the arrival of newly independent nation-states, did the UN embrace anticolonialism, notwithstanding the power asymmetries reflected in the Security Council.[3] Given that the evolution of peace operations and, in parallel, the authority of the UN Secretary-General were intimately connected with decolonisation and North–South relations,[4] these paradoxical capacities expose contradiction or indecision at the centre of modern politics that Rob Walker identifies in the negotiation between claims to state sovereignty and claims to international authority (or systemic necessity). Walker points to the location where political judgements are made – a site of intense politics where one finds practices of inclusion and exclusion that continuously draw and redraw lines of discrimination, particularly between inside and outside.[5]

It seems that more often than not scholars of international peace interventions (whether problem-solving or critical) assume to know where this line is situated between international forces of intervention and local subjects of intervention. Cynthia Weber argues that in discussions of intervention the discrimination between inside and outside is conceived theoretically as necessary. The *a priori* assumption about the existence and stability of the line enables judgements about the transgression of state sovereignty. It then becomes a simple matter of judging whether the line was crossed or not, thus silencing the historical practices through which sovereignty and intervention came to be, and thus which particular meanings of the state found expression.[6] As I argue elsewhere, this enables a spatial imagination that makes possible tales of international saviours coming to protect powerless victims of conflict *and* tales of international (or liberal) imperialists coming to dominate and govern victims of international intervention.[7] Partly to show that peace interventions are more complex than the imposition of peace or governance from above, Oliver Richmond has rightly emphasised the agency of local actors. He argues that a focus on 'local' agency points to practices of resistance or co-option that suggest alternatives to the hegemonic liberal peace and to the ongoing formation of a 'hybrid peace'.[8] However, as Audra Mitchell argues, Richmond struggles to move away from the 'local/international' distinction, thus associating the 'everyday' and ideals of resistance to 'local' actors and 'power/control' to 'international' actors.[9] One of the effects of adopting a theoretical posture that presumes the local/international distinction is the caricature of 'the relationships between international and local actors, sometimes even processes, mechanisms, and structures', thus excluding 'the critique of "local" transnationalised actors that can benefit or aggravate the relationship between an international militarised peace agenda and capitalism'.[10]

If 'local' agency is integrated into analyses of international peace interventions, it cannot be as agents who only suffer or react to such interventions. As Mitchell writes, in the literature on peace and conflict studies the everyday is discussed by 'attributing the "quality" dimension to "local" actors and the "control" aspect to "international" actors', thus reifying the power relations between the two.[11] The concept of hybridity, deployed to highlight and empower 'local' agency, seems to rely too readily on this 'local/international' binary, thus undermining its critical edge as it runs the risk of reaffirming a particular understanding of the distinction between 'local' and 'international'. This seems particularly true at the level of elite negotiations where, for instance, it is never clear whether heads of states such as Gbagbo, Ouattara, or the then French president, Nicolas Sarkozy, act as 'local/national' or 'international' agents. In Côte d'Ivoire, the very political struggles and dynamics of the conflict were intertwined and embedded in 'regional' dynamics and the politics of 'international' peace intervention practices. In Côte d'Ivoire, the 'international community' did not come into a situation where 'local' agencies were clearly established or where the inside/outside line was clear-cut. In the 1990s and throughout Gbagbo's presidency (at least until the 2007 Pretoria Accords), the concept of *ivoirité* was deployed by elites in attempts to define and determine 'true' Ivorians from foreigners,[12] and also as a means to protect Ivorian sovereignty from perceived undue influence from France and international others. Most importantly, while the Ivorian conflict is too often discussed by scholars and media experts as a national conflict, it involves complex regional dynamics. As François Gaulme argues, the regional dimensions may have received surprisingly little scholarly attention, but they remain both crucial and obvious. More than two decades of civil wars in West Africa produced various effects from which Côte d'Ivoire was not isolated. National political struggles, economic relationships (with the Ivorian economy as the regional economic centre), important population movements, and social and political intergenerational tensions involved numerous and complex 'regional' dynamics.[13] In this context, France was already present and embedded in 'local' and 'regional' politics, dynamics and structures, pointing to transversal and horizontal connections and lingering neocolonial hierarchies that the local/international distinction obscures.[14] Furthermore, ECOWAS has been a site where one can find these local/international (or should it be regional?) tensions inherent in the Ivorian conflict. Historically, its member states have been divided between Francophone members with special relationships with France and Anglophone members that have often criticised French influence over their Francophone colleagues.[15] These ECOWAS dynamics were made more complex from the late 1980s by the various conflictual relationships between West African regimes, trans-border ready-to-hire militias, rising xenophobic and violent practices, and the fact that Côte d'Ivoire has been a regional economic powerhouse and the place where many ECOWAS citizens continue to work and live.

This suggests that 'hybridity' not only predated the international peace interventions of the 2000s in Côte d'Ivoire, but cannot be easily conceived according to a stable local/international line that distinguishes parties to the conflict from peacebuilders. Diverse 'local' agencies (various competing national and regional elites, but also genuine social movements and political opposition groups) played a key role in setting the limits and the conditions of possibility of international interventions by working with, against, or in spite of the limitations imposed by international peace interventions. Analyses of the conflict in Côte d'Ivoire without an examination of the changing conditions that emerged from the imposed 'peace' by international forces are insufficient, just as analyses of international peace interventions since 2002 are insufficient without an examination of how 'local' agents worked with, against, or in spite of them.

Hybridity seems too easily captured by mainstream peace practices to reaffirm the local/international discrimination – because hybridity needs the distinction to exist as a concept. Instead, a focus on agency and the ways in which it is formed, enabled and transformed, moves the analysis beyond the 'local/international' binary, problematises this binary without dismissing its political significance, and points to how agents conceive, capture, and enable their agency as 'local' or 'international'. Below, in the analysis of the international politics of intervention in Côte d'Ivoire, the question of political agency is intimately linked to the question of (legitimate) violence. This is not to argue that there is a direct causal relationship between agency and violence, but to highlight how specific instances of violence point to moments of a changing, moving, and enabling of political agency. In the interpretation of agency here I stress its contingent and negotiable nature.

Agency is enabled, transformed, and negotiated through practices, including but not limited to violent intervention practices. There is no *a priori* and strict local/international distinction (if one considers the transnational connections of elites, for instance, in both peace negotiations and movements of global capital) nor is there a strict line between 'power/ control' actors and 'resistance' actors. As Mike McGovern writes of Côte d'Ivoire, 'there is considerable creativity invested in the struggle to gain and maintain power in African states'. He adds that if 'we are to embrace African agency, we must acknowledge that it is not so different from agency as exercised ... anywhere else: it contains admirable as well as regrettable elements'.[16] He argues that it is no longer enough to counter Western racist stereotypes, just as I argue that it is not enough to criticise the particular hegemonic content of Western or international intervention. Indeed, in the context of the Ivorian conflict, it seems difficult to interpret violence as a strict case of inside violence – the Ivorian conflict and its 'root causes' – that is distinguishable from the case of outside intervention as deployed by 'international' forces. Both kinds of violence were intertwined and defined each other. And in the ways violence was deployed lay (competing) claims to legitimate violence, political agency and authority. Peace became a rhetorical device for asserting such claims.

'Neither war nor peace'

After the 1999 Christmas Eve *coup d'état* by General Robert Guéï that overthrew the government of Henri Konan Bédié, Gbagbo was elected president in 2000 under conditions that he himself called 'calamitous'. The main opposition parties boycotted the presidential election in light of Guéï's attempts to stage an electoral coup, thus giving way to a Guéï–Gbagbo confrontation that the latter won. Gbagbo was sworn in on 26 October amid street violence, firefights, and attacks on Ouattara's residence after his refusal to recognise Gbagbo's electoral victory. Gbagbo was president, but his legitimacy and authority needed to be ascertained. While the French government recognised him through its ambassador Francis Lot, the United States, South Africa, the Organization of African Unity, and the UN called for new elections. The contested legitimacy of Gbagbo's regime – of Gbagbo's agency as president – set the stage for the 19 September 2002 rebellion, but it would also become, implicitly, the key issue of the various international peace negotiations to come.

It started with simultaneous attacks against military installations in Abidjan, Bouaké, and Korhogo by approximately 800 soldiers ostensibly protesting against their demobilisation due in early 2003. Loyal governmental forces quickly regained control of the situation in Abidjan, but could not do so in the north and west of the country where the rebels took control of more cities while their ranks swelled with other dissatisfied soldiers and civilians. By the end of September, rebel forces had consolidated their control of the northern half of the country and created a political organisation, the Mouvement patriotique de Côte d'Ivoire (MPCI), with Guillaume Soro as spokesman. Gbagbo refused to share power with an armed rebellion and expected the French government to activate the defence accord between the countries. Instead, on 29 September ECOWAS mobilised a contact group comprising Togo, Mali, Niger, Ghana, Nigeria and Guinea-Bissau that was presided over by Togo's Gnassingbé Eyadéma. For Gbagbo, this ECOWAS-led mediation raised the fear of a deeper regional involvement by countries hostile to his regime that supported the rebels and/or his political opponent

Ouattara. He foresaw that peace negotiations would transform the rebels into legitimate political agents by protecting their territorial gains.[17] But after negotiating a ceasefire on 17 October, the ECOWAS contact group was unable to overcome obstacles and internal rivalries that made the experience laborious and uncertain.[18] However, it was the intransigence of the rebels who, armed with the belief in their military superiority (a conviction supported by some French officials), demanded Gbagbo's resignation, revision of the constitution and new elections. In turn, the government demanded that rebels disarm and respect the integrity of Ivorian territory. No one compromised and the ECOWAS-led peace talks broke off.[19] Things became more complicated when the war started again on 28 November where previously unknown rebel groups, Mouvement populaire ivoirien du Grand Ouest (MPIGO) and Mouvement de la Justice et de la Paix (MJP), opened a second front on the border between Liberia and Côte d'Ivoire. It was later confirmed that these groups were largely composed of Liberian mercenaries and militias. The French stopped their initial advance. After a comprehensive ceasefire agreement in May 2003, Ivorian government and rebel forces, with French and ECOWAS peacekeepers, launched a joint operation in the west of the country against these Liberian militias. The opening of this second front exposed the regional dynamics of the conflict that had grown in complexity since the late 1980s, with the involvement of Liberia and Burkina Faso being clearly important factors.[20]

While ECOWAS emphasised the difficulties involved in drawing a clear line between the 'local' and 'international' limits of the conflict (conceptually, by increasing the difficulties in locating the 'regional' between 'local' and 'international'), the French military intervention illustrated the stakes involved in making the distinction and its effects on agency. The French government refused to intervene directly in favour of Gbagbo, arguing that it was an 'internal affair' with no outside involvement, but still offered logistical, communication and transport support within the framework of 'normal' military cooperation between the countries. On 22 September 2002, the French military deployed 'impartial' troops to Côte d'Ivoire to stop the fighting. The new Operation Licorne was to set up 'the necessary conditions in search of a political solution'[21] and 'to allow Ivorians to define political solutions'.[22] French Minister of Defence Michèle Alliot-Marie argued that 'a show of force avoids resorting to force'; the logic being that French force was inherently legitimate to deter opposition parties from using force to attain power.[23] French troops established a 'zone of trust' (*zone de confiance*) which was put to the test a few times by rebel forces.[24]

Paradoxically, the French military interposition might have prevented a civil war and limited the bloodshed, but it also imposed basic parameters for the future peace negotiations. In dividing the country in two, it legitimised the north–south narrative of confrontation,[25] thus enabling the agency of rebels to become Forces Nouvelles (FN) as a legitimate political opposition and interlocutors in peace negotiations.[26] According to Stephen Smith, in

Paris the legitimacy of the northern armed rebellion evolved rapidly from denial to formal recognition: 'As the months went by, the territory conquered by the [MPCI] transformed itself into a source of legitimacy in the eyes of France.'[27] The use of force, or the perceived legitimacy of such force, was central to French diplomacy. President Jacques Chirac, known for disliking Gbagbo, allegedly claimed that '[Gbagbo] imagines that he has an army when he does not have one anymore; he believes [himself] to be power when he is not anymore'.[28] After visiting the rebels in Bouaké, Foreign Affairs Minister Dominique de Villepin argued that it was imperative 'to propose to those [MPCI] with the bulk of military power, sufficiently attractive responsibilities to get them to accept disarmament'.[29] Contradicting his political leaders, Chief of Staff General Bentegeat reported that Ivorian government air capabilities offered 'tangible military results' and that their rapid intervention force was 'very sturdy'.[30]

Rebel and French violence (and/or its threat) enabled agency by changing or constituting the conditions of possibility for it, but this was facilitated and based upon a spatial inside/outside discrimination that established the possibility of political judgement. On the one hand, the debate was over the 'outside' influence that supported the rebels, notably the involvement of Burkina Faso as financial backer that had allowed the rebels to organise and overtly prepare their coup in Ouagadougou. The Gbagbo government sought French military support under the bilateral defence agreement in view of this external support, but the French rejected this interpretation instead emphasising an interpretation of the conflict as a *ivoiro–ivoirien* civil war. Consequently, on the other hand, the French would claim impartiality as an international party to the local Ivorian conflict, notwithstanding Burkina Faso's support and the problem of Liberian militias in the west. The French use of force was premised on the assumption that it was legitimate violence for peace and that, consequently, the French government could impose or decide who got to deploy violence legitimately in Côte d'Ivoire. The French-imposed zone of trust that divided the country in two produced a political space for a 'North' distinguishable from the 'South' that was identified, associated, and thus represented by the rebels and Gbagbo's government respectively; a spatial grid that would later be reinforced by the deployment of ECOWAS and UN troops. Having two politically legitimate groups thus created the conditions that rendered an international (or French) political solution possible. Contrary to the logic of the French Minister of Defence, the French intervention suggested how, by using force, a short-cut to power was achievable. This process of legitimising an armed rebellion was formalised in January 2003 on the basis of the Linas–Marcoussis Accords. The Accords gave important presidential powers to the Prime Minister who would lead a new government of national reconciliation, allocated the Ministry of Defence and the Ministry of the Interior to the rebels, and stipulated that elections were the way out of the crisis.[31]

In the post-1960 world, Francophone African heads of state had come to expect French help or rescue when needed.[32] The French decision not to activate the defence accords in Côte d'Ivoire in 2002 was thus unsurprisingly interpreted by Gbagbo and his supporters as a betrayal and as part of the various attempts at discrediting and removing him from power, including empowering the rebels.[33] After Linas–Marcoussis and under the new conditions imposed by 'international' forces, Gbagbo responded to his adversaries in two interconnected ways. First, he mobilised state and 'street' violence ('Young Patriots', pro-Gbagbo militias, and 'street generals' such as Charles Blé Goudé and Eugène Djué[34]) and he encouraged and justified this (arguably limited) violence with an anti-colonial and nationalist rhetoric about the need and desire for a 'second decolonisation'. This so-called 'Patriotic Galaxy' also sometimes worked with government security forces, as in March 2004 when opposition parties staged a protest march that was quickly broken up by security forces and civilian militias.[35] Second, while this anti-colonial position focused on France, it was extended to all international actors, who were portrayed as instruments of French and/or Western hegemony. In this framework, Gbagbo's government could present itself as the defender of Ivorian sovereignty against 'outside' or 'international' influence. On multiple occasions, shows of popular support against perceived imperialist designs and limited acts of violence targeted both Ivorian political opponents and French and UN actors in attempts to curb international meddling and to increase Gbagbo's ability to negotiate with more powerful actors the limits of his political authority and freedom of action.

While the majority of commentators and experts seem to underplay or ignore this, Gbagbo's popular support was not all show. Various forms of resentment and political criticism and opposition had deep roots. With time, Gbagbo's anti-colonial rhetoric and tactics seemingly increased his legitimacy and authority as president, defender of Ivorian sovereignty, and leader of a 'second decolonisation' as he touched on sensitive issues to many Ivorians.[36] In these Ivorian–international negotiations over peace, there were two turning points leading to the 2010–2011 post-election crisis that both gave credibility to Gbagbo's representations and enabled, transformed, and/or (dis)empowered agency. The first was the events of November 2004. In October, it became obvious that the peace process was breaking down as the due date for disarmament approached. Indeed, on the 30th, the UN Secretary-General Special Representative, Albert Tévoédjré, accused Gbagbo of preparing for war.[37] On 4 November, he did go to war when the Ivorian army (FANCI) launched Operation Dignité to re-conquer the North. The offensive was not a surprise as preparations had been going on for weeks. According to D'Ersu, Chirac had called Gbagbo on the 3rd to rebuke him and warn him that the French army would respond. The Elysée, Ministry of Defence, and Foreign Minister Michel Barnier were strongly set against Operation Dignité, but French ambassador to Côte d'Ivoire Gildas Le Lidec and Barnier's cabinet reckoned that it might put an end to a stagnant political situation.[38] In any case, neither French nor UNOCI forces reacted to the end of the ceasefire.[39] In fact, partisans of the FN attacked the French camp near the city of Man on 6 November. This attack was overshadowed, however, by the FANCI air bombardment of Bouaké that hit a French barracks, killing nine French soldiers and an American citizen, and injuring 38 French soldiers. On the orders of General Henri Poncet, commander of Licorne forces, with General Bentegeat's approval, the FANCI aircraft were destroyed after landing.[40] Chirac then ordered the total destruction of the remaining Ivorian air force without consulting or warning the UN. According to Amnesty International, the majority of Ivorians interpreted the French actions as unjustified because they had not yet heard about the initial French casualties.[41] Rumours of a French coup spread when French forces took control of the Abidjan airport. The ensuing violence targeted Europeans and especially French citizens and property,[42] leading to a large-scale evacuation of French and European nationals and culminating at the Hotel Ivoire where, on 9 November, French forces fired on a crowd of protesters. The reasons for such a reaction are unclear. As tensions mounted, the French military argued that its soldiers acted in self-defence, while Ivorian protesters and gendarmerie claimed that French forces opened fire 'precipitously, if not indeed in panic'.[43] In sum, French actions gave credibility to Gbagbo's rhetoric and representations and united (for a moment) Ivorians against French and international meddling. The relative powers of various agencies were reshuffled: France could not claim to be an 'international impartial' agent for peace anymore thus opening the door to African-led negotiations and the UN and AU use of sanctions and other coercive mechanisms against Gbagbo. More importantly, it created more room for Gbagbo to manoeuvre within or against the conditions of possibility imposed by international peace interventionism, notably because he could exploit the divisions within Africa itself over the relative weight to be given to Ivorian sovereignty and international authority. Political negotiations were rewriting the lines between the 'local' and the 'international', thus in the process enabling or transforming agency.

The second turning point was the 2007 Ouagadougou Accords. The French had been discredited in 2004, the UN was increasingly the target of anti-colonial criticism and sometimes of violent protests, African-led negotiations had been unable to disrupt Gbagbo's delaying tactics, elections were repeatedly postponed, the war economy and associated economic interests had been consolidated (to the benefit of both parties to the conflict), and thus the situation had settled into what many commentators called a state of 'neither war nor peace'. As McGovern argues:

> Ivorian elites and intercalaries have many incentives to maintain a situation of neither war nor peace, in which instances of relatively low-level violence are a built-in part of the social and political equation, necessitating the state of emergency that acts as cover for various forms of profiteering.[44]

The April 2005 Pretoria Accords, under the aegis of then-South African President Thabo Mbeki, called for presidential elections in October and for the UN to be involved in their organisation. UN Security Council Resolution 1603 (2005) created the position of UN High Representative whose responsibilities were to verify all stages of the electoral process. However, after the elections were postponed twice, and at French insistence, the UN Security Council responded with Resolution 1721 (2006) to strengthen the powers of Prime Minister Banny and insist again on elections as a way out of the crisis. Gbagbo countered with a peace plan on 19 December 2006 that sought to do away with international influence, divide the Ivorian political opposition (between FN and the official opposition parties), and take back the initiative by insisting on inter-Ivorian dialogue. The timing was almost perfect for Gbagbo: his two main international adversaries, Chirac and UN Secretary-General Kofi Annan, were leaving their office in 2007, South Africa was to be a member of the UN Security Council and Burkina Faso's Blaise Compaoré was to become president of ECOWAS in January. Facilitated by Compaoré and supported in the Security Council by South Africa, the Ouagadougou Accords were based on prior agreements (and the need for elections, identification mechanisms, and disarmament). They also abolished the zone of trust – thus disabling 'international' authority – and made FN's Guillaume Soro prime minister – thus confirming that the ex-rebels recognised Gbagbo's presidency and *vice versa*. This 'local' peace accord generated much optimism because it changed the rapport de force between 'local' and 'international' actors, suggesting that the 'international community' had abdicated its influence to an African solution. However, as the International Crisis Group (ICG) noted, it would also make it harder if not impossible for Gbagbo and Soro to blame international interventions for the possible failure of this newest peace initiative.[45] Indeed, the Accords had displaced and rewritten the inside/outside line as it changed the *rapport de force* between 'local' and 'international' actors. As Gbagbo had confirmed and consolidated his agency as president, he had also implicitly accepted the inherent responsibility and consequences of this agency under conditions of international peace interventionism. One such key condition was the UN mandate to monitor and validate the next election, initially scheduled for October 2005 but held in 2010.

Regime change

After 2004, violence was used in a relatively limited fashion in Côte d'Ivoire before the 2010–2011 post-election crisis, but was nevertheless an instrument of negotiation between the claimants of Ivorian sovereignty and the claimants of international authority. This violence, however, found its meaning and political possibility as the enabler of agency in representations and conceptualisations based upon the local/international distinction. French and UN troops could deploy it to define their role as humanitarians and/or agents of international authority. Gbagbo's government and the Forces Nouvelles both claimed to use force in a manner that defended the Ivorian people and/or Ivorian sovereignty. Gbagbo was able to capture and manipulate these representations and their political effects to his advantage until the 2010 post-election crisis, but then seemingly underestimated the limits of his tactics and representations under the changing conditions of international interventionism.

As early as 2005, the ICG remarked that the personal dimension of the conflict and Gbagbo's attitude of winning everything at all cost needed to be taken seriously.[46] In October 2010, Gbagbo said in an interview to Jeune Afrique that his party's objective was 'we win or we win'. It seems that he had no intention of leaving office, no matter what the election results, believing that in Africa a leader does not give up power voluntarily. Elections were meant to increase his legitimacy and decrease international meddling. His usual delaying tactics did not work in 2011 because in the end, as McGovern explains, international 'unanimity countered Gbagbo's strategy of playing for time, hoping that African–European or inter-African schisms would provide him with some sort of mitigated legitimacy'.[47]

Regime change was not inevitable and 'international unanimity' not so easily formed. Regime change was made possible by a combination of two factors: the strong international legitimacy given to Ouattara as the elected president; and the ways he acquired the means of using legitimate force by creating the Forces républicaines de la Côte d'Ivoire (FRCI – as formalised by decree on 17 March 2011). The first issue is embedded in the international politics of intervention and negotiations between claims to Ivorian sovereignty and claims to international authority. Who gets to decide on the legitimate president of Côte d'Ivoire, and the acceptable parameters of a national political order? The UN had supervised the 2010 election and confirmed the results according to the Pretoria Accords of 2005. Secretary-General Ban Ki-moon responded fiercely to Gbagbo's challenge by demanding that he step down and by asserting that '[f]acing this direct and unacceptable challenge to the legitimacy of the United Nations, the world community cannot stand by'.[48]

This 'world community' reacted relatively strongly to Gbagbo's refusal to leave office, but this 'world' or 'international' community must be deconstructed. For example, the role of African governments and regional organisations increases the difficulty of drawing the local/international line.[49] On 7 December, ECOWAS approved the election results, demanded that Gbagbo leave office immediately, and suspended Côte d'Ivoire from the organisation. Two days later, the Peace and Security Council of the AU recognised Ouattara as the elected President, asked Gbagbo to transfer his power to Ouattara immediately, and suspended Côte d'Ivoire from the AU. On the 20th, the Council of the EU adopted targeted sanctions against personalities of the regime, including Gbagbo and his wife. On the 23rd the Council of Ministers of the Union économique et monétaire ouest-africaine specified that only representatives of the Ouattara government would have access to the country's accounts, while the World Bank suspended its programmes and froze its aid to Côte d'Ivoire. On 25 January, the interim Governor of the Central Bank of West African States closed its bank branches within the country. To what extent this strategy of economic starvation worked to solve the crisis is hard to tell, but it undermined Gbagbo's ability to pay civil servants, soldiers and various political allies. With the UN, AU, ECOWAS, EU and Organisation internationale de la Francophonie having recognised Ouattara's electoral victory, Gbagbo was quickly being isolated internationally.

However, contrary to Thomas Bassett and Scott Straus's claim that there was 'strong and consistent positions of the AU and ECOWAS toward the Côte d'Ivoire crisis',[50] there were intense debates within these institutions. The AU was the last international organisation to react on 9 December, strongly urging Gbagbo 'to respect the results of the election'.[51] Gbagbo had African allies, having developed close relationships with some African heads of states, notably President Santos of Angola who benefitted from the expulsion of Angolan rebels from Ivorian territory. The *Economist* even reported that Santos lent 300 soldiers to Gbagbo for close protection purposes.[52] After Nigeria threatened Gbagbo with an ECOWAS military action in December 2010, but especially a month later when Nigeria urged the UN Security Council to sanction an AU military intervention, cracks in the African consensus began to show. In particular, Ghanaian President Atta Mills surprised Western diplomats when he bluntly refused and opposed military action to oust Gbagbo. After meeting with both Gbagbo and Ouattara, Mills did not want to take sides. For him, a military intervention meant jeopardising his country's business interests with its neighbour, the lives of about one million Ghanaians living in Côte d'Ivoire, and a possible refugee crisis in Ghana. Ugandan President Yoweri Museveni urged restraint and his government argued that contested elections should be investigated instead of just declaring a winner.[53] South Africa also changed its position in January, supporting a power-sharing solution. Influenced by Thabo Mbeki's interpretation of the crisis as a French-led, neocolonial intervention that should be opposed, South African President Jacob Zuma abruptly reversed his government's stance when he questioned the results of the elections on 21 January. From then until March, South Africa opposed the Nigerian-led support for military intervention and instead proposed itself as a mediator and suggested a power-sharing solution between Gbagbo and Ouattara,[54] even at some point hinting at its own military intervention.[55]

As tensions rose and the violence increased in the first months of 2011, so did the stakes of international intervention. The crisis exposed the horizontal and transversal political dynamics and the personal dimensions of political elite negotiations over 'international' and 'African/regional' peace interventionism. With the mounting violence increasingly targeting civilians in Abidjan in particular,[56] Gbagbo's agency as legitimate president and defender of Ivorian sovereignty abated. Gbagbo's stubbornness further isolated him. On 10 March, the AU reaffirmed its recognition of Ouattara as the legitimate president, making untenable the positions of Gbagbo's remaining allies.[57] Later in March both South Africa and Angola dropped Gbagbo.[58] This African consensus opened the door for further 'international' intervention. On the one hand, Sarkozy had not wanted to intervene without UN approval and African support – cooperation with Nigeria as the leader of ECOWAS being a top priority.[59] On the other hand, Russian and Chinese resistance to intervention in the UN Security Council abated as African organisations and governments showed agreement. This pivotal African role can be variously interpreted. Alex Vines argues that 'the only initially promising aspect of this situation has been that of leadership from emerging African institutions', while Mbeki wrote that 'the AU has asserted the ability of the major powers to intervene to resolve these challenges by using their various capacities to legitimize their actions by persuading the United Nations to authorise their self-serving interventions'.[60] In any case, it seemed that the escalating violence shifted politically effective agency away from Gbagbo and further towards actors who claimed to represent 'international' authority. French agency as 'international' peace broker was particularly empowered by its political position in the UN Security Council and as a military power in Côte d'Ivoire.

Yet, as Gbagbo was losing grip on power and the legitimacy to use violence, the international intervention that changed a regime could not have happened, it seems, without the transformation of an ex-rebel army (FN) into a republican one (FRCI). The post-election crisis was, at first, the struggle between an elected president without legitimate force and an illegitimate president that stayed in power because of the military forces under his command. As Moussa Fofana argues, the crisis led to an alliance between Ouattara and Soro and the FN. According to Fofana, as early as January 2011, the FN discussed a military solution and, after a meeting in January of ECOWAS member army chiefs, Ouattara might have made deals with Nigeria, Senegal and Burkina Faso to provide rebels with weapons. Fofana argues that a peaceful resolution might have excluded Soro and the FN from the benefits of a new political order after years of being one of the main beneficiaries of the 'neither war nor peace' situation. This alliance solved the problem of external military intervention, creating the condition for an Ivorian solution to the crisis and giving Ouattara the military forces he needed to confront Gbagbo.[61] Yet, it is rather unlikely that this alliance would have been possible without the transformation of the conditions of possibility for legitimate violence and its associated shifts of agency that came out of the formation of an 'international' consensus. With the diplomatic and international situation rapidly turning in his favour, Ouattara was able to transform the FN into (arguably) the legitimate military force needed to support his political claims.[62]

The FRCI launched an offensive on 28 March, encountering little resistance until it reached Abidjan, except by not-so-local militias and mercenaries at Duékoué in the west of the country.[63] Two days later, France and Nigeria sponsored UNSC Resolution 1975 (2011) authorising UNOCI and Licorne forces 'to use all necessary means to carry out its mandate to protect civilians under imminent threat of physical violence, within its capabilities and its areas of deployment, including to prevent the use of heavy weapons against the civilian population'.[64] The dominant interpretation of the text engaged the 'impartial forces' on the side of the electoral winner and an ex-rebel army.[65]

Conclusion

After years of negotiations over the respective limits of Ivorian sovereignty and international authority, in the name of peace and Ivorian democracy, French–UN violence was deployed and performed the authority of an 'international community' to impose peace and regime change. Alex Bellamy and Paul Williams argued that the 'Security Council's responses to the crises in Côte d'Ivoire and Libya need to be seen in the context of its increasing willingness to authorize coalitions and "blue-helmet" peacekeeping operations to use all necessary means for human protection purposes'.[66] Certainly, the legitimacy of the April 2011 intervention will be debated for years to come, but in Côte d'Ivoire this seems to be a superficial conclusion in light of the complexity and variety of political considerations that were being negotiated. Rather, the case of Côte d'Ivoire calls into question the possibility of a universal concept such as human security/protection applicable to all conflicts. It emphasises the contingency of intense negotiations. The case evidences the increasingly important role played by African regional organisations and rapidly changing 'international' peace practices. Yet, it is far from clear what these transformations mean for the reorganisation of power internationally, for the politics and practices of intervention in Africa, and for the social, economic, cultural and political evolution of Côte d'Ivoire and West Africa more generally. Peace and 'human protection' discourses easily become rhetorical devices for legitimising violence, guide post-conflict societal development, and provide neat post-facto explanations. The asymmetrical characteristics underpinning peacekeeping and peacebuilding practices (including discourse practices) are well documented.

This chapter suggested that behind claims to legitimate violence are ontological commitments about agency. These commitments must be analysed and deconstructed because they have fundamental political consequences for the limits imposed on the formation of, and the possibility for, agency. It is here that the common anti-imperial or post-colonial critique seems insufficient. In theory, agency is assigned *a priori*. We are supposed to know who or what agency is local or international and what this identification entails. In practice, agency is performed, authorised, institutionalised. It is claimed, resisted, challenged, negotiated and/or transformed through human actions and reactions. To assign the quality of 'local' or 'international' to agency is to neglect how a specific agency becomes local or international, or moves from one to the other, in a specific context, and thus how the minimal conditions of its possibilities are established and negotiated. For instance, as Gbagbo was both 'local' actor in a conflict and an 'international' actor in peace negotiations, so too for the commonly understood 'international' interlocutors, like the French and African governments, who were often both direct actors in the conflict and 'international' peacekeepers. Before negotiations over peace, there are intense negotiations, interactions and struggles over legitimate agency where contradictions and tensions seem particularly obvious in the use of violence.

Ultimately, political judgement over the legitimacy of regime change in Côte d'Ivoire is commonly framed spatially between claims to Ivorian sovereignty and claims to international authority, but realised temporally between the immediate moment of crisis – when decisions are made and implemented and so much and so many lives are at stake that it seems difficult to argue against intervention – and the long-term and structural conditions of possibility that lead so many to believe that international military intervention was deemed necessary in 2011. The analysis here suggests that the question is not about defining, imposing or building peace per se, but first about the minimal conditions of possibility for establishing, enabling and transforming agency under conditions of liberal peace interventionism.

Acknowledgements

I thank Tony Chafer, Geneviève Parent, Florian Kühn, Michael Pugh, Mandy Turner and the anonymous reviewers of IPK for their comments and support in improving this chapter, and the Social Sciences and Humanities Research Council of Canada for their financial support. This chapter is an updated version of the article of the same name that appeared in *International Peacekeeping*, vol. 19, no. 4, August 2012, Taylor & Francis Ltd, www.tandfonline.com, reprinted by permission of the publisher.

Notes

1 See, e.g., Roger Mac Ginty, *International Peacebuilding and Local Resistance*, New York: Palgrave Macmillan, 2011.
2 Ali Mazrui, 'The United Nations and Some African Political Attitudes', *International Organization*, vol. 18, no. 3, 1964, p. 504. Also Adekeye Adebajo (ed.), *From Global Apartheid to Global Village: Africa and the United Nations*, Scottsville: University of KwaZulu-Natal Press, 2009.
3 Mark Mazower, *No Enchanted Place: The End of Empire and the Ideological Origins of the United Nations*, Princeton, NJ: Princeton University Press, 2009.
4 Anne Orford, *International Authority and the Responsibility to Protect*, Cambridge: Cambridge University Press, 2011.
5 R. B. J. Walker, *After the Globe, Before the World*, New York: Routledge, 2010.
6 Cynthia Weber, 'Reconsidering Statehood: Examining the Sovereignty/intervention Boundary', *Review of International Studies*, vol. 18, no. 3, 1992, pp. 207–212.

7 Bruno Charbonneau, 'Dreams of Empire: France, Europe, and the New Interventionism in Africa', *Modern and Contemporary France*, vol. 16, no. 3, 2008, pp. 279–295.
8 See, *inter alia*, Oliver Richmond, *A Post-Liberal Peace*, New York: Routledge, 2011.
9 Audra Mitchell, 'Quality/Control: International Peace Interventions and the "Everyday"', *Review of International Studies*, vol. 37, no. 4, 2011, pp. 1623–1645.
10 Bruno Charbonneau, 'The Imperial Legacy of International Peacebuilding: The Case of Francophone Africa', *Review of International Studies*, vol. 40, no. 3, 2014, p. 629.
11 Mitchell (note 9 above), p. 1633.
12 This is not to say that *ivoirité* is a purely elitist phenomenon. The questions of identity, identification and citizenship are commonly understood as constituting the central dynamics of the conflict. See Ruth Marshall-Fratani, 'The War of "Who Is Who": Autochthony, Nationalism, and Citizenship in the Ivorian Crisis', *African Studies Review*, vol. 49, no. 2, 2006, pp. 9–43; Sara Berry, 'Property, Authority and Citizenship: Land Claims, Politics and the Dynamics of Social Division in West Africa', *Development and Change*, vol. 40, no. 1, 2009, pp. 23–45.
13 François Gaulme, 'La Côte d'Ivoire entre guerre et paix' ['Côte d'Ivoire between War and Peace'], *Études*, vol. 407, nos. 7–8, 2007, pp. 9–19.
14 On the specificity of peace operations in Francophone Africa, see Bruno Charbonneau and Tony Chafer (eds), *Peace Operations in the Francophone World: Global Governance Meets Post-Colonialism*, New York: Routledge, 2014.
15 Tony Chafer, 'The UK and France in West Africa: Towards Convergence?', *African Security*, vol. 6, nos. 3–4, 2013, pp. 234–256.
16 Mike McGovern, *Making War in Côte d'Ivoire*, Chicago, IL: University of Chicago Press, 2011, pp. 203–204.
17 Hugo Sada, 'Le conflit ivoirien: enjeux régionaux et maintien de la paix en Afrique' ['The Ivorian Conflict: Regional Issues and Peacekeeping in Africa'] *Politique Etrangère*, vol. 68, no. 2, 2003, p. 323.
18 In particular, the battle for leadership was fierce between Senegale President Abdoulaye Wade, whose country had been excluded from the contact group, and Togo's Eyadéma. ECOWAS deployed troops in January which were later integrated into UNOCI.
19 UN Security Council, *Report of the Secretary-General on Côte d'Ivoire*, UN doc. S/2003/374, 26 March 2003, p. 4.
20 Gaulme (note 13 above).
21 Sénat, France, *Rapport d'information au nom de la commission des Affaires étrangères, de la défense et des forces armées sur la gestion des crises en Afrique subsaharienne* [*Foreign Affairs, Defence, and Armed Forces Information Report on Crisis Management in Sub-Saharan Africa*], no. 450, 3 July 2006, p. 44.
22 Assemblée nationale, France, *Commission des Affaires étrangères*, Compte rendu no. 30, 29 January 2003.
23 Assemblée nationale, France, *Commission des Affaires étrangères*, Compte rendu no. 10, 9 November 2004.
24 Assemblée nationale, France, *Commission de la Défense nationale et des Forces armées*, Compte rendu no. 26, 21 January 2003.
25 The–north-south confrontation has been overemphasized and often misrepresented as a religious division. There are North–South tensions, but these are complex and transforming, and each 'region' has a diverse population. Years of conflict and elite instrumentalization of this confrontation, however, have in some respects consolidated the division.
26 The MPCI, MPIGO, and MJP formed the *Forces Nouvelles* on 22 Dec. 2002.
27 Stephen Smith, 'La politique d'engagement de la France à l'épreuve de la Côte d'Ivoire' ['France's Policy of Engagement Tested in Côte d'Ivoire'], *Politique africaine*, vol. 89, March, 2003, pp. 119–120.

28 Quoted in Francis Laloupo, 'La Côte d'Ivoire ou l'échiquier des énigmes', *African Geopolitics*, no. 13, 2004 (at: www.african-geopolitics.org).
29 Assemblée nationale (note 24 above).
30 Assemblée nationale (note 22 above).
31 The Marcoussis Accord became the negotiating basis for all subsequent peace accords. In interviews with French officials in 2004 and 2007, the failure of the French-led Marcoussis Accords was laid at Gbagbo's feet. In 2011, however, several French officials at the Ministry of Foreign Affairs admitted that the French patronizing attitude toward Gbagbo was partly to blame. Author's interviews, Paris, November 2004, September 2007, April–May 2011.
32 See Bruno Charbonneau, *France and the New Imperialism: Security Policy in Sub-Saharan Africa*, Alderhost: Ashgate, 2008.
33 During the Marcoussis negotiations, President Chirac even brandished the possibility of bringing Gbagbo to the International Criminal Court.
34 On the 'street' movements and violence, see Richard Banégas, 'Côte d'Ivoire: Patriotism, Ethnonationalism and Other African Modes of Self-Writing', *African Affairs*, vol. 105, no. 421, 2006, pp. 535–552; Richard Banégas, 'Post-election Crisis in Côte d'Ivoire: the *Gbonhi* War', *African Affairs*, vol. 110, no. 440, 2011, pp. 457–468.
35 International Crisis Group, *Côte d'Ivoire: pas de paix en vue* [*Côte d'Ivoire: No Peace in Sight*], Rapport Afrique no. 82, Dakar/Brussels: International Crisis Group, 2004.
36 His 2010 election results are a strong indication of that: in the first round, he received 38.3 per cent of the vote and 45.9 per cent in the second round. See also McGovern (note 16 above). Banégas (note 34 above) argues that the Young Patriots are composed of young men with genuine political demands, and not simply 'thugs' as they are often portrayed.
37 UN Security Council, *Third Progress Report of the Secretary-General on the United Nations Operation in Côte d'Ivoire*, S/2004/962, 9 December 2004, p. 3.
38 Laurent D'Ersu, 'La crise ivoirienne: une intrigue franco-française' ['The Ivorian Crisis: A Franco-French Intrigue'], *Politique africaine*, vol. 105, March, 2007, p. 98.
39 UNOCI was created on 9 March 2004 by UN Security Council Resolution 1528 that authorized the initial deployment of 6,240 military troops and 350 police officers under a Chapter VII mandate.
40 D'Ersu (note 38 above), p. 86.
41 Amnesty International, *Côte d'Ivoire: Clashes Between Peacekeeping Forces and Civilians; Lessons for the Future*, AI Index AFR 31/005/2006, Abidjan: Amnesty International, 19 September 2006,.
42 Over 20,000 French citizens lived in CI before 2004 and over 8,000 of them were evacuated by 18 November.
43 Amnesty International (note 41 above). See also Charbonneau (note 32 above), pp. 166–169. More than 20 Ivorians were killed according to the French government or 64 according to the Gbagbo's government.
44 McGovern (note 16 above), p. 197.
45 International Crisis Group, *Côte d'Ivoire: faut-il croire à l'accord de Ouagadougou?* [*Côte d'Ivoire: Should We Believe in the Ouagadougou Accord?*], Rapport Afrique no. 127, Dakar/Brussels: International Crisis Group, 2007.
46 International Crisis Group, *Côte d'Ivoire: le pire est peut-être à venir* [*Côte d'Ivoire: The Worst May Be Yet to Come*], Rapport Afrique no. 90, Dakar/Brussels: International Crisis Group, 2005, p. 6.
47 Mike McGovern, 'The Ivorian Endgame' *Foreign Affairs*, 14 April 2011 (at: www.foreignaffairs.com/articles/67728/mike-mcgovern/the-ivorian-endgame?page=show).
48 'UN Chief Warns of "Real Risk" of Ivory Coast Civil War', *BBC News*, 22 December 2010 (at: www.bbc.co.uk/news/world-africa-12056444).

49 For more on the role of African regional organisations in Côte d'Ivoire, see Fabienne Hara and Gilles Yabi, 'Côte d'Ivoire, 2002-2011', in Jane Boulden (ed.), *Responding to Conflict in Africa: The United Nations and Regional Organizations*, New York, Palgrave, pp. 145-176.
50 Thomas Bassett and Scott Straus, 'Defending Democracy in Côte d'Ivoire', *Foreign Affairs*, vol. 90, no. 4, 2011, pp. 130-140.
51 Peace and Security Council of the African Union, 'Communiqué', 252th Meeting, Addis Ababa, 9 December 2010.
52 'Turmoil in Côte d'Ivoire', *The Economist*, Abidjan, 10 March 2011.
53 Scott Baldauf, 'African Union Leaders divided about Ivory Coast intervention', *The Christian Science Monitor*, 26 January 2011.
54 On South Africa-Nigeria dynamics during the crisis, see Vincent Darracq, 'Jeux de puissance en Afrique: Le Nigeria et l'Afrique du Sud face à la crise ivoirienne' ['Power Games in Africa: Nigeria and South Africa Facing the Ivorian Crisis'], *Politique étrangère*, vol. 2, summer, 2011, pp. 361-374.
55 Baudelaire Mieu, 'Côte d'Ivoire: préparation d'une intervention de l'Afrique du Sud à Abidjan?' ['Côte d'Ivoire: Preparation of a South African Intervention in Abidjan?'], *Jeune Afrique*, 6 April 2011.
56 See UN Security Council, *Twenty-Seventh Progress Report of the Secretary-General on the United Nations Operation in Côte d'Ivoire*, UN doc. S/2011/211, 30 March 2011.
57 Peace and Security Council of the African Union, 'Communiqué', 265th Meeting, Addis Ababa, 10 March 2011.
58 'Côte d'Ivoire: Laurent Gbagbo lâché par l'Angola?' ['Côte d'Ivoire: Laurent Gbagbo Abandoned by Angola?'], *Jeune Afrique*, 23 March 2011.
59 Interviews by the author, Ministère des Affaires étrangères et européennes, Paris, April-May 2011.
60 Alex Vines, 'Côte d'Ivoire: Power Gridlock', *The World Today*, vol. 67, no. 3, 2011, p. 24; Thabo Mbeki, 'What the World Got Wrong in Côte d'Ivoire', *Foreign Policy*, 29 April 2011.
61 Moussa Fofana, 'Des Forces Nouvelles aux Forces républicaines de Côte d'Ivoire' ['From New Forces to Republican Forces in Côte d'Ivoire'], *Politique africaine*, vol. 122, June 2011, pp. 161-178.
62 The timing might have also worked into Ouattara's favour. At the time, the world was witnessing the 'Arab Spring' and on 17 March the UN Security Council Resolution 1973 (2011) authorized the use of force in Libya.
63 See Christophe Boisbouvier, 'Côte d'Ivoire: les secrets d'une offensive éclair' ['Côte d'Ivoire: Secrets of a Blitzkrieg'], *Jeune Afrique*, 8 April 2011.
64 UN Security Council, Resolution 1975, UN doc. S/Res/1975, 30 March 2011. Except for the emphasis on 'heavy weapons against the civilian population', Resolution 1975 was simply reiterating the Chapter VII mandate.
65 Brazil, China, India, and Russia had a more restrictive interpretation emphasizing the neutrality of peacekeepers. See Alex Bellamy and Paul Williams, 'The New Politics of Protection? Côte d'Ivoire, Libya and the Responsibility to Protect', *International Affairs*, vol. 87, no. 4, 2011, pp. 835-837.
66 *Ibid.*, pp. 828-829.

10 Enemy images, coercive socio-engineering and civil war in Iraq

Toby Dodge

On 10 June 2014, after four days of fighting, Da'esh (ad-Dawlah al-Islāmīyah fil-'Iraq wa ash-Shām, or the Islamic State in Iraq and the Levant), took control of Iraq's second city Mosul. Da'esh then fought their way out of Nineveh Province, heading down the main highway towards Baghdad. Their fighters also pushed into Diyala Province, which borders Iran to the east, while simultaneously consolidating the group's position in Anbar province, bordering Syria.

The violence that engulfed Iraq in June 2014 cannot be explained simply or primarily as the act of one extremely violent terrorist group. The speed with which the Iraqi government lost control of northwest Iraq indicates this new upsurge in mass violence was more akin to a multifaceted and widespread uprising than the outcome of one radical jihadist group's actions. The gravity of the present crisis, with the Iraqi army quickly overwhelmed in Iraq's second city and then losing control of large tracts of territory to the north of Baghdad, has put the sustainability of the country's post-invasion political settlement in doubt, the security of the whole country and with it the future of Iraq itself. The roots of this crisis lie in the political settlement that was used by the Bush administration to order Iraq after it had removed the Ba'athist regime in 2003. The rise of Da'esh and Iraq's renewed civil war spring directly from the profound mistakes made by the US occupation as it attempted to rebuild and reform the Iraqi state.

However, there has been a tendency, in both journalistic coverage and academic analyses, to stress the inter-communal nature of the conflict.[1] This 'primordialisation' of Iraq has the advantage of both absolving US policy makers of blame for the rise of Da'esh and the civil war as well as playing to deeper, longer running, Orientalist stereotypes of the Middle East. In this narrative, the United States had sought to bring democracy to Iraq but irrational, violent Arabs were more intent on killing each other than enjoying the benefits of American-delivered freedom and capitalism. Over a decade after the invasion, a much more nuanced analysis of the causes of Iraq's post-war descent into violence is possible. This avoids the Orientalist idea of the inevitability of ancient hatreds leading the rise of radical Islam and civil war. Instead, it is anchored in a detailed examination of the evolution of

US policy towards post-war Iraq. This approach identifies the political settlement imposed upon the country by US policy after the invasion as the central driver of conflict. Iraq's new political settlement, initially constructed under the US occupation, then expanded and institutionalised by a group of formerly-exiled politicians empowered by their allies, was based around a 'victor's peace' and an 'exclusive elite bargain'. The new structures of governance and politics were deliberately constructed to exclude those thought to be members of, or complicit with, the old ruling elite. It is this victor's peace, deliberately created to exclude a section of society, that explains Iraq's descent into civil war and then the rise of Da'esh. This chapter details the effects of this exclusive elite bargain but also explains its causes. The origins of Iraq's post-war political settlement can be traced back to the ideational understanding of Iraq shared by the dominant decision-makers in the Bush administration. George W. Bush, Secretary of Defence Donald Rumsfeld and key advisers at the Pentagon, Paul Wolfowitz and Douglas Feith, all made sense of Iraq and America's role in the country by deploying a 'diabolical enemy image' schema. This allowed these key decision makers to ideationally order a complex and alien society of which they knew very little prior to the invasion. It also shaped the moral sense of certainty that both propelled the US government to invade Iraq but also drove its post-war sense of mission. However, this schema also encouraged the United States to pick certain groups of people to form Iraq's new ruling elite, and more importantly to exclude others.

Cognition, enemy images and the historiography of US involvement in Iraq

Given both the hubris and optimism that drove US forces into Iraq in 2003, scholarship on American policy in Baghdad needs to explain why, as Anatol Lieven put it, the US insisted on 'kicking to pieces the hill of which it is king',[2] the counter-productive policy decisions made during the first year of the occupation, and the resulting escalation in violence from 2004 to 2007 and again from 2013 to 2014.

There has certainly been a massive volume of literature published on the US relationship with Iraq in the run up to the invasion and in its continuing bloody aftermath. However, a curiously small amount has actually focused on trying to explain what drove the specifics of the US policy process from 2001 to 2011. Instead, the literature can be divided into three major categories. The first is by eyewitness journalists explaining how the occupation and then civil war unfolded on the ground, the application of policy making by the occupation authorities in Baghdad, or the policy making process itself in Washington, DC. The best of these offers an invaluable source of information for further academic study but were not written as deeply analytical or consciously academic texts.[3] The second set of works were written by US policy makers once they had left government service. On the one hand, the vast majority of these works are acts of transparent self-justification, blame shifting and attempts to shape as positive a historical record of the protagonists role as possible. On the other hand, they offer an invaluable source on actions taken and the intent behind them. As will become apparent below, these works of self-justification, once subject to critical analysis, are more revealing about the ideational drivers of policy than their authors had obviously intended.

The final set of works on US policy are academic texts, of which, however, only a small number actually deal directly with what shaped the US policy making process. The majority are instead exercises in international relations (IR), focusing on the large structural drivers of US policy. Raymond Hinnebusch's work, originating from a leftist position, represents the best example of this approach. However, a rationalist, utility maximising intent is inferred from what are assumed to be the US hegemonic goals in the region.

> The seizure of Iraq's pivotal oil fields would make appeasement of the Arabs superfluous; Iraq could be used to break OPEC and destabilize unfriendly Muslim oil states. ... the seizure of Iraq would allow the US to secure access to Arab oil without Arab alliances and consent and to remove the last remaining constraints on total US commitment to the achievement of 'Greater Israel'.[4]

There are three problems with such an approach. First, the United States is anthropomorphised, conceived of as a highly rational unitary actor. It is aware of the long-term threats to its global and regional position and deploys its unrivalled power to meet them. Second, evidence for this thesis is largely inferred from actions taken. Debates within the highest levels of government, the often incoherent policymaking process itself and unintended consequences are either left unexamined or taken for granted. Given the huge costs that the United States suffered in Iraq, amounting to a major foreign policy defeat, these oversights are troubling.

A second academic approach to the foreign policy of the Bush administration and its attitude towards Iraq, places explanatory stress on the ideational drivers of policy. The best example of this is the work of Jean-Francois Drolet.[5] By focusing on the influence of ideology, this body of work escapes the limitations of more mainstream approaches within IR. However, it rarely follows through from archaeological investigations into the ideational roots of foreign policy behaviour to how those ideas actually shape the policymaking choices of key individuals within government. The result is a major disconnect between the ideational drivers of decision makers, the decisions they ultimately take and the consequences.

A third body of academic literature does indeed focus on the policy making process both in Washington but also in Baghdad.[6] However, the works that seek to do this from a leftist position have a tendency to reproduce a number of the underlying assumptions of Hinnebusch's approach. The US hegemon is perceived to be in dogged pursuit of its rationalist interest-maximising goals. Depending on the degree of ruthless brutality assigned to US intent, the violence that accompanied the fulfilment of these goals was either an unintended outcome of policy incoherence or an acceptable cost.[7] Such a highly rationalist approach marginalises the power that the ideational has in the shaping of foreign policy decision-making. The policy mistakes are attributed to either imperfect information or resource constraints. The fact that the decision makers themselves may not be pursuing a rational strategy of utility-maximisation is not countenanced.

In order to overcome these gaps in the historiography of the US involvement in Iraq, the powerful insights of the ideational approach to US foreign policy need to be combined with insights gained from foreign policy analysis (FPA).[8] Within IR and FPA, two separate and distinct approaches, the cognitive and constructivist, have placed the ideational at the centre of explaining decision-making. The combination of both approaches may yield a more coherent and detailed explanation for the ongoing development of US policy in Iraq after the initial invasion and during the nine years that US troops occupied the country.

At first glance, the combination of cognitive and constructivist approaches would appear intellectually counter-intuitive, to say the least. The cognitive approach has an individualist ontology and a rationalist epistemology. Constructivism, on the other hand, stresses the causative power of ideational structures and the 'co-constitutive' relationship between structures and agents.[9]

Although different, both approaches suffer from their own intellectual lacunae. The cognitive study of decision-making, because of its individualist ontology, finds it difficult, if not impossible, to factor in the societal dynamics that ultimately structure collective meaning and shape an individual's approach to information processing.[10] On the other hand, within constructivism, the individual level of analysis tends to be marginalised or disappear altogether, with a tendency to focus on the causative powers of the ideational.[11] The utilisation of insights from both approaches, while recognising the ontological and epistemological tensions inherent in this, would allow for the study of ideational influences on individuals involved in the foreign policy decision-making process while tracing those influences back to the socially produced structures that give those ideas inter-subjective meaning.

At the decision-making level, the cognitive school argues that individuals are 'cognitive misers', enforcing a stable meaning on a highly complex and over-determined reality by subconsciously filtering out data that is considered superfluous.[12] Belief systems not only filter and prioritise information, they also impose normative appraisals on situations, imposing coherence through ideologically-shaped judgment.[13] Once a belief system has been formed, it solidifies around the defence of 'cognitive consistency'.[14] The individual defends the internal consistency of their belief system by discrediting information that does not make sense within its own boundaries. Ironically, this process of 'cognitive consistency' is likely to be much more rigid in expert policy makers. By their very profession they process large volumes of information to make sense of situations and do so at speed.[15] Foreign policy decision makers are likely to have a complex but also exclusionary belief system. In spite of the time spent by the cognitive school mapping the role and complexity of belief systems, the analytical dominance of an individualist ontology and rationalist epistemology means belief systems are seen as idiosyncratic, produced by each person's specific life experiences and education.

The constructivist approach, concerned about the mutually constitutive relationship between structure and agency, focuses on how inter-subjective meaning is created among a group of decision makers and beyond that within a society and across the globe.[16] Jutta Weldes stresses the role of articulation in this process where,

> particular phenomena, whether objects, events or social relations, are represented in specific ways and given particular meaning on which action is then based. With their successful repeated articulation, these linguistic elements come to seem as though they are inherently or necessarily connected and the meanings they produce come to seem natural, to be an accurate description of reality.[17]

The *via media* between the individualist approach of the cognitive school and the constructivist approach that sees meaning as produced inter-subjectively, is the category of the 'other'. The cognitive school places the negatively defined other at the centre of an individual's belief system and the system's defence of its cognitive consistency. It helps reduce cognitive dissonance as the moral juxtaposition between self and other by simplifying information about other entities, categorising them not only as allies or foes but more simply as good and bad.[18] However, constructivism would focus on the inter-subjective societal processes where the other becomes the 'antithesis of core values and beliefs' for the whole country.[19] This allows a society, in this case the United States after 9/11, to be celebrated as morally superior, acting with unquestionable motives.[20] This is contrasted with the 'other', who is either sociologically 'immature' or morally degenerate.[21] If the others are categorised thus, then their motives are always self-serving and negative. For this basic dualism to be ideationally sustainable, its meaning has to be anchored in a society's morality, its collective perception of itself, its place within international politics and its relationship to its others. From within literary theory Edward Said has labelled this 'Orientalism', 'European culture gained in strength and identity by setting itself off against the Orient as a sort of surrogate and even underground self'.[22] From within FPA, Brett Silverstein and Robert Holt label it 'folk theory', where 'there is only this one type of war. There is always one right, justified, and innocent side – ours, even if we are committing unprovoked genocide – and the other side is always actuated by evil motives.'[23]

Following the cognitive school, the placing of a 'diabolical enemy image' at the centre of a belief system leads to an aggressive defence of cognitive consistency. The decision-making process becomes constricted, both perceptions and facts are blurred, and appraisals of the enemy inflexible.[24] The enemy appears to possess all the traits of an ideal-typical enemy, new discordant information is denied once it has been processed from within an unchallenged and highly rigid belief system.[25] Following Said, the power of this diabolical enemy image is enhanced when it is anchored in cultural and racist stereotypes that have long shaped Western interactions with the 'Orient' and that have given violent intrusions into the non-Western world a sense of moral purpose and clarity.

It is the centrality of the 'diabolical enemy image' to decision makers and the society which they claim to represent, that shapes the pursuit of a 'victor's peace'. In a victor's peace, the conflict winner continues to deploy violence after an official ceasefire with the aim of solidifying and guaranteeing its dominance. With the 'diabolical enemy image' at the centre of the victor's belief system, conflicts arising from a victor's peace are perceived by its protagonist as an ideological struggle between good and evil with success only achieved by total victory. Once the initial military struggle is over, state power is deployed to 'cleanse' society of the vanquished foe, purging the societal and political organisations associated with the old order.[26] The loser's peace, on the other hand, is a direct result of the enemy's exclusion. It is marked by an upsurge of grassroots, non-state asymmetrical violence. Here local elites, excluded by the victor's peace, have little choice but to deploy violence in an effort to gain a place at the governing table or overthrow the post victory settlement in its entirety.

US policy in Iraq from 2003 onwards and its effects can be explained by the deployment of both the cognitive and constructivist approaches to foreign policy analysis. Iraq, as the key proving ground for the Bush doctrine, was to be coercively re-engineered. However, from within the belief system dominating decision making in Washington and policy application in Baghdad, the 'hope of democracy, development, free markets, and free trade' could only be guaranteed by the complete defeat of the 'diabolical enemy', the Ba'athist ruling elite which had run the state since 1968. It was this understanding of Iraqi politics and how to reform it that led to the unleashing of a victor's peace after regime change had been successfully carried out. The 'diabolical enemy image and its victor's peace meant organised violence was deployed by both those now controlling the state to ensure their success and those excluded from any power to overthrow it.

The enemy image and the belief system of the Bush administration

The role and power that Iraq as a 'diabolical enemy image' occupied in the administration's belief system underpinned the Bush presidency's reaction to the attacks in September 2001. Although it was quickly apparent that Osama bin Laden at the head of al-Qaeda had been responsible for the attacks using a base within Afghanistan, Iraq was ushered into the policy discussions concerning the response. By 21 November 2001, seventy-two days after the attacks, Bush had already asked Rumsfeld what plans he had in hand to invade Iraq.[27] By January 2002, Bush lumped terrorists and their state allies into one 'axis of evil'.[28] In Bush's memoirs, he makes plain that Saddam Hussein gave coherence to his perception of Iraq as an enemy image by personifying Iraqi 'evil' in Bush's mind. Further, it was also 'his henchmen' and government that 'tortured innocent people, raped political opponents in front of their families, scalded dissidents with acid, and dumped tens of thousands of Iraqis into mass graves'.[29] He then quotes discussions with Elie Wiesel, a Holocaust survivor, in which he compared Saddam Hussein's brutality to the Nazi genocide, with Wiesel advising the president 'you have a moral obligation to act against evil'.[30] Here the 'other' is defined in morally absolutist terms. The irrational evil of Saddam Hussein and his henchmen was such that any action against them was bathed in a moral absolutism, placed beyond reproach or suggestions of duplicitous or self-serving motives.

Beyond the president himself, the 'diabolical enemy image' of Iraq was reproduced in remarkably similar fashion across the decision-making elite in Washington. By 2002, Iraq planning was dominated by the Department of Defence. Within the Pentagon, Rumsfeld designated the office run by Feith, Under-Secretary of Defence, as responsible for all post-war planning and security.[31] This was formalised in an executive order issued by Bush in January 2003.

For Rumsfeld, as for Bush, the Ba'ath Party was best understood through historical comparison to the Nazi Party in Germany and the Communist Party in the Soviet Union.[32] In the autumn of 2003, this historical analogy was powerfully deployed by Rumsfeld's deputy, Paul Wolfowitz, to stop any attempt to modify the victors' peace by more fully integrating the Sunni community into Iraq's post-war political process. He wrote three words on the policy proposal before returning it to Rumsfeld, 'They are Nazis!'[33]

Feith was the most important individual in the government handling Iraq policy. It was his office that drafted policy for post-regime change Iraq and ensured it was implemented. In his memoirs, written shortly after leaving government in 2005, Feith laid out what is probably the most coherent description of the Ba'ath Party as a 'diabolical enemy image' at the centre of the administration's belief system, giving it both coherence and cognitive consistency. First, as with Bush, Rumsfeld and Wolfowitz, the Ba'ath Party was compared to the Nazis in Germany. It 'had become a synonym for the Iraqi regime, more or less as the Nazi Party was the German regime under Adolf Hitler'. However, in Feith's mind, its sins were even greater because, whereas the Nazis 'had run Germany for a dozen years; the Ba'athists had tyrannised Iraq for more than thirty'.[34]

US decision-making power in Baghdad was even more concentrated than in Washington. For the first twelve months of the occupation, from May 2003 to April 2004, L. Paul Bremer III, the head of the Coalition Provisional Authority (CPA), had paramount authority across the entire country.[35] The instructions he was given before arriving were minimal, nearly all oral and were not augmented while he was in Baghdad.[36] The enemy image at the centre of Bremer's belief system, laid out in his memoir of the year he spent ruling Iraq, is built around the same central schema that shaped the perceptions of Bush, Rumsfeld, Wolfowitz and Feith. The Ba'ath Party was repeatedly compared to both the Nazis and the Communist Party of the Soviet Union, with Saddam playing the role of Hitler but for three times as long.[37]

It was through these assertive coherent, inter-subjective schemas that the most influential US decision-makers understood Iraq, Saddam Hussein and the Ba'ath Party: there was no room for ambiguity. Ba'ath Party members had no redeeming features. At best they had been the knowing and willing vehicle through which Saddam had unleashed horror on the Iraqi population. At worst their active involvement in torture, rape and murder went well beyond complicity. The reform programme put in place by Bremer in 2003 and 2004 was targeted against a party membership seen as no better than the Nazis in Germany. Their removal from power thus became a moral necessity. Once Saddam Hussein was safely in US custody in December 2003, it was the Ba'ath Party itself that became the main threat, target and obstacle to re-engineering Iraq, the Party being then blamed for the rising insurgency. But the damning of a party whose peak membership comprised over two million Iraqis, was highly problematic for US policy. How to interact with a state infrastructure populated, at its higher echelons, with a majority of former party members, and how to understand a society ruled by them for 35 years. What level of complicity does that bring to ordinary citizens beyond the two million people who joined the party itself?

However, as the Wolfowitz quote indicates, party membership or at least sympathy and fellow travelling was extended, explicitly and by inference, to the Sunni section of Iraqi society as a whole. Bremer, when briefing Bush on declining security in June 2003, described the 'Sunni heartlands' of west and north Iraq as containing '[l]ots of sore losers'.[38] Feith was repeatedly critical of those he saw as adopting 'the Sunni perspective' for being 'inclined to look somewhat benignly on Baathists' and favour cutting a deal with them: 'Such a deal might generally gratify Sunni Arabs, whose political predominance in Iraq the Baathists ensured.'[39] Policy was shaped by analytically collapsing the Sunni population of Iraq into the diabolical enemy image formed around the Ba'ath Party. Both were to be treated in the same way and defined as the enemy other, giving clarity to perceptions of Iraqi society and moral certainty to US policy.

These dominant perceptions of the Ba'ath Party, central to the US belief system of the main policy makers working on Iraq, laid the groundwork for the victor's peace. As the examples of Wolfowitz, Feith and Bremer indicate, policy was drafted, accepted or rejected, by using the enemy image of the Ba'ath Party to gain coherence and defend cognitive consistency. Moreover, there is clear evidence that Iraq's Sunni community were cognitively categorised with the Ba'ath Party, and were fixed and dammed accordingly. The ramifications for US policy making and its effects in Iraq are clear. Not just the former ruling elite, but members of a mass party and a large religious group in society were to be actively excluded from power as a central pillar of US plans to transform Iraq and 'let freedom reign'.

Laying the foundations for the victor' peace: de-Ba'athification

Given the central role that the demonisation of the Iraqi Ba'ath Party played in the belief system of key members of the Bush administration, it is little surprise that political exclusion was the first policy to be enacted once the CPA was created. The one explicit order, drafted by Feith in the Pentagon that Bremer took with him for implementation in Baghdad, was the de-Ba'athification of Iraqi society. The document banned the top four levels of the Ba'ath Party's membership from holding any government job. It also banned *any* former member of the Ba'ath from occupying jobs in the top three management levels of government institutions.[40] Feith stressed that '[w]e've got to show all the Iraqis that we're serious about building a New Iraq'. The policy was to be implemented 'even if it causes administrative inconvenience'.[41] For Feith, de-Ba'athification was the cornerstone of building a new Iraq, the central role that the Ba'ath played in his belief system meant that the damage caused by purging them from the Iraqi state was of little concern compared with the greater moral good of their exclusion.

The de-Ba'athification of Iraqi society was specifically designed to drive the old ruling elite and those associated with it out of office and marginalise them in society. In an economy dominated by state employment, excluding large numbers of individuals from working for the government was tantamount to legislating for their forced impoverishment. The effects went well beyond the costs of 'administrative inconvenience' that Feith had been happy to pay. First, to quote Lieutenant-General Sanchez (Commander of Coalition forces in Iraq when the order was issued), de-Ba'athification '[e]liminated the entire government and civic capacity of the nation. Organisations involving justice, defense, interior, communications, schools, universities, and hospitals were all either completely shut down or severely crippled, because anybody with any experience was now out of a job.'[42]

A second consequence had even greater impact on Iraq. In May 2003, just after the de-Ba'athification edict was issued, I conducted a series of interviews with mid-level and senior Ba'athists in the Baghdad suburb of Ghazaliya. The effects of the edict were easy to detect. At first there was bewilderment. A senior Ba'athist exclaimed, 'Why can't he leave us alone? We are like the Communist Party of the Soviet Union, worn out and ideologically defeated.'[43] But within days of the edict the sense of defeat mutated into defiance and reorganisation. De-Ba'athification was perceived as needless and vindictive persecution that went well beyond the party and affected the Sunni section of the population. It triggered a concerted attempt at organisation and then violent confrontation; the fight for a losers' peace had begun.

Politically securing the victor's peace: the exclusive elite bargain in Iraq

The formation of the Iraqi Governing Council (IGC) in July 2003 was the first step taken by the US occupation in building a post-regime change political order, to be the cornerstone of a sustainable transformation of Iraq. Given the influence of the enemy image in the belief systems of decision makers it is little surprise that the IGC completely excluded anyone associated with the previous regime. However, the ideational dynamics shaping the enemy image led to a Governing Council which also minimised the role of Sunnis in its ranks and indeed those who were resident in Iraq before 2003. The political order represented an exclusive elite bargain between a small, and formerly exiled, group of returning politicians.

Elite bargains are frequently placed at the centre of successful negotiations to end internal conflicts and move towards a subsequent consolidation of democracy. For these bargains to function as intended, the elites involved must be 'principle decision makers', politically, economically and militarily – and crucially have the ability to deliver the leadership of dominant social groups in society.[44] The bargain between them involves the building of a consensus around 'the basic procedures and norms by which politics will henceforth be played'.[45] Inclusive settlements integrate as broad a section of the existing national elites as possible into a ruling coalition. This gives the organisations they represent access to the state's institutions, jobs and largesse. The politicians can then use state resources, rents and employment opportunities as patronage to sustain a strong base of support in society for the settlement.[46]

However, when applying the notion of elite bargains to conflict-prone states, Stefan Lindemann makes the perceptive distinction between elite bargains which are inclusive and hence promote stability, and those which are exclusive and prone to driving countries back into conflict.[47] Exclusive bargains involve a narrow set of elites, excluding key politicians and the groups they seek to represent, thereby fostering 'antagonism and violent conflict'.[48] In Iraq, the post-invasion political settlement was shaped by the perception of the Ba'ath Party and beyond that the Sunni community were enemies to be excluded. It was hence designed to exclude key indigenous political elites from any role in government. This, combined with a campaign of violent persecution, drove sections of those elites underground and then into open rebellion against the new political settlement and those it empowered to run the state.

Moves towards forming the IGC began at the end of May 2003. In the aftermath of a United Nations Security Council resolution on Iraq, Bremer sent Rumsfeld a memorandum committing the CPA to building an interim government consisting of about 30 Iraqis. Bremer set out his ambitions to make the government 'broadly representative of all major strands of Iraqi society (internals and exiles, Shia, Kurd, Turkman, Christian, tribal, men and women)'. The 'representative' categories Bremer mentions are instructive; in this first iteration they certainly include gender, some religious and ethnic groups, but notably exclude Sunnis.[49] Bremer's Anglo-American governance team then spent six weeks identifying 'women, tribal, and religious leaders we could consider for the membership'.[50] During this process, Bremer acknowledged the need 'to find effective, patriotic Sunni members'. However, this new search brought Bremer and his team 'face to face with a major structural problem inherent in Iraq's post-Liberation politics: a lack of credible Sunni leaders. Almost all politically active Sunnis had been co-opted into Saddam's security services, of Baath Party, or killed as traitors.'[51] Bremer's comment indicates his belief system and the place the Ba'ath occupied in it. First, by inference, the only politically active Sunnis still alive in Iraq had previously been co-opted into the security services or Ba'ath Party. Second, if they had been co-opted, they could not be considered credible leaders. From this perspective, Iraq's Sunni community was either not politically active, dead, or tainted by Ba'athist co-option.

When the membership of the IGC was announced in July 2003, the effect of the enemy image at the heart of Bremer's decision making was easily detected. First, of the five members of the IGC identified as Arab 'Sunni', only two, Naseer al-Chaderchi and Mohsen Abdel Hamid, were members of any organised political party.[52] Al-Chaderchi was 70 when asked to join the IGC. His party had been set up by his father in the 1950s and 1960s but quickly lapsed into political irrelevance after regime change. Hamid, conversely, was Secretary-General of the Iraqi Islamic Party (IIP). The IIP's role in the IGC and every government it has served in since was to deliver a tame and neutered 'Sunni vote', to bring that section of the population, from which the former ruling elite was meant to have originated, into the new post-war political settlement on a fractured and subservient basis.

A great deal of evidence suggests that from 2003 onwards the IIP singularly failed to play this role because it was not representative of the social constituency assigned to it by Bremer's team. The IIP's close association with the US occupation and the new governing structures meant it was repeatedly out-flanked by more autonomous and representative political forces in the struggle to mobilise the Sunni section of society. Beyond the IIP, the six parties that gained prominence in exile by allying themselves with the United States took control of the council.[53] Finally, 14 of the 22 council members were long-term exiles or had lived in the Kurdish Regional Government enclave outside Iraqi state control from 1991 onwards.

The exclusive elite bargain placed by Bremer at the centre of the IGC quickly dominated the Iraqi state. On 11 November 2003, in the face of increasing violence and an approaching US presidential campaign, Bremer was summoned to Washington where it was decided that sovereignty would be handed back to Iraqis no later than June 2004. What became known as the 15 November Agreement (the date the IGC was told about the plan and gave its assent), would give interim power to a new government ahead of national elections. This hasty transition plan triggered vocal opposition from Grand Ayatollah Ali al-Sistani, the most powerful religious authority in the country. Al-Sistani, aware that in Iraqi history 'temporary' unelected governments had a tendency to transform themselves into permanent dictatorships, demanded that any sovereign government of Iraq must be directly elected.

At this moment a decision maker with a radically different understanding of Iraqi society was called in to break the impasse between the US government and al-Sistani. In early 2004, UN diplomat Lakhdar Brahimi was asked to negotiate a compromise between al-Sistani, the Coalition Provisional Authority and the IGC that would allow the hand-over of sovereignty to take place. Brahimi's approach to Iraqi politics stood in stark contrast to that of Bremer and his governance team. On three extended research trips to Iraq, Brahimi's team went to great lengths to consult with as diverse and representative a cross section of Iraqi society as possible.[54] The conclusions Brahimi reached after his first trip in February 2004, indicated the extent to which Iraq politics had become dangerously polarised,

> In the Sunni community and among the secular elite, there are perceptions that they are witnessing a decisive shift in the balance of power as a result of which they will lose in the new political arrangements that are being put in place. ... minority groups feel that a majoritarian system will put them at a huge disadvantage, while women's groups are concerned that the gains made under the secular regimes of the past are under threat from a new system dominated by religious-based parties.[55]

Brahimi made clear the outcome if Iraqi politics was allowed to develop as it had under the US occupation: 'I have appealed to the members of the Governing Council and to Iraqis in every part of Iraq to be conscious that civil wars do not happen because a person makes a decision, "Today, I'm going to start a civil war".'[56]

Socio-engineering and civil war in Iraq 209

To avert this outcome Brahimi drew up a transition plan that would have directly challenged the effects of the enemy image at the centre of US decision making. It was specifically designed to unpick the exclusive elite bargain, bring in the now fractured and excluded Sunni community, and hence rework and broaden the nascent elite bargain. First, Brahimi recommended that a new caretaker government, comprising many former Ba'athist technocrats, should be selected. They would manage the government during the interregnum before elections in 2005. This would force the IGC to switch its energies from government to society, making all political groupings build national political organisations that would act as a channel for public opinion, linking as much of the polity as possible to its government. Finally, Brahimi wanted to convene a national conference, consisting of 1,000–1,500 delegates. This would start the process of national dialogue, instituting consultative channels between society and the state. It would also provide a venue within which those who had been excluded by the US occupation could be brought into the political process, integrating the more radical and alienated voices in the run up to elections.[57]

Unsurprisingly, because Brahimi's plan ran directly counter to their enemy images, US policy makers favoured its rejection.[58] Brahimi's choices for the new government's prime minister and president were vetoed by Bush because there was a danger that they would not 'stand up and thank the American people for their sacrifice in liberating Iraq'.[59] Instead, the premiership was given to a long time exile and habitué of Washington, Iyad Allawi, the head of one of the six formerly exiled parties which had dominated the IGC. The vice-presidencies went to another two of the six parties, Ibrahim al-Jaafari, head of the Dawa Islamic Party, and Rowsch Shaways, senior member of the Kurdistan Democratic Party. Ministerial posts were then liberally divided among the other leading parties on the IGC.

In spite of Brahimi's best efforts and his warning of an imminent civil war, the parties empowered by the United States and placed at the centre of the exclusive elite bargain negotiated in July 2003, had successfully secured their grip on power, thereby committing themselves to furtherance of a victor's peace. Those excluded by the enemy image and targeted by the victor's peace were deliberately drummed out of government service and pushed to the political and economic margins of Iraqi society. The extent and content of the 'diabolical enemy image' that gave coherence to US perceptions of Iraq meant the exclusions went well beyond Ba'athists to include swathes of the Sunni community itself.

After Brahimi's departure from Baghdad, the exclusive elite bargain came under threat once again during the national elections of 2010. In the run-up to the 2010 national elections, the veteran Iraqi politician Ayad Allawi set out to challenge the pact through electoral mobilisation. Allawi built a broad-based coalition, the Iraqi National Movement (Iraqiya), around 18 parties that combined senior politicians enjoying national recognition with local personalities and regional political organisations which could effectively mobilise voters in their communities.

The potentially revolutionary effects of Iraqiya's 2010 election campaign triggered an aggressive defence of the existing system by those who had benefited from it most. This was a blatant attempt at triggering a return to the sectarian politics and exclusive elite bargain of the previous seven years. Its proponents hoped that this would solidify voting blocs along religious and ethnic lines to deliver the desired election results. To this end, the first steps were taken two months before the vote. In early January 2010, the Justice and Accountability Commission, the government agency charged with implementing the de-Ba'athification process set in motion by the Americans, issued edicts to ban 511 individual candidates and 14 party lists from the elections.[60]

However, such a blatant attempt at shaping the elections had the opposite effect to the one intended. The use of de-Ba'athification as an electoral tool drove those opposed to the post-2003 election system to the ballot box in large numbers. This, combined with Iraqiya's united electoral front and a strong local organisation, delivered a potentially revolutionary result. Iraqiya won 91 seats, compared to 89 for the then prime minister, Nuri al Maliki's State of Law coalition and 70 for the Shia electoral coalition, the Iraqi National Alliance. Iraqiya took 80 per cent of the Sunni vote, but was also the only electoral coalition to secure seats in areas dominated by both Sunni and Shia voters, winning 12 seats in Shia-majority areas.[61] Such a strong, overtly secular vote raised the possibility in March 2010 that Iraq's exclusive elite pact could be swept aside and a new, more inclusive political dispensation built.

Given the fractious and unconstitutional nature of the election campaign, the close result and the potentially revolutionary ramifications of the outcome, it is no surprise that the process of government formation was bitter, punctuated by mistrust and very time-consuming. Negotiations lasted 249 days from polling until the formation of the government (compared with 156 days in 2005). A deal was finally struck in November 2010 that brought Iraqiya into another government of national unity, attempting to curb the threat it posed by allocating it government ministries.

However, the co-optation of senior Iraqiya politicians did not prove enough to temper the threat they posed to the exclusive elite pact. In December 2011 and again in December 2012, the houses of Vice President Tariq al-Hashemi and then Minister of Finance, Rafi al-Issawi, were raided and their bodyguards taken into custody on charges of terrorism. Hashemi was then allowed to flee the country into exile but his bodyguards confessed to terrorism offences and Hashemi was sentenced in absentia to be executed. Hashemi was not a particularly effective or popular politician. As a result, his arrest resulted in little popular protest. Issawi, on the other hand, had a strong political constituency in his home province of Anbar and had won international respect for his effective and non-partisan management of the Ministry of Finance.

The raid on Issawi's house in December 2012 and his subsequent resignation as Minister of Finance in March 2013 triggered mass protests across the Sunni-dominated northwest of Iraq. The move against Issawi mobilised the Sunni section of Iraqi society because they had felt increasingly excluded from national politics since the 2010 national elections, cut off from the benefits of oil wealth and discriminated against by the Iraqi security forces. From December 2012 to April 2013, tens of thousands of people demonstrated in Anbar's two biggest cities, Fallujah and Ramadi. Protests quickly spread into the neighbouring provinces of Diyala and Nineveh.

The government brought in the Iraqi army to break up the demonstrations. This suppression caused the deaths of nine people at the end of January 2013 and a further 40 in April. The use of state-sponsored violence to break up popular protest left a legacy of resentment and alienation among Iraq's Sunni population and galvanised hostility toward Maliki's government and, in turn, the Iraqi state. This legacy has been expertly exploited by Da'esh. The steady rise in politically motivated violence during 2013 and 2014 can be seen as a direct result of the suppression of the protest movement but also the underlying grievances that initially triggered the demonstrations.

It is this profound sense of alienation felt by the Sunni sections of Iraq's population which forms the major driver of Da'esh's revolt. De-Ba'athification, started under the US occupation but accelerated by subsequent Iraqi governments, led Iraq's Sunnis to feel persecuted by the state. It is unsurprising that the protests of 2012 and the harsh government-backed crackdown occurred in the areas where Da'esh has since come to dominate. In the aftermath of the 2010 election, an election in which Sunni turnout was high, those who voted saw their key political representatives driven from the government on trumped up charges of terrorism.

Conclusions

The consequences of a victor's peace: Iraq's civil war

The looting that dominated Baghdad in the immediate aftermath of the war reflected US coercive weakness and its inability to impose the ideational vision dictated by the belief systems of its key decision makers. This vacuum in both governance and security was exacerbated by the decision to pursue such a thoroughgoing de-Ba'athification process. If the looters in Baghdad took away the fixtures and fittings of the Iraqi state, US policy similarly destroyed what was left of its institutional memory. The de-Ba'athification was an attempt to drive what was left of the old governing elites, their technocratic allies and the Sunni community out of state institutions – a direct result of the way Iraq was ideationally ordered from within the American decision makers' belief system. Beyond the ideational, neither the US occupation nor the nascent new Iraqi state were materially strong enough to impose this post-war settlement, and the civil war it triggered was a struggle between those seeking to impose a victor's peace and those fighting for a loser's peace.

The first political group to exploit the US military's inability to control the country were the insurgents, a disparate movement of independent groups fighting to drive the US out and overthrow the victor's peace. The motivation that mobilised and united these separate groups was their collective exclusion from the post-war political order. As such, US troops were initially their main target, but as these were redeployed to decrease their vulnerability and political visibility, insurgents increasingly focused on Iraqis who served in the new police force and army. By August 2003, car bombs became a weapon of choice, with the increasingly sectarian mass casualty attacks driving Iraq towards civil war.

The dynamic of alienation and exclusion fuelling an increasing spiral of violence, was accentuated from 2006 onwards by Da'esh taking control of the movement. The insurgency had begun in a diffuse and reactive fashion. By 2005, the insurgency began to consolidate around a small number of larger, better organised and funded groups.[62] In 2006 there was a further consolidation when the forerunner of Da'esh, the Islamic State in Iraq, was formed as an umbrella organisation for a number of radical Sunni Islamist groups fighting under an explicitly sectarian banner. They exploited and exacerbated political exclusion by using the language of sectarian extremism. By using mass casualty attacks targeted against Iraq's Shia population, Da'esh achieved its aim of driving the country into a sectarian civil war.[63]

On the other side of the equation, the formerly-exiled political parties placed at the centre of the exclusive elite bargain by the US, used their election victories in 2005 to violently impose a victor's peace on the whole country. Between 2005 and 2006, the Ministry of Interior became the main vehicle for imposing a victor's peace. At this time the Ministry of Defence and the Iraqi army were perceived by Iraqi politicians in government to be under US control. The Ministry of Interior, on the other hand, appeared to be independent of US scrutiny and it controlled the Special Police Commandos (later renamed the National Police), judged to be the most effective fighting force in the country.[64] Through 2005–2006, the commandos acted as a sectarian death squad, frequently resorting to extra-judicial execution and torture.[65] Complaints reached their peak in November 2005, when US forces raided a Ministry of Interior 'detention facility' and found 170 detainees (166 of whom were Sunnis) 'held in appalling conditions'.[66] Following this, several confirmed cases of secret detention facilities and the widespread use of torture came to light.[67]

The struggle between a victor's and loser's peace reached its height in 2006, when the 50,000-strong militia the Jaish al-Mahdi (JAM), Muqtada al-Sadr's military organisation, become the main group murdering Sunnis in Baghdad. From mid-2006 onwards, its death squads used Sadr City, a slum of two million people in eastern Baghdad, as a platform from which to drive the Sunni population out of Baghdad. Each night JAM members would sweep across the north and west of Baghdad in a pincer movement, which bore all the hallmarks of a well-planned operation, to attack the Sunni-dominated areas of western Baghdad. Under the cover of darkness, convoys of armed men would leave Sadr City moving into mixed or predominately Sunni neighbourhoods. As many as 60 men at a time would be seized. Their bodies, bearing the signs of torture, would be dumped the next morning on the city's periphery.[68] The ultimate aim was to drastically reduce the numbers of Sunni residents in Baghdad. Previously affluent suburbs on the western side of the Tigris, such as Mansour and Yarmouk, were targeted for violent population transfer. The militia campaigns of murder and intimidation coincided with the withdrawal of banking services and healthcare provision from Sunni residential areas on the west bank of the river. There is strong evidence to suggest that government services were withdrawn as part of a coordinated campaign to drive Sunnis from Baghdad.[69]

The death and destruction wrought on Iraq after Bush declared an end to the invasion in May 2003, clearly qualifies as a civil war. By June 2012 that conflict has cost at least 107,000 civilian lives.[70] Media punditry and governmental responses to such wholesale carnage have tended to deploy primordial explanations for the violence. An emphasis on the ethno-sectarian divisions in Iraqi society shifts the blame away from those who invaded the country and encouraged the bloody aftermath of regime change by their imposition of a victor's peace and an exclusive elite bargain. Such attempts at absolution are anchored in the dominant Orientalist stereotypes that provide easy, if racist, explanations of complex situations. However, a close examination of how the Iraqi civil war started decentres ethno-sectarian divisions seeing them as, at best, second order explanations. In their place, as a central cause of post-war violence was the deliberate exclusion of a section of Iraq's society driven by the dominant enemy images that shaped US decision making in 2003 and 2004. These policies gave rise to the exclusive elite bargain imposed on the country by the United States and its formerly exiled Iraqi allies, and then to the civil war that ripped the country apart after 2005.

Acknowledgements

This chapter is an updated version of the article of the same name that appeared in *International Peacekeeping*, vol. 19, no. 4, August 2012, Taylor & Francis Ltd, www.tandfonline.com, reprinted by permission of the publisher.

Notes

1 See, e.g., Leslie H. Gelb, 'Divide Iraq into Three States', *International Herald Tribune*, 26 November 2004; Peter W. Galbraith, 'How to Get Out of Iraq', *New York Review of Books*, 13 May 2004; Peter W. Galbraith, *The End of Iraq: How American Incompetence Created a War without End*, New York: Simon & Schuster, 2006.
2 Anatol Lieven, *America Right or Wrong: An Anatomy of American Nationalism*, Oxford: Oxford University Press, 2004, p. 2.
3 The best of these include, Anthony Shadid, *Night Draws Near: Iraq's People in the Shadow of America's War*, New York: Henry Holt, 2005; Nir Rosen, *Aftermath: Following the Bloodshed of America's Wars in the Muslim World*, New York: Nation Books, 2010; George Packer, *Assassins' Gate: America in Iraq*, New York: Farrar, Straus & Giroux, 2005; Rajiv Chandrasekaran, *Imperial Life in the Emerald City: Inside Baghdad's Green Zone*, London: Bloomsbury, 2007; Thomas E. Ricks, *Fiasco: The American Military Adventure in Iraq*, London: Allen Lane, 2006; *The Gamble: General Petreaus and the Untold Story of the American Surge in Iraq, 2006-2008*, London: Penguin, 2009.
4 Raymond Hinnebusch, 'The US Invasion of Iraq: Explanations and Implications', *Critique: Critical Middle Eastern Studies*, vol. 16, no. 3, 2007, pp. 209–228. Also, Toby Dodge, 'The Sardinian, the Texan and the Tikriti: Gramsci, the comparative autonomy of the Middle Eastern state and regime change in Iraq', *International Politics*, vol. 43, no. 4, 2006, pp. 453–473.
5 Jean-François Drolet, *American Neoconservatism: The Politics and Culture of a Reactionary Idealism*, London: Hurst, 2011. Also, Edward Rhodes, 'The Imperial Logic of Bush's Liberal Agenda', *Survival*, vol. 45, no. 1, 2003, pp. 131–154; Michael C. Williams, 'What is the National Interest? The Neoconservative Challenge in IR Theory', *European Journal of International Relations*, 2005, vol. 11, no. 3, pp. 307–337; Tony Smith, *A Pact with the devil: Washington's Bid for World Supremacy and the Betrayal of the American Promise*, New York: Routledge, 2007.
6 The most empirically detailed account is James Dobbins, Seth G. Jones, Benjamin Runkle and Siddharth Mohandas, *Occupying Iraq: A History of the Coalition Provisional Authority*, Santa Monica, CA: RAND, 2009.
7 On the latter, see Michael Schwartz, *War Without End: The Iraqi War in Context*, Chicago, IL: Haymarket Books, 2008; on the former, Eric Herring and Glen Rangwala, *Iraq in Fragments: The Occupation and Its Legacy*, London: Hurst, 2006.
8 For an earlier attempt at this approach using different intellectual tools see, Toby Dodge, 'The Ideological Roots of Failure: The Application of Kinetic Neo-Liberalism to Iraq', *International Affairs*, vol. 86, no. 6, November 2010, pp. 1269–1286.
9 David Patrick Houghton, 'Reinvigorating the Study of Foreign Policy Decision Making: Toward a Constructivist Approach', *Foreign Policy Analysis*, vol. 3, no. 1, 2007, p. 28.
10 See, e.g., Deborah Welch Larson, 'The Role of Belief Systems and Schemas in Foreign Policy Decision-Making', *Political Psychology*, vol. 15, no. 1, 1994, p. 25. The partial exception to this is early work on operational codes, especially Alexander L. George, 'The "Operational Code": A Neglected Approach to the Study of Political Leaders and Decision-Making', *International Studies Quarterly*, vol. 13, no. 2, 1969, pp. 190–222.
11 Most obviously in Alexander Wendt, *Social Theory of International Politics*, Cambridge: Cambridge University Press, 1999.
12 Jerel A. Rosati, 'The Power of Human Cognition in the Study of World Politics', *International Studies Review*, vol. 2, no. 3, 2000, pp. 56, 59.
13 Shannon Lindsey Blanton, 'Images in Conflict: The Case of Ronald Reagan and El Salvador', *International Studies Quarterly*, vol. 40, no. 1, 1996, pp. 22, 25.

14 Rosati (note 12 above), p. 52.
15 *Ibid.*, p. 56.
16 Jutta Weldes, 'Constructing National Interests', *European Journal of International Relations*, vol. 2, no. 3, 1996, pp. 281–282.
17 *Ibid.*, p. 285.
18 Blanton (note 13 above), p. 25.
19 David J. Finlay, Ole R. Holsti and Richard R. Fagen, *Enemies in Politics*, Chicago, IL: Rand McNally, 1967, p. 7.
20 See, Edward W. Said, *Orientalism: Western Concepts of the Orient*, London: Penguin, 1991, p. 237.
21 On the distinction between the two in Orientalist discourse see, Toby Dodge, 'Stephen Hemsley Longrigg et ses contemporains: le despotisme oriental et les Britanniques en Irak: 1914–1932', *Monde Arabe, Maghreb–Machrek*, no. 240, 2010, pp. 33–58.
22 Said (note 20 above), p. 1.
23 Brett Silverstein and Robert R. Holt, 'Research on Enemy Images: Present Status and Future Prospects', *Journal of Social Issues*, vol. 45, no. 2, 1989, p. 171.
24 Finlay *et al.* (note 19 above), p. 16.
25 See Gerald N. Sande, George R. Goethals, Lisa Ferrari and Leila T. Worth, 'Value-Guided Attributions: Maintaining the Moral Self-Image and the Diabolical Enemy-Image', *Journal of Social Issues*, vol. 45, no. 2, 1989, p. 93; Blanton (note 13 above), p. 26.
26 See Astri Suhrke, 'Peace in Between', in Astri Suhrke and Mats Berdal (eds), *The Peace In Between: Post-war Violence and Peacebuilding*, Abingdon: Routledge, 2011, pp. 1–24. For earlier codifications of a victor's peace see Oliver P. Richmond, *The Transformation of Peace*, Basingstoke: Palgrave Macmillan, 2005, pp. 30, 210.
27 Bob Woodward, *Plan of Attack*, New York: Simon & Shuster, 2004, p. 1.
28 George W. Bush, 'President Delivers State of the Union Address', Washington, DC, 29 January 2002 (at: http://georgewbush-whitehouse.archives.gov/news/releases/2002/01/20020129-11.html).
29 George W. Bush, *Decision Points*, London: Random House, 2010, p. 228.
30 Ibid., pp. 427–428.
31 Bob Woodward, *State of Denial*, New York: Simon & Schuster, 2006, pp. 90–91.
32 Donald Rumsfeld, *Known and Unknown: A Memoir*, New York: Sentinel, 2011, p. 514.
33 Quoted in Mark Perry, *How to Lose the War on Terror*, London: Hurst, 2010, p. 13.
34 Douglas J. Feith, *War and Decision: Inside the Pentagon at the Dawn of the War on Terrorism*, New York: Harper, 2008, pp. 419, 430.
35 Bremer got specific assurance from Bush on this. See L. Paul Bremer III with Malcolm McConnell, *My Year in Iraq: The Struggle to Build a Future of Hope*, New York: Simon & Schuster, 2006.
36 Dobbins *et al.* (note 6 above), p. xiii.
37 Bremer with McConnell (note 35 above), pp. 38, 51, 53.
38 *Ibid.*, p. 71.
39 Feith (note 34 above), pp. 419, 430.
40 See Chandrasekaran (note 3 above), pp. 76–77.
41 Quoted in Bremer with McConnell (note 35 above), p. 39.
42 Quoted in Special Inspector General for Iraq Reconstruction, 'Hard Lessons: The Iraq Reconstruction Experience' (at: www.sigir.mil/publications/hardLessons.html), p. 74.
43 Interview by the author with a senior Ba'athist official, Ghazaliya, Baghdad, May, 2003.
44 See Michael Burton, Richard Gunther and John Higley, 'Introduction', in John Higley and Richard Gunther (eds), *Elites and Democratic Consolidation in Latin America and Southern Europe*, Cambridge: Cambridge University Press, 1992, p. 8.

45 Higley and Gunther, 'Preface', in *ibid.*, p. xi.
46 See Stefan Lindemann, *Do Inclusive Elite Bargains Matter? A Research Framework for Understanding the Causes of Civil War in Sub-Saharan Africa*, Discussion Paper 15, London: Crisis States Research Centre, LSE, February 2008, (at: www.crisisstates.com/download/dp/dp15.pdf), pp. 2, 10.
47 *Ibid.*
48 *Ibid.*, pp. 2, 21.
49 Bremer with McConnell (note 35 above), p. 84
50 *Ibid.*, p. 86.
51 *Ibid.*, p. 93.
52 See BBC News, 'The Iraqi Governing Council', 14 July 2003 (at http://news.bbc.co.uk/1/hi/world/middle_east/3062897.stm).
53 These were the Kurdistan Democratic Party, the Patriotic Union of Kurdistan, the Iraqi National Congress, the Iraqi National Alliance, Islamic Supreme Council of Iraq and the Dawa Islamic Party.
54 See Lakhdar Brahimi, 'Briefing of the Special Adviser to the Secretary-General', UN doc. S/2004/461, 7 June 2004.
55 Lakhdar Brahimi, 'The Political Transition in Iraq: Report of the Fact-finding Mission', UN doc. S/2004/140, 23 February 2004, p. 4.
56 Hamza Hendawi, 'Iraq May Be Slipping Into Civil War', *Associated Press*, 16 February 2004 (at: http://news.google.com/newspapers?nid=1988&dat=20040216&id=20giAAAAIBAJ&sjid=C60FAAAAIBAJ&pg=2207,4016303).
57 On the Brahimi plan, see 'Statement of the Special Adviser to the Secretary-General, to the Security Council on the Political Transition Process in Iraq', 27 April 2004 (at: www.navend.de/aktuell/pdf/2004-05-10/Brahimi27April.pdf); Brahimi (notes 53 and 54 above); Julian Borger, 'UN Envoy Presents Plan for New Rule in Iraq', *The Guardian* (London), 28 April 2004.
58 See Bremer with McConnell (note 35 above), pp. 348–349.
59 *Ibid.*, p. 359.
60 Salam Faraj, 'Iraq Election Officials Bar Nearly 500 Candidates from Poll', *AFP*, 15 January 2010 (at: www.google.com/hostednews/afp/article/ALeqM5iq5fJFplxZiPms3wzK1upE0lpP1A).
61 On the 2010 election results, see International Crisis Group, *Iraq's Secular Opposition: The Rise and Decline of al-Iraqiya*, Middle East Report 127, 31 July, 2012 (at: www.crisisgroup.org/~/media/Files/Middle%20East%20North%20Africa/Iraq%20Syria%20Lebanon/Iraq/127-iraqs-secular-opposition-the-rise-and-decline-of-al-iraqiya.pdf), pp. 12–13; Adeed Dawisha, 'Iraq: A Vote Against Sectarianism', *Journal of Democracy*, vol. 21, no. 3, July 2010, p. 36; Joel Wing, 'Iraq's Politics: Not Much Has Changed by 2010 Elections', *Musings on Iraq*, 21 May 2010 (at: http://musingsoniraq.blogspot.co.uk/2010/05/iraqs-politics-not-much-changed-by-2010.html).
62 See Mohammed M. Hafez, *Suicide Bombers in Iraq: The Strategy and Ideology of Martyrdom*, Washington, DC: United States Institute of Peace, 2007, p. 52.
63 See Dexter Filkins, 'Memo Urges Qaeda to Wage War in Iraq', *International Herald Tribune*, 10 February 2004; Justin Huggler, 'Is This Man the Mastermind of the Massacres?', *The Independent on Sunday*, 7 March 2004.
64 See interview with Matthew Sherman, Deputy Senior Adviser to Iraq's Ministry of Interior December 2003–January 2006 (at: www.pbs.org/wgbh/pages/frontline/gangsofiraq/interviews/sherman.html); Matt Sherman and Roger D. Carstens, *Independent Task Force on Progress and Reform*, Williamsburg, VA: Institute for the Theory and Practice of International Relations at the College of William and Mary, 14 November 2008, p. 2.

65 See, e.g., Hannah Allam, 'Wolf Brigade the Most Loved and Feared of Iraqi Security Forces', 21 May 2005 (at: http://wolfsongalaska.org/chorus/node/363); Sabrina Tavernise, Qais Mizher, Omar al-Naemi and Sahar Nageeb, 'Alarmed by Raids, Neighbors Stand Guard in Iraq', *New York Times*, 10 May 2006.
66 Amnesty International, Beyond Abu Ghraib: Detention and Torture in Iraq, London: Amnesty International, March 2006, p. 4. See also Associated Press, 'Iraq Inquiry Says Detainees Appear to Have Been Tortured', *The New York Times*, 15 November 2005.
67 See interview with Sherman (note 64 above).
68 Patrick J. McDonnell, 'Following a Death Trail to Sadr City: US Forces Think the Kidnap-and-Kill Forays Haunting Iraq Originate in the Insular Shiite Stronghold of Baghdad', *Los Angeles Times*, 24 October 2006.
69 See David Kilcullen, *The Accidental Guerrilla: Fighting Small Wars in the Midst of a Big One*, London: Hurst, 2009, p. 126.
70 See Iraq Body Count (at: www.iraqbodycount.org).

11 Libya in the shadow of Iraq
The 'Old Guard' versus the *thuwwar* in the battle for stability

Nicolas Pelham

Throughout their revolt of 2011, Libyan anti-Qaddafi forces struggled to reconcile two competing tendencies battling for supremacy both in their upper echelons and among their grassroots. One vision aspired to a wholesale overhaul of the existing order in which the dispossessed would 'inherit the earth', the other aspired to retain the existing order and its broad hierarchies albeit without the presence of the ruling family at its helm. While fighters headed to the front driven to differing degrees by ideals and personal greed at the fantastic assets that awaited their conquest, politicians tried to impose a semblance of order on the territory the fighters had prized from Qaddafi's grasp. With almost a million square kilometres under rebel control by April 2011, this crystallized into a struggle between the militia forces who overthrew Qaddafi, known to Libyans as *thuwwar*, and the politicians who sought to inherit post-revolution Libya, who hankered after stability with which to govern and rebuild. With little demonstrable sign of demobilization, disarmament and reintegration following Qaddafi's downfall in October 2011, the continued presence of militias in the public arena offset the National Transitional Council's (NTC) plans for transition. When elections approached in July 2012, the two rival forces viewed the ballot box as the process by which authority could be transferred back from the self-appointed brigades to an elected political body. But these elections did not provide a viable route towards peace and reconciliation – in fact, they solidified the *thuwwar*'s opposition to the NTC, and signalled Libya's descent into civil war.

And yet the relationship between the *thuwwar* and the NTC was fraught from the beginning. When the NTC wooed the old regime to defect, the *thuwwar* forcibly opposed their inclusion. Within months of persuading Major-General Abdel Fatah Younes, a former Qaddafi interior minister and commander of the Saiqa Special Forces, to join the rebels as commander-in-chief in March 2011, a militia group killed him. However, the militias had become too powerful to bypass. When Tripoli and the west of the country fell into rebel hands in August 2011, the incoming NTC relied on the militias as an essential stop-gap to fill the vacuum and prevent pro-Qaddafi forces from launching a comeback. This move led to the institutionalization and further empowerment of the *thuwwar*. Under pressure from the militias, the incoming authorities devolved local security to local military councils, broadly run by the militias, and carved up control of its 6,000 kilometres of borders among them, in many cases recognizing what had already become a fait accompli. In the absence of a criminal justice system and the destruction of many prisons, the NTC further recognized the militia's powers of de facto detention and incarceration of 8,000 people. With no judicial service operational to bring them to justice, as of January 2015 thousands continued to languish in their cells. Commanders wielded the powers of policemen, judges and executioners. Thus, de facto, Libya was ruled by multiple decentralised military dictatorships with no separation of powers.

To the fledgling government, however, the militias increasingly became less instruments of stabilization than obstacles to its efforts to re-establish central authority. Tensions intensified between governing pragmatists, who sought an inclusive approach to the former regime, and militiamen, who rejected any measure which would compromise their hold on the ground. The latter were particularly unnerved by the NTC's transition from Benghazi to the capital, Tripoli, following Qaddafi's flight in August 2011, and its adoption of a British-backed government stabilization plan compiled over the previous three months, designed to serve as the transition's 'roadmap'. The plan highlighted the lessons learnt from Iraq, and warned of the pitfalls that had followed Saddam's overthrow when the governor, US administrator Paul Bremer, drunk on the hubris of victory, gutted his state by dismissing Ba'ath party members en masse from government employ and abolishing the armed forces, moves which rendered the state dysfunctional and sparked rebellion (see Chapter 10 of this book, by Toby Dodge). But while foreign advisers were concerned not to replay the failures of a past intervention, by seeking to go in the opposite direction they sowed the seeds for the NTC's failure in Libya. By embracing the old elite in such an extensive way, the new regime increasingly alienated those who had led the rebellion and claimed to be its mantle-bearers.

Reining in the *thuwwar*

In accordance with the plan, the government favoured maintaining all but the most senior levels of the former civil and security services over the rebellious undisciplined *thuwwar*. The defence ministry released plans for a 100,000-man army, of which the bulk was drawn from the pre-existing security forces, and restricted recruitment of demobilized *thuwwar* to 25 per cent of the force. Similarly the Supreme Security Council (SSC), an agency the Interior Ministry agency established to recruit members of the *thuwwar* into the security forces, claimed that 32,000 of Qaddafi's 88,000-strong police force had returned to work, making them the majority of the post-revolution police force that officials anticipated would number around 50,000.

Libya's fledgling government displayed other signs of their readiness to revive the old order, echoing Egypt's post-Mubarak Supreme Command of the Armed Forces (SCAF) which had removed the pinnacle of the security regime, but kept the apparatus beneath it intact. Senior army commanders, who were often of Arab Bedouin stock, projected their reach into the periphery often by wooing the very tribes from which they stemmed. On 24 April 2012, in the Saharan town of Sebha, I met Khalifa Haftar the former commander of Qaddafi's brutal but unsuccessful war in the 1980s against Chad (who subsequently fled into US exile, only to return in 2011 to support the revolution). After travelling south in a 30-car convoy, he feasted with hundreds of tribesmen from the Warfalla, Libya's largest tribe, which had remained loyal to the Qaddafi regime even after the Colonel fled Tripoli. After the requisite mutton, Haftar gave a terse address appealing for support 'to stop the *fitna*', or dissension, and uphold the local authority.

When the night-time celebratory firing of heavy weapons continued for weeks after Qaddafi's flight, Tripolitanians began to view the jubilant militiamen from elsewhere in Libya, particularly Zintan and Misrata, less as liberators than occupiers. The fledgling authorities made concerted efforts to clear the cities of the checkpoints the *thuwwar* had erected across the capital, and to reclaim their most lucrative holdings, particularly the ports, border terminals and airports they had seized. In mid-April 2012, after months of painstaking negotiation and false starts, the NTC claimed – prematurely – to have recovered control of Tripoli's international airport from Zintan's militia, and its inner city airport, Benita, from Souq al-Juma, the militia of a central Tripoli suburb. Far from instituting a new order, the government maintained the pre-revolutionary institutions for its rule, justifying its actions by arguing that as an unelected body it lacked the authority to institute change. 'Not before the elections' became a mantra for the deferral of demands to revamp Libya – from tenders for new housing projects to replacing the obstructionist system for issuing visas for journalists. Consequently, for the most part, the government was a relic of the Qaddafi regime. Ministers openly acknowledged their lack of control over a recalcitrant middle management steeped in decades of Qaddafism, which made even simple procedures seem Herculean. The choice of an exiled professor, Abdelrahim al-Keib, as prime minister compounded the government's inability to stamp a fresh imprint on Libya. Widely perceived as pleasant but weak, the self-effacing Keib suffered from an oversized sense of his own lack of legitimacy and leadership experience.

The *thuwwar*, perceiving the government as skeletal and its plans as a threat to their status and pre-eminence, launched a rearguard action to keep Libya in their hands. The bitterness they felt at their rejection was heightened by claims that when they finally conquered Qaddafi's hometown of Sirte in October 2011, the NTC scuppered their attempts to stage a celebratory march to Tripoli by promising a heroes' welcome in Benghazi, as if they were no longer welcome in the capital.

Resentful that their men had risked their lives for a revolution that others had hijacked, *thuwwar* commanders looked to their arms to assert their claims. Posing as the revolution's moral arbiters, they called for expunging the rotten regime root-and-branch, with a reconfiguration no less comprehensive than the de-Ba'athification that followed the overthrow of Saddam Hussein. In successive Congresses held during spring 2012 in the *thuwwar*-dominated towns of Misrata and Benghazi, hundreds of militiamen presented their demarches to the government. Their tone grew markedly hostile. While government ministers participated in the first congress, they stayed away from the second. Held in Benghazi on 24–25 April 2012, the latter, which I attended, provided a platform for a succession of belligerent militiamen to lambast the NTC. '*Thuwwar* of Libya unite', cried the chairman, in an appeal to join forces against the governing body. In their final session, delegates resolved to halt any hand over of weapons 'to those who try to kill us', an illusion to the old armed forces, many of whom, particularly from the Saadi federation of tribes in the eastern Green Mountains, had defected to the NTC with their commanders at the outset of the revolution. They insisted that any dissolution of the militias should be deferred to the end of the constitutional process which, at that point, was scheduled for 2013. 'The *thuwwar* are afraid that if they abandon their weapons, Qaddafi's henchmen will strike back', explained Faraj Sweihli, a Misrata militia commander who retained his base inside Tripoli until November 2013 despite government attempts at eviction.

Foremost among *thuwwar* grievances was the demand for public sector employment. In the eyes of the *thuwwar*, the NTC's inclusive approach to former regime forces, coupled with their order to the militias to disband, would strip them of the status and employment they had acquired by dint of the revolution. The *thuwwar* were also unnerved by government negotiations on outsourcing Libya's border defences to foreign private security companies. Aegis, a London-based security company which in 2004 won the world's largest private security contract from the US Coalition in Iraq, offered to establish a border force in exchange for a US$5 billion contract (the offer was declined). The 'lessons of Iraq' that Western advisers were keen to impress on the NTC, noted one Libyan critic wryly, did not extend to the issue of Western carpetbaggers soliciting contracts. Delegates also wanted the government to purge existing ranks of the armed forces and civil service of Qaddafi's *azlam*, or cadres, in what they envisaged would be a Libyan version of de-Ba'athification. In early 2012, *thuwwar* commanders lashed out at government plans for recruitment of an army based on the old corps, accusing it of raising a fifth column. The armed forces, they alleged, would be riddled with pro-Qaddafi forces, and possibly in cahoots with Qaddafi's offspring. They also resented the pre-eminence of some of its Qaddafi-era cadres. For example, Mustafa Abdel Jalil, the chairman of the NTC, had been Qaddafi's justice minister when the revolution began; and the NTC appointed government's first minister, Mahmoud Jibril, was the economic guru in Jama'at Seif, the supposedly reformist coterie of Seif al-Islam Qaddafi.

As he rolled a cigarette, Hussein Qarish, a garage mechanic who had joined Misrata's militia, wistfully imagined a post in the diplomatic corps, tracking Qaddafi's former cohorts in Libya's embassies: 'We want to enter the ministries and cleanse them of the regime', he said. There was further consternation at the government's failure to restart public sector projects. Construction cranes in full swing before the revolution hung motionless, testimony to a flight of all but half a million of an estimated 3.5 million foreign workers in Libya in 2010. Even so, many in Benghazi protested that officials preferred Asian migrants over local workers. Radio stations broadcast news of the labour minister's deal to import Sudanese workers, and Bangladeshis cleaned oil company offices while Libyans protested at their gates at the lack of jobs. A fighter from Shahat, a Green Mountain town where black prisoners were incarcerated on suspicion of fighting for Qaddafi, vented his anger at sub-Saharan migration: 'We don't want Africans in our country spreading diseases. Get out. *Allahu Akbar.*'

The second demand of the *thuwwar* was for greater budgetary support. Militiamen resented what they saw as the NTC's aspiration to take over the country's oil revenues estimated at some US$5 billion monthly, ports and copious assets, including an estimated US$200 billion of investments, after the *thuwwar* had won them in battle. Their concerns were exacerbated by the NTC's lack of transparency over its disbursement of oil income and fear that it was monopolising the proceeds. Originally comprising of nine members, the NTC had grown to 86 by late April 2012, thus spawning new members with scant public redress. Even its employees found its methods opaque. 'I have no idea who the NTC is', said a security official. 'We don't know their names. We don't have their CVs. Many think that the bulk is remnants of the old regime.'

Government schemes that were designed to ease tensions often inflamed them. A doctor addressed delegates at the second Benghazi Congress, documenting how health ministry clerks and Libyan diplomats had billed the government for US$30,000 for a visit to a Viennese dentist, and pocketed the difference. The only female speaker at the Congress – a businesswoman turned 'Boudicca' who claimed to have fired the first shots at Sirte in a bid to revive the flagging front – denounced officials taking holidays using stipends allocated for medical treatment abroad for the war wounded. Most damaging of all, the government suspended a one-off handout of 4,000 dinars (US$3,200) for married fighters and 2,800 dinars for bachelors in the spring of 2012 amid widespread reports of corruption. In April 2012, 66 officials were dismissed, accused of awarding themselves much of the 1.8 billion dinar (US$1.4 billion) pay-outs after forging the names of hundreds of thousands of applicants, far in excess of the tens of thousands who played a role in the colonel's downfall. The then-Labour minister, Mustafa Rujbani, said the list of *thuwwar* he received seeking government posts was riddled with duplicates and fictional names. A member of the NTC's military committee, who said that no more than 7,000 men had fought in battles against Qaddafi's forces, claimed that anyone who cried *Allahu Akbar* had added their name. Yet delegates from the Congress podium warned that the suspension of payments would be considered as a declaration of war.

The *thuwwar*'s third demand was for decentralization and the bridging of inequalities between the capital and the provinces. Many *thuwwar*, particularly those based in the periphery, expressed concern at what they saw as the NTC's proclivity for centralization and suppression of ethnic and sectarian diversity after the colonel's overthrow. A delegation of Imazighen, or Berbers, criticized the government for appointing only a single Amazigh minister, and then that was only after a month of protests. 'They promised to give us our language and minority rights when we rose up and they needed us', said a delegate from Yefren, an Amazigh stronghold nestled in the Nafusa mountains. 'But once they gained power, they were no longer interested.' In a sign of their distrust for central authority, feuding tribes opted less for NTC intervention than tribal mediation to resolve their differences. To NTC consternation, two feuding towns near the Tunisian border – Riqdaleen and Zawara – summoned a tribal *lijnat al-Islah*, or reconciliation committee, which consisted of 70 elders drawn from 20 tribes across Libya, to negotiate a *hudna*, or ceasefire. In Sebha, community leaders intervened to curb ethnic violence, long before government arrived on the scene.

The anger was at its most visceral in Benghazi, the birthplace of the uprising that toppled Qaddafi in February 2011. Once Tripoli fell, Libya's new leaders and Western advisers relocated to the plusher capital, abandoning Benghazi, in a move that had overtones of the former regime. Within a year of the revolt, Benghazi's initial exuberance had turned to despair. 'Almost everyone has moved to Tripoli', said one of the few remaining foreign consuls in April 2012. Benghazi languished without signs of renewal. In March 2012, 3,000 tribal leaders, militia commanders and local politicians gathered in Benghazi to declare the creation of a new federal region in Cyrenaica, or Barqa, Libya's oil-rich east.

For all their grandstanding, the *thuwwar* were even less accountable for the power and copious weapons that they wielded than the NTC. Doubts surrounding the revolutionary credentials of some Congress delegates were as persistent as those surrounding the NTC's members. Many participants hailed from parts of Libya which were among the last to fall to the rebels. Alongside a militia commander from Jufra, Qaddafi's garrison town in central Libya, was a delegation from Qaddafi's home town of Sirte – both of which had been strong supporters of the colonel and his regime.

Moreover, for all their show of unity, the *thuwwar* struggled to maintain a common front. As frustration mounted and competition for assets, arms, and control of smuggling and trans-Saharan and trans-Maghrebian trade routes intensified, some militias turned their arms on each other. Border skirmishes erupted around western and southern trading hubs, pitting Arabs against Black Toubou tribes, and Arabs against Imazighen, who during the revolution had fought together. The lack of a central authority further heightened old ethnic rivalries that predated the state. Hitherto only Italian fascism and the colonel's dictatorship had managed to keep the vast country united, and unlike neighbouring Tunisia, Libya lacked national and federal political institutions which might have provided the foundations for a modern unitary state. From April to June 2012, Arab tribes in the southern towns of Kufra and Sebha pounded Toubou shanties with artillery shells, which led to hundreds of deaths. 'Everyone is afraid and everyone is buying arms. The NTC and the government are too weak to protect us', said Eissa al-Hamissi, a film-maker who recorded the transition from revolution to an ethnic struggle for control of the trade route to Tunisia between his hometown of Zawara (an Amazigh stronghold on the Mediterranean coast) and the nearby Arab town of Riqdaleen.

For all the infighting, the arsenals the militias had assembled enabled them to frequently overpower the weaker forces of the NTC. Despite nominal deference to central government, military councils frequently continued to act autonomously. Militias staged military pageants, and paraded their caches as shows of force to ward off army or other attempts to challenge their authority. In February 2012, the militia of the Awlad Suleiman, an Arab tribe, marked the first anniversary of liberation by parading its war-loot through the town, including 50 tanks and scores of 'Grad' missiles. The Jufra militia leader mentioned above claimed to have captured 600 tanks from the arsenal that Qaddafi's security forces had left behind.

The struggle for authority

In the first months of the revolution, there were indications that the *thuwwar* and the government could have established a working relationship. Militias ceded formal control at many of the country's entry points, while retaining a covert presence by donning army uniforms and repainting their vehicles the crimson and white colours of the security forces. Zawara's militia continued to operate the Ras Jdir crossing to Tunisia, alongside government forces. Government demands in April 2012 that militias hand over responsibility for some 3,000 detainees was achieved in part by painting state insignia on the gates of militia prisons. A Salafi fighter in Benghazi who was hired by the Interior Ministry's SSC to integrate *thuwwar* into the security forces cited religious precedent for how former foes could be merged into a single force. If the Prophet Mohammed could integrate Khalid bin Walid, the former commander of Mecca's army of Unbelievers, into his army and dispatch him to conquer Syria for Islam, he argued, how could the *thuwwar* reject their own countrymen? 'Libya does not have enough native experts to throw them away', he said.

When the scheduled elections in the summer of 2012 came nearer, however, the relationship between the NTC and the militias became dangerously frayed. Inside the new security forces, rivalries between the old regime forces and the militiamen recruited by the SSC intensified. And across the country, militias defied the NTC's order to disband by 2 April 2012. Government predictions that the term 'militia' would disappear from Libya's lexicon within two months of the order proved fanciful. Even in Tripoli, where the government focused its efforts, rogue militias continued to occupy key military installations in defiance of NTC orders to leave. Despite its costly construction of a high-security cell, the NTC retreated from its demands that Zintan's militia hand over its prize catch, Qaddafi's son Seif al-Islam, for trial, and detained an international lawyer and four officials from the International Criminal Court who sought to visit him. Signs bearing the term 'holy property' peppered the capital's prime properties, as militiamen citing the Quranic Sura of Ansar, insisted that the Prophet had sanctioned the acquisition of spoils of war. The religious affairs minister griped that he was powerless to prevent fanatics capturing the country's mosques, because he lacked a militia of his own.

Despite its ambitious plans, the government failed to gain control of its borders. Emboldened militias secured revenue from smuggling across all Libya's frontiers, particularly with neighbours in the Sahel. Subsidized petrol, flour and guns went out; alcohol and migrants came in. Few figures are available for the flow, but if Libya consumed all the fuel and flour it produces its population would be among the world's most obese: according to government figures, Libyans consumed an average of 37 loaves of bread and enough petrol for to fill their tanks twice each week. In addition, cross-border demand for weapons from Qaddafi's looted armouries boosted earnings potential, stoking fresh violence in northern Mali and the Sinai Peninsula.

As the militias grew stronger, so in turn the government weakened, which hastened the erosion of state control. Some pooled resources and combined to form rapid reaction forces able to move faster and in larger numbers than the new army, and thereby project their influence. The Libyan Shield, a force comprising seven militias, sent its fighters to Kufra, a Saharan trading-post en route to Darfur, to bolster the capabilities of the local Arab tribe, the Zuwayy, against the Toubou (who were their rivals for control of the sub-Saharan trade routes). Though the army also sent forces, they were too few in number to act as a neutral buffer. Even after the army negotiated a ceasefire on 20 April 2012, Libya Shield militiamen drove around Kufra flying the Prophet Mohammed's black flag of Jihad. The Shield's commander, Wissam Ben Hamid, refused to accept army orders to halt fire, and periodically shelled Toubou shanties on behalf of the Arab tribe. Similarly in the west, militias formed a composite 1,750-man force, drawn from 20 militias, thus creating another arm of Libya Shield.

On several occasions the rivalry between government and militia forces spilled into violence. Government installations in April and May 2012 came under repeated attack. In Darna, in eastern Libya, a military commander newly appointed by the NTC was shot dead at a petrol station the day before he was due to take charge. The armoured car of the UN Representative, Ian Martin, was attacked as it drew up outside the SSC's offices in Benghazi for talks on security sector reform. Militiamen also stormed the state prison cell where the authorities were holding Islamists suspected of perpetrating the assassination of the former Saiqa commander, Abdel Fattah Younes. When they failed, a militiaman hurled a bomb at its gates. On 8 May 2012, two hundred armed men attempted to storm Prime Minister Keib's cabinet office while he was meeting the defence minister, killing one of Keib's bodyguards. Fearing for their lives, ministers and NTC members toyed with resignation. Gunfire cut through the late evening chatter at the Rixos, Tripoli's luxury hotel where the NTC had taken up residence.

There was a further escalation in June 2012, when the NTC's foreign backers came under attack. The US and British consulates and the ICRC compound were all targeted in Benghazi. A British diplomatic convoy in Sebha was struck by a rocket-propelled grenade. Militias again fought over Tripoli's international airport, a sign of the incremental factionalism into which Libya had slipped.

As it lurched from placating the Old Guard to appeasing the *thuwwar*, NTC chairman Mustafa Abdel Jalil harangued officials for failing 'to absorb the revolutionaries'. In April 2012, the NTC offered the *thuwwar* blanket amnesties for any crimes committed during the war, restored its stipends and added bonuses, sanctioned the intervention of militia forces in such troublespots as Bani Walid (a former regime garrison town), and backed the creation of a Patriotism and Integrity Commission (a counterpart to Iraq's De-Ba'athification Commission) which was assigned responsibility for vetting electoral candidates and government officials.

But such conciliatory measures failed to stem the deterioration. The more ground the government conceded, the more empowered the militias became. Defying fears, Libya's electoral process proceeded remarkably smoothly. With UN assistance, over 70 per cent of an estimated 3.4 million electorate registered to vote within barely three weeks. Nevertheless, there were worrying signs that the militias preferred bullets over ballots. In the Saharan town of Murzuq, the scene of particularly violent ethnic clashes between blacks and Arabs, an Arab candidate was shot dead on 18 May 2012, as tensions rose over whether blacks stripped of their citizenship under Qaddafi would be allowed to vote. 'Who will respect the results, when everyone has a gun?', asked an Amazigh activist from Zawara. Some commanders feared that an elected government would enjoy the popular mandate that the NTC lacked and thus be more able to press for their demobilization. In a possible sign of official wavering, the initial election date of June 2012 was delayed by several weeks.

Conclusion

In July 2012, Libya held its first multiparty general elections for a General National Congress that brought the government of Ali Zeidan, a human rights lawyer, to power. Empowered to issue contracts and implement reconstruction plans, an elected government should have been well-placed to broaden its support base. Had the government invested more of its energy in kick-starting the economy by reviving the private sector, militiamen might have sought job opportunities elsewhere.

But by seeking to buy the militia's silence with handouts, the government merely empowered the centrifugal forces pulling at Libya's seams. The absence of an accepted truth and reconciliation commission intensified the debate and disagreement about the country's past, and prompted a growing number of armed and aggrieved Libyans to seek justice with their own hands. And as the post-revolutionary strife intensified, older struggles pitting the ethnic, tribal and religious differences that Colonel Qaddafi had suppressed over his four-decade rule, filled the vacuum left by the NTC's failure to lay the institutional foundations of a modern state.

Although Libya's multiple armed groups allowed the 2012 election to proceed, by the time of the next election, two years later in June 2014, Libya's constitutional process was no longer able to contain their power. Nervous of letting ballots not bullets decide Libya's fate, Barqa's self-declared military council erected roadblocks near Sirte to prevent access for election officers. In an attempt to scupper a vote that armed groups in the east feared would give undue influence to the more populous west, the elections commission offices were overrun in Benghazi, and a helicopter carrying ballot papers was attacked. Libya's oil exports plummeted as militiamen in the Gulf of Sirte took over the terminals. And in August 2014, a conglomeration of militias known as Libya Dawn swept control of Tripoli in the wake of the June 2014 elections, forcing the newly-elected House of Representatives and the armed forces to flee to Tobruk, on the far east of the country near the Egyptian border, which precipitated a renewed bout of fighting between the forces who waved the banner of revolution and those who professed to represent stability based on certainties of the past. Future historians might yet write a postscript to the effect that in their zeal to correct the past, Libya's new authorities overcompensated for the mistakes the Western power made in Iraq and Afghanistan, thereby alienating the revolutionary forces that it had acted militarily to sweep into power.

The decision of Western powers to intervene militarily to oust Libya's dictator but thereafter disengage – thereby ducking responsibility for the maelstrom they unleashed – had consequences which rippled far beyond Libya. Western support for Libya's revolutionaries encouraged Syrians to follow their example, but the anticipated support for their rebellion never came (see Chapter 13 of this book, by Christopher Phillips). Arguably Iraqi Sunnis also followed suit, with their mass protests against Maliki's rule.

When it failed to materialise, armed groups waving the flag of religion took their place. The chaos prevailing not only in Libya but in the broader region owes much to Western military intervention, which promised a new era of statehood meeting the needs of the Middle East's people (not leaders), but failed to deliver.

Acknowledgements

This chapter is based on an updated version of an eyewitness account published as an article of the same name that appeared in *International Peacekeeping*, vol. 19, no. 4, August 2012, Taylor & Francis Ltd, www.tandfonline.com, reprinted by permission of the publisher.

12 Defending neoliberal Mali
French military intervention and the management of contested political narratives

Bruno Charbonneau and Jonathan Sears

The French military intervention in Mali, which began on 11 January 2013, exposed the complex dynamics of Malian politics, the rising regional threat of 'terrorist' and illicit networks in the Sahel, the limits of African conflict management organisations, and the mechanisms of French militarism in Africa. Generally, comments and analyses have so far focused on the problem of Mali's 'state failure' and its articulation with a 'terrorist' threat. The legitimacy and necessity of the French military interposition have hinged on this articulation. According to French President François Hollande, the request of interim Malian President Dioncounda Traoré for French military intervention was justified on the basis of an external terrorist threat. The same request by President François Bozizé of the Central African Republic (CAR) was rejected on the basis that France would not 'protect a regime' against the Séléka rebels because this crisis was considered, in Paris, an internal CAR affair. Both states suffered a *coup d'état* and showed their chronic incapacity to face serious security threats, but only Mali received massive French and international attention and support.[1]

For many analysts, the situation in Mali reflects the state's inability to respond to security threats, and thus the policy grammar directs attention to the 'terrorist threat' and 'state failure'. Warfare and security-building measures are conceptualised as strategies and instruments of state policy. French military intervention and the subsequent UN military deployment are conceived as a necessary and reasonable response to 'state failure' and the potential dangers of a disordered world filled with 'terrorists', 'jihadists', 'extremists', and 'Islamists'. The 2013 French and international intervention can be construed as Mali's liberation from 'groups of terrorists and extremists'.[2] As Roland Marchal noted, the names given to the northern Malian groups are often deployed incorrectly and interchangeably. In Mali, terms such as 'salafist' distinguish 'radical' Islamists from groups and actors who articulate a more 'republican' Islam.[3] Consensus on international military intervention in Mali emerged given an absence of obvious, legitimate interlocutors with negotiable interests in Mali's north. However, this and similar interpretations require already-institutionalised identities and identity spaces and thereby hinder the methodical analysis of both the conditions of possibility for military intervention and the ontological purposes of the

French war. As with many analyses of military intervention, the problem's formulation enables and enacts judgments about the legitimacy of deploying international military violence.[4] In the Malian case, interrelated tropes about 'global terrorism' and Islamist violence in Africa were emphasised. Narratives of alleged globalised and monolithic characteristics of the Islamist threat obscure context-specific dynamics and the local embeddedness of Islamist and other rebel groups in Mali. Legitimising discourses come with institutionalised identities available to military and statebuilding intervention that mask the politically contested nature and the effects of defining the problems as 'state failure' and 'global terrorism'.

This is where the ontological aims of warfare appear: in its affirmation, imposition, and reproduction of specific identities and institutional configurations.[5] In the words of Michael Shapiro, such aims 'are overcoded by official and bureaucratic discourses in modern states' that legitimate military violence on the basis of security interests and mask the 'identity stakes driving hostilities'.[6] Indeed, the Malian state 'weakness' in carrying out its sovereign and welfare activities is inextricably linked to its 'failure' in imposing and consolidating a hegemonic national identity. Multiple sites of authority and legitimacy-seeking make the nation- and statebuilding processes in Mali a crucial dimension of the post-French war context. In a sense, Malians are faced with longing for the relative social peace of 1992–2007, occasioned by effective (though not uncontested) legitimation of domination, by a political class oriented to the experience of southern and urban populations.[7] Instead, they face the messier and potentially violent realities of coercion-hegemony coming to prominence over the democratic experiments with persuasion-hegemony.

The French war might have been necessary to stop an armed rebellion,[8] but deploying international military violence in the name of peace and security has inevitably reshaped both the crisis and Mali's future. Hence, this chapter seeks to emphasise the ontological effects of the war, notably in how it establishes limits to the formation of national identity and the Malian state and manages contested political possibilities. This focus is in part to deprive the war of its necessity, but also to reveal how the official 'war-against-terrorism' rationale for the war erases the context-specific dynamics that led to the crisis in the first place. Identifying as problematic the foundational analytic assumption that Mali is a fully-formed, democratic nation-state, the chapter further argues that democratic citizen identity formation is a continuous process. As such, the French war cannot 'save Mali from terrorism' per se, but more accurately contribute to the Malian processes of national identity and statebuilding by responding militarily to the challenges of multiple non-state sites of authority and legitimacy-seeking.

Background to the French war

The most direct events leading to the French war started in January 2012 when the Mouvement national de libération de l'Azawad (MNLA) attacked

Malian positions in the country's north. The armed rebellion was soon joined by the Islamist armed group of Ansar Eddine,[9] led by the Tuareg leader Iyad ag Ghali, and by the Mouvement de l'unicité du jihad en Afrique de l'Ouest (MUJAO). Both groups had established links with Al-Qaeda in the Islamist Maghreb (AQMI) during the previous decade. Between January and March, the Islamic groups gained in strength and, by the end of June, were able to oust the MNLA rebels, thus illustrating the fluidity of the rebel groups and their alliances. From July 2012 until the January 2013 French military intervention, Ansar Eddine, MUJAO and AQMI controlled all three northern regions of Kidal, Timbuktu and Gao.[10]

The situation in the north was worsened by the reaction in the country's capital, Bamako. On 22 March 2012, Captain Amadou Haya Sanogo led a mutiny that turned into a coup d'état against the regime of President Amadou Toumani Touré (ATT). Sanogo argued that the regime's inability to respond to the rebellion, the worsening situation in the north, and the very poor condition of the Malian army legitimated the coup. He promised that the Malian army would take back the north and reassert Malian sovereignty, but only succeeded in exacerbating the crisis. From then on, the crisis developed along two parallel tracks with no necessary links between them.[11] In Bamako, political elites focused on their political game, divided as they were between the camps of interim President Dioncounda Traoré, Prime Minister Cheick Modibo Diarra[12] and Captain Sanogo. The coup d'état left Mali deeply divided, but not necessarily on a neat north–south axis or a secular–Islamist divide. These widespread clichés obscure the complexities of the crises and the effects of an 'erosion of democracy, rise of criminality, and impunity of state officials' that 'opened the door for various groups to flourish in the north, gaining territory and, in some instances, popular legitimacy'.[13] The crises of political legitimacy in Mali continue to be expressed in dissatisfaction with government corruption, debate-stifling 'consensus', and ineffective development programmes. Widely-expressed desires to curb corruption and revitalise public life feed into the increasingly broad appeal of religiously-framed discourses about deficits in the moral authority of Mali's political leadership.

The complexity of the changing alliances of the northern groups, the uncertainty of political power and authority in Bamako, and the varied and varying agendas of all partly explain the indecision and lack of concerted international action in 2012. On the day of his inauguration (15 May 2012), President Hollande put Mali at the top of the French foreign affairs to-do list, arguing that his predecessor neglected the risks that destabilisation in Mali represented.[14] But French diplomats seemed unable to persuade their Western allies at the UN, notably the Americans, who were unconvinced that the Sahel groups were a threat to US security interests.[15] Only in July, after the destruction of the Timbuktu mausoleum, was French ambassador to the UN, Gérard Araud, successful in passing a cautious resolution that took note of the request of the Economic Community of West African States (ECOWAS) and the African Union for a UN mandate authorising the deployment of a stabilisation force. This resolution further requested that the Secretary-General 'develop and implement in consultation with regional organisations, a United Nations integrated strategy for the Sahel region encompassing security, governance, development, human rights and humanitarian issues'.[16]

This prudent resolution did not incite rapid and willing international action. The deployment of ECOWAS troops was delayed by the Sanogo junta's opposition to an international intervention, by ECOWAS members that doubted the organisation's intervention capacity and negotiated financial aid packages and political advantage, and by members of the UN Security Council, especially the United States, that questioned the operational capacity, ability, and objectives of the ECOWAS force. In November, the Secretary-General expressed his fears that a poorly conceived and executed military deployment could exacerbate 'an already extremely fragile humanitarian situation' and 'risk ruining any chance of a negotiated political solution to the crisis'.[17] After long negotiations between France and the United States in particular, on 20 December the Security Council adopted Resolution 2085, which authorised the deployment of an African-led International Support Mission in Mali (AFISMA) for an initial period of one year.[18] At the time, there was no plan to re-conquer the North. The Malian army was to be trained and work with AFISMA forces, but coming events transformed the crisis into a French war.

The French war on terrorism

Throughout the fall of 2012, President Hollande repeated numerous times that his government would not 'put boots on the ground'. But his government became increasingly frustrated by the reluctance of the UN Security Council and the United States, the European Union's lack of interest, and the inconclusiveness of ECOWAS meetings whose members showed little interest in finding a solution.[19] UNSC Resolution 2085 (20 December 2012) authorised an African force, but offered no timetable or mechanism to generate troops. The French government nevertheless had a few allies. President of Niger, Mahamadou Issoufou, argued strongly for a quick military operation to save his country from 'contagion'. African presidents Macky Sall (Senegal) and Alpha Condé (Guinea) also favoured such a solution.[20]

The official and public reason for launching the French war was that the situation evolved 'at the speed of light' when the rebels moved south toward, allegedly, Bamako.[21] In 2013, Hollande transformed his discourse: 'the very existence of this friendly nation is at stake. Military operations will last for as long as required ... Terrorists must know that France will always be there when it's a matter not of its fundamental interests but the right of a population ... to live in freedom and democracy'.[22] With few exceptions, discussions of the conflict in Mali have been framed in terms of the strategic necessity to respond to the Islamist threat in Africa.[23] The hostage scenario at the In Amenas facility in Algeria (16 January 2013) was interpreted as supporting the claim that the Malian conflict was linked to the globalised Islamist al-Qaeda networks, and therefore that the ungoverned spaces of the Sahel were a threat for the West and Western interests. British Prime Minister David Cameron linked Mali to the so-called 'same threat' found in Pakistan and Afghanistan, framing it in terms of 'a generational struggle' against extremists.[24]

However, as Caitriona Dowd and Clionadh Raleigh argued, responses to the conflict were 'emblematic of the de-contextualised approach analysts, politicians, and policy makers have taken in assessing violence in Africa'.[25] Analytical platitudes have their political uses. In the case of Mali, they neglected the 'fractious nature of diverse Islamist groups using force to achieve (often vaguely specified) goals',[26] the local specificity and historical emergence of the conflict, the local appeal and embeddedness of Islamist groups, and the role of international actors in failing to produce and sustain desirable future possibilities for Malian politics. The emphasis on Islamist and 'terrorist' violence authorised and legitimised French and international intervention, but it also enabled power redistribution within Mali: 'Interim authorities clearly capitalised on a widespread perception of an Islamist threat, and it effectively garnered international support for the Malian government at a time when its domestic standing was doubtful.'[27]

Despite official statements and media reports about the global threat that the Malian Islamist rebels represented, the situation was more complicated than a 'terrorist' attack and was rooted in Malian dynamics. On 9-10 January 2013, the situation in Bamako was tense. Political movements, most of them having been created after the March 2012 coup d'état, which they supported, called for the immediate creation of a national and sovereign platform for change in Mali. They also demanded that interim President Traoré leave office and that the north be liberated from the Islamists. According to several reports, the demonstrations were to continue for a few days and produce an insurrectional climate that would bring back the Kati military (i.e. the 'Green Berets' loyal to Captain Sanogo) to the political centre. Different rumours of a coup against Traoré included one about an agreement between the Islamists of Iyad ag Ghali and marginalised political actors in Bamako to take over the country.[28]

While it is impossible to assert the veracity of the rumours that Sanogo was behind the planned coup, or that the Islamist groups were part of the planning and execution, it seems very unlikely that the French government and the UN were unaware of the possibility of another coup. The increasing tension in Bamako coincided with the advance of rebel forces toward Mopti, the Sevare airport, and Konna. The attack broke the implicit agreement with the government, reached in the spring of 2012, that no armed groups would cross the north–south boundary.[29] The Malian army's inability to oppose the rebel advance drove President Traoré to write to Paris requesting French military intervention. The letter, whose final and revised version apparently originated from Paris,[30] asked for intelligence gathering and air support for Malian troops (but no ground troops). For the French government, this letter legalised the military operation. The decision to intervene militarily was taken on 10 January 2013 and officially started on 11 January.[31] On 22 May 2013, testifying in front of the National Assembly defense commission, Chief of Staff of the Armies Admiral Edouard Guillaud stated that the directives given in January were 'to stop the offensive toward Bamako and thus preserve the existence of the Malian state; to destroy – which means in military language to neutralise 60 per cent of the enemy forces – and disorganise the terrorist network; to help in re-establishing the territorial integrity and unity of Mali; and to seek hostages, notably ours'.[32] According to Roland Marchal, the 'French expected their intervention to solve once and for all the question of what to do with coup makers'.[33] Interim President Traoré was to strengthen his authority, Captain Sanogo was to quietly disappear from the political scene, and Islamists were to be destroyed so that the 'legitimate' representatives of the north (i.e. the MNLA, essentially, according to the French) were to become partners for peace.

Things did not quite go according to plan. In the second half of 2013, Malian political elites were still trying to understand, negotiate and adjust to the conditions produced by the French operation. The regions of Gao and Kidal were experiencing terrorist attacks (notably in October 2013 and in June 2014). Kidal, in particular, has been the object of many negotiations and tensions. Controlled by the MNLA, its leadership allowed the presence of French troops (who protected the airport), but not of the Malian army. An agreement was reached on 18 June 2013 to allow for the presence of the Malian state and army in Kidal, but the city has become the symbol of French interference in Mali. The French demand for national elections to be held on 28 July 2013 reinforced the impression that the French were imposing their own agenda. As Marchal wrote, the 'discrepancy between military progress and political stasis may be the most important problem today for the international community in Mali'.[34]

There is no doubt that the French war transformed everything. Yet, an analytical focus on the so-called 'terrorist' threat lends itself too easily toward the diagnosis of 'state failure' and its implicit programme of action (i.e. statebuilding). The first priority of the UN mission (MINUSMA) is the 'Stabilization of key population centres and support for the reestablishment of State authority throughout the country'.[35] The legitimacy of the French war and the UN mandate rests on this technocratic articulation between the diagnosis/problem and the solution. International warfare in Mali might be construed as necessary against salafist insurgents, but it is also an attempt at defining the Malian political subject, with little to no regard for the deep history of resistance to the imposition of colonising powers and projects in Mali.

To debate, on the basis of security considerations alone, whether military violence is a legitimate response overemphasises formal politics, de-contextualises terrorism, and obscures domestic issues also at stake, such as socio-economic justice, identity and livelihoods. These are the issues by which the Malian state's administrative and welfare activities are linked to its attempts to project and consolidate a hegemonic national political identity. In turn, these attempts confront multiple sites of, and struggles between, state-sanctioned and 'traditional' moral authority, and between state and non-state actors' legitimacy-seeking. Thus the nation- and statebuilding processes in Mali are a crucial dimension of the post-French military intervention context.

Crises and neoliberal democratic statebuilding in Mali

Given that international intervention seeks to return Mali to *la vie normale*, this normality invites interrogation. If the French 'saved' Mali, we must study what it claims to have 'saved'. If MINUSMA is working to restore state authority, we must examine the form this authority has taken and could take in the future. Mali's armed forces were unable to claim a monopoly of violence to maintain territorial control of the country during the events of 2011–2013, and it is far from clear that they could claim it in late 2014. Following the French operation Serval, the establishment of MINUSMA invites consideration of ongoing governance and development challenges to the prospects of pluralist democratic rule in Mali, as well as the longer-term processes of sustainable nation-state building.

Democratic governance

How did problems of domestic governance articulate with 'growing sociocultural cleavage between urban elites and the rest of the population'[36] to give rise to challenges 'not only for Malian democracy, but for Mali as a secular, multi-ethnic state'?[37] The period of executive dominance is marked by a vision of democratisation as minimally good governance and largely procedural electoralism to support economic liberalisation: a key part of the legacies of Mali's guidance and discipline by the International Monetary Fund, World Bank and major bilateral and multilateral donors. Development initiatives tied to economic restructuring have further centralised power, concentrated wealth and intensified the economic and social divisions between rural and urban populations, and also within urban areas. Although GDP growth was 'relatively high in 2001–2010', the legacies of restructuring in '[e]conomic stagnation, the rise in poverty, the breakdown of public services',[38] are still felt as overall GDP growth in 1990–2010 struggled to match population growth.[39] With these antecedents, state actors have struggled greatly to balance longer-term development investment with the immediate needs of Mali's most vulnerable populations, among whom 50 per cent still live daily on less than US$1.25 (purchasing power parity).[40]

The political importance of growing socio-cultural cleavages is clearer in light of divisions among the leadership of the movement against Moussa Traoré's regime (1968–1991). The early post-1991 narrative of Mali's democratic consolidation emphasised the 'People's Revolution' movement's diverse membership. This emphasis and enthusiasm has tended to obscure the 'rapid alternations between expressions of national unanimity and sharp divisions across one divide or another'.[41] Divisions among the movement's leaders marginalised the more revolutionary democrats who bore the legacies of anti-colonial and anti-authoritarian populism, and allowed reformer democrats and liberal formalists to consolidate their influence. Reformer democrats, mostly upper-middle and middle class intellectuals and professionals (e.g. doctors, lawyers, teachers), 'swam in two waters' and 'had one foot in the *ancien régime* and one in the stirrup of the insurgents'.[42] Numerous in the higher levels of the Malian state, they were 'very little inclined to accept and even less to accomplish deep socio-political changes'. The liberal formalists included an administrative ruling class embedded firmly in the *ancien régime* upper and upper-middle classes, and who often 'associated social rights with anarchy'.[43] In brief, the most radical anti-dictatorship actors were marginalised by those who sought the legitimation of an ongoing neoliberal regime, now electorally. Thus was forestalled Mali's 'second independence'. Those who pre-empted meaningful pluralism in the Third Republic were well represented in the national conference of July–August 1991: 'members of a specific social fraction: educated, urban, professional employees, many of them centered in the public service'.[44] They structured the minimal reforms that shifted from economic liberalisation under dictatorship to electorally legitimated economic liberalisation. This elite democracy largely eschewed the transformative aspirations of Mali's most marginalised populations. The 'broad coalitions of relatively privileged citizens' who agitated for democratic transition saw it 'as a means to defend their privileges and not to bring about popular democracy, involving all segments of the population'.[45] Today, precisely 'because of their proximity and entanglement with the State', Bamako-based non-governmental groups (including those providing public services), reproduce views common to 'donor-oriented, professional civil society' actors, and more generally have 'lost sight of the country's grassroots realities and regional dynamics'.[46] This contributes to a form of ideological homogenisation among the heirs of a formalist and market-oriented vision of Mali's post-authoritarian, post-Cold War possibilities in governance and statebuilding, a vision affirmed by international donors (including donor states and multilateral organisations such as the World Bank and UN).

Well before its transition from authoritarianism in 1991–1992, Mali's development as a nation-state was shaped by post-Second World War dynamics of decolonisation and independence. Thus democratisation and statebuilding are part of a 60-year history from pre-colonial, to colonial, to post-colonial authoritarian rule, to post-authoritarian political and economic liberalisation. Even without exploring the histories of decolonisation and militant nationalism in the region,[47] the daily realities of rural and minority communities are clearly disconnected from the dominant views of political elites economically reliant on international donors. Thanks to these influential elites, Mali's 'donor darling' status has further obscured persistent shortcomings in democratic governance.[48] Domestic and international policy viewpoints converge, mediated through Mali's long-standing aid dependence and model aid recipient status in partnerships with bilateral donor and multilateral aid agencies. These donor-led 'partnerships' have tended to 'lessen the accountability of the executive branch of government'.[49] Managerial 'good governance' has been compromising democratic consolidation on a national level for nearly a decade. Now, as it was with the overly enthusiastic and uncritical domestic and international views of Mali's early post-transition period (1992–1997), elections in July–August 2013 are again being overemphasised as a feature of progressive democratic consolidation. Enthusiasm for procedural electoralism is again set to ignore the 'several structural and longstanding threats to democratic consolidation in Mali',[50] which international security and development aid has done little to address. Electorally legitimating the international military intervention reinforces a system of militarised global governance unable to account or allow for differences internal to the Malian polity that exacerbate these threats.

Establishing a culture of consensus

Since the early 1990s, socio-cultural elements have significantly complemented Mali's electorally legitimated post-Cold War statebuilding. Through the later Alpha Oumar Konaré years (1997–2002) and early ATT period (2002–2005), appeals to socio-cultural legacies of social cohesion, 'resolution', and 'unity' tended to obscure entrenched injustices of violation, exploitation and structural inequality.[51] These broad discourses of 'reconciliation' appear crucial to the cultural politics of legitimating economic liberalisation through minimal–procedural democratisation, and, though not uncriticised, of extending the state's administration across the territory through both coercive and persuasive means.

The idea of ostensibly 'national' culture as a potential 'anchor' to legitimise neoliberal economics and politics has been well articulated for and with allies and donors, such as France and the United States. For proponents of neoliberalism, resistance to economic liberalisation reforms is to be overcome by adapting 'democracy to familiar cultural forms'.[52] Given that 'the legitimation of the market depends on *finding the factors* that determine support for neoliberal reforms',[53] political class actors in state and non-state spheres have narrated such cultural forms and factors in a discourse of national political culture. This so-called 'Malian' culture, which allegedly holds advantages for democratic consolidation, is centred on the political, economic and demographic centre of southern Mali, and resonates little with minority populations, particularly those of north Mali and of the littoral populations on the Niger River bend.[54]

Linked to broader claims about compatible cultural democracy in Africa,[55] narratives of common historical experience across different populations have overstated the inclusivity of Mali's post-authoritarian nation-state building project. From the start of the independence period, Mali's leaders attempted to forge an abstract sense of national identity with flags, anthems, the idea of a national 'people's army', and a modern nation-wide school system.[56] Ideas about education for political development in Sub-Saharan Africa, while no longer anti-colonial or even anti-capitalist in tone, remain strongly tied to the 'ideological re-education of African society to create the new African who can contribute effectively to the realisation of nationalist objectives'.[57]

A political historiography of 'national identity'

To enable Malian state authority to be accepted as able and legitimate to manage inequalities and conflicts, political class actors through the independence period sought to elaborate the formation of citizen consciousness. Among the legacies of presidents Modibo Keita (1960–1968) and Moussa Traoré (1968–1991) were 30 years of 'civic and moral education' stressing unity and discipline of 'member-militants' within the state, disseminating a centralist ideology, and enforcing harsh measures of internal party and social discipline.[58] In the post-authoritarian period (Konaré and ATT), democracy promotion took up this complex legacy of a centralised, clientelistic state both to encourage and to discipline Mali's citizen-participants in its public life. The project to educate and mobilise Malians to participate in elections received broad and enthusiastic support from international donors and NGOs. With its capacities and donors' support, the state, together with sponsored civil society actors, has been able since the 1990s to sustain programmes of 'democracy promotion', which acculturated citizens into a sense belonging to the Malian polity, if mainly as voters in elections. Such an identity has taken hold mostly with donor-oriented political class actors in civil society and government. These mainly Francophone and Bamanan-speaking actors – largely educated, urban and professional – have dominated national political culture in Mali during the decades of democratisation. Domestic and foreign government and NGO actors' citizen awareness activities have predominantly emphasised formal citizen identity commensurate with procedural democracy: election participation within the institutional consolidation of a minimal liberal state.

By emphasising formal citizen identity, the Konaré and ATT regimes aimed to manage the possibly disorderly popular demands invigorated by the political liberalisation of the 1990s. Such management sought narrowly conceived political class cohesion at the expense of linking formal politics to concerns and activities of the mass population. To minimise the influence of ethno-linguistic diversity and inequality, post-1991 regimes stressed social harmony, and further reproduced a mythological unity of Malians' ostensibly 'national characteristics' within an idea of 'greater Mali'.[59]

The story of Sundiata Keïta founding and ruling the Mali Empire (*Maliba*, 'Greater Mali') in the thirteenth to fifteenth centuries has been represented as an important 'contemporary political symbol in the context of Malian democratization'.[60] Such political symbolism and historiography frames the 'founding epic of the nation'[61] as a 'Malian, indeed African, non-aggression pact', and further claims that 'all of these elements, internalized in the collective memory, are brought to the surface and invoked to protect Mali from ethnic conflict'.[62] Such analyses articulate democratisation with 'Malian traditional society' as 'a unique political culture that may have provided Mali with a democratic advantage over other African nations'.[63]

Malian historian and writer Adame Ba Konaré (wife of former president Konaré) exemplifies the nationalist historiography, stressing that the Sundiata epic remains 'more than lived history' because his deeds 'are cultural ingredients defined for all time'.[64] Reading history thus, she claims that the interdependence of norms and practices governing economic and political relationships has forged a 'veritable Malian identity of common characteristics and values that are internalized and shared'.[65] This problematic historiography – because partial and oriented to the south of Mali – has influenced contemporary political discourse in multiple spheres and organisations of the state administration, as well as donor-oriented local civil society organisations and foreign NGOs.[66] This historiography also exemplifies the selective articulation of Mali's dominant, Mandé/Bamanan cultural heritage, with a liberal formalist orientation to the electoral legitimation of ongoing statebuilding. This orientation tends to exaggerate commonalities and minimise differences and conflicts in the complex ideological and material transformation of social and political identities.

In 2013, in the period of post-coup, post-insurgency and post-intervention, a renewed emphasis on the region's imperial historiography appears poised again to inform a preoccupation with 'unity' and 'integration'.[67] The election of Ibrahim Boubacar Keïta (IBK) as president in 2013 will do little to mute the nation- and statebuilding symbolism that has in the past weakened meaningful pluralism. Indeed, in such a political cultural climate, the Malian administration and its donor-partners seem unlikely to attempt to 'valorize local cultures while avoiding the steam roller that is the national narrative of the Mali Empire'.[68] These domestic and foreign elites fail to appreciate fully that the notion that the Mali empire formed a pre-modern basis for international diplomacy, democracy, and human rights, is 'more mythical than historic' and has 'never been the cultural crucible of the north'.[69]

Those who take exception to this national and nationalist narrative continue to build on indigenous mechanisms of social regulation, based on coexisting and interacting 'normative orders with different sources of legitimacy and authority'.[70] The invigoration of alternative, non-state sites of social regulation, including claims to moral authority from religious or traditional/customary bases, revives fundamental questions about the ongoing formation of the Malian polity. These persuasive/norm-setting and coercive/disciplinary alternatives continue to challenge not merely the legitimacy of a particular government and its foreign donor-partners, but also the scope of the nation-state's legitimate (capable and acceptable) authority. It is thus not an overstatement to claim that 'the major intellectual issue in the reconstruction of Mali is this: to redefine another narrative that blends together multiple epics of which one and all could be proud'.[71] Pride, belonging and investment in the Malian polity cannot be taken for granted, and thus neither can the uncontested legitimacy of the Malian authorities.

Together, executive dominance, failed efforts to decentralise power, and growing socio-cultural cleavages make up the Malian context, in which demands for self-determination and autonomy react to broader political and economic conditions. A decade of decentralisation has 'done little to resolve the tension between state and customary authority or between the administrative drive toward uniformity and control' and the vibrant local social systems 'where there is a long history of self-governance and resistance to the state'.[72] Added to these administrative elements are the contours of contemporary cultural politics. Even if existing Malian territory remains non-negotiable, legacies of competing nationalisms will persist.[73] Successive Tuareg rebellions (1962–1964, 1990–1995, 2006), ethno-linguistically mobilised self-defence forces (e.g. Gandy Koy, Ganda Izo), and self-help responses to socio-economic cleavages, these culturally-mediated struggles of post-authoritarian transition and continue to condition Mali's development as a coherently sovereign nation-state.

These dynamics are re-emerging from the past 20 years' attempts to legitimate neoliberal democracy in Africa.[74] The domestic–foreign partnership 'project' of neoliberal political and economic development confronts specifically moral dimensions of legitimacy-seeking. Making space for elections still leaves open Malians' dissatisfaction with their experience of democratisation. Citing corruption, administrative inefficiency, clientelist opportunism, and 'consensus' politics, Malians found resonance in the promises of moral purification and order made in 2012 by putschists and Islamists alike.[75] Although military intervention provided much desired social order, struggles for moral authority – across the territory, not only in the north – are still central. President IBK is seeking legitimacy by embodying the identity of a 'fierce opponent of the overthrown former president Amadou Toumani Touré and his catastrophic management of the country' in order to 'symbolize a complete break with the corrupt former regime'.[76] As much as national and international elites may want to see this challenge met,[77] opportunities 'to engage in serious reforms and inclusive dialogue' appear to be dwindling; renewed clientelist practices seek 'short-term stability at the expense of long-term cohesion and inclusiveness'.[78]

International statebuilding and peacebuilding in Mali

Hence, it is in this historical and contemporary context we can analyse the transformation of the conflict and the claim that the French military intervention might have 'saved' Malian democracy and allowed the July 2013 presidential election.

The 2013 French war might be construed as the liberation of Mali from salafist insurgents or as an example of neocolonialism.[79] French troops were applauded by Malians; François Hollande was welcomed in Bamako and Timbuktu as a national hero; French Minister of Foreign Affairs Laurent Fabius gloated over the 'great success' of the operation and over the authorisation to deploy a UN peacekeeping force; French Minister of Defense Jean-Yves Le Drian kept repeating that 'France can be proud'; interim President Traoré did not miss an opportunity to be seen shaking hands with Hollande; and the international consensus over the necessity and success of the military operation was sustained (with the exception of Morsi's Egypt). While there is little evidence to support the interpretation that this was a (traditional) neocolonial action, the presence of the French army in MNLA-controlled Kidal when the Malian army was kept out, the imposition of elections on 28 July,[80] renewed violence in the fall of 2013 and spring of 2014, the suicide attack killing two and injuring seven UN peacekeepers in August 2014, the radicalisation of former Touareg leader Iyad ag Ghali,[81] and tensions between IBK's government, France and international financial institutions,[82] have given credence to rising Malian critiques of French involvement. However, this common binary interpretative frame (humanitarian versus neocolonial) comes at a cost: it externalises the problem of intervention, romanticises local agency, and forecloses investigation into the articulation between global militarised practices and transnational neoliberal governance.[83] Malian democratic governance was internationalised since its beginning in the early 1990s. Its failures in 2012 have not led to debating its value, but to its militarisation.

The current moment links to historical struggles around the foundations of the post-authoritarian nation-state of Mali, including administration and state–society relations, in light of the challenges for sustainable development and pluralist governance. Even more so than security problems, Mali faces the challenges of rebuilding and reforming not only the administrative control of the population, but also the legitimacy of that administration, as it attempts to implement security sector reform, meaningful inter-communal dialogue, and anti-corruption measures. Identifying a paradox at the interface of national and international sources of legitimacy, French political scientist Michel Galy insists that Mali's 'democracy under guardianship' has tended to empower politico-religious actors to criticise the Malian state's shortcomings while assisted by France, which has 'endorsed a long series of rigged elections before international community and regional bodies'.[84]

It may be that status quo ante bellum can no longer be envisioned as a durable future, given that its desirability and meanings are uneven across the national territory. It may be a significant point of debate whether an entirely or specifically 'liberal system/way of rule' is currently threatened, or if the 'liberal peace' is being imposed.[85] Nonetheless, whatever Mali's future, the French and international military intervention and continued presence has already established strategic relationships and set down key limitations. One is that Mali is and will be a secular state, because 'French military intervention seems to have basically frozen' the debate on the role of Islam in politics.[86] In light of the ubiquity of Islam-based discourses of moral authority and legitimacy, excluding faith-based voices from public life will present problems for the consolidation of peace in Mali. Indeed, according to Gregory Mann, 'arguments grounded in Islam are now much closer to being hegemonic than those grounded in the Malian state' and foreground the question about the capacity of a secular state to provide justice.[87] Another difficult limitation is that the international legitimacy of Malian sovereignty requires elections and a specific mode of governance for international aid resources to keep flowing. Mali's modus vivendi of the last decade, supported by international donor-partners, has stalled administrative decentralisation, instrumentalised economic development initiatives, and sustained elite-level patron-clientelism. Most clearly evident in Mali's north, the consequences of this governance mode indicate broader, systemic challenges to the administrative capacities and symbolic/persuasive influence of Malian state authority.

The successful prosecution of the French war and the subsequent hastily organised elections combine to legitimise the actions of the Malian state and international actors, and may further galvanise mainstream (possibly even majority) support for the consolidation of the neoliberal governance mode. Malian and French state authorities legitimised military intervention with 'terrorist' discourses and have sought electoral legitimation (July–August 2013) of the decision to intervene, as well as a return to status quo ante bellum of security and development aid partnerships. To the extent that such a return to pre-war conditions does not respond in a meaningful way to Mali's truncated political pluralism, the façade of 'democratic governance', which the coup and insurgency broke through, risks being re-established. Significantly, although the international legitimacy of Malian sovereignty requires elections and a specific mode of governance, the domestic legitimacy of Malian state sovereignty confronts multiple sites and types of struggle and contestation. The point at which international and domestic sources of legitimacy collide will continue to be the location of intense political negotiations and struggles. For instance, the strategic selection of dialogue partners from among regional and local elites has so far excluded dissenters from the processes necessary for the refoundation of the Malian state (see, for instance, the composition of the Commission for Dialogue). Without meaningful dissent and deliberation within political processes, those who feel unheard will continue to find alternative channels to pursue their interests and desires (e.g. identity-based mobilisation). Thus the incomplete development of pluralism in Mali presents risks to state integrity from within, risks that the French intervention, however legitimate, has obscured.

Conclusion

The French military intervention in Mali confirms the militarisation of peace and the 'aggressive attempt to introduce liberal values' into peace operations,[88] albeit in the specific context of Francophone Africa.[89] Certainly, the French war led to the further militarisation of the region on two counts: the UN deployed a significant military force in Mali (12,000 authorised troops) and the French military redeployed its military throughout the Sahel. Operation Serval was officially terminated on 13 July 2014 to be replaced by 'a larger and more permanent operation to fight against terrorism in the Sahel'. Operation Barkhane is composed of 3,000 French military troops in Mali, Mauritania, Chad, Niger and Burkina Faso, with its headquarters in Chad's capital N'djamena (where the French military has been since 1986). According to the Minister of Defence, the Barkhane force will be composed of 20 helicopters, 200 armoured vehicles, 10 transport airplanes, six fighter jets and three drones.[90]

While the electoral legitimisation of a specific mode of development and governance is not unique to Mali, what is striking is both the relative political and logistical ease and speed of the French military intervention and the Malian and international consensus supporting it. The historical specificity, the material capacities, and the diplomatic resources of French militarism in Africa allow the French state to deploy such force and, thus, to continue influencing political, economic, and cultural struggles and processes in Mali and elsewhere in Francophone Africa.[91] It seems unlikely that any other state than France could have deployed 4,000 troops in Mali on such short notice, with such efficiency, and with such strong regional support (particularly from Niger, Senegal, and Guinea). While in other contexts the deployment of such force was judged to be neocolonial (as in Côte d'Ivoire in 2011[92]), the management of contested political narratives in Mali through French military means received unambiguous support. This support, however, came only after everything else had apparently failed, notably the UN Security Council reluctance to act and authorise an African force and the failure of African regional organisations (notably the African Union) to get organised. It may be an important point of debate whether the initial international (the US, European, and African) resistance to intervene militarily in Mali indicates the limits of the 'liberal peace', but once the French government decided to launch Operation Serval, 'peace' through militarisation and democratic governance was aggressively pursued and supported by a broad range of African and non-African decision-makers, opinion-leaders, states, and international organisations. Despite opening debates over the merits of military intervention to solve the Malian crises, the French war found legitimacy and opportunity in the 'liberal peace' values of peace operations, 'war-against-terrorism' discourses, and their exclusionary practices, although raising the issue of (the possibility of) distinguishing UN peacekeeping from 'parallel' French counterinsurgency operations.[93]

The likelihood that salafist insurgents will return makes it impossible to predict the full consequences of such violence and counter-violence. The French war against such 'terrorists' is liable further to galvanise support for the southern-oriented and neoliberal mode of good governance. Thus, existing and violence-prone socio-cultural cleavages risk being deepened further rather than addressed and defused. To the extent that international conceptions of legitimate authority diverge from those rooted in Malian dynamics, the internationally-supported and recognised electoral process may persist in failing to integrate marginalised and minority communities. These inter-communal cleavages have been racialised and have become violent. For example, in 2012, slave-descended international human rights activist Ibrahim ag Ibaltanat noted that when 'the Islamist rebels seized power in northern Mali in April, many people in the slave-descended community [were] kidnapped, stoned to death, whipped, or forced into labour'.[94] Thus neatly illustrating that 'some people benefit from the political economy of war. In the north, there are quite a few interests lined up against peace'.[95]

While it seems likely that Malians will face prolonged international peacebuilding and statebuilding activities, the crucial fallacy would be to see Malians' rejection of relatively authoritarian governance and/or of radical Islamist governance as identical to an embrace of liberalism or Western norms of governance. Analysts need to interrogate rather than affirm a specifically neoliberal form of internationally-supported statebuilding and the superficial domestic electoralism that supports it. Far from there being no alternatives, multiple non-state sites of authority and legitimacy-seeking remain significant grounds for challenges. Through these challenges, state and non-state actors seek to reproduce and contest the legitimacy and authority of Mali's authorities. Clearer now are the conflict-prone legacies of competing ideas about the 'state' that might 'fail', and about the forms that post-colonial nationalism and post-Cold War statebuilding might take.

Acknowledgements

The authors would like to thank Florian Kühn, Mandy Turner and the anonymous peer reviewers for their encouragement, careful reading and constructive comments.

Notes

1 The Séléka rebel coalition attacked the capital Bangui in December 2012 and overthrew the Bozizé regime on 22 March 2013. France has a long history of military presence in the country. It has maintained 250 soldiers in Bangui since 2003 to support MICOMAX, but reinforced its military presence by 450 soldiers coming from its Gabonese base in March 2013. During President Hollande's visit to South Africa (14–16 October 2013), during which South Africa asked the French president to intervene militarily in CAR, there were discussions to increase the number of soldiers between 750 and 1,000. In December 2013, Operation Sangaris was launched. As of August 2014, the French contingent was at 2,000 soldiers in CAR. All numbers come from the French Ministry of Defence website (at: www.defense.gouv.fr/operations/centrafrique/operation-boali/l-operation-boali).
2 This is how the UN Security Council names the northern Malian groups in its Resolution 2100, UN doc. S/Res/2100, 2013.
3 Roland Marchal, *Is a Military Intervention in Mali Inevitable?*, Oslo: NOREF, October 2012; Hannah Armstrong, 'A Tale of Two Islamisms: Another Kind of Islamism Gains Ground in Southern Mali', *New York Times blog*, 25 January 2013 (at: http://latitude.blogs.nytimes.com/2013/01/25/another-kind-of-islamism-gains-ground-in-southern-mali/?_r=0).
4 See Bruno Charbonneau, 'Dreams of Empire: France, Europe and the New Interventionism in Africa', *Modern and Contemporary France*, vol. 16, no. 3, 2008, pp. 279–295.
5 On the effects of war on political formation and particularly on the construction of truth and knowledge, see Tarak Barkawi and Shane Brighton, 'Powers of War: Fighting, Knowledge, and Critique', *International Political Sociology*, vol. 5, no. 2, 2011, pp. 126–143.
6 Michael Shapiro, 'Warring Bodies and Bodies Politics: Tribal versus State Societies', *Body and Society*, vol. 1, no. 1, 1995, p. 111.
7 Nicolas van de Walle, *Foreign Aid in Dangerous Places: The Donors and Mali's Democracy*, Working Paper 61, Helsinki: UNU-WIDER, July 2012 (at: www.wider.unu.edu/publications/working-papers/2012/en_GB/wp2012-061/). Cf. Jamie Bleck and Nicholas van de Walle, 'Parties and Issues in Francophone West Africa: Towards a Theory of Non-Mobilization', *Democratization*, vol. 18, no. 5, 2011, pp. 1125–1145.
8 Accusations of French neocolonialism in the Malian case have been relatively rare, and generally unconvincing. Stephen Smith has called such critics 'lazy' because they simply rely on past French military adventures in Africa; Stephen Smith, 'In Search of Monsters', *London Review of Books*, vol. 35, no. 3, 2013 (at: www.lrb.co.uk/v35/n03/stephen-w-smith/in-search-of-monsters). While the evidence so far does not support the claim that this was a French neocolonial action (in the traditional sense of an invasion designed to advance French interests), the military deployment is still grounded in the assertion of global liberal governance norms, as the rest of the chapter shows.
9 Ansar Eddine has many transliterations (e.g. Ansar Dine, Ançar Dine, Ansar al-Din, and Ansar ul-Din). Iyad ag Ghaly's insurgent movement is not the same as Cherif Ousmane Madani Haidara's 30-year-old movement in southern Mali, called Ansar Dine.
10 For a summary of the first half of 2012, see International Crisis Group, *Mali: éviter l'escalade*, Rapport Afrique no. 189, Dakar/Brussels: International Crisis Group, 18 July 2012.
11 Marchal (note 3 above).
12 Diarra was forced to resign on 10 December 2012 after being briefly arrested by military personnel loyal to Sanogo.

13 Susanna Wing, 'Briefing Mali: Politics of a Crisis', *African Affairs*, vol. 112, no. 448, 2013, p. 481.
14 'Mali: histoire secrète d'une guerre surprise', *Le Nouvel Observateur*, 10 February 2013 (at: http://globe.blogs.nouvelobs.com/archive/2013/02/08/mali-histoire-secrete-d-une-guerre-surprise.html).
15 Informal discussion, National Intelligence Council high-level officer, Washington, DC, 14 March 2014.
16 United Nations Security Council, 'Resolution 2056', UN doc. S/Res/2056, 5 July 2012.
17 United Nations Security Council, 'Report of the Secretary-General on the situation in Mali', UN doc. S/2012/894, 28 November 2012, p. 20.
18 United Nations Security Council, 'Resolution 2085', UN doc. S/Res/2085, 20 December 2012.
19 Roland Marchal, 'Briefing: Military (Mis)adventures in Mali', *African Affairs*, vol. 112, no. 448, 2013, p. 488.
20 According to the French newspaper, *Le Nouvel Observateur*, after UNSC Resolution 2071 was adopted on 12 October, the French government received calls from several African governments who did not believe that AFISMA could perform its mission. At the end of October, France changed its strategy and planned its military support of the African force, including the presence of French troops on the ground. 'Mali: histoire secrète d'une guerre surprise', *Le Nouvel Observateur*, 10 February 2013 (at: http://globe.blogs.nouvelobs.com/archive/2013/02/08/mali-histoire-secrete-d-une-guerre-surprise.html).
21 The French government and media reports claimed that the rebels threatened Bamako, but this is highly unlikely. The small rebel forces (estimates varied greatly) could hardly have controlled both the north and a capital of 2 million people.
22 Cited in Smith (note 8 above).
23 On the production of dominant narratives about security threats coming from Africa, notably terrorist and Islamist related violence, see Malinda Smith (ed.), *Securing Africa: Post-9/11 Discourses on Terrorism*, Burlington, VT: Ashgate, 2010.
24 'UK to Consider Boosting French Mali Operation Support', *BBC News*, 22 January 2013 (at: www.bbc.co.uk/news/uk-politics-21136882).
25 Caitriona Dowd and Clionadh Raleigh, 'Briefing: The Myth of Global Islamic Terrorism and Local Conflict in Mali and the Sahel', *African Affairs*, vol. 112, no. 448, p. 499.
26 *Ibid.*, p. 501.
27 Isaline Bergamaschi, 'French Military Intervention in Mali: Inevitable, Consensual yet Insufficient', *Stability*, vol. 2, no. 2, 2013, p. 6.
28 See International Crisis Group, *Mali: sécuriser, dialoguer et réformer en profondeur*, Rapport Afrique no. 201, Dakar/Brussels: International Crisis Group, 11 April 2013, pp. 5–6; Marchal (note 19 above), p. 486; *Le Nouvel Observateur* (note 20 above).
29 André Bourgeot, 'Rébellions et djihadisme dans le septentrion malien', in Doulaye Konaté (ed.), *Le Mali entre doutes et espoirs: Réflexions sur la Nation à l'épreuve de la crise du Nord*, Bamako: Éditions Tombouctou, 2013.
30 According to *Le Nouvel Observateur* (note 20 above). If it was confirmed that Paris wrote the letter, this would not be a first in the history of Franco-African relations.
31 For a good (but incomplete) summary of the French Serval operation, see International Crisis Group (note 28 above), pp. 7–15.
32 Assemblée nationale (France), 'Audition de l'amiral Édouard Guillaud sur les enseignements de l'opération Serval', Commission de la défense nationale et des forces armées, Compte rendu 74, 22 May 2013.
33 Marchal (note 19 above), p. 495.

34 Roland Marchal, 'Mali: Visions of War', *Stability*, vol. 2, no. 2, 2013, p. 1.
35 United Nations Security Council, 'Resolution 2100', UN doc. S/Res/2100, 25 April 2013, p. 7.
36 Van de Walle (note 7 above), p. 3.
37 Gregory Mann, 'Mali: Democracy, the Coup and the Anti-globalization Left – Right Questions, Wrong Answers?' *African Arguments*, 18 April 2012 (at: http://africanarguments.org/2012/04/18/mali-democracy-the-coup-and-the-anti-globalization-left-right-questions-wrong-answers-by-gregory-mann/).
38 Nicholas van de Walle, *African Economies and the Politics of Permanent Crisis, 1979–1999*, New York: Cambridge University Press, 2001, p. 231.
39 International Monetary Fund, *Mali*, Country Report no. 13/44, Washington, DC: IMF, February 2013, pp. 34, 36 (at: www.imf.org/external/pubs/ft/scr/2013/cr1344.pdf).
40 *Ibid.*, p. 31.
41 Patrick Manning, *Francophone Sub-Saharan Africa, 1880–1995*, New York: Cambridge University Press, 1998, p. 186. See also René Otayek (ed.), *Afrique: les identités contre la démocratie?* Vol. 10, *Autrepart: Cahiers des sciences humaines nouvelles*, Paris: IRD Editions, 1999.
42 Shaka Bagayoko, *Le Cheminement du Mali vers un espace politique pluriel*, Bamako: Centre Djoliba, 1999, p. 25. Bagayoko's 'insurgés' does not mean violent militants, but rather the ensemble of those rising up against the dictatorship.
43 *Ibid.*, pp. 25–26.
44 Manning (note 41 above), p. 190. See also Claude Fay, 'La Democratie Au Mali: Ou Le Pouvoir En Pature', *Cahiers d'Etudes Africaines*, vol. 35, no. 1, 1995, pp. 19–53.
45 Roger Pfister, 'Political Changes – Road to democracy?', in B. Sottas and L. V. Vischer (eds), *L'Afrique part tous les matins: Stratégies pour dépasser le bricolage quotidien*, Bern: Peter Lang, 1995, p. 251.
46 Isaline Bergamaschi, 'The Fall of a Donor Darling: The Role of Aid in Mali's Crisis', *Journal of Modern African Studies*, vol. 52, no. 3, 2014, pp. 347–378.
47 See Baz Lecocq, *Disputed Desert: Decolonisation, Competing Nationalisms and Tuareg Rebellions in Northern Mali*, Leiden: Brill Academic, 2010; Bruce Hall, *A History of Race in Muslim West Africa, 1600–1960*, New York: Cambridge University Press, 2010.
48 Isaline Bergamaschi, 'The Role of Governance and Aid in Mali's Crisis', *Al Jazeera English*, 31 March 2013 (at: www.aljazeera.com/indepth/opinion/2013/03/201331412468880930.html). See also Alexis Roy, 'Mali: instrumentalisation de la société civile', *Alternatives Sud*, vol. 17, no. 4, 2010, pp. 111–118 (at: www.cetri.be/IMG/pdf/Mali.pdf).
49 Van de Walle (note 7 above).
50 *Ibid.*, p. 3.
51 Virginie Baudais and Grégory Chauzal, 'Les partis politiques et "l'indépendance partisane" d'Amadou Toumani Touré', *Politique africaine*, vol. 104, 2006, pp. 61–80. See also Julien Gavelle, Johanna Siméant and Laure Traoré, 'Le court terme de la légitimité: prises de position, rumeurs et perceptions entre janvier et septembre 2012 à Bamako', *Politique africaine*, vol. 130, no. 2, 2013, pp. 23–46.
52 Malians' preferences 'challenge the market economy paradigm' preferring 'economic democracy' that 'satisfies the basic economic needs of all citizens'. Massa Coulibaly and Amadou Diarra, 'Démocratie et Légitimation du Marché: Rapport d'Enquête Afrobaromètre au Mali: Décembre 2002', *Afrobarometer Working Papers*, no. 35, 2004, pp. 35.
53 *Ibid.*, p. 36, emphasis added.
54 Hall (note 47 above). See also Grégory Giraud, 'Cinquante ans de tensions dans la zone sahélo-saharienne', in Michel Galy (ed.), *La guerre au Mali*, Paris: La Découverte, 2013.

55 Daniel T. Osabu-Kle, *Compatible Cultural Democracy: The Key to Development in Africa*, New York: Broadview Press, 2000. See also Ousmane Sy, Michel Sauquet and Martin Vielajus, 'Entre tradition et modernité, quelle gouvernance pour l'Afrique?', Actes du colloque de Bamako, 23–25 January 2007. Sy, formerly Mali's interior minister, is also coordinator of the Alliance for Rebuilding Governance in Africa (ARGA).
56 Chris Cutter, 'Nation-Building in Mali', PhD thesis, University of California, Los Angeles, 1971, p. 96.
57 Osabu-Kle (note 55 above), p. 107.
58 Seydou Badian Kouyaté, *Les dirigeants d'Afrique noire face à leur people*, Paris: Maspero, 1964.
59 Jonathan M. Sears, 'Deepening democracy and cultural context in the Republic of Mali', PhD thesis, Queen's University Kingston, Ontario, 2007, pp. 57–61.
60 Z. K. Smith, 'Relationships between Poverty Reduction Approaches and Donor Support for Democracy: The Case of Mali', in J. S. Holmes (ed.), *New Approaches to Comparative Politics*, Lanham, MD: Lexington Books, 2003, p. 39.
61 Z. K. Smith, 'Mali's Decade of Democracy', *Journal of Democracy*, vol. 2, no. 3, 2001, p. 76.
62 Adame Bâ Konaré, 'Perspectives on History and Culture: The Case of Mali', in R. James Bingen, David Robinson and John M. Staatz (eds), *Democracy and Development in Mali*, East Lansing, MI: Michigan State University Press, 2000, p. 22.
63 Smith (note 61 above), p. 76.
64 Konaré (note 62 above), p. 16.
65 *Ibid.*, p. 15.
66 Sears (note 59 above), pp. 52, 162, 180, tracks the 'Greater Mali' tropes through various government, media, and NGO sources. Cf. J. McGuire, 'Sunjata and the Negotiation of Postcolonial Mande Identity', in Robert Austen (ed.), *In Search of Sunjata: The Mande Oral Epic as History, Literature, and Performance*, Bloomington, IN: Indiana University Press, 1999.
67 D. T. Niane cited in 'Crise malienne, Djibril Tamsir Niane: La solution passe par l'unité et une force de défense commune', *Le Soleil*, 12 February 2013 (at: http://fr.allafrica.com/stories/201302120892.html).
68 Gilles Holder, 'Au Mali, la guerre des islamismes', *Le Monde*, 28 January 2013 (at: http://actualite.portail.free.fr/societe/28-01-2013/au-mali-la-guerre-des-islamismes/).
69 *Ibid.*
70 Charles E. Benjamin, 'Legal Pluralism and Decentralization: Natural Resource Management in Mali', *World Development*, vol. 36, no. 11, 2008, p. 2255. See also Moussa Djire and Abdel Kader Dicko, *Les conventions locales face aux enjeux de la décentralisation au Mali*, Paris: Karthala, 2007.
71 Holder (note 68 above).
72 Benjamin (note 70 above), pp. 2260, 2267.
73 Charles Grémont, André Marty, Rhissa Ag Moussa and Younoussa Hamara Touré, *Les liens sociaux au Nord-Mali: Entre fleuve et dunes*, Paris: Karthala-IRAM, 2004. See also IRIN, 'Mali: Chronologie du conflit dans le nord du pays', Nations Unies Bureau de la Coordination des Affaires Humanitaires, 10 April 2012 (at: www.irinnews.org/fr/report/95263/mali-chronologie-du-conflit-dans-le-nord-du-pays).
74 Bruce J. Berman, 'Ethnicity and Democracy in Africa', Working Paper no. 22, Tokyo: Japan International Cooperation Agency Research Institute, 2010, pp. 3–32 (at: http://jica-ri.jica.go.jp/publication/assets/JICA-RI_WP_no. 22_2010.pdf).
75 Wing (note 13 above).

76 Sarah Diffalah, 'Mali. Les quatre défis du prochain président', *Le Nouvel Observateur*, 10 August 2013 (at: http://tempsreel.nouvelobs.com/monde/20130809.OBS2773/mali-les-quatre-defis-du-prochain-president.html).
77 'La France salue la formation du nouveau gouvernement malien', *Xinhua*, 9 September 2013 (at: http://french.cri.cn/621/2013/09/09/562s341043.htm); 'Propos de M. Fabius, Mali – Conférence de presse conjointe de M. Laurent Fabius, ministre des affaires étrangères, et du Premier ministre du Mali', Déclarations officielles de politique étrangère, 7 February 2014 (at: http://basedoc.diplomatie.gouv.fr/vues/Kiosque/FranceDiplomatie/kiosque.php?fichier=bafr2014-02-07.html#Chapitre5).
78 International Crisis Group, 'Mali: Reform or Relapse', 10 January 2014 (at: http://www.crisisgroup.org/en/regions/africa/west-africa/mali/210-mali-reform-or-relapse.aspx).
79 'Bruce Hall on the Battle for Timbuktu', interview by James Todd, Duke University, Durham, NC, 8 February 2013 (at: http://youtu.be/lNZrLCXcN4c).
80 Jeune Afrique revealed that at the end of June 2013 interim President Traoré asked to postpone the elections until October, but the French government refused. 'Présidentielle malienne: qui a fixé la date du premier tour au 28 juillet?', *Jeune Afrique*, 24 July 2013 (at: www.jeuneafrique.com/Article/JA2741p008.xml0/).
81 The once leader of the Touareg independence movement reappeared in August 2014 in a video, claiming allegiance to the radical Islamist agenda associated with al-Qaeda. Dorothée Thiénot, 'Le chef d'Ansar Eddine, Iyad ag Ghali, refait surface', *Jeune Afrique*, 6 August 2014 (at: www.jeuneafrique.com/Article/ARTJAWEB20140806185355/terrorisme-iyad-ag-ghali-video-youtubele-chef-d-ansar-eddine-iyad-ag-ghali-refait-surface.html).
82 Tensions with France concerned the signing of a defence agreement and the purpose and permanence of French military bases in the country. Tensions with international financial institutions rose when IBK purchased a new presidential jet.
83 Bruno Charbonneau, 'The Imperial Legacy of International Peacebuilding: The Case of Francophone Africa', *Review of International Studies*, vol. 40, no. 3, 2014, pp. 607–630.
84 Michel Galy, 'Introduction. Guerre au Mali, une intervention bien française', in Michel Galy (ed.), *La guerre au Mali*, Paris: La Découverte, 2013, p. 21.
85 We discuss this issue in: Bruno Charbonneau and Jonathan Sears, 'Fighting for Liberal Peace in Mali? The Limits of International Military Intervention', *Journal of Intervention and Statebuilding*, vol. 8, nos. 2–3, 2014.
86 Marchal (note 34 above), p. 3.
87 Gregory Mann, 'Mali: Which Way Forward?', *African Arguments*, 5 May 2013 (at: http://africanarguments.org/2013/05/14/mali-which-way-forward-a-chat-with-bruce-hall-baz-lecocq-gregory-mann-and-bruce-whitehouse/).
88 Michael Pugh, 'Reflections on Aggressive Peace', *International Peacekeeping*, vol. 19, no. 4, 2012, pp. 410–425.
89 Bruno Charbonneau and Tony Chafer (eds), *Peace Operations in the Francophone World: Global Governance Meets Post-Colonialism*, New York: Routledge, 2014.
90 'Mali: Le Drian annonce la fin de Serval remplacée par l'opération Barkhane contre le terrorisme au Sahel', *Jeune Afrique*, 13 July 2014 (at: www.jeuneafrique.com/Article/DEPAFP20140713104503).
91 See Bruno Charbonneau, *France and the New Imperialism: Security Policy in Sub-Saharan Africa*, Aldershot: Ashgate, 2008.
92 Bruno Charbonneau, 'War and Peace in Côte d'Ivoire: Violence, Agency, and the Local/International Line'. *International Peacekeeping*, vol. 19, no. 4, pp. 508–524.

93 This was an issue of significant concern at the UN Department of Peacekeeping Operation. Interview, official UN DPKO Mali desk, UN Secretariat, New York, 10 December 2013.
94 Geoffrey York, 'Mali chaos gives rise to slavery persecution', *Globe and Mail*, 11 November 2012 (at: www.theglobeandmail.com/news/world/mali-chaos-gives-rise-to-slavery-persecution/article5186368/).
95 Bruce Hall, in Baz Lecocq and Gregory Mann (eds), 'Mali: How Bad Can it Get?', *African Arguments*, 3 April 2012 (at: http://africanarguments.org/2012/04/05/mali-how-bad-can-it-get-a-conversation-with-isaie-dougnon-bruce-hall-baz-lecocq-gregory-mann-and-bruce-whitehouse/).

13 Intervention and non-intervention in the Syria crisis

Christopher Phillips

From March 2011, when protestors in the southern Syrian town of Deraa took to the streets initiating an uprising against President Bashar al-Assad, until August 2014, well over 150,000 are estimated to have died. Almost three million refugees have fled abroad, while more than six million more are internally displaced.[1] These figures dwarf those killed and displaced by Muammar Qaddafi's forces in Libya in 2011 and those targeted by Slobodan Milosevic in Kosovo in 1998–1999. But while these latter two intra-state crises prompted direct military intervention from Western governments, Syria's has not. The Assad regime has deployed brutal force against civilian areas, while the opposition has become more armed, divided and radical, committing its own, smaller-scale atrocities. Syria increasingly resembles the kind of humanitarian and security disaster that many academics and politicians insisted belonged in the past, while the international community is seemingly inert. Yet even though direct military action has been absent, it is a myth to claim there has been no international intervention in Syria. On the contrary, while the crisis has domestic origins, from the very beginning international actors have utilised an arsenal of intervention tools. Far from inert, this chapter contends that external actors, whether in support of Assad or his enemies, have played a major role in shaping the nature and scale of the crisis.

This chapter will examine external intervention in Syria from 2011 to 2014 by considering three questions. First, why has there been no Western direct military intervention, as deployed in Libya? Second, what forms of intervention have taken place and what impact have they had? Third, as a concluding point, does the Syria case offer clues as to the nature of future interventions in the Middle East? To address these, the chapter is split into six sections and a conclusion. The first section offers a brief synopsis of the Syrian crisis. The second section considers how academics and policy makers have defined 'intervention' and engages in the debates regarding the responsibility to protect (R2P) doctrine. It highlights the ambiguous character of R2P and the difficulty of gathering international support in cases such as Syria where it clashes with the interests of 'great powers', specifically the five permanent members of the UN Security Council (P5). I then examine the policies of the US and Russia, the only states capable of initiating or blocking a major military action in Syria, and explains why direct military intervention has not been forthcoming. The following section looks at the intervention short of direct military action conducted by Assad's Western enemies, principally the US, Britain and France. The fifth section offers an examination of Assad's regional enemies, notably Saudi Arabia, Qatar, Turkey and Israel. The sixth section then analyses the role of Assad's international allies: Russia, Iran, Iraq and the Lebanese militia, Hezbollah. In each of these sections the different intervention tools each has deployed, from diplomatic sanctions to sending troops, will be explored. These illustrate how a conflict often characterised as one that has failed to prompt external intervention, has in fact attracted decisive intervention from day one.

The Syria crisis

The Syrian crisis would almost certainly not have happened were it not for the Arab Spring. Syrians have lived under a Ba'athist dictatorship since 1963, but a combination of a feared security service, the co-option of certain sectarian and economic groups, and some genuine enthusiasm for Bashar al-Assad who succeeded his father as president in 2000 meant dissent was rare. However, there were long-term resentments against the regime, not least the perceived privileged position of Assad's Alawi sect (12 per cent of the population) and the indignity regularly meted out by security forces. More recently, Assad's crony-capitalist liberalising programme had hit the rural peasantry hard, most of which are Sunni Arabs who are underrepresented in positions of power despite constituting 65 per cent of the population. It was therefore hardly surprising that it was in a neglected rural Sunni market town, Deraa, where the uprising began in March 2011, when teenagers graffitied anti-regime slogans, inspired by the Tunisian and Egyptian revolutions.[2] When they were arrested and tortured by security forces, the townsfolk, similarly inspired, demonstrated. Yet, unlike in Tunisia and Egypt where security forces were more cautious, Assad's men responded with live fire. Protestors were killed, but their funerals attracted more protests, where yet more unarmed civilians were gunned down. This response sparked demonstrations elsewhere in the country, which the regime met with similar brutality. Within weeks, hundreds had been killed. Yet Assad showed no public remorse, offering only superficial concessions as the repression continued. Within a month, the tone of protest had shifted: from demanding reform to regime change.

Assad claimed that 'armed gangs' were infiltrating the demonstrations, compelling security forces to shoot back. Demonstrators countered that these were government thugs, the '*shabiha*' (ghosts), acting as agents provocateurs. Most evidence supports the protestors' claims that they were initially unarmed, but this gradually changed in the latter half of 2011. The regime's violence pushed some oppositionists to arm. In June, 120 regime forces were reported killed in the northern town of Jisr al-Shughour. Soon afterwards, as a stream of (mostly Sunni) soldiers deserted Assad's army, defected officers formed the Free Syria Army (FSA), committing to defeat Assad militarily. Various local armed groups emerged, adopting the 'FSA' banner and the first major clashes with the regime occurred in Rastan in September 2011. While non-violent demonstrations continued, they became fewer as the regime arrested peaceful organisers. The Syrian National Council (SNC), the opposition in exile dominated by émigrés formed in Istanbul in August 2011, struggled to keep up as armed elements that owed them little loyalty came to dominate opposition forces on the ground. The exact moment that the uprising became a civil war is unclear, but by early 2012 the slide towards violence was irreversible.[3]

The tone of the rebellion shifted too as Islamists became more visible. This was partly the result of earlier, more secular demonstrators being arrested or fleeing abroad, but it also reflected the dominance of armed groups. Though the new militias gathered around the secular FSA's banner, they were locally based, independent and mostly Islamist. As the war escalated, more and more radical groups emerged, including many Salafists and Jihadists who refused to accept FSA leadership. As Salafists and Jihadists proved the most disciplined and effective fighters, they came to dominate the rebels, feeling bold enough by September 2013 to denounce the FSA leadership and their exiled allies, the Syrian Opposition Coalition allies (SOC, which succeeded the SNC in December 2012). From 2013 onwards, some rebel groups had started fighting each other as well as Assad for a variety of reasons including competing ideologies, control of key resources, personal rivalries, or on the encouragement of external allies. While the emergence of the radical jihadist Islamic State in Iraq and Syria (ISIS) as the most powerful rebel group in Syria (and neighbouring Iraq) in 2014 prompted some renewed unity among the remaining opposition factions, divisions and sporadic fighting continued. Meanwhile, many Syrians remained loyal to Assad, often Alawis, Christians (8 per cent), Druze (3 per cent) and secular Sunnis. Assad initially won their support by falsely painting the opposition as Islamist radicals that would exact revenge on non-Sunnis and secularists were they to gain power. Sadly, the subsequent rise of Jihadists made this a self-fulfilling prophesy.

Despite ebbs and flows on the ground, by mid-2014, after over three years of civil war, Syria was divided militarily and politically. While fighting continued and territory changed hands, the prospect of the war's conclusion looked a long way off. The loose collection of rebel militia, dominated by Islamists but fighting among themselves, held chunks of the north including much of the commercial capital, Aleppo. However, much of the eastern territory they had previously 'liberated' from Assad was conquered in turn by ISIS who threatened the north as well. The regime retained the coast, the south and most of the capital, Damascus, and was expanding towards

Aleppo though also wary of the ISIS threat in the East, which it had initially welcomed as it fanned disunity among the rebels. Kurdish militia, independent of all sides, had carved out an autonomous region in the north-east, but was battling ISIS to retain it. Many parts of Syria, whether under rebel, regime, ISIS or Kurdish control, resembled a failed state.

Intervention and 'the responsibility to protect'

The grim descent into violence prompted many politicians and commentators, particularly in the West, to question the lack of external intervention. Such commentators limit their definition of 'intervention' to direct military action, meaning the deployment of the intervening states' own militaries. Recent precedents of such actions are the no-fly zones established in Iraq in 1991 and Libya in 2011. Yet this definition ignores the multiple activities undertaken by external actors short of direct military action. What about, for example, military action that is 'indirect', such as a state sending weapons but not troops? Or 'direct' action that is not military, such as economic or diplomatic sanctions? A central claim of this chapter is that by focusing too much on the absence of Western direct military intervention, commentators have ignored the other forms of interventions that have shaped the Syria conflict. A broader definition of 'intervention' is therefore needed. Here, 'intervention' is regarded as 'activity undertaken by a state, group within a state or international organisation which interferes in the domestic affairs of another state'.[4] Such 'interference' can cover a range of subversions from disparaging remarks through to outright war or annexation, and date as far back to the foundation of the modern international state system.[5] The Middle East and Syria, moreover, have been no strangers to interference, with Damascus facing various sanctions and boycotts since the 1980s.

Before looking at the interventions that have occurred, it is necessary to explain why direct military intervention has not taken place. This is particularly intriguing given that the Syrian crisis coincided with an apparently similar case when force was deployed: the United Nations Security Council authorising a no-fly zone over Libya, the first time direct military action had been authorised under chapter VII of the UN Charter against the wishes of a sovereign state. However, the Libya case was exceptional, rather than the signifier of a new era of muscular liberal intervention.

Much of the controversy over the UN decision to directly militarily intervene in Libya but not in Syria comes from the debate over the R2P doctrine. Academic advocates of R2P base the concept on a reformed interpretation of sovereignty to include responsibility, arguing that states can sacrifice sovereignty if they fail to protect the welfare of their citizens or prevent human suffering from spreading over their borders.[6] In such circumstances, the UN or any state, could and should intervene. In the 2000s, the UN adopted and codified R2P in three stages. First, the International Commission on Intervention and State Sovereignty (ICISS), in 2001, suggested that direct military intervention could be legitimate when 'major harm to civilians is occurring or immediately apprehended, and the state in question is unable or unwilling to end the harm, or is itself the perpetrator'.[7] Then the Outcome Document of the 2005 World Summit in New York, later endorsed by the UN General Assembly, called for collective action when 'national authorities manifestly fail to protect their populations from genocide, war crimes, ethnic cleansing and crimes against humanity'.[8] In 2009, the UN Secretary-General then added a third document, entitled 'Implementing the Responsibility to Protect', in which he reiterated the need for 'Member States to respond collectively in a timely and decisive manner when a state is manifestly failing to provide such protection.'[9]

To many supporters of R2P, such as Anne-Marie Slaughter, these three documents provide a framework for legal direct military intervention for humanitarian purposes. They argue that the Libya intervention was, as US national security adviser and R2P advocate Susan Rice claimed, 'inspired by R2P', and have called for similar action in Syria.[10] Yet Aidan Hehir argues that this codification of R2P actually makes direct military intervention more difficult. Along with limiting the causes of intervention to four highly debatable concepts – 'genocide, war crimes, ethnic cleansing and crimes against humanity' – the Outcome Document reinforces the power of the UN Security Council. It permits the P5 to veto any action against their allies or themselves – as, indeed, has happened in Syria with Russia and China using vetoes. The R2P documents give no details on who would implement any approved direct military intervention, and there are no plans for the creation of an independent UN military force.[11] Any agreement on intervention remains bound by the willingness of the more heavily-armed states to provide force.

UN Security Council Resolution 1973 (hereafter UN1973), the resolution authorising intervention in Libya, echoes much of the Outcome Document's language. It reiterates 'the responsibility of the Libyan authorities to protect the Libyan population,' and states that the regime's, 'widespread and systematic attacks ... may amount to crimes against humanity' – one of the four crimes to which R2P was resolved to respond.[12] In this case, the major flaws of R2P identified by Hehir were overcome: the P5 sanctioned it (though China and Russia abstained); there was willingness by powerful members (NATO) to provide military force; and one of the four 'crimes' (crimes against humanity) was identified (though UN1973 only stated that crimes against humanity 'may' have been committed). However, there was no actual mention of R2P in the resolution. As Justin Morris has shown, even Britain and the US, who have previously supported the idea of R2P, justified their actions in terms of national interests rather than responsibility.[13] This suggests that UN1973 did not usher in a new era of R2P. Even when the restrictions identified by Hehir were overcome, in the exceptional circumstances of the Libya crisis, R2P was still not officially invoked. Indeed, the reluctance by the US and others to refer to R2P implies recognition of its controversy, especially from Russia and China, and that the acceptance of a new understanding of sovereignty to include responsibility is still a long way off.

This is not to suggest that R2P is irrelevant or 'dead', but that the Libya case should not be identified as having set a new international norm of humanitarian intervention.[14] Despite (or in Hehir's view because of) attempts to codify R2P, its application remains selective according to the will of the P5. Libya was a particular case where national interests aligned with R2P, yet Syria is a case, like Darfur or Sri Lanka before it, where members of the P5 are reluctant to endorse direct military intervention. Although it is difficult to detach the Syrian case from the Libya one and, indeed, the Libyan experience greatly affected the course of the Syrian crisis, it is nevertheless necessary to do so when considering the absence of direct military intervention. R2P, despite its lofty ideals, seems likely to be applied in a case-by-case rather than universal basis given the structural weaknesses identified by Hehir and its inability to outstrip national interests as the prime driver of international politics.

The Syria case: direct military intervention is unpalatable

Direct military intervention thus remains dependent on the will of the P5 to act, whether with UN approval or not, something that advocates of R2P have failed to surmount. To explain why no such action has taken place in Syria, we must therefore examine the motives of the key states that could have made it happen: Russia and the US. Russia, in conjunction with China, has prevented any attempts to condemn the Assad regime at the UN, ensuring that no motion could proceed even if there was the will from other states. At the same time, the United States, the only opponent of Assad realistically capable of acting unilaterally in Syria without UN endorsement, has been reluctant to do so. While Libya was a case particularly favourable for direct military intervention, Syria was the opposite.

Russia's stance on Syria has been influenced by Libya. Given President Vladimir Putin's long-standing belief in preserving the 'constitutional order', Russia's abstention on UN1973, which effectively permitted direct military action, was surprising.[15] However, as seen by Moscow's approval of Western action in Afghanistan in 2001, when Russian interests are not threatened Putin has been willing to cooperate. Yet as the Libya operation progressed, Russia accused NATO of overstepping its UN mandate, pursuing regime change rather than the humanitarian protection Putin thought he had approved. Consequently, Putin responded to any talk of similar action in Syria with distrust.

Moreover, Assad's Syria was far more important to Russia than Qaddafi's Libya. While Qaddafi was long an international pariah, despite occasional expedient flirtations with the US, Syria has been Moscow's closest Middle

Eastern ally for decades. As Roy Allison has argued, many aspects of this alliance were more symbolic than material. Russian trade with Syria is insignificant, and arms exports accounted for only 5 per cent of Russian arms deliveries abroad, less than those sold to Assad's enemies in Israel and Turkey.[16] Similarly, the Russian naval base in the Syrian port of Tartus is tiny. However, symbolically, Moscow wants to retain its only Mediterranean base. Alliance with Syria has given Russia a foothold in the Middle East – a region it partly dominated during the Cold War. Giving this up would be a serious geostrategic error, particularly as US power seems to be waning in the region. There were also domestic reasons for backing Assad. Moscow feared an Islamist victory in Syria might boost Russian Jihadists, particular in the North Caucasus, barely 800km from Syria. Finally, there was a pragmatic strand: Assad's regime appeared far stronger than the opposition. While Libya's regime disintegrated within weeks, Syria's core remained strong, with military defections slow at first and key leaders remaining loyal. While the Libyan opposition united quickly, presenting themselves as a viable government-in-waiting, Syria's was fragmented. Accepting UN1973 may have represented a realistic assessment by Russia that Qaddafi was on the way out, even though it opposed NATO's attempts to hurry the process, but Assad was far more important and appeared stronger.

Russia's behaviour at the UN reflected its determination to prevent Western direct military intervention in Syria. In May and June 2011, Russia blocked draft resolutions by Britain and France to condemn Damascus' use of force. In February 2012, Russia, alongside China, vetoed a Security Council resolution from the Arab League calling on Assad to step down. A British-proposed resolution to extend the application of Western economic sanctions on Syria to include all UN members suffered a similar fate in June 2012. As late as May 2014, Russia joined with China to veto a UN Security Council resolution for the International Criminal Court (ICC) to investigate the conflict. Yet Russia has not been completely obstinate, backing resolutions 2042 and 2043 that endorsed the UN-led 'Annan Plan' to send observers to Syria in April 2012. It also endorsed the June 2012 UN-backed Action Group for Syria's 'Geneva Communiqué' that called for a negotiated solution to the crisis and the 'Geneva II' peace talks between the regime and the SOC in January and February 2014. However, contrary to hopes from the US, Moscow placed no pressure on Assad to grant concessions and the talks swiftly broke down. Indeed, Russia has consistently opposed anything that might weaken Assad or lead to direct military intervention. In November 2011, Russian Foreign Minister Sergei Lavrov stated bluntly that given the action in Libya had been used to support one side in a civil war, 'I don't think we will allow anything of that sort to be repeated'.[17] Lavrov's acknowledgement that it is within Russia's power as a veto-holding member of the UN Security Council to 'allow' direct military intervention or not, reiterates how any action is contingent on the will of the P5.

However, while Russia (and China) created an impasse at the UN, leading NATO members were cautious about direct military intervention anyway. Prominent individuals, such as US Republican Senator John McCain, made the case for a no-fly-zone while French Foreign Minister Alain Juppe suggested 'humanitarian corridors', but this had little bearing on policy.[18] Russian and Chinese resistance at the UN prevented the kind of momentum gathered by UN1973. Lack of international support for direct military intervention was not helped by the absence in Syria of a united opposition that could offer a viable alternative in the way the Libyan NTC had done.[19] And so the divisions seen in the Security Council in the run up to Kosovo in 1999 and Iraq in 2003 were not repeated, when the US and Britain pushed for intervention in the face of Russian-led opposition. The US, and by extension NATO (except for Turkey), was reluctant to intervene due to the particularity of the Syrian case and geostrategic concerns in the region.

Unlike Libya, Syria sits on several, often overlapping, geostrategic faultlines, particularly sensitive to the US. Alongside its long-standing alliance with Russia, Syria is a close ally of Iran, a source of tension for the US and its regional allies Saudi Arabia and Israel. As a majority Sunni country but with a government dominated by the minority Alawites, a distant offshoot of Shiism, Syria resides on the growing fault-line between these Muslim sects, who are being increasingly manipulated by Iran and Saudi Arabia in their regional 'Cold War'.[20] Moreover, it borders two of the US's closest allies, Israel and Turkey, and three potentially unstable states, Lebanon, Jordan and Iraq, meaning that any spill-over could have serious repercussions.

While such fault-lines would prompt caution at any time, the Syria crisis came amid an era of diminished Western, particularly US, influence in the region. There is growing evidence that US power in the Middle East is declining.[21] While it retains a strong military presence in the Gulf, the result of the imperial overstretch of the Iraq occupation, lack of resources after the global financial crisis and the fall of key allies after the Arab Spring suggests that the post-Cold War era of *Pax Americana* in the Middle East may be over. The US must now compete with other actors, such as Russia or regional players like Turkey, Qatar, Saudi Arabia and Iran. The particular fault-lines in Syria make this more pronounced but the reluctance of the US to be dragged in is also symptomatic of a more cautious US engagement with the region. This may be more due to lack of will than a permanent structural shift, with President Obama particularly disinclined to follow the Middle East adventures of his predecessor George W. Bush. However, the increased assertiveness of regional actors and Russia's influence in Syria suggests that a 'post-American' Middle East could be a more enduring legacy of the crisis.

The reasons for Obama's reluctance for direct military action are manifold. One is the legacy of his predecessor's unilateralism, which cost the US regional credibility and prompted war-weariness among the US public. There were barely any demonstrations in US cities demanding action.

When the prospect of US military strikes was raised in 2013 after Assad's alleged use of chemical weapons, the overwhelming majority polled were against NATO involvement.[22] This included Congress who looked set to humiliatingly oppose Obama's plans only for the vote to be called off when the US accepted a Russian-initiated plan for Assad to chemically disarm instead. Another deterrent is the scale and cost of direct military intervention in Syria. After UN1973 it became clear that, despite Obama's intentions to 'lead from behind', the US's NATO allies did not have the military capacity to lead. Libya showed that large-scale Western interventions could only take place if Washington provided the majority of forces. That campaign cost the US$1.6 billion. A similar campaign in Syria would be considerably more expensive, and was estimated by Joint Chiefs of Staff General Martin E. Dempsey to require at least 70,000 servicemen.[23] Logistically, Syria is more populous than Libya, with 22 million rather than 6 million, and its cities are dispersed over a diverse landscape, unlike Libya, which had an easier operational terrain. Assad's defences are stronger, composed of Russian surface-to-air missiles – armaments Putin has deliberately strengthened since 2011.[24] Finally, there were serious questions over whether direct military intervention would actually succeed. Divisions within the Syrian opposition prompted fears that regime change would most likely lead to anarchy. The Libyan opposition has struggled to re-impose order after Qaddafi's fall and it did not have to deal with a heterogeneous population like Syria's. The chances of ethnic and sectarian violence if the state collapses in Syria is therefore even higher.

Despite a general reluctance, the US has occasionally threatened to use force unilaterally against Assad. Obama threatened force in August 2012 if Assad deployed chemical weapons, and then planned a military strike when they were allegedly used in East Ghoutta in Damascus in August-September 2013. However, these were to be limited retaliatory strikes for violating the White House's 'red line', rather than a concerted military campaign for regime change or humanitarian reasons, as deployed in Libya. Moreover, the willingness of Obama to cancel these operations in the face of domestic and international opposition, for example via the face-saving Russian deal, suggests wariness about direct military intervention even with limited strikes. Indeed, the episode in late summer 2013 seemed to confirm that the US had no appetite for direct military intervention against Assad.

The stunning rise of ISIS in 2014, crossing the Syrian-Iraqi border to take over Mosul, prompted a belated military response from Obama in northern Iraq, launching airstrikes in August to protect Kurdish allies. This raised the possibility of similar strikes on ISIS' positions in eastern Syria. However, in announcing the strikes Obama emphasised the need to protect US personnel on the ground in Iraq and his cooperation with both Baghdad and Irbil, neither of which apply to Syria.[25] Moreover, if any strike in Syria did come, it would likely be defined through a narrow, security lens targeting a terrorist non-state actor – Assad's enemy, no less. This would be more akin to drone strikes in Yemen and Pakistan, rather than the direct military intervention in a civil war against a sovereign regime proposed in 2012-13.

By other means: Western intervention in Syria

While direct military intervention has largely been ruled out, alternative intervention techniques have been readily utilised. While commentators have been distracted by debates over direct military intervention, various other acts of interventionism have shaped the Syrian civil war. The interveners can be divided into three groups. The first is made up of the US, Britain and France, often in conjunction with the EU, who have primarily used diplomatic and economic tools against Damascus and eventually showed a reluctant willingness to help Syria's armed rebels. The second group involves Assad's regional enemies, notably Saudi Arabia, Qatar and Turkey, who led efforts to recognise, finance and eventually arm the rebels. Another enemy, Israel, deployed direct military intervention for defensive reasons, but seemed less enthusiastic about trying to influence the course of the conflict. The third group is made up of Assad's allies: Russia, Iran, Iraq and Hezbollah, whose support has ranged from early diplomatic protection through to finance, weaponry and manpower.

Western governments initially hoped that diplomatic and economic pressure could push Assad to stop the violence or, alternatively, persuade elements of the regime to overthrow him, as occurred in Egypt. However, having spent most of the 2000s isolating Assad, Western states did not have the same leverage they had in Egypt. Moreover, Assad's regime was used to withstanding sanctions. Western governments underestimated the resilience of the 'coup-proofed' regime that Hafez al-Assad had built, wrongly expecting it to disintegrate under pressure.[26] Consequently Western sanctions had little effect. Yet rather than shift tactics, frustrated Western states continued to ratchet up pressure believing the regime would eventually crack.

Despite their historically difficult relationship, in a sign that they feared instability in Syria, Western states initially adopted a soft line with Assad. But as crackdowns escalated, on 29 April 2011 the US expanded its sanctions on Syrian institutions and individuals, and added Assad's name on 18 May. The EU replicated these moves, creating its own list on 17 May and adding Assad on 23 May. These lists steadily grew, with the EU alone initiating over 20 rounds, freezing the foreign assets of 180 individuals and 54 institutions by the end of 2012.[27] However, with no sign that Assad was shifting or that a coup was imminent, on 18 August, the US, France, Britain and Germany simultaneously called on Assad to stand down. In hindsight these early diplomatic moves appear misguided, based, as they were, on the false assumption, briefed in the White House and State Department in 2011, that the regime would easily fold; believing Syria to be the latest 'domino' in the Arab Spring. Instead, Western governments expended key diplomatic cards for little gain as this removed the possibility of future negotiations with Assad

(Non-)intervention in the Syria crisis 261

without losing face. Soon afterwards the US and (more importantly given the vital trade with the Netherlands, Italy and Germany) the EU banned imports of Syrian oil – the source of 20 per cent of government revenue.[28] However, while this crippled the Syrian economy, the crackdown continued.

Having removed the possibility of negotiation, Western leaders increased their support for Assad's opponents, meeting the main opposition group, the Syrian National Council (SNC) that formed in Istanbul in August 2011. However, while the NTC in Libya was recognised as the 'sole legitimate government of Libya' by France, Britain and the US even before Qaddafi fell, the SNC was merely deemed, 'a leading and legitimate representative of Syrians seeking a peaceful democratic transition,' by the US.[29] Many doubted the SNC's ability to unite different opposition groups and, unlike the NTC, it held no territory. Even when the opposition was repackaged into the National Coalition for Syrian Revolutionary and Opposition Forces (SOC) in November 2012, there was only cautious recognition. The US declared it 'a legitimate representative of the Syrian people,' but not 'of Syria'.[30] The shadow of Iraq and Libya influenced Western thinking. Policy makers were wary of backing an ineffectual exile group with little support on the ground, as the US had with Ahmed Chalabi's Iraqi National Congress in 2003. Moreover, with direct military intervention no longer an option, the US and its Western allies were reluctant to offer the SNC/SOC the same recognition as they had the NTC in Libya as it would increase the expectations to follow up with a similar military campaign.

Western direct military intervention in Libya played a key role in transforming the Syria crisis from an uprising into a civil war, as it emboldened rebels to take up arms. Early protests in Syria were modelled on the peaceful methods that successfully overthrew dictatorships in Tunisia and Egypt. The move to arm in summer 2011 was mostly the result of the repeated brutality of Assad's forces, not seen in Tunisia or Egypt, and the detention of many of the peaceful leaders. However, at the same time NATO and Libya's rebels were offering an alternative model of violent opposition supported by external direct military intervention. It is no coincidence that the first major armed group, the Free Syrian Army (FSA) was formed in August 2011 at the peak of the Libya conflict. Nor that one of the first statements released by its nominal leader, Colonel Ri'ad al-Asaad, was a call for weapons and a no-fly zone from the international community.[31] Western leaders can hardly be blamed for this turn, as it was mostly down to the optimistic interpretation of UN1973 by Syria's rebels that such intervention would be replicated. However, Western voices such as French Foreign Minister Alain Juppe irresponsibly raised expectations of 'humanitarian corridors'. While Obama and others could have stated that direct military intervention was unlikely, possibly tempering the rush to arm by rebels, this would have undermined Western strategy to pressure the regime into collapse.

By early 2013, neither diplomatic pressure, economic sanctions nor supporting the exiled opposition groups had succeeded in toppling Assad.

Indirect military support for the rebel fighters was thus cautiously explored. There was division in the White House, with Obama rejecting CIA chief General David Petraeus's plan in summer 2012 to arm and train the rebels. However, fears that weapons would end up in the hands of the Jihadists fighting Assad were eventually overcome as the 'moderate' rebels lost ground to radicals. Although the US denies allegations that the CIA were covertly helping to funnel weapons via Turkey since early 2012, it publically sent $60 million in 'non-lethal' aid to the FSA's Supreme Military Council (FSA-SMC) via its flagging ally, the SOC, in March 2013.[32] Soon afterwards, in May 2013, Britain and France successfully lobbied the EU to lift its arms embargo on Syria's rebels and in June Obama authorised a modest cache of US arms to be sent to the FSA-SMC.[33] Then, after the successes of ISIS in 2014, Obama asked Congress to approve a further $500 million in military training and equipment for vetted moderate militia, though this was not due to be sanctioned and delivered until 2015. Despite appearances, the move to arm the rebels was a continuation of previous strategies rather than a shift in favour of a military solution. It was first designed to boost the 'moderate' FSA-SMC, to stem the success of jihadists, especially ISIS after 2014. Second, it was intended to continue and extend the pressure on Assad to compromise or quit, by showing that the West was willing to arm his enemies.

However, again many of these moves were based on miscalculations that ended up shaping the conflict. The weapons sent to the 'moderate' rebels were too few to have the impact needed to prevent fighters haemorrhaging to more radical groups. If anything it did more damage by making them look like Western stooges. The moderates were further undermined when Obama reversed his pledge to launch air strikes after the Goutta chemical weapons attack. Not surprisingly, soon afterwards, in September 2013, eleven of the largest militia, including several groups that had previously fought with the FSA, denounced both the SOC and the FSA. Similarly, the threat of arming the rebels had the reverse impact intended. Having agreed to a Russian suggestion to attend proposed peace talks, the lifting of the EU arms embargo prompted a *volte face* from Damascus. Reports then surfaced that Russia had shipped a new batch of S-300 SAM missiles in response. Assad's forces also stepped up their military campaign to make gains before any Western arms arrived, scoring a major victory in the battle for Qusayr in May–June 2013. Whether intended or not, Western intervention, particularly their miscalculations, had a major impact on the course of the conflict.

Assad's regional enemies: Turkish, Saudi and Qatari intervention

While Assad's main regional opponents, Turkey, Saudi Arabia and Qatar, have been more willing to help the rebels than their Western allies, they too have shown caution. Each opposes Assad for a different reason. Turkey, which forged a close relationship with Syria in the late 2000s, initially insisted it could persuade Assad to reform. Yet when this failed, an angry and humiliated Prime Minister Recep Tayipp Erdogan dramatically cut ties with Assad and backed the opposition in late summer 2011.[34] Beyond Erdogan's personal stake, ensuring a friendly government in Syria was also initially part of Ankara's 'strategic depth' policy for increasing Turkey's influence in the region. With that policy faltering in parallel with the chaos in Syria, Ankara increasingly saw the crisis through a security lens, hoping to contain the fighting, refugees and general disorder crossing its longest border. This danger was revealed in May 2013 when two car bombs killed 53 in the border town of Reyhanli, allegedly by a group of pro-Assad Turks. Turkey also fears that instability in Syria's Kurdish region could exacerbate its own Kurdish issue. While Erdogan had started a peace process with PKK separatists in 2012, were it to break down, fighters could potentially exploit chaos in Syria to launch attacks into Turkey.

Qatar also turned on its former ally, Assad, with a wider strategy in mind. The gas-rich emirate quickly saw in the Arab Spring the potential to boost its regional influence: forging close ties with emerging Islamists, particularly the Muslim Brotherhood in Egypt and Tunisia, and supporting Libya's rebels. In Syria, the Qatari-owned al-Jazeera news channel reported the Deraa protests from an anti-Assad angle from the beginning. As seen by the absence of coverage when protests broke out in neighbouring ally Bahrain, Qatar is able to influence the channel's editorial policy when it is in its national interests. Saudi Arabia, in contrast, was more reluctant to encourage the Syrian public against Assad at first, fearing the Arab Spring could unleash protest at home. However, once the Syrian unrest began, Riyadh saw the opportunity to weaken its enemy Iran by defeating Tehran's allies in Damascus. Saudi and Qatari media have also portrayed the Syria unrest as a sectarian clash. This narrative sees the Sunni majority rising up against the Shia (Alawi) rulers. This might be a genuine representation of their rulers' sectarian, Wahabist ideology, or alternatively a cynical ploy to gain mass support from Arab Sunnis against Shia Iran.

Saudi Arabia, Qatar and Turkey initially echoed the West's diplomatic approach by withdrawing their ambassadors from Damascus in August 2011. With traditional Arab heavyweights Egypt and Syria incapacitated by domestic instability, in November Saudi and Qatar were able to push through an Arab League peace plan that involved Assad standing down. When this was rejected by Syria, it was suspended from the League. At the same time, Arab League sanctions were announced by Qatari Prime Minister and Foreign Minister Sheikh Hamad bin Jassim al-Thani, due to Qatar's official role holding the League's rotating presidency, but also indicating Doha's rising influence. Turkey, not an Arab League member but active in the Organisation of the Islamic Conference (OIC) that also condemned Assad's violence in August 2011, announced that it would implement similar sanctions and endorsed the Arab League's Syria plan and its successor, the UN's eventually aborted 'Annan plan'.[35]

However, this did little to deter Assad. The sanctions were poorly implemented by Syria's allies and key trading partners, Lebanon and Iraq. Syria's economy nosedived, but this was more due to the war and Western oil sanctions. Frustrated by the lack of progress, Turkey, Saudi and Qatar deployed alternative intervention tools earlier than the West. Even before it cut relations with the Assad government, Turkey allowed both the SNC and FSA to be based within its territory. Turkey's ruling AKP had previously forged ties with their ideological fellow travellers Syria's exiled Muslim Brotherhood, and ensured they dominated the newly-formed SNC. Although this led to charges that it was a Turkish proxy, by January 2012 the SNC was receiving financial support from Saudi Arabia and Qatar as well, the latter also having long-standing links with the Syrian Muslim Brotherhood.

A major departure from Western strategy came in spring 2012 when the Gulf states increased support for the armed opposition. By early June, Western journalists were witnessing Saudi and Qatari representatives handing over arms on the Turkish–Syrian border.[36] Riyadh offered salaries to rebel fighters, administered through the SNC, to encourage defections from Assad's army. Once again, this intervention helped shape the character of the armed rebels, with several groups adopting Islamist ideologies to increase their chances of receiving Gulf arms.[37] Considerable funding also came from private donations from Syrians and others living abroad, particularly via Kuwait, with many backing jihadist groups such as Jubhat al-Nusra and, allegedly, Islamic State in Iraq and Syria (ISIS). Turkey, whose military had occasionally clashed with Assad's forces, including the shooting down of a Turkish jet, also increased its support for the armed rebels. The FSA leadership in Hatay were given greater freedom to cross into Syria to coordinate, although increasingly these leaders were marginalised as Islamist militia dominated.[38] Turkish officials denied offering more than logistical support, but multiple reports from the border contradict this.[39] This surge in support for the armed rebels, reportedly coordinated through the US's Incirlik airbase in Turkey with US approval, coincided with gains on the ground in summer 2012. FSA rebels adopted sophisticated tactics only possible with external advice and assistance, such as targeting under-defended airbases to counter Assad's superior air power.

However, Turkey, Qatar and Saudi Arabia were inconsistent. Despite each calling for Western direct military action, none were willing to commit forces. Turkey feared Russian or Iranian retaliation if it attacked Syria, while Qatar and Saudi Arabia have limited troops. They increasingly pressed the US to allow them to deliver heavy weaponry, but Washington, as their weapons supplier, consistently refused. Arms have been sent sporadically, but rebels complained of short supplies. In a conflict dominated by regional militia, the three states have tended to support different groups, undermining rebel unity. Turkey and Qatar supported 'moderate' Islamists connected to the Syrian Muslim Brotherhood, but also allegedly facilitated jihadist activity, including JAN and even ISIS, recognising they were the strongest anti-Assad forces. In contrast, Saudi Arabia, which loathes the Muslim Brotherhood and publicly fell out with Turkey and Qatar over backing an anti-Brotherhood coup in Egypt in summer 2013, backed Salafist militia as a counterweight both inside and outside the FSA umbrella. It also staunchly opposed the jihadists, fearing domestic blowback. In late 2013, Saudi Arabia shifted its principle backing to the newly-formed 'Islamic Front', a Salafi-dominated umbrella group of non-jihadists attempting to gain recognition as the main armed opposition. Soon afterwards major clashes broke out between Islamic Front and ISIS, in an attempt by the Saudi-backed rebels to check the jihadists' growing power, although this front gradually dissolved as ISIS fought back in mid-2014. In many ways, the rebels' various divisions reflect the lack of unity among their external backers, another means by which intervention has shaped the civil war.

Israel's stance is also of interest. Uniquely among Assad's enemies, Israel has resorted to direct military action: bombing several arms convoys and facilities since early 2013 intending to prevent Damascus transferring weapons to Hezbollah.[40] Yet unlike Assad's other foes, Israel has no enthusiasm for the opposition. Though Assad is an enemy, the Syrian–Israeli border has been quiet since 1973, and Israel fears instability in Syria will change that. It also worries that the collapse of the Assad regime might see its weapons transferred to Hezbollah, although these fears subsided after the 2013 UN chemical weapons plan. At the same time, a victory for Islamists could lead to renewed conflict anyway.[41] Israel thus is acting in a reactive, defensive manner, and has shaped the conflict less profoundly than other actors.

Assad's allies: intervention from Russia, Iran, Hezbollah and Iraq

The most consistent interventionists in the Syria crisis have been Assad's principle allies: Russia and Iran, with the latter often acting in conjunction with its regional allies, Hezbollah and, to a lesser extent, Iraq. As discussed, Russia provided diplomatic support at the UN. Even when the deadlock was eventually broken on chemical weapons in summer 2013, Moscow ensured a favourable outcome for Damascus. Russia has further aided Assad economically and militarily. In reaction to EU sanctions that prevented an Austrian bank from printing Syria's banknotes, for example, Moscow delivered over 30 tonnes of new notes ensuring that salaries could be paid.[42] Similarly, a generous line of credit was agreed for arms supplies. Moscow insists it is honouring pre-existing contracts. Previous orders have been honoured, such as the SS-N-26 Yakhont air defence missiles, sent in 2011 and 2013, or the repair of Mi-24 Helicopter gunships. However, there were reports of new purchases, including a US$550 million contract for advanced counterinsurgency jets, later put on hold.[43] In a symbolic show of force,

Russia also sent a flotilla of warships to Tartus in summer 2012 and sent military advisors to operate the new SAM batteries.

The other major power supporting Assad is Iran. This alliance of convenience that formed after the Iranian Revolution of 1979, against common enemies in Iraq and Israel, evolved ever closer in the 2000s and is now vital to Assad's survival.[44] Although Islamist Iran has little ideological affinity with the secular Ba'athist regime, its alliance with Syria is a major regional strategic asset as it offers a key supply line to Hezbollah in Lebanon to keep pressure on one enemy, Israel, and reduce the influence of another, Saudi Arabia. Tehran aided Damascus's attempts to crush early protests, providing riot equipment and offering technical assistance in cyber warfare against the opposition's social media.[45] Financial support has been provided, including $9 billion in aid by early 2012 alone and a $3.6 billion credit facility agreed in mid-2013.[46] Iran joined Russia in restocking Assad's arsenal, as well as sending military advisors. And up to 15,000 Iranian troops have fought in Syria, under the command of Republican Guard commander, Qassem Suleimani, according to reports.[47] While Iran denies direct military intervention, opposition fighters claim to have heard 'regime forces' speaking Farsi.[48] With stakes so high for Iran, and Assad's forces weakened by two years of fighting and over 100,000 defections, an Iranian military presence is plausible.

In contrast, Hezbollah has openly admitted having a military presence in Syria. The Lebanese Shia militia and party has readily followed the line of its Iranian patron also recognising the existential threat Syria's uprising poses to its own future. Hezbollah leader Hassan Nasrallah stated its fighters were in Syria, despite it costing him hard-earned domestic and regional popularity among Sunnis. While Hezbollah has been reportedly advising Assad since 2011, officially its first fighters in Syria were there independently. By 2013, however, Hezbollah was openly fighting in Qusayr. Nasrallah justified intervention stating the need to save Syria from, 'the hands of America, Israel and the takfiris [Sunni jihadists]'.[49] Crucially, Hezbollah and Iran helped reorganise the regime's military into a more effective force, resulting in the Qusayr victory. They also funded and trained new militias, the Basij-like Jaysh al-Sha'abi (people's army) and reorganised Assad's military structure, forming the eventually vital National Defence Force reserve unit in 2013.

Finally, Iraq has played an unlikely role in supporting Assad. Though Prime Minister Nuri al-Maliki was close to Iran and broadly acquiesced to Tehran's strategy, he was no mere client.[50] Nor was Maliki a friend of Assad, having previously accused Syria of allowing insurgents into Iraq. However, he feared that triumph for the Sunni-led Syrian opposition may renew rebellion among Iraq's own minority Sunnis, especially given how many Syrian militias, such as Jubhat al-Nusra and ISIS, hosted Iraqi fighters. Syria's Kurds also alarmed Maliki. To focus his attention elsewhere, Assad withdrew from Syria's eastern Kurdish provinces in 2012 and, since then, the long-oppressed Kurds have been running their own affairs, independent of both the regime and the opposition. Any gains for Syria's Kurds threatened to boost the separatist impulses of Iraq's oil-rich autonomous Kurdish region. Thus Iraq facilitated Iran's logistical support for Assad, permitting Iranian cargo planes and trucks to pass through its land and air space. Baghdad also gave direct economic and diplomatic support by providing cheap fuel, defying Arab League sanctions. Moreover, Maliki gave his blessing when, as part of its reorganisation and supplementing of the Syrian military, Iran recruited thousands of Iraqi Shia fighters to fight in Syria.[51] While these interventions certainly helped Assad survive, they ultimately failed to prevent the spill-over Maliki feared with ISIS's 2014 seizing of Mosul prompting a major Iraqi crisis and, ironically, the prime minister's own downfall.

Conclusion

This chapter has critically explored three questions concerning intervention in the Syria crisis. The first focused on why there has been no Western direct military intervention. It was argued that there are three main reasons for this. First, the notion of responsibility to protect (R2P), whether due to its narrow codification or a lack of genuine support from key powers, is not sufficiently established as an international norm to trump the strategic interests of the five permanent members of the UN Security Council (P5). Second, to ensure that no momentum for intervening could gather, Russia, with support from China, has blocked any UN attempts to condemn the Assad regime. Finally, and arguably most importantly, the one state with the ability to lead a major direct military intervention, the US, has been reluctant to do so. The particularities of the Syrian case, the geostrategic faultlines it sits on, the potential for the proliferation of chemical weapons and jihadist groups, Syria's uncompromising terrain, Assad's superior defences, lack of public support and a reduction in US regional influence have all deterred the Obama administration.

The second question concerned the forms of external intervention that have taken place and what impact they have had on the conflict. It was argued that 'intervention' as a concept needs a broader definition than direct military action. Interference has been a staple of international relations since the emergence of the modern state system and Syria was on the receiving end long before 2011. Since the crisis began, already-existing levers of influence were greatly expanded by both Assad's enemies and allies, and these have played a key role in shaping the conflict. Western direct military intervention in Libya, and the fact that leaders appeared unwilling to refute hopes that a similar no-fly zone would be launched in Syria, raised expectations among the rebels and helped militarise Syria's uprising. The subsequent inability of the West to meet these expectations, and the rebels' reliance for weapons and money on private Gulf actors and the governments of Qatar, Saudi Arabia and Turkey, played a role in their gradual Islamisation and radicalisation. At the same time, it is unlikely that the Assad regime would have survived were it not for the diplomatic, military and financial support of key allies Russia, Iran, Iraq and Hezbollah. The Syria crisis had domestic origins, but external actors have greatly shaped its course and character.

The third question related to whether the Syrian case offers any clues as to the shape of future interventions in the Middle East. Three observations can be made. First, the Syria case should not be used, as some have, to claim that R2P is dead. As seen by the Libya case, the doctrine is continually evolving and its codification has paradoxically made implementation difficult. The fact that the Syria crisis fell outside its practical scope, given P5 objections, does not mean that in different circumstances elsewhere it may not be applied. The Syria case does, however, confirm that R2P is a selective, case-by-case doctrine and its goal of building an international system where sovereignty is based on responsibility is a long way off. The second observation to arise from the Syrian case is on whether or not the focus on direct military intervention has detracted attention from the other interventions that have taken place. Alternative interventions as outlined here can have huge impacts, not just in terms of facts on the ground, but also in terms of shaping attitudes and approaches. More research is required on the impact of these kinds of interventions in such crises.

Finally, the diverse kinds of intervention seen in the Syria crisis might prove an increasing trend in the Middle East for years to come. As discussed, the Syria crisis has exposed the diminution of Western influence in the region, caused by the Iraq war, the global financial crisis, and the Arab Spring. It has signalled increased Russian willingness to act in the region, and has also highlighted the activity of regional actors Saudi Arabia, Qatar and Turkey. It has also served to show to Iran the fragility of its regional position. Even if there is a solution to the Syria crisis, the Middle East is unlikely to stabilise in the short term, as evidenced by continued instability in Libya, Egypt, Yemen, Lebanon and, especially, Iraq. With so many actors, including the United States, having a stake in these states, whether for security, strategic or ideological reasons, deploying the various intervention tools short of direct military action identified in Syria in this chapter might emerge as a norm in the region.

Acknowledgements

I would like express my thanks to Mandy Turner, Florian Kühn, Lee Jones, Andrew Jillions and the anonymous peer reviewers for extremely helpful comments on earlier drafts of this chapter.

Notes

1 UNHCR figures at the time of writing, August 2014 (at: http://data.unhcr.org/syrianrefugees/regional.php).
2 Stephen Starr, *Revolt in Syria*, London: Hurst, 2012, p. 3.
3 Emile Hokayem, *Syria's Uprising and the Fracturing of the Levant*, London: Routledge, 2013, p. 81.
4 R. J. Vincent, *Non-Intervention and International Order*, Princeton, NJ: Princeton University Press, 1974, p. 13.
5 Lee Jones, *ASEAN, Sovereignty and Intervention in Southeast Asia*, London: Palgrave Macmillan, 2012, p. 31; George Lawson and Luca Tardelli. 'The Past, Present, and Future of Intervention', *Review of International Studies*, vol. 39, no. 5, 2013, pp. 1233–1253.
6 The key works on this debate include: Lee Feinstein and Anne Marie Slaughter, 'A Duty to Prevent', *Foreign Affairs*, vol. 83, no. 1, 2004, pp. 136–150; David Chandler, 'The Responsibility to Protect? Imposing the "Liberal Peace"', *International Peacekeeping*, vol. 11, no. 1, 2004, pp. 59–81; Philip Cunliffe, 'Sovereignty and the politics of Responsibility', in Christopher J. Bickerton, Philip Cunliffe and Alex Gourevitch (eds), *Politics without Sovereignty: a Critique of Contemporary International Relations*, London: UCL Press, 2007; R. Jackson, *Sovereignty*, Cambridge: Polity, 2007; Jennifer Welsh (ed.), *Humanitarian Intervention and International Relations*, New York: Oxford University Press, 2004.
7 ICISS, *The Responsibility to Protect*, Ottawa: International Development Research Centre, December 2001, p. 16 (at: http://responsibilitytoprotect.org/ICISS%20Report.pdf).
8 UNGA, *Outcome Document of World Summit*, New York: UN General Assembly, UN doc. A/60/L.1, 15 September 2005 (at: http://responsibilitytoprotect.org/world%20summit%20outcome%20doc%202005(1).pdf)
9 Justin Morris, 'Libya and Syria: R2P and the Spectre of the Swinging Pendulum', *International Affairs*, vol. 89, no. 5, 2013, pp. 1265–1283.
10 Anne-Marie Slaughter, 'Syrian Intervention is Justifiable, and Just', *Washington Post*, 8 June 2012 (at: http://articles.washingtonpost.com/2012-06-08/opinions/35462325_1_syrian-state-bashar-nato-planes).
11 Aiden Hehir, *The Responsibility to Protect*, London: Palgrave Macmillan, 2012, p. 52.
12 'UN Security Council Resolution 1973 (2011) on Libya – Full Text', *The Guardian*, 17 March 2011 (at: www.theguardian.com/world/2011/mar/17/un-security-council-resolution).
13 Morris (note 9 above).
14 Stewart M. Patrick, 'RIP for R2P? Syria and the Dilemmas of Humanitarian Intervention', *The Internationalist*, 12 June 2012 (at: http://blogs.cfr.org/patrick/2012/06/12/rip-for-r2p-syria-and-the-dilemmas-of-humanitarian-intervention).
15 Roy Allison, 'Russia and Syria: Explaining Alignment with a Regime in Crisis', *International Affairs*, vol. 89, no. 4, 2013, pp. 795–823.
16 *Ibid.*
17 'Russia Will Not Allow Libya-Style Military Intervention in Syria', *Middle East Online*, 1 November 2011 (at: www.middle-east-online.com/english/?id=48833).
18 'France Outlines Syria Humanitarian Corridor Proposal', *Reuters*, 24 November 2011 (at: http://uk.reuters.com/article/2011/11/24/uk-france-syria-idUKTRE7AN0KC20111124).
19 Yezid Sayigh, 'The Syrian Opposition's Leadership Problem', Carnegie Endowment for International Peace, 3 April 2013 (at: http://carnegieendowment.org/2013/04/03/syrian-opposition-s-leadership-problem/fx6v#).

20 Morten Valbjørn and André Bank, 'The New Arab Cold War: Rediscovering the Arab Dimension of Middle East Regional Politics', *Review of International Studies*, vol. 38, no. 1, 2012, pp. 3–24.
21 Fawaz Gerges, *Obama and the Middle East: The End of America's Moment?*, London: Palgrave, 2012, p. 2.
22 Andy Sullivan, 'US Public Opposes Syria Intervention as Obama Presses Congress', *Reuters*, 3 September 2013 (at: www.reuters.com/article/2013/09/03/us-syria-crisis-usa-idUSBRE97T0NB20130903).
23 Mark Mazetti, Robert F. Worth and Michael R. Gordon, 'Obama's Uncertain Path Amid Syria Bloodshed', *New York Times*, 22 October 2013 (at: www.nytimes.com/2013/10/23/world/middleeast/obamas-uncertain-path-amid-syria-bloodshed.html).
24 Allison (note 15 above).
25 David Hudson, 'The President Gives an Update on the Situation in Iraq', The White House Blog, 9 August 2014 (at: www.whitehouse.gov/blog/2014/08/09/president-gives-update-situation-iraq).
26 J. T. Quinlivan, 'Coup-Proofing: Its Practice and Consequences in the Middle East', *International Security*, vol. 24, no. 2, 1999, pp. 131–165.
27 'Consolidated List of Financial Sanctions Targets in the UK', HM Treasury (at: www.hm-treasury.gov.uk/d/syria.htm).
28 David Lesch, *Syria the Fall of the House of Assad*, New Haven, CT: Yale University Press, 2012, p. 159.
29 *Ibid.*, p. 170.
30 'US Recognises Syria Opposition Coalition Says Obama', *BBC News*, 12 December 2012 (at: www.bbc.co.uk/news/world-middle-east-20690148).
31 'War is Only Option to Topple Syrian Leader: Colonel', *Reuters*, 10 July 2011 (at: www.reuters.com/article/2011/10/07/us-turkey-syria-colonel-idUSTRE79640Q 20111007).
32 Seymour M. Hersch, 'The Red Line and the Rat Line', *The London Review of Books*, vol. 36, no. 8, 17 April 2014; 'Syria Rebels to Get Direct Non-Lethal Support from US for 1st Time, Secretary Kerry Announces', *CBS News*, 28 February 2013 (at: www.cbsnews.com/8301-202_162-57571757/syria-rebels-to-get-direct-non-lethal-support-from-u.s-for-1st-time-secretary-kerry-announces/).
33 Mazetti *et al.* (note 23 above).
34 Christopher Phillips, *Into the Quagmire: Turkey's Frustrated Syria Policy*, Briefing Paper, London: Chatham House, December 2012 (at: www.chathamhouse.org/publications/papers/view/188137).
35 *Ibid.*
36 Rania Abuzaid, 'Opening the Weapons Tap: Syria's Rebels Await Fresh and Free Ammo', *Time*, 22 June 2012 (at: http://world.time.com/2012/06/22/opening-the-weapons-tap-syrias-rebels-await-fresh-and-free-ammo/#ixzz2j7zkZnQl).
37 'Syria's Salafists: Getting Stronger?' *The Economist*, 20 October 2012.
38 Aaron Lund, 'The Free Syrian Army Doesn't Exist', *Syria Comment*, 16 March 2013 (at: www.joshualandis.com/blog/the-free-syrian-army-doesnt-exist/).
39 Phillips (note 34 above).
40 'Israeli Warplanes Bomb Syrian Weapons Convoy to Lebanon, Say Officials', *The Guardian*, 4 May 2013 (at: www.theguardian.com/world/2013/may/04/israel-syria-weapons-lebanon).
41 Eyal Zisser, 'The Deadlocked Syria Crisis', *Strategic Assessment*, vol. 16, no. 2, 2013, pp. 35–45.
42 Shaun Walker, 'Plane Loads of Cash: Flight Records Reveal Russia Flew 30 Tonnes of Bank Notes to Syrian Regime', *The Independent*, 26 November 2012 (at: www.independent.co.uk/news/world/europe/plane-loads-of-cash-flight-records-reveal-russia-flew-30-tonnes-of-bank-notes-to-syrian-regime-8352790.html).

43 Allison (note 15 above).
44 Jubin M. Goodarzi, *Syria and Iran: Diplomatic Alliance and Power Politics in the Middle East*, London: I. B. Tauris, 2006, pp. 1–10.
45 Deborah Amos, 'Pro-Assad "Army" Wages Cyberwar In Syria', *NPR*, 25 September 2011 (at:www.npr.org/2011/09/25/140746510/pro-assad-army-wages-cyberwar-in-syria).
46 'Iran Grants Syria $3.6 Billion Credit Facility to Buy Oil Products', *Reuters*, 31 July 2013 (at: http://uk.reuters.com/article/2013/07/31/us-syria-iran-idUSBRE96U0GZ20130731).
47 'Report: Top Iran Military Official Aiding Assad's Crackdown on Syria Opposition', *Haaretz*, 6 February 2012 (at: www.haaretz.com/news/middle-east/report-top-iran-military-official-aiding-assad-s-crackdown-on-syria-opposition-1.411402).
48 'Videos Show Iranian Officers Supervising Syrian Soldiers', *France 24*, 13 September 2013 (at: http://observers.france24.com/content/20130913-videos-iranian-supervising-syrian-soldiers).
49 Loveday Morris, 'Hezbollah Chief Defends Group's Involvement in Syrian War', *Washington Post*, 25 May 2013 (at: www.washingtonpost.com/world/middle_east/hezbollah-chief-admits-and-defends-groups-involvement-in-syrian-war/2013/05/25/3748965a-c55e-11e2-9fe2-6ee52d0eb7c1_story.html).
50 Toby Dodge, *Iraq: From War to a New Authoritarianism*, London: Routledge, 2012, p. 162.
51 Mona Mahmood and Martin Chulov, 'Syrian War Widens Sunni-Shia Schism as Foreign Jihadis Join Fight for Shrines', *The Guardian*, 4 June 2013 (at: www.theguardian.com/world/2013/jun/04/syria-islamic-sunni-shia-shrines-volunteers).

Index

Page numbers in italic indicate tables.

Abdullah, Abdullah 174
Abidjan 179, 183, 187, 190–1
Abu Ghraib 104, 212n66
accountability xii, 12, 28, 31, 71, 85, 87, 89, 97, 99, 103–4, 131–2, 164, 171, 176, 210, 223, 237
accumulation by dispossession 6, 9, 43, 50, 89; 'gendered' 106
Afghan Independent Human Rights Commission 166
Afghan National Police (ANP) 171
Afghanistan 1, 11, 13, 23, 43, 52, 60, 70, 78, 80, 85, 97, 163–178, 204, 227, 233, 256, ; Bilateral Status Agreement (BSA) 173; corruption 171; democratization 171n31, 174; foreign forces 101; peacebuilding 163, 175; Provincial Reconstruction Teams (PRTs) 53, 142; rentier state 171n32; security 155, 165–9, 171, 173; Strategic Framework Agreement 164; weak state 166, 168; women 94, 96–99, 168, 170, 174;
Africa xi, xiii: civil wars 181–2; colonialism 65, 67–8; conflicts 182, 229; democracy 238; elections 179, 187, 189; Francophone 183, 243; intervention 13, 65, 222, 229, 232, 243; imperialism 64, 68 *see also* colonialism; Islamism 233; peacekeeping 82–3; power 182; regionalism 189–93, 243; territory 64; women 103–4
African International Support Mission in Mali (AFISMA) 232
African Union (AU) 13, 82–3, 179, 187, 189–91, 232, 243

agency xiii, 102, 182
'aid as peacebuilding' 165
aid: Afghanistan 43, 163–78; Cambodia xii, 118–9, 121–2; and COIN 32, 141, 172; corruption 172; Côte d'Ivoire 190; delivery 3–4, 151; dependence 12, 28, 130, 172, 237; donors 10, 84, 89, 119; fragile states 10, 12, 164; humanitarian 148, 151, 175; Israel 153; Mali 232, 237, 242; and military 167, 171–2; NGOs 27–8, 174; Palestinians 12–3, 148, 150–5; and Potemkin states 28; Somalia 79; Syria 262, 266 *see also* donors
Alabama 51
Alawites 252–3, 258, 263
Albania 65
Albanian Kosovars 86
Aleppo (Syria) 253–4
Algeria 233; French colonialism 2
alienation 82, 211–2
al-Jaafari, Ibrahim 209
al-Jazeera xiii, 263
Allawi, Iyad 209
Alliot-Marie, Michèle 184
Al-Qaeda 165, 169, 173, 203, 231, 233
Al-Qaeda in the Islamic Maghreb (AQMI) 231
Al-Sistani, Ali 208
America *see* US
Anbar Province (Iraq) 197, 211
Angola 190–1
Annan, Kofi 80–1, 87, 188
Annan Plan 257, 264
Ansar Eddine 231
anti-colonialism 13, 66, 141–2, 180, 186–7, 236, 238

Index 273

anti-imperialism 63, 107, 192
Aoi, Chiyuki 99
Arab League 257, 263-4, 267
Arab Spring 1, 94, 191n62, 252, 258, 260, 263, 268
Arafat, Yasser 150, 152-3
arbitration 135
army: Colonial 67; demobilisation of 120; development 67-8; function of 153n109
ASEAN (Association of Southeast Asian Nations) 122
Ashdown, Paddy 61
Assad, Bashar al- 15, 83, 251-3, 256-7, 259-68
Assad, Hafez al- 260
asymmetries; conflict 51, 147; of power 72, 77, 147, 180; peacekeeping 192; violence 202
atlanticism 77, 80
atrocity 97, 123, 251; crimes 94; sexual 105
authoritarian elite 12; governance 244; government 118-9; policing 135; rule 237
authoritarianism 71, 105, 118, 128, 135, 153, 236
authority 13-4, 22, 31, 50, 69, 82, 124, 164, 168, 179-80, 183, 186-9, 191-3, 218-20, 223-4, 230-1, 234, 240, 244; command 87; exclusion from 103; local 220, 244; moral 15, 231, 235, 242; quest for 89, 224; religious 208, 240-2; state 45, 164, 234-5, 238, 242
autonomous rational individuals 28, 89
autonomous 32; coping 14; forces 208; Palestinian zones 147; region 254, 267
autonomy 32, 69, 72, 144, 224, 240
'axis of evil' 203

Ba'ath/Baath Party (Iraq) 14, 42, 197, 202-7, 209, 219; De-Baathification 14, 42, 205-6, 210-1, 221, 226
Ba'ath/Baath Party (Syria) 252, 266
Baghdad xiii, 104, 197-9, 202-3, 205-6, 209, 211, 213, 259, 267,
Balkans 65, 70, 78, 80, 85
Bamako (Mali) 231-4, 236, 241
Bandung (Indonesia) 149
Bangladesh 65; workers 222
bargaining 135; labour 134
Barkawi, Tarak 68
Barkhane, Operation 243
BDS *see* Boycott, Divestment and Sanctions (BDS) movement

Bellamy, Alex 68, 192
benchmark 25, 59, 98
Benghazi (Libya) 219, 223-4, 226-7; congress 221-2
Berdal, Mats 77, 82
Berlin Congress (1884-1885) 68
bilateral development assistance 118, 121, 128-9, 134, 235, 237
military cooperation 173, 185
Bilateral Status Agreement (BSA) 173
binary 21, 25; frame 241; gender 102; local/international 181-2; ordering 25; resistance 107; war-peace 46
biopolitics 45-6
bipolarity 87
Blair, Tony 1-2, 77
Bliesemann de Guevara, Berit 82
Bonn Agreement 13, 165, 168-9, 174
borders 7, 14, 29, 43, 49, 53, 89, 121, 123, 150, 165, 182, 184, 197, 219-21, 223-5, 227, 254, 258-9, 263-5
Bosnia and Herzegovina (BiH) 3, 61, 80, 85; army 80; elections; High Representative 61; peacebuilding 70; Peace Implementation Council 87; rape 94; Serb forces 80
Boutros-Ghali, Boutros 80, 123
Boycott, Divestment and Sanctions (BDS) movement 146-7, 152
Brahimi, Lakhdar 80, 168, 208-9
Brahimi Report, panel on peacekeeping reform (UNSG) 80, 88, 143
Brazil 86, 192n65
Bremer, Paul 14, 204-5, 207-8, 219
BRICs (Brazil Russia India China) 86
Britain/British *see* UK
British Colonial Development Act 142; colonialism 63, 65, 67, 142; empire 70; imperialism 63, 68;
British Indian Army 65, 67
Burkina Faso 184-5, 188, 191, 243
Bush administration 14, 169, 197-9, 203, 205; doctrine 202
Bush, George H. W. 222
Bush, George W. 2, 97, 198, 203-4, 209, 213, 258
business 26, 85, 147; Cambodia 119-21, 131; corporate 88; Palestinian elites 152; environment 84; Israel 146; men 103; and military 119, 135, 190; models 85, 104; private 120; protection 85; tycoons 131; women 222
Buzan, Barry 29

Index

Call, Charles 88
camaraderie ix, 101
Cambodia 1, 6, 11–2, 53–4n61, 71, 103, 117–138; expropriation 120, 129, 135; unions 129–30, 132–5; violence 119, 124–5, 129, 135–6
Cameron, David 233
capacity 2, 135: agency 99; building 28, 109, 118, 130, 135, 144, 164; Cambodia 121, 124–5; imperial 180; institutional 25; intervention 232–3; local 84; military 171, 259; organisational 23, 28; productive 85; state 15, 168, 205, 229, 242
capital 3–4, 24; accumulation 9, 44, 53, 84–5; circulation 32; and coercion 24; density 7, 121; European 7; industrial 50; production 6 *see also* primitive accumulation
capitalism 5, 10, 13, 30, 44, 77, 197; anti- 238; classes 29; and neo-colonialism 109; corporate 89; crony 152, 252; 'disaster' 44; expansion 7, 22, 29, 44; global 46, 87, 149, 182; liberal 16; monopoly 43, 46; predatory 11, 118–9, 128, 130, 135; trade 6; and war 44, 89, 181
capitalist consociation 29; core 7, 9, 29, 85; 'economies of scale' 6; elites 31; exchange; investment 6, 44, 85; market 8, 10; relations 6, 32
Capstone Doctrine 82
Central African Republic (CAR) 229
Central Intelligence Agency (CIA) 80, 165, 262
Chalabi, Ahmed 261
Chandler, David 72
Charbonneau, Bruno 5, 13, 15
Chesterman, Simon 61
China 53, 65, 83, 86, 121–2, 128, 136, 173, 191n65, 255–8, 267
Chirac, Jacques 185–8
choice 31, 71–2, 105, 129, 199, 209, 220
citizenship 7, 12, 24n27, 26, 45, 50, 85, 97, 104, 120, 131, 140, 145, 149, 181n12, 226, 230, 238
civil society 12, 26, 102–3, 119–20, 126, 130–3, 140, 147, 174–5, 236, 238–9
civil society organizations (CSOs) 128, 130, 132
civil wars 3, 24n27: Cambodia 119, 125; Côte d'Ivoire 185; insurgency 143; Iraq 14, 197–8, 208–9, 211–2; Libya 218; Syria 253, 257, 260–1, 265; US/American 9, 40, 42, 47–8, 51–3; West Africa 181, 184

civilian police *see* police
civilian population/civilians 24n27, 26, 51, 80–2, 87, 100–1, 143, 166–7, 179, 183, 190, 192n64; casualties 165, 170n28, 171, 175, 213, 251–2, 255
civilisation 6, 15, 52, 61, 77–8
clans 79, 103
Clark, Wesley 81n22
clash of civilisations 6; ethnic 226; military 264; sectarian 263, 265
client states 86
clientelism 26, 240–2
clientelist state 68, 238, 266
Clinton, Hillary 87n9
Clinton administration 80
Coalition Provisional Authority (CPA) (Iraq) 204–5, 207
coalitions 14, 50, 79–80, 83, 86, 122, 165–6, 171, 192, 205–6, 209–10, 221, 229n1, 236, 253, 261
coercion 4, 10, 24, 45, 68, 77, 80, 187, 197, 202, 211, 230, 237
cognition 198, 200, 202
'cognitive consistency' 201, 203, 205
COIN (counterinsurgency operations) *see also* insurgencies
Cold War 5, 66, 141; intervention 118; Kampuchea 122; peace 21; peacebuilding 70; peace practice 30, 67; Russia 257; security 27 *see also* post-Cold War
collapse 7, 49, 87, 120, 122, 128, 261, 265; states 81, 259
colonial control 6, 45, 67, 150; expansion 44, 63; peace 12, 140, 154–5; policing 8, 65; practices 139–40, 144, 149
colonialism 6, 10, 26, 45, 60–3, 65, 71, 95; anti- 13, 66, 141–2, 180, 186–7, 236, 238; and UN 7
colonization 3, 12, 145, 150–1, 154 *see also* decolonisation; imperialism; neo-colonialism; post-colonialism
combatants 51
community 3, 31, 135, 147, 163, 165, 223; black 50; councils 31; development 103; donor/aid 163–4, 166, 172; international 10, 25n40, 61, 66, 82–3, 97–9, 106–7n79, 166, 181, 188–9, 192, 234, 242, 251, 261; peacebuilding 143; property 89, security 21–2, 25–6, 29, 31; Sunni 203, 205, 207–9, 212

Index 275

competing elites 182; ideologies 23, 30, 244, 253; nationalism 10, 240; NGOs 129
competition 10, 23, 29, 42-3, 53, 84, 87, 174, 223, 258
comprehensive approach (NATO) 167; peace plan 69; settlement 120, 184
Condé, Alpha 232
Confederate armies 49-50
conflict prevention 142
conflict-prone states 96, 206, 244
conflicts 6-7, 9, 12-3, 21, 27, 39-44, 47, 53, 64, 78, 88, 107, 127, 143, 149, 184, 239, 265; and civil society 102; context 3, 142, 197; dynamics 82, 97, 167, 181, 184, 198, 233; economy 106, 135; inter-state 143; land 127; local 63, 171, 175, military 39; and peacekeeping 94, 182; protracted 67; and reconstruction 41; societies 28, 64, 85, 106; transformation 241; social 28, 51, 54; women 100, 102-3, 105
Congo 66, 79, 94, 106-7; UN peacekeeping 66, 86;
Connor, Joseph E. 88
consociation 29
consolidation; capitalism 29; democracy 206, 236-8; peace 64, 242; state authority 45
constitutional assembly 120; order 26, 48, 256; process 221, 227; reform 184
constitution: Afghanistan 97, 174; Bosnia and Herzegovina (BiH) 84; Cambodia 120; Côte d'Ivoire 184; Egypt 94; Iraq 210; republican (Kant) 26
contestation 47, 54, 84, 100, 103, 109, 119, 129, 173, 183, 230, 242-4
Cooper, Robert 69-70
core vs periphery 4, 6-7, 9, 27, 29-31, 61, 63, 70, 85, 220, 223
corporatist policies 149
corruption 15, 85; Afghanistan 171; Cambodia 131; failed states 85; Guinea-Bissau; human rights 132; Libya 15, 222; Mali 231, 240-1; Palestine 153
Côte d'Ivoire 5, 100, 179-196, 243; aid programmes 190; and AU (African Union) 189; international community 181; and ECOWAS (Economic Community of West African States) 189-90; intervention 11, 13, 179-80, 182, 191-2; peacekeeping 192; refugees 190; violence 182, 184-5, 188; women 105

Counterinsurgency Field Manual (CFM) 143
counter-insurgency 10, 12, 65, 81-2, 139-4, 147-9, 154, 167, 172; guide (US government) 141-2; operations (COIN) 32, 139, 146, 172, 244, 265; and peacebuilding 144, 150-1, 155 *see also* insurgency
coup d'état 79; Burkina Faso 185; Central African Republic 229; Côte d'Ivoire 183, 187; Mali 231, 233-4, 239, 242; Syria 260
Crimea 87
Croatia 80
crusade against evil 2
Cuba 52
Cunliffe, Philip 9-10
customary institutions 25, 28, 85, 103, 105, 119-20, 127, 129, 136, 240
Cyprus 80

Da'esh (ad-Dawlah al-Islāmīyah fīl-'Iraq wa ash-Shām – Islamic State in Iraq and the Levant) 1, 14, 16, 83, 197-8, 211-2, 253-4, 259, 262, 264-7
Damascus (Syria) 253-4, 259-60, 262-3
Darfur 94, 101, 225, 256 *see also* Sudan
Dawa Islamic Party 209
de Coning, Cedric 99
debt; consumer 152; crises 85; driven capitalism 89; Palestine 153; repayment 84; toxic 85
decentralization 15, 72, 223, 240, 242
decolonization 5, 8, 53, 78, 180, 186, 236-7
demobilization 15, 120, 135, 183, 218-9, 226
democracy 25, 117, 206: Afghanistan 98, 165, 168, 171; Cambodia 117, 121, 127-8, 132; and colonialism 12; Côte d'Ivoire 192; elite 236; government 124, 176; and guardianship 241; intervention 1; Iraq 197, 206; legitimate state 87; liberal 12, 31, 83, 87, 127-28, 149, 174; Mali 230-2, 235-9, 241; mask 96; Palestine 153; peacekeeping 67; and pluralism 121; promotion 140, 238; reform 103; statebuilding 98, 167; women 104 *see also* elections
Democratic Republic of Congo (DRC) *see* Congo
democratic governance 154, 235, 237, 242, 244 *see also* governance

democratic peace 15, 26–7; transition 261
Deng, Francis 88
dependence 73, 86, 129, 152, 171 *see also* aid dependence
Deraa (Syria) 251–2, 263
detention 140, 148, 171, 212, 219, 261
deterrence 10, 73, 147, 259, 267
Deutsch, Karl 29
development 4, 12, 27, 52, 103, 128–9, 142, 176, 192, 242; accountability 171; Afghanistan 164, 167, 170; assistance 150–2, 237; Cambodia 118, 120–1, 128, 130; effectiveness 231; humanitarian 172; infrastructure 152; Iraq 202; Mali 235–6, 240; neoliberal 7, 15; Palestine 139–41, 148, 153–5; Sahel region 232; and security 28, 77, 87, 141–3; sustainability 241–2; UN 10, 84, 88; uneven 7; USA 52; women 170
developmentalism 68, 149
'diabolical enemy image' 14, 198, 202–4, 209
discrimination 13, 80, 107, 180, 182, 185, 211
Dodge, Toby 2, 14, 85, 219
donors 4, 10, 12, 28, 31, 77, 89, 95, 130, 132, 142, 144, 150–1, 153, 163–4, 168: Afghanistan 163, 174, 176; Cambodia 12, 118–9, 121, 129; civil society 236, 239; 'darling' 237; Mali 15, 235; multilateral 95, 118, 121, 151, 235–7; OECD 143, 150; Palestine 139; peacebuilding 139, 141, 143–4, 148; women 102–3, 118; World Bank 84, 132, 235 *see also* aid; Western donors
Doyle, Michael 61, 65, 68, 73, 88
DPKO *see UN Department of Peacekeeping Operations*
DRC (Democratic Republic of Congo) *see* Congo
drones 41, 43, 173, 175, 243, 260
Druze 144n46, 253
Duffield, Mark 4, 164

early colonialism *see* colonialism
East Jerusalem 145, 154
East Timor 71
Eastern Bloc 66, 122, 125
Economic Community of West African States (ECOWAS) 13, 179, 181–5, 188–91, 231–2

economic: abstract models 26, 72–3, 149; change ix, 8, 26, 42, 46, 48, 119; class 119; dysfunction 85; development 15, 121, 128, 240; imperialism 64; inequalities 96, 154; justice 89, 235; liberalisation 83, 227, 235–8; logics 28, 64; policy 3, 87, 89, 142; production 41; reforms 15, 121; reproduction 4, 24, 29, 31, 77; rights 89, 127, 130; sanctions 254, 257, 260–1
economy 1, 39: Cambodia 118, 128; Côte d'Ivoire 181–2, 192; Iraq 205, 209; Israel 146, 148; Mali 243; military 46; neoliberal 12, 15, 77, 84, 117, 151–2, 155; opium 165, 171; Palestine 139, 147, 150–3; peacebuilding 10, 63, 167; security 45, 141, 173; Syria 252, 261, 264; USA 9; and war 44, 106, 146, 171, 174, 244; way of life 32; and women 11, 97, 106
education 4, 30, 50, 98, 123, 125, 130, 201, 238
Egypt xiii, 24n27, 94, 142, 220, 227, 241, 252, 260–1, 263, 265, 268
El Salvador 89n63
elections 77, 107, 117, 120, 173, 179; Afghanistan 97–8, 173–4; Cambodia 117, 120, 127, 135; Congo (DRC) 107; Côte d'Ivoire 179, 183, 187–91; Egypt 94; Gaza 152, 153; Iraq 208–12; Libya 218, 220, 225–7; Louisiana 51; Mali 234, 237–42; Southern States 52; UN monitoring 77; *see also* democracy
elites 1, 3, 13–4, 24, 30, 53, 86, 89, 96, 120, 141, 144, 153, 184n25, 203, 207–8, 212–3; Afghanistan 170; authoritarian 12; business 31, 152; Cambodian 118–9; co-option 4, 9, 29; corrupt 12, 171; democracy 236; international 1; local 3, 5, 12–3, 73, 89, 150, 182, 202, 207, 242; Mali 234; networks 128–9, 182; pacts 210; Palestine 150–3; ruling 14, 32, 135, 198, 202, 205–7; settlement 198, 206; state 211, 219; transnational 239–40; warrior 23, 85, 187; Western 2
emancipation 9, 30, 32, 49n47, 52, 95, 108, 124; anti- 22–3, 29; of women 97, 99
empire 8, 10, 27, 41, 45, 59–62, 64–5n26, 68–70, 72–4, 78, 141, 180, 239,

Enlightenment, the 8, 22, 24, 26, 47
Enloe, Cynthia 66
Erdogan, Recep Tayyip 263
Ethiopia 104
ethnic cleansing 255 *see also* genocide; mass atrocities
ethnic conflict 239; diversity 223, 227; groups 207, 210; violence 171, 223, 226, 259
ethnicity 84, 100, 235
eurocentrism 78
European Union (EU): Afghanistan 97; Chad 86; colonialism 69, 87; Côte d'Ivoire 190; Council 189; gender 100; Israel 146; Kosovo 85; nation-building 70; peacebuilding 72, 143; Somalia 73; Syria 260-2, 265; and UN 151; and USA 86, 151, 260
exclusion *see* politics of inclusion/exclusion
export 85, 132, 134, 146, 154, 227, 257
expropriation 6, 22, 120, 129, 135, 145
extremists 229, 233

factions 117, 122, 163, 168, 170, 175, 226, 253
Fahim, Marshal Mohammed 169
'failed states' 10, 83, 85, 164, 166, 254 *see also* fragile states; weak states
FANCI (Forces Armées Nationales de Côte d'Ivoire) *see* Ivorian Army
Fateh 148, 152
Feith, Douglas 198, 203-5
feminism 8; anti-militarist 100; binary 102, 104; critical 96-7; language 97; liberal 11, 94-6, 98-100, 106-9; post-colonial 11, 95-6, 98, 107-9; feminist discourse 8
Ferguson, Adam 26
Flint, Colin 9
force, use of 4, 10, 13, 62-3, 69, 73, 78-82, 168, 179, 184-5, 189, 224, 233, 243, 257, 259, 265
Forces républicaines de la Côte d'Ivoire (FRCI) 189, 191
foreign direct investment (FDI) 89
Foucault, Michel 45
fragile states; aid 142; state capacities 142; and security 143; *see also* failed states; weak states
France 13, 66, 78, 96, 133, 179, 181-2, 185-7, 192, 229, 232, 237, 241-3, 252, 257, 260-2
free markets 85, 95-6, 118, 120-1, 202
Free Syrian Army (FSA) 16, 253, 261-2, 264-5

Index 277

Free Trade Union of Workers of the Kingdom of Cambodia (FTUWKC) 133-135
French army 186, 241
French colonialism 2, 67
friendly government 142, 263; nation 232

G8 7
Galtung, Johan 44, 94
garment industry 132
Garment Manufacturers' Association of Cambodia 133
gas 263
Gaulme, François 181
Gaza Strip 101, 146-8, 150, 152-4
Gbagbo, Laurent 13, 179, 181, 183-5n31, 188-91, 193
gender categories 207; dichotomy 106; discourse 11, 94, 103-4; identity 100; inequality 11, 41-2, 98-9; protection 96; and security 95
gendered institutions 96; logics of protectionism 11, 105; spring 94; peace 95; power relations 95, 97, 106
genocide 39, 80, 88, 202-3, 255, *see also* ethnic cleansing; mass atrocities
Germany 53, 203-4, 260-1
Ghana 87, 183-4, 190
globalisation 27, 68, 106
'good governance' *see* governance
Governance 12, 15, 22, 25, 29, 50, 72, 87, 103, 130-1, 134, 139, 153, 155, 180, 207-8, 211, 232, 235-6, 242-3: authoritarian 244; community 165; democratic 235, 237, 242, 244; Global 8-10, 15, 22, 28, 149, 237; 'Good' 86, 95, 125, 128, 131, 144, 151-4, 170, 172, 235, 237, 244; islamist 244; national 62; neoliberal 15, 44, 142, 241; pluralist 241-2; proxy 61, 71; reform 28, 132; resource 7, 12, 127-8; security 96; strategies 140, 155, structures 139, 148, 151, 198; Western 31
governments 2, 144, 146-7: authoritarian 118; and capitalism 85, 119, 133-4, 149; corruption 131, 231; Côte d'Ivoire 183-6, 189; elite 14, 61, 86, 207; -in-waiting (Syria) 257; Israel 144, 146-7;

Kosovo; legitimacy 79, 103, 128, 147, 164–5, 171, 176, 225–7, 240, 261; liberal 10, 12, 22, 31–2, 70, 72, 121–4, 176, 243; Mali 233; and peace 24–5n32, 105–6, 119, 125, 129, 203, 211, 223–4; power 4, 198; recipient 4, 130, 132, 212, 238; reform 219; Syria 83; transitional (Afghanistan) 167, 169–70; transitional (Congo) 107; transitional (Iraq) 42, 207–10; and UN 66, 71, 81; US Federal 9, 48; women in 97, 107;
Grad missiles 224
grand assembly (Loya Jirga) 173
Grant, Ulysses 52
grassroots actors 102, 118, 131, 218; violence 202
'greed and grievance' 28
Guatemala 66
Guéhenno, Jean-Marie 71–2, 83
Guinea-Bissau 183
Gulf: of Sirte 227; states 264, 268
gunboat diplomacy 86

Haiti 64, 79–80
Hamas 148, 152–3
Harvey, David 6, 43, 50
Harrison, Graham 4
health care 39, 50, 213; ministry 222
'hearts and minds' 147, 172
heavy weapons 179, 192, 220, 264
Hegel, G. W. F. 26n46
Hehir, Aidan 255–6
Helmand Province (Afghanistan) 171
Hezbollah 252, 260, 265–6, 268
Higate, Paul 104
High Level Panel on Threats, Challenges, and Change (UN) 143
Hinnebusch, Raymond 199–200
Hobbes, Thomas 24
Hobson, John 63
Hollande, François 229n1, 231–2, 241
Hudson, Heidi 11
Hughes, Caroline 6, 11–2
human rights 8, 11–2, 65–6, 78, 86–7, 95, 99, 104, 117, 120–7, 129–30, 132, 154, 164, 166–8, 170–1, 174–5, 232, 239, 244
'human terrain teams' 172
humanitarian aid *see* aid
humanitarian intervention 65n26, 81, 256
Hun Sen 133
Hussein, Saddam 14, 203–4, 221

Hutu regime 80
Huysmans, Jeff 95
hybrid identity 108; 'peace' 5, 181; operations 80
'hybridity' 149, 182
hypermasculinity 104, 106

ICISS *see* International Commission on Intervention and State Sovereignty
ideology 3, 6, 8, 16, 26–7, 30, 40, 45n27, 47, 49n47, 52–3, 72, 77, 84, 87, 118, 152, 172, 175, 199, 202, 206, 236, 238–9, 253, 263–4, 266, 268
Ignatieff, Michael 61–3, 69–70
imperial altruism 63; expansion 63, 70; geopolitics 63; historiography 239; multilateralism 8, 10, 65, 74, 149; political economy 63; power 3, 60, 68, 73, 78, 142; practices 8, 44, 73; roots of UN 7; war 10, 81, 142; violence 6
imperialism 9–10, 42–44, 54, 59, 60–2, 64–7, 70–1, 78, 86, 98; 'liberal' 61, 63, 69, 180; and peacebuilding 62, 67, 71, 107, 180; structural imperatives of 46; and UN 79; *see also* neo-imperialism; anti-imperialism
Implementing the Responsibility to Protect (UNSG) 255
In Larger Freedom (UN) 141
inclusion *see* politics of inclusion/exclusion
inclusive settlements 206, 219, 238, 240–1
indigenous forces 25n32, 67–8, 103; human rights associations 123; ownership 164, 239; political elites 207
individual rights 22, 100
inequalities 30, 44, 96, 98, 100, 133, 223, 238
inferior 2, 98 *see also* Other
influence 3, 7, 16, 23, 27, 29–30, 32, 45, 63–4, 66, 68–9, 73, 78, 82, 84, 86, 100, 125, 131, 150, 172, 181–2, 185–6, 188, 199–200, 206, 225, 227, 236, 239, 242, 256, 258, 260–1, 263, 266–8
informal economies 89, 97; imperialism 44; power 7, 72–3; practices
insecurity 95, 143, 167–8; women's 108; *see also* security sector reform (SSR)
institutional approaches 27, 164; capacity 25; culture 104; design 28; identities 229–30; power 4, 25; practices 90; structure 30, 150; violence 39

institutionalism 89
institution-building 150, 164
institutions: Bretton Woods 78; capitalist 46, 85; customary law 103; gendered 96; global 44; hollow 77; masculinist 106; military 45, 101; Palestinian 139, 150, 153; post-conflict 71; security 27, 100, 104, 153; state 39, 50, 61, 65, 205–6, 212, 224, 227; supra-national 28, 30; UN 86, 101
insurgency 14, 42, 81, 135, 140, 142, 146, 149, 154, 169–70, 172, 204, 212, 239, 242 *see also* counterinsurgency operations (COIN)
integration; capitalist 89; 'league of peace' 26; post-war 40, 48, 239; 'skewed' 146, 150;Western 22, 26, 29
International Commission on Intervention and State Sovereignty (ICISS) 2–3n7, 97, 254
International Committee on the Reconstruction of Cambodia 121
'international community' 10, 25n40, 61, 66, 82–3n31, 97–9, 106–7n79, 166, 181, 188–9, 192, 234, 242, 251, 261
International Criminal Court (ICC) 186n33, 225, 257
International Crisis Group (ICG) 88, 169, 188–9
international donors *see* donors
International Financial Institutions (IFIs) 84, 89, 96, 121, 241
international funding 129
international interactions 23
international intervention 8, 12, 16, 163, 235; colonial peace 155, 180, 183; and economy 120; failure 188; legitimisation 21; peacebuilding 8, 11, 62, 71, 182; practice 127; regime change 179, 191
International Labour Organisation (ILO) 134–5
international law 22, 25, 62, 78–9, 86–7, 100
International Monetary Fund (IMF) 7, 9, 15
International Security Assistance Force (ISAF) 163, 166–74
international security 81, 96, 105, 143, 237
international system 3–7, 10, 16, 22, 25, 73, 87, 268
inter-state conflict 143; peace 24
intervention *see* international intervention

intifada; first 146–50; second 147–50, 152–3
intra-state conflicts 82, 251
Iraq War 14, 265; (1991) 80
Iraq 1, 52, 252, 258, 265; asymmetrical colonial encounters 45; Coalition Provisional Authority; complexity 2; constitution 84; elite pact 210; foreign forces; insurgency; invasion 11, 42, 60, 169, 198, 203, 213, 258; 'Islamic State' 83, 197, 253, 259; Kurds 207–8, 267; lessons learnt 219, 221; Mosul 197, 259; oil 199, 267; police 212; post-war settlement 14, 198, 207; 'Provincial Reconstruction Teams' 53; regime change 23, 97; R2P; security 155, 169, 211; Shia 207, 210, 212, 267; specialists 2, 202; Sunni community 203–5, 207, 211, 227, 266; statebuilding 85; Transitional Administrative Law; war (1991) 80; women 99, 207
Iraqi army 197, 211–2
Iraqi Governing Council (IGC) 206
Iraqi Islamic Party (IIP) 207
Iraqi National Alliance 208n53, 210
Iraqi National Congress (INC) 208n53, 261
Iraqi National Movement (Iraqiya) 209
Irbil (Iraq) 259
irrational evil 203
Islamic Conference 263
Islamic Front 265
Islamic State *see* Da'esh
Islamic State in Iraq and Syria (ISIS) *see* Da'esh
Islamist groups 203, 233–4, 240, 253, 257, 263; militia 226, 264; terrorism 15, 212, 229–30; threat 229, 230, 233, 244
Israel 12, 101, 139–40, 144–55, 199, 252, 257–8, 260, 265–6; economy 146–7; Supreme Court 145 *see also* Oslo Accords; Palestinians
Israel Defense Forces (IDF) 101, 144, 146–8
Issoufou, Mahamadou 232
Italy 224, 261
Ivorian Army (FANCI - Forces Armées Nationales de Côte d'Ivoire) 186
Ivory Coast *see* Côte d'Ivoire

Japan 30
Jerusalem 146 *see also* East Jerusalem

280 Index

Jewish settlements 154
Joffe, George 2
Jubhat al-Nusra (JAN) 264–6
Jufra militia 224
justice, delivery of 103, 106, 134, 171, 205, 219, 227, 242; economic 89, 235, 237; ministry of 98; social 118, 165, 170, 235; traditional 89; transitional 171

Kabul 166–70
Kaldor, Mary 143
Kampuchea 122 see also Cambodia
Kant, Immanuel 24, 26
Karzai, Hamid 97, 169, 173
Kashmir 78
Keita, Modibo 238
Keïta, Ibrahim Boubacar (IBK) 239
Keïta, Sundiata 239
Kenya 165
Kerry, John 174
Keynesianism 30
Khmer Rouge 117, 119, 121–3
Kilcullen, David 141–2
Ki-moon, Ban 189
'kinetic' 140, 148
Kipling, Rudyard 16
Kirsch, Scott 9
Knesset 154
Kosovo 87–8, 251, 258
Krasner, Stephen D. 3
Kühn, Florian P. 8–9, 82
Ku Klux Klan 50
Kurdish militia 254; region (Syria) 263, 267
Kurdish Regional Government 208
Kurdistan Democratic Party 209

Lao People's Democratic Republic 122
Latin America 142
Lavrov, Sergei 257
law enforcement 106 see also police
Lawson, George 4
leadership 8, 62, 79–80, 104, 145, 169–79, 191, 206, 220, 231, 234, 236, 253, 264
League of Nations 78
League of Peace (Kant) 24, 26
Lebanon 79, 258, 264, 266, 268
legitimacy 13, 23, 64: biopolitics 45; deficit 171, 220; donor 132; electoral process 189, 236–7, 239, 242; failed states 164; international 241–2;

intervention 2, 74, 88, 179, 192, 229–30, 237, 243, 255; mandate 234; moral 15, 242; normative orders 240; 'vs legality' 2; liberal imperialism 63, 66, 244; local 82, 231; peacebuilding 10, 59–60, 71, 73, 150–1, 163, 176; political 13, 62–3, 179, 184–5, 193, 238; rule 61–2; terrorism 52; UN 64, 67, 80; use of force 13, 26, 128, 167, 171, 179, 182–3, 185, 189, 191–2, 235
liberal democracy 121, 127
liberal feminist ideas see feminism
liberal internationalism 9, 29
liberal peacebuilding 11, 68, 107–9; 118, 129–30, 151: Cambodia 118–9, 129–30, 135; gendering 94–6, 98, 104–5, 107–9; oPT 151
liberal triumphalism 117
liberalisation 10, 83, 86, 238; economic 235–7
Liberia 100; conflict 184; militias 185; gender-based violence 107n79
Libya 1, 78, 218, 254: constitution 227; elections 226–7; gender discourse 94; intervention 11, 15–6, 78, 107, 253–4, 259, 261, 267; militias 220, 225, 227; national defence 14; National Transitional Council (NTC) 218–9, 223, 226, 258, 261; oil 223, 227; peacekeeping 192; post-revolutionary 14, 218; regime change 1, 11, 23, 83, 94; R2P 15, 255–6, 268; Supreme Security Council (SSC) 219; tribes 220, 223, 225; violence 15, 94n8, 228, 261; women 94n8
Lieven, Anatol 198
Linas-Marcoussis Accords 185–6
Lindemann, Stefan 206
local agency 28, 164; romanticised 241
local ownership: discourse 86, 104; liberal forms 7, 120; women 104
local/international 5, 12–3, 27–8, 68, 71, 73, 84–6, 89, 99, 102–4, 107–8, 119, 125, 140, 147, 149, 164–5, 168, 175–6, 179–185, 187–9, 192–3, 202, 222, 230, 241–2
'Lockean heartland' 29; 'state' 22
Locke, John 2, 22, 29
logical framework 59, 141
Loridon, Jean-Michel 117
loya jirga (grand assembly) 173
Luck, Edward 88
Lugard, Frederick 63

McGovern, Mike 182, 187, 189
Mali 1, 15, 183, 229–250; army 231–4, 241; election 237; French intervention 11, 229, 231, 234–5, 241, 244; 'Greater' (*maliba*) 239; identity 139; neoliberal development 15, 229, 236–7; peace 15; 'people's army' 238, 'state failure' 229, 243; terrorism 230, 233, 241; violence 225, 230
Maliki, Nuri al- 210–1, 227, 266–7
Mann, Gregory 242
Marchal, Roland 229, 234
market economy 174, 237n52,
Marshall Plan 50
Marx, Karl 6, 49, 89
Marxism 43–4
masculinity 100, 106, 108; militarised 101, 104–5; pastoral 102, 105
mass atrocities 97 *see also* ethnic cleansing; genocide
Mazrui, Ali 180
Mbeki, Thabo 188, 190–1
Médecins Sans Frontières (MSF) 164
micro-credit 85
Middle East 1, 81, 151, 197, 228, 251, 254, 257–8, 268; Quartet 1, 81 *see also* named countries
Migdal, Joel 26n42
militarisation 9–10, 13, 15, 39–41, 45–6, 54, 77–79, 86–89, 101, 105, 125, 142, 172, 181, 237, 241, 243, 267
military: and aid 167; balancing 184–5; and civilians 45n27, 170, 172; expeditions 44, 65–6; intervention 2–3, 15, 68, 95, 140–2, 163, 166, 184, 190–1, 193, 228–35, 237, 240–4, 251–2, 254–62, 266–8; logistics 78–9; male/masculinist 101, 104; occupation 4, 52; post-conflict 202; relations 25n32; peacekeeping 13, 27, 61, 63, 142, 175; strategy 140, 165; valorisation of 101; violence 4, 80–2, 145–6, 230, 235
militias 13–4, 51, 82, 171, 182, 184–6, 191, 213, 218–9, 224, 252–4, 262, 264–6
Mill, John Stuart 2, 25
Mills, Atta 190
Milošević, Slobodan 251
mining 66
minorities 168, 170, 208, 219, 223, 237–8, 244, 258, 266
Misrata (Libya) 220–2
mission civilisatrice 8, 61, 63, 149
Mississippi 49–50, 52

Mitchell, Audra 181
modality: assistance 171; of peacebuilding 10, 60, 62, 64
modernity 1–2, 63
modernisation 27, 29
money 24, 89, 133, 268
monopoly: capitalism 43, 46; economic 150, 152–3; of violence 23, 25n40, 26, 167–8, 171, 235
monopolisation: of discourse 87; of income 222
More Secure World: Our Shared Responsibility, A (UN) 141
Morris, Justin 255
Mostar 85
Mouvement de l'unicité du jihad en Afrique de l'Ouest (MUJAO) 231
Mouvement de la Justice et de la Paix (MJP) 184
Mouvement national de libération de l'Azawad (MNLA) 230–1, 234, 241
Mouvement patriotique de Côte d'Ivoire (MPCI) 183
Mouvement populaire ivoirien du Grand Ouest (MPIGO) 184
Mozambique 69, 106
multinational force 168–9
Multinational Force (Lebanon) 79
Mungwa, Alice 103
Museveni, Yoweri 190
Muslim Brotherhood 263–5
Muslims 2, 144n46; 145, 199, 258
myth 5, 239, 251; of gendered spring 94; liberal 9, 32; of rationality 24; religious 145

9/11 attacks 201
National Army of Democratic Kampuchea 122
national security 4, 78
national self-determination 69, 70–1, 73, 86, 154–5, 240
National Transitional Council (Libya) 14, 218
nationalism 53, 172, 240; militant 237; post-colonial 244
nation-building 70, 166
NATO 29, 67, 261: Afghanistan 13, 163, 167, 169, 172–3; Libya 255–6; and militias 13; Russia relations 16, 27, 257–8; and UN 78, 80–1, 83, 87–8; and women's rights 99, 101
natural resource extraction 120

Index 281

Index

neocolonialism 109, 139, 181, 190, 237, 241, 243
neo-imperialism 59–60, 69, 73
neoliberal economics 12, 77, 84, 89n63, 117, 151–2, 155, 237; development model 7, 15, 240; ideology 84, 97, 118; peace 85; reconstruction 44, 53; statebuilding 85, 235–6, 246; strategies 15, 84; transnational governance 15, 95, 119, 142, 149, 241–2
neoliberalism 5, 9, 29, 84, 237; Mali 229; and post-colonialism 108; and sexual violence 106; and war 46, 244
neo-patrimonial state 153
nepotism 153
Netherlands 261
New International Economic Order (NIEO) 149
NGOs 8, 27, 43, 53, 96, 123, 124, 126, 128–32, 163, 168, 172, 174, 238–9
Nigeria 183, 190–2
no-fly zone 254, 258, 261, 267
non-intervention 30, 251
non-Western periphery 27; societies 28, 30, 202; women 106
normalisation of capitalism 30
normative agenda 30, 100; codes 104; discourse 25; orders 240; vision 163, 200
North Atlantic Treaty Organization *see* NATO
North Carolina 51
Northern Alliance 169
Northern Ireland 42
North-South relations 50, 180, 184n25, 185

Obama administration 67, 83, 173, 258–9, 262, 267
Obama, Barack 259, 261–2
occupation 4, 14, 40, 52, 62, 122, 139, 145–8, 150–3, 170, 197–8, 204, 206, 208–9, 211–2, 258
occupied Palestinian territories (oPt) 11–2, 139, 156
OECD (Organisation for Economic Cooperation and Development) 143, 150n95
oil; Arab 199; Iraq 199, 267; Libya 222–3, 227, 261; rents 211, 222, 227
Old Guard (Libya) 14, 218, 226
ONUB (UN Operation in Burundi) 83
Operation Barkhane 243; Cast Lead 148; Defensive Shield 148; Dignité 186; Enduring Freedom 80, 165;
Licorne 184, 187, 192; Protective Edge 101, 148, Restore Hope 79; Sangaris 229n1; Serval 235, 243
opium economy 165
opposition parties 128, 183–4, 186, 188
oPt (occupied Palestinian territories) 11–2, 139, 156
Organisation of the Islamic Conference (OIC) 263
Organization of African Unity 183
Orientalism (Said) 1, 11, 14, 25, 46, 95, 197, 201, 213
Oslo Accords 139, 145–7, 150 151, 153–4 *see also* Israel; Palestinians
Other 2, 9, 14, 16, 25n37, 28, 95, 98–9, 103, 164, 201–3; othering 25, 46, 96
Ottoman Empire 65n26
Ouagadougou 185; Accords 105, 187–88
Ouattara, Alassane 179, 181, 183–4, 189–91
overstretch 80; imperial 258

P5 (permanent 5 members of the UN Security Council) 80, 122, 251, 255–7, 267–8
pagoda committees 130
Pakistan 16, 65, 79, 173, 233, 260
Palestine Liberation Organization (PLO) 139, 145, 150–1
Palestine 1, 11–2, 45, 86, 139–40, 154–5; historic 144–5; insurgency 140, 149, 154–5 *see also* occupied Palestinian territory (oPt)
Palestinian Authority (PA) 86, 146–7, 149–54; diaspora 150; economy 147, 152–3; heritage 145; leadership 145, 150–1, 155; Reform and Development Plan 153; resistance 148; security force 153; workers 146, 148; zones 147
Palestinians 86, 101, 144, 146 *see also* Israel; Oslo Accords
Panama 52
Paris Declaration on Aid Effectiveness 155
Paris Economic Protocol (PEP) 146, 152
Paris Peace Accord (1991) 120–3
Paris Peace Conference 52
Paris, Roland 59–63, 65, 68, 71, 73
parliamentary democracy 171; elections 97; oversight 28; quotas 98, 105
patriarchy 11, 97, 100, 103–4, 106
patronage: Cambodia 126, 128, 136; Hezbollah 266; Iraq 206; Mali 242; politics 104

Pax Americana 7, 258
PCR *see* post-war/post-conflict reconstruction
peace accords 69, 79, 107, 120–3, 188; agreements 10, 69, 84, 96, 151; treaties 42, 145 *also* named countries
peace process 11, 81, 84, 86, 95, 101, 105, 108–9; Cambodia 121–3, 127; Côte d'Ivoire 186; Israel-Palestinian 151; PKK 263 *see also* Oslo Accords
peace; activists 21; aggressive 10–1, 77–93; alternative forms 9, 30, 46; ambiguity 29; and capitalism 135, 181; colonial 12, 140, 155, 180; democratic 15; discourse 84, 95, 99, 151, 165, 183; dividend 119; double-edged sword of 94–114; and emancipation 32; *eternal* 21; 'experts' 32, 88; exploring 8; gender and 94–5; genealogy of 23; geographies 46, 63; global 9; governing 4; human rights 123; 'hybrid' 5, 181; imposing 8, 11, 180, 182, 192, 242; making 23, 52, 95, 102; militarised 13, 41, 77–9, 86–7, 181, 243; internationalisation 30; particular 6, 16; 'partners for peace' 151–2, 234; policy 17; politics 9, 28–9, 31–2, 40, 45, 47; post-war 39, 42, 48, 52; of the powerful 9; practice 11, 22, 26, 30–1, 61, 100, 140, 192; preventing 2; and reconciliation 218; reconstruction 52, 54; research 26, 32, 60–1, 87, 181; securitisation 27; security 39, 101, 230; and state 24, 77; strategies 8; sustainable 139; theory 26; type of 7, 9, 23, 26, 30, 94, 117, 136, 140, 182; tyrannical 8; unequal 16; violent 8, 10, 23, 44n22, 78, 117, 155, 180, 185; visions 13, 27, 32, 40, 46, 163; and war 9, 16, 21, 23–4, 39–41, 43, 45–6, 54, 127, 163–178, 187 *see also* victor's peace
peacebuilders 6, 109, 182; 'natural' 102;
peacebuilding i, ix, 1, 3, 5, 10–2, 46, 59, 94–9; and colonialism 61, 150, 154, 180; Commission (World Bank) 87–8; as counterinsurgency 139–62; economy 89, 152; EU 72, 143; and imperialism 59–62, 67, 70–1, 73, 107; industry 152–3, 175; institutionalization 1–2, 149, 154; insurgent victories; local frameworks 163–4, 175, 182, 188; missions 3, 8, 13, 63, 117, 139; operations 61–3, 65, 69, 71; policy 139, 149; post-conquest 60, 63, 70, 74; post-settlement 59–61, 70, 72, 74; stabilisation 12; statebuilding 13, 170–1, 241, 244; toolbox 140; and UN 65–70, 72–3, 82, 143; women's groups
peacekeepers 10, 13, 192, 241
peacekeeping 10, 27, 59–76, 78, 166, 184; AU 83; blue beret/helmet 80–1, 83, 192; economic rationale for 64, 89; forces 80–1, 167–9; and NATO 83, 163, 167; sexual exploitation 99, 105
Pelham, Nicolas 14–5
pension funds 136
periphery *see* core vs periphery
Petraeus, David 143, 262
petrol 225–6 *see also* oil
Philippines 52
Phillips, Christopher 3, 15, 227
Phnom Penh 119, 121–2, 125, 127–8, 132–4
PKK (Partiya Karkerên Kurdistanê) 263
Polanski, Roman 77
police 68, 100, 129, 135, 153n109; Afghanistan 171; female 100; Iraq 212; Kosovo 85; Libya 119; state 153; UN 66, 71 *see also* law enforcement
political accountability 68; economy 5, 7, 10–2, 25n36, 29, 44, 63, 77–8, 84, 87, 89, 97, 99, 106, 131, 134–5, 140, 146, 149–50, 153–5, 175, 244; elites 3, 13, 190, 207, 231, 234; leadership 231; orders 10, 14, 69, 72, 108, 118, 120, 189, 191, 206, 212; parties 42, 207, 212; power 118, 120, 231; practices 3, 29, 71; representation 32, 154, 211; settlements 14, 120, 163, 175, 197–8, 207; violence 39–40, 48, 51, 129
politics: 'consensus' 240; electoral 174; everyday 108; of expert technocracy 31; of gender 100; global 25, 45; of identity 42; of inclusion/exclusion 11, 96, 103; internal 3; of international institutions 7; of intervention 2–3, 5, 8, 12, 155, 192; of nation states 7, 21, 23–4, 46; of peace 9, 26, 28–32, 40, 45, 180–2, 189; post-conflict 50; power 41; racial 42; of representation 11, 96, 102, 108; UN 21; of the 'winning side' 9; world 7, 21, 74
populism 119, 128, 236

post-Cold War 4, 8–9, 66, 83, 96, 141; cosmopolitanism 123; military 88; optimism 143, 236, 258; peacebuilding 139; peacekeeping 61, 66; statebuilding 237, 244; UN 10, 96 *see also* Cold War
post-colonial feminism 11, 95–6, 98, 107–9; governance 103; states 68, 80, 149 *see also* colonialism
post-colonialism 12, 53, 141, 155, 192, 244
post-conflict: aid conditionalities 84, dynamics 43; geographies 45; institutions 71, 108; reconstruction 8–9, 39, 41, 53, 68, 84, 98, 118, 167; societies 10, 40, 64, 71, 120, 167; spaces 53–4; violence 106; vision 14
post-war; geographies 40, 48; institutions 52n58; period 39; political order 14, 118, 212; political settlement 14, 198, 207, 212; reconstruction 8–9, 40–4, 47, 51–4; spaces 39–40, 43; stabilisation 48; statebuilding 167; transformation 48
'Potemkin states' 28
poverty 235; feminisation of 97; gendered 97; and insecurity 143; and rebellion 28n64
Poverty Eradication and Community Empowerment (PEACE) 165
power: air 1, 167, 264; asymmetric 72, 77, 99, 135, 147, 180; balance of 208; Christian 2; colonial 8, 141; competing elites 5, 23; disparities 7; emancipatory 30; gendered 97, 100; hierarchy 84, 134–5, 233; and hybridity 181; imperial 3, 60, 67–8, 70–1, 73, 78, 142; informal 72–3; 'killing' 140; knowledge 88, 200; male 105; military 13, 39–41, 80, 173, 185, 191, 227; separation of 219; -sharing 174, 183, 190; 'soft' 172; structures 23, 108, 119, 144, 151
Pretoria Accords 181, 188–9
primitive accumulation 6–7, 43, 119, 136, 154 *see also* capitalism
privatisation 10, 84–5, 106n72, 118, 121, 129, 131
Privatisation Agency of Kosovo (PAK) 85
privilege 2, 4–5, 64, 77, 83, 87, 132, 134, 143, 150, 236, 252
problem-solving 78, 96, 100, 106, 180
property ownership 3, 12, 22, 24, 89, 118–20, 148
protect: responsibility to *see* R2P

protectionism 11, 85, 102–3, 105, 149
Provincial Councils (Afghanistan) 98
Provincial Reconstruction Teams (PRTs) 52, 142, 167, 172
Proxy forces 82; governance 61, 71
public opinion 28, 67, 81, 209
order 136 *see* police; security sector reform (SSR)
public oversight 28; property 89, 148; sector employment 221; sector projects 222; services 25n40; 235–6
Pugh, Michael 10, 141–2
Putin, Vladimir 256, 259

Qaddafi, Muammar 14, 83, 107, 218–27, 251, 256–7, 259, 261
Qaeda, al- *see* Al-Qaeda
Qatar 174, 252, 258, 260, 262–5, 268
Quartet, The 1, 87
'quasi-colonial presence' 61, 65
quasi-states 145

R2P (responsibility to protect) 15, 94, 97, 251, 254–6, 267–8
race 41, 50, 98, 100, 105
Ramallah 154
RAND study 142, 154
rape 94, 97, 100, 105–7, 204
Rashid, Ahmed 166
rationalisation 28, 103
rationality 4, 24, 26–8, 199–200
rationalist epistemology 200–1
rebel elites 86; forces 105, 183–4, 191–2, 230–1, 233, 253, 264; militias 14, 253, 262; movements 79, 184; victories 218
reconciliation 21, 31, 152, 174, 185, 218, 223, 227, 237
reforms 32 50, 61, 103, 124–5, 132, 153, 197, 204, 252, 263; Iraq 14; judicial 84, 131; security sector reform (SSR) 26, 102, 140, 143–4, 155, 226, 241; of structures 85
refugees 77, 80, 123, 127, 154, 167, 190, 251, 263
regime change 1, 10–1, 13, 16, 21, 23, 30, 60, 77, 80–1, 85–7, 94–5, 97, 166, 179, 188–9, 191–3, 202–3, 206–7, 213, 252, 256, 259–61
regional actors 3, 5, 13, 83, 118, 121–2, 132, 175, 242–3, 252, 258, 260, 262–5, 268; economy 11–2, 43–4, 52, 64, 152, 181–2; interventions 11, 181, 183–4, 190, 232, 243; security 63, 227–8

reintegration 218
religious authorities 208; freedom 1; groups 205, 207, 240, 242; mythology 145; norms 28, 231; parties 208; voters 210
rentier state 12, 171, 176
representation 11, 22, 26, 32, 94–6, 98–108, 129, 154, 164, 179, 187–8, 202, 206–8, 234, 236, 252, 261, 263–4
resilience 260
resources 6–7, 12, 24, 42, 44, 80, 84, 103, 118–20, 127–9, 131, 135, 144–5, 150, 154–5, 172, 174, 200, 206, 225, 242–3, 253, 258
resource governance 7, 12, 127–8
responsibility to protect (R2P) *see* R2P (responsibility to protect)
revenues 146, 222, 225, 261
revolution 3, 14, 47–8, 53, 210, 218–28, 236, 252, 261, 266
Rice, Susan 67, 94n8, 255
Richmond, Oliver 86, 180–1
risk 3, 15, 25, 28, 31n84, 69, 79–81, 85, 101, 121, 168, 172, 231–2, 242–4; management 31; 'states at' 26
'roadmap'; Afghanistan regional 175; Israel-Palestinian 151–3; Libya 219
Robinson, Mary 168
Roy, Sara 146
rule of law 26, 96, 107n79, 125, 143–4, 167
rules of engagement (ROE) 82
ruling elites 14, 135, 198, 202, 205, 207
Rumsfeld, Donald 198, 203–4, 207
Russia 16, 83, 86, 191–2n65, 252, 255–60, 262, 264–8
Rwanda 79–80, 104–6

Sadr, Muqtadr al- 213
Sahel 225, 229, 231–3, 243
Said, Edward 25, 46, 201–2
Sall, Macky 232
Sambanis, Nicholas 61, 65
Sam Rainsy Party (SRP) 133
sanctions 3–2, 147, 164–5, 187, 189, 252, 254, 257, 260–1, 263–5, 267
Sarkozy, Nicolas 181, 191
Sartori, Andrew 22
Saudi Arabia 252, 258, 260, 262–6, 268
savage *see* Other
schools 51, 97, 167, 205, 238
Scottish Enlightenment 26
Sears, Jonathan 15
secessionists 66

sectarian extremism 212, 259, 263; politics 42, 210, 213, 223, 252, 263
secular elites 208, 210; groups 253; laws; state 15, 231, 235, 242, 266
secularisation 27–8
security sector reform (SSR) 26, 102–5, 140, 143–4, 153, 155, 226, 241
security 14, 63, 70, 78, 86–7, 99–100, 165, 170, 174–5, 197, 211, 229, 237, 241, 251, 259, 263; community 7, 21–2, 25–6, 29, 31; of expectations 26; forces 128–9, 186, 207, 211, 219, 224–5, 252; governance 96, 139; institutions 27, 83, 100, 103–4; Israel and Palestinians 145, 153–5; local 219; management 9, 12, 140–5, 153–5; militarised 46, 79–80, 147; national 4; and peace 39, 95, 101, 139, 230; post war 167, 203; regional 63; state 27, 143; and violence 23; and war 45
security-development nexus 28, 77, 143, 151, 155, 232, 237, 242; -peacebuilding nexus 13
self-determination 69–71, 73, 86, 154–5, 240
self-help 240
self-justification 199
Separation Wall/Barrier 140, 147
September 11 2001 *see* 9/11 attacks
Serbia 83
sexual and gender-based violence (SGBV) 11, 94, 96, 102, 105–7n79
shabiha (ghosts) 252
Shapiro, Michael 230
Sharon, Ariel 144
Shaways, Rowsch 209
Shia 207, 210, 212, 258, 263, 266–7
Sierra Leone 84, 100
Six-Day-War 146
Smith, Stephen 184
social contract 86, 149; justice 118, 165; movements 7, 118–9, 182; services 39; structures 24, 175
socialism 53, 141
society 1–2, 4, 6, 9–10, 12, 14, 16, 22–31, 39–41, 44–5, 48, 53–4, 62, 64, 71–3, 77–8, 85, 89, 99–103, 106, 118–20, 124–8, 130–3, 139–40, 143–4, 147, 149–51, 155, 168, 174–5, 192, 198, 200–2, 204–9, 211, 213, 236, 238–9, 241
socio-economic rights 89, 235
soldiers *see* combatants

Index

Somalia 79–82
South Africa 86, 183, 188, 190–1, 229n1
South Sudan 53
sovereignty 21, 24, 30, 72, 97, 139, 146, 149–50, 180–1, 186–93, 208, 231, 242, 254, 256, 268; discourse 3; 'organised hypocrisy' 3
Soviet Bloc *see* Eastern Bloc
Soviet Union 7, 53, 87, 120, 125, 203–6
Special Police Commandos (Iraq) 212
Spivak, Gayatri 95, 98
Sri Lanka 256
stabilisation 12, 21, 48, 66 -7, 139, 141, 144, 151, 154, 170
standard of civilisation 6, 25, 61
Stasi 79
state failure 25n40, 79, 81, 164, 166, 219, 225, 229–30, 234, 244, 254 *see also* failed states
state fragility 99 *see also* fragile states
statebuilding 13, 170–1: approaches 143–4; capitalist 26, 77; failed states 230, 234; and imperialism 72, 240; and nationalism 244; and/as peacebuilding 85–6, 96, 140, 143; post war 167; process 13; and women 104
state: accountability 97, 231; authority 45, 103, 164, 171, 224, 234–5, 238–40, 242; capacity 15, 125, 168–9, 171; and capitalism 32, 205; collapse 259; concept 4–5, 28, 52, 85–6, 119, 180; control of 202; elites 128; financing 12, 171, 176, 205–6; form 9, 39, 153, 240; formation 9, 54; homogeneity 235; ideal-type 28; imperial 70, 72–3, 154; institutions 39, 45, 50, 86, 153, 212, 227, 239; Lockean 22; military 144; 'of nations' (*civitas gentium*) 26; 'neoliberal' 85, 244; 'night watchman' 22n10; and peace 21, 23, 43, 234; power 14, 21, 46, 140, 168, 202; and society 12, 21, 41, 132, 206, 209, 237, 240–1, 244; sovereignty 8, 24, 180, 240–2, 254; super structure 22; system 63, 254, 267; territory 30, 45–6, 145, 234; terror 40 *see also* failed states; hybridity, weak states
subaltern 5, 67, 95, 98–9, 103
subordination 72–3, 95, 98, 106
Sudan *see* South Sudan
Sudanese workers 222
Suez 78
Suhrke, Astri 12

Sun City Peace Accord 107
Sunni heartlands 204
Sunni: countries 258; Muslims 14, 203–213, 227, 252, 263, 266; soldiers 253
Syria 197, 224, 227, 251–271; Free Syrian Army (FSA) 16, 253, 261–2, 264–5
Syrian National Council (SNC) 253, 261, 264
Syrian Opposition Coalition 253, 261

Taliban 80, 97, 163–6, 169, 173–4; post-Taliban order 171–2
Tanzania 97, 165
Tardelli, Luca 4
Tartus (Syria, Russian naval base) 257, 266
taxation 28, 64, 85, 146
technocratic approaches 32, 98, 212, 234
terrorism 15, 40, 81, 142, 210–11, 230, 232–5, 243–4
Tévoédjré, Albert 186
Thailand 122
Thakur, Ramesh 99
thuwwar 218–228
Tilly, Charles 45
Timbuktu 231, 241
Timor-Leste *see* East Timor
Tocqueville, Alexis de 2–3
Togo 183
Touré, Amadou Toumani (ATT) 231, 237–8, 240
Toynbee, Arnold 52
trade union 129, 130–5; movement 132
trading monopolies 153
traditional structures 29, 77, 103, 118, 235, 239
training: expertise 88, 119, 125, 131; human rights 120; military 39, 41, 142, 163, 173, 262
transitional administration 10, 68; government 107, 167, 169; justice 171; period 122–4
transparency 72, 95, 164, 175, 199, 222
Traoré, Dioncounda 229, 231, 233–4, 236, 238, 241
tribal leaders 207, 223; lineage 172; mediation 223
True, Jacqui 107
Turner, Mandy 12
Turkey 252, 257–8, 260, 262–5, 268

Index 287

Uganda 97, 100, 104, 190
UK 30, 52, 63, 78, 82, 87, 252, 255, 257–8, 260–2; Afghanistan 142, 171, 233; and Allies 66, 96; Army 81; Department for International Development (DFID) 142; Foreign and Commonwealth Office (FCO) 56, 67, 142, 169, 226; imperial counterinsurgency 142
UN Charter 69, 82, 254
UN Department of Peacekeeping Operations (DPKO) 79, 82, 87
UN Development Program (UNDP) 84, 164–5
UN Education, Scientific and Cultural Organization (UNESCO) 86
UN General Assembly 78, 82, 122–3, 255
UN High Commissioner for Human Rights 168
UN High Commission for Refugees 77
UN High-Level Panel on Threats, Challenges and Change 143
UN Interim Security Force for Abyei (UNISFA) 83
UN Mission in Cambodia (UNTAC) 11, 12, 117–38
UN Mission in Sierra Leone (UNAMSIL) 83
UN Mission in Sudan (UNMIS) 83
UN Multidimensional Integrated Stabilization Mission in Mali (MINUSMA) 234–5
UN Office for the Coordination of Humanitarian Assistance (UNOCHA) 77
UN Operation in Burundi (ONUB) 83
UN Operation in Côte d'Ivoire (UNOCI) 187, 192
UN Organization Stabilization Mission in the DR Congo (MONUSCO) 83
UN Peacebuilding Commission 87–8, 143
UN Protection Force (UNPROFOR) 79
UN Secretary General (UNSG) 80–1, 86, 123, 232, 255
UN Security Council (UNSC) 15, 16, 66, 78, 79–80, 82–4, 88, 100, 122, 165, 166, 168, 180, 188–92, 207, 232, 243, 251, 254–5, 257–8, 267; Permanent Five *see* P5
UN Special Representative of the Secretary-General (SRSG) 80, 125, 168, 186
UN: administration 68, 81, 86; Afghanistan 165–6, 170, 175; Cambodia 122–6; colonial roots 7; and development 10; as corporate business 88; and gender 95–6, 100–6, 109; global governance 8, 10; imperialism 7–8, 25–7, 64–6, 71–2, 77–9, 180, 187; legitimacy 64, 67, 81–2, 87; mandate 16, 80, 117, 188, 232, 234, 256; and NATO 83, 88; overseeing elections 188–90, 226; Israel-Palestine 151; sanctions 164–5; Secretariat 79–80, 88; Special Advisers 88; Syria 251, 254–8, 265, 267
unequal relations 72, 132
ungoverned spaces 233
Unified Task Force 79
Uruzgan Province (Afghanistan) 171
US Agency for International Development (USAID) 88, 142
US Army *see* US military
US Army/Marine Corps Counterinsurgency Field Manual (FM-324) 143
US Department of Defense (DoD) 142
US Government Counterinsurgency Guide 141–2
US Institute for Peace (USIP) 88
US State Department 142; Bureau of Conflict and Stabilization Operations 78; Office of the Coordinator for Counterterrorism 141
US: Afghanistan 164–175; 'backyard' 64, 142; Cambodia 122, 132–4; Civil War 40, 47–8; hegemony 7, 52, 52, 199, 200; elites 14; foreign policy 13–14, 52, 78, 142, 198–200, 202, 208, 231, 252; geopolitics 53, 257, 267; imperialism 62, 66, 74, 78, 141; intervention 9, 12, 14, 42, 163, 166, 169, 211; Iraq 11, 59–60, 197–213, 219, 221, 255; Israel-Palestine 151–3; Libya 220; military forces 49–50, 79, 81, 122, 165–73, 200, 212, 259; R2P 255; racial politics 42; and Russia 256–8; Senate 67, 169; Syria 16, 256–67

valorisation: of the military 101; of local cultures 239
veterans 45, 51, 134
victimisation 11, 98, 107
victor's peace 9, 12, 14, 30, 198, 202, 205–6, 209, 211–13
Village Leagues, Palestinian 148

violence ix, 1, 4, 6, 8–10, 13–16, 23, 31, 40–42, 45–6, 48, 50–54, 84, 101, 104, 117, 119, 124–5, 128–9, 135–6, 145–9, 180, 202, 226, 233, 235, 244, 253–4; Afghanistan 163, 165, 168, 170, 171; asymmetrical 202; Côte d'Ivoire 179, 182–3, 185–8, 190–3; cultural 95, 244; epistemic 96; ethnic 223, 259; gender-based 11, 94, 98–100, 102, 105–7; Iraq 169, 197–8, 208, 211–13; Israel 155; Mali 225, 230, 241; as peace 10, 78; societal 140–1, 144; state monopoly 23–4, 26, 39, 53, 235; structural 30, 40, 43–45, 84, 147–8; Syria 260, 263
violent conflict *see* conflict; *see also* violence; war
violent dispossession 6–7, 11, 144
voters 51; black 52; Cambodia 117; Iraq 210; Mali 238; women 98

Wahabism 263
Walker, Rob 180
war 3, 6, 9, 12, 16, 21, 23, 24; -and-aid economy 171, 174; and capitalism 29–30, 43–4, 46, 49; elites 85, 170, 191; and gender equality 101; legitimisation of 23, 30, 166; liberal 23, 46; -reconstruction-peace 43, 47; financing 64, 163, 170, 173, 223; Iraq 14, 169, 268; 'on terror' 6, 40, 43, 46, 97, 128, 163, 168, 230; 'operations other than' 81; political economy of 106, 146, 163, 174, 187, 225, 263; termination 117; 'total' 41, 45; veterans 45; of words 51 *see also* conflict
warlords 103, 165, 168
water 120, 145; privatisation of 129
Watts, Michael 44
weak states 25–7, 30; Afghanistan 168–71; Iraq 224–5; Mali 15, 230; and Western norms 81; *see also* failed states; fragile states
Weber, Cynthia 180
Weber, Max 25n39
welfare 86; activities 230; of citizens 254; distribution 89; gains 30
West Bank 145–8, 150–4, 213
Western: organisations 27; bloc 89; democracy; discourse 1, 2, 25, 28, 67, 81, 87, 98–9, 125, 139–40, 233, 261; donors 4, 12, 95, 139, 141, 144, 148, 150, 152–3, 172–3; governance 22, 31–2, 244; intervention 1, 6, 10–11, 13, 15, 23, 26, 31, 65, 67, 70, 79, 87, 139–40, 149, 152–5, 183, 221, 227–8, 251–4, 257, 259–62, 264, 267–8; protectionism 105; security community 21, 27, 147; societies 4, 6, 22, 31, 66; states 6, 16, 22, 25–6, 29, 31, 66, 67, 68, 79, 128, 142, 260–1; superiority 6–9, 16, 25–30, 61, 77–9, 130, 151, 202; racism 14, 183; values 8, 125
'white man's burden' 16
Whitworth, Sandra 104
Wiesel, Elie 203
Wolesi Jirga (Afghan parliament lower house) 97
Wolfowitz, Paul 53, 198, 203–5
women: advancement of 94; Afghanistan 97–99, 165–6; agency 11, 94–7, 100–5; Bosnia and Herzegovina 94; disempowerment 11, 96; from global south 11, 97–8, 106; human rights 95–9, 104, 174; influence; Iraq 207; military and 101, 104–5; peacebuilding 100–3; in peace processes 105, 109; protection of 11, 94–9, 106–9, 170; quota 97–8, 100, 104; 'subaltern' 98–9, 103
Women, Peace and Security (WPS) 100
World Bank 7, 9, 15, 40, 47, 53, 84, 132, 235; Cambodia 130–1; Côte d'Ivoire 190; Palestinian aid 148, 151; and security 87
World Summit (2005) 97, 255
World Summit Outcome (UN) 255
World Trade Organization (WTO) 84
World War One (WWI) 42, 44, 52, 53, 62, 67
World War Two (WWII) 42, 52, 62, 67, 119; post 7, 9, 30, 33, 47, 53, 236

Yemen 16, 94, 260, 268
Yugoslavia 79, 84

Zimbabwe 104
Zionism 53, 145
Žižek, Slavoj 3
zone of conflict 29–31; of peace 29–31
Zuma, Jacob 190